C 02737786J R

JSCSC Library

Date: 11 JUN 2002

Class Mark:
32(100) ADA

Hobson Library
316739

GLOBALIZATION AND EMERGING TRENDS IN AFRICAN STATES' FOREIGN POLICY-MAKING PROCESS

The Making of Modern Africa
Series Editors: Abebe Zegeye and John Higginson

Electoral Territoriality in Southern Africa
Stephen Rule

Community Health Needs in South Africa
Ntombenhle Protasia Khoti Torkington

Consolidation of Democracy in Africa
A view from the South
Edited by Hussein Solomon and Ian Liebenberg

Ghana in Search of Development
The challenge of governance, economic management and institution building
Dan-Bright S. Dzorgbo

Regional and Local Economic Development in South Africa
The experience of the Eastern Cape
Etienne Louis Nel

Agrarian Economy, State and Society in Contemporary Tanzania
Edited by Peter G. Forster and Sam Maghimbi

Entrepreneurial Ethics and Trust
Cultural foundations and networks in the Nigerian plastic industry
Yakubu Zakaria

Growth or Stagnation? South Africa heading for the year 2000
Mats Lundahl

Sudan's Predicament
Civil war, displacement and ecological degradation
Edited by Girma Kebbede

Globalization and Emerging Trends in African States' Foreign Policy-Making Process
A comparative perspective of Southern Africa

Edited by
KORWA GOMBE ADAR AND ROK AJULU
Rhodes University, South Africa

Ashgate

© Korwa Gombe Adar and Rok Ajulu 2002

All rights reserved. No part of this publication may be reproduced, stored in a retrieval system or transmitted in any form or by any means, electronic, mechanical, photocopying, recording or otherwise without the prior permission of the publisher.

Published by
Ashgate Publishing Limited
Gower House
Croft Road
Aldershot
Hampshire GU11 3HR
England

Ashgate Publishing Company
131 Main Street
Burlington, VT 05401-5600 USA

Ashgate website: http://www.ashgate.com

British Library Cataloguing in Publication Data
Globalization and emerging trends in African states'
    foreign policy-making process : a comparative perspective
    of Southern Africa. - (The making of modern Africa)
    1. Africa, Southern - Foreign relations - Case studies
    I. Adar, Korwa Gombe II. Ajulu, Rok
    327.6'8

Library of Congress Control Number: 2001095873

ISBN 0 7546 1822 6

Printed and bound in Great Britain by Antony Rowe Ltd., Chippenham, Wiltshire

Contents

List of Figures and Tables   *vii*
Editors and Contributors   *viii*
Acknowledgements   *x*
List of Acronyms   *xi*

1 Southern African States' Foreign Policy and Foreign Policy-Making Process: An Introductory Contextualisation
Korwa G. Adar and Rok Ajulu   1

PART I: COUNTRY CASE STUDIES

2 Dysfunctional Foreign Policy: Angola's Unsuccessful Quest for Security since Independence
Assis Malaquias   13

3 Globalization and Foreign Economic Policy-Making in Botswana
James J. Zaffiro   34

4 Survival in a Rough Neighbourhood: Lesotho's Foreign Policy in the Era of Globalization
Rok Ajulu   51

5 Continuity and Change in Malawi's Foreign Policy-Making
Jonathan Mayuyuka Kaunda   71

6 From Ramgoolam to Ramgoolam: An Analysis of the Mauritian Foreign Policy-Making Process
Rosabelle Laville   91

7 Mozambique's Foreign Policy: From Ideological Conflict to Pragmatic Cooperation
Oscar Gakuo Mwangi   117

8   Towards an Understanding of the Foreign Policy-Making Process of a New State: The Case of Namibia
Frank Khachina Matanga   135

9   Untangling the "Gamble on Investment": Élite Perceptions of Globalization and South Africa's Foreign Policy during the Mandela Era
Philip Nel   153

10   Facing the New Millennium: South Africa's Foreign Policy in a Globalizing World
Garth le Pere and Anthoni van Nieuwkerk   173

11   Contextualising Foreign Policy-Making in the Kingdom of Swaziland
Albert Domson-Lindsey   211

12   Zambian Foreign Policy-Making Process in the Post-1991 Multi-Party Dispensation: the Chiluba Presidency
Korwa G. Adar   240

13   Post-Cold War Zimbabwe's Foreign Policy and Foreign Policy-Making Process
Korwa G. Adar, Rok Ajulu and Moses O. Onyango   263

PART II: REGIONAL AND GLOBAL CASE STUDIES

14   How Far, Where To? Regionalism, the Southern African Development Community and Decision-Making into the Millennium
Paul-Henri Bischoff   283

15   Britain and Southern Africa: A 'Third Way' or Business as Usual?
Rita Abrahamsen and Paul Williams   307

16   Continuity and Change in the United States' Foreign Policy Towards Southern Africa
Peter J. Schraeder   329

Index   350

List of Figures and Tables

Figure 7.1	The Structure of Foreign Policy-making in Mozambique	128
Figure 8.1	Foreign Policy-making Process: the Actors (Namibia)	144
Table 9.1	Mean Scores for Two Questions (V217 & V218) by Party Support and by Positional Sector, 1997-1998	161
Table 9.2	Investor-friendly Liberalisation Index (S.A.)	164
Table 9.3	State-based Redistributive Index (S.A.)	166
Figure 10.1	South African Foreign Policy-making Environments	180
Figure 10.2	South African Foreign Policy-making: the Actors	187
Table 10.1	Decision-making Styles: a Comparison of the Old and New	196
Figure 12.1	A Schematic Model of Zambian Foreign Policy-making	252
Table 12.1	Zambian Military Expenditure and Armed Forces	258
Figure 14.1	Proposed SADC Organ Structure (1999)	291
Table 14.1	Military Expenditure by the Members of the Southern African Development Community	293
Table 14.2	Armed Forces of the Members of the Southern African Development Community	294

Editors and Contributors

Editors

KORWA G. ADAR is Associate Professor of International Studies in the International Studies Unit of the Department of Political Studies, Rhodes University, South Africa. He received his MSc in Political Science from Indiana State University, and MA and PhD in International Studies from the University of South Carolina, USA. Prior to joining Rhodes University in 1997, he taught at the University of Nairobi (1987-1994) and at the United States International University-Africa, Nairobi, Kenya (1994-1997). He is the author of many book chapters as well as of articles which have appeared in numerous internationally refereed journals such as the *Journal of Third World Studies*; *African Security Review*; *African Sociological Review*; *African Journal of Conflict Resolution*; *Journal of the Third World Spectrum* and *African Studies Quarterly*. He is the author of *Kenyan Foreign Policy Behavior Towards Somalia, 1963-1983* (Lanham: University Press of America, 1994) and a co-editor of *The United States and Africa: From Independence to the End of the Cold War* (Nairobi: East African Educational Publishers, 1995). He was the recipient of the 1992 Fulbright Research Grant for African Scholars. He is currently working on a book entitled *Global Commons and Collective Interests: African States and the Law of the Sea Convention*.

ROK AJULU is a Senior Lecturer in African Politics and Political Economy in the International Studies Unit of the Department of Political Studies at Rhodes University. He holds a PhD from Sussex University. He has taught at a number of universities, most recently at Leeds, before joining Rhodes in January 1994. A contributing editor to the *Review of African Political Economy* and an associate editor of *Africa World Review*, he is the author of a number of book chapters as well as of numerous articles in internationally refereed journals. He is currently working on a book on the political economy of democratisation in Kenya.

Contributors

RITA ABRAHAMSEN, Department of International Politics, University of Wales, Aberystwyth, UK.

PAUL-HENRI BISCHOFF, Department of Political Studies, International Studies Unit, Rhodes University, South Africa.

ALBERT DOMSON-LINDSEY, Department of Political Studies, Rhodes University, South Africa.

JONATHAN MAYUYUKA KAUNDA, Department of Political and Administrative Studies, University of Botswana, Botswana.

ROSABELLE LAVILLE, Department of Anthropology, Rhodes University, South Africa.

GARTH LE PERE, Institute of Global Dialogue, Johannesburg, South Africa.

ASSIS MALAQUIAS, Department of Government, St Lawrence University, New York, USA.

FRANK KHACHINA MATANGA, Department of Government, University of Maseno, Kenya.

OSCAR GAKUO MWANGI, Department of Political Studies, Rhodes University, South Africa.

PHILIP NEL, Department of Political Studies, University of Stellenbosch, South Africa.

MOSES O. ONYANGO, Department of Political Studies, Rhodes University, South Africa.

PETER J. SCHRAEDER, Department of Political Science, Loyola University of Chicago, USA.

ANTHONI VAN NIEUWKERK, Department of International Relations, University of Witwatersrand, South Africa.

PAUL WILLIAMS, Department of International Politics, University of Wales, Aberystwyth, UK.

JAMES J. ZAFFIRO, Department of Political Science, Central College, Pella, Iowa, USA.

Acknowledgements

The authors are greatly indebted to the constructive and supportive comments offered by many reviewers on earlier drafts of this manuscript. Whilst it is not possible to mention the names of all those who provided their expertise, the following people deserve to be singled out: Fred Hendricks, Nixon Kariithi, Tawana Kupe, Paul Maylam, Robin Palmer, Roger Southall, Lynette Steenveld, Louise Vincent, and Laurence Wright, Rhodes University; Eddy Maloka, African Institute of South Africa; and Chisepo Mphaisha, University of the Western Cape.

Korwa G. Adar expresses his gratitude to Mr Jens Kapoma, Deputy Permanent Secretary (Political), Ministry of Foreign Affairs, Zambia, Mr Joe Muntanga, Deputy Principal Clerk, Zambian National Assembly, Isaac R.B. Manda, Director, Zambian Institute of Diplomacy and International Studies, for their insights on the Zambian foreign policy-making process; and Ms Tembi C.C. Mtine, Chief Librarian, and Mr Augustine D. Lubozhya, Deputy Chief Librarian, Zambian National Assembly Library, for making it possible for me to use the National Assembly Library; and Laurent C.W. Kaela, Head of the Department of Political and Administration Studies at the University of Zambia. The further assistance of Amanda Wortmann and Zodwa Ramafalo of the African Institute of South Africa is gratefully acknowledged.

Special thanks is due to Marion Baxter, Institute for the Study of English in Africa (ISEA), Rhodes University, for preliminary editing of the text and for providing the necessary desktop publishing services; and also to Cecilia Blight of the Cory Library, Rhodes University for proof-reading the manuscript. We also extend our appreciation to John Landman, Geography Department, Rhodes University, for producing the detailed map of Southern Africa. Odette Cumming, Secretary of the Political Studies Department, Rhodes University, provided much appreciated secretarial services.

The final production of the manuscript could not have been possible without the generous financial support we received from the Rhodes University Joint Research Council.

Korwa G. Adar
Rok Ajulu

List of Acronyms

AAF - Angola Armed Forces
ACP - Africa, the Caribbean and the Pacific
ACRI - Africa Crisis Response Initiative
ADB - African Development Bank
AFDL - Alliance des Forces Democratiques pour la Liberation du Congo
AFL-CIO - American Federation of Labour and Congress of Industrial Organizations
AFM - Armed Forces Movement (Mocambique)
AFORD - Alliance for Democracy
AGOA - Africa Growth and Opportunity Act
ANC - African National Congress (South Africa)
ASAS - Association of Southern African States
ASEAN - Association of South East Asian States
ATDCG - Africa Trade and Development Coordinating Group
AZ - Agenda for Zambia

BAC - Basutoland African Congress
BBC - British Broadcasting Corporation
BCP - Basutoland Congress Party
BDC - Botswana Development Corporation
BDF - Botswana Defence Force
BECI - Botswana Export Credit Insurance
BEDIA - Botswana Export Development and Investment Authority
BEDU - Botswana Enterprise Development Unit
BI - Barden International
BLNS - Botswana, Lesotho, Namibia, Swaziland
BMAP - Botswana Management Assistance Programme
BMATT - British Military Advisory and Training Team
BNP - Basutoland Congress Party
BNPC - Botswana National Productivity Centre
BNTZ - Botswana National Development Centre
BoB - Bank of Botswana
BOCCIM - Botswana Confederation of Commerce, Industry and Manpower
BPA - Basutoland Progressive Association
BPF - Barotse Patriotic Front
BPSDP - Botswana Private Sector Development Project

CBC - Congressional Black Caucus
CCM - Choma Cha Mapinduzi
CCZ - Christian Council of Zambia
CDASJ - Christian Democratic Action for Social Justice

CFU - Commercial Farmers' Union
CIA - Central Intelligence Agency
CIS - Community of Independent States
CLA - Caprivi Liberation Army
CLM - Caprivi Liberation Movement
CNU - Caucus for National Unity
COMESA - Common Market for Eastern & Southern Africa
COMIRA - Comite Militar de Resistencia de Angola (Military Committee for Angolan Resistance)
COSATU - Congress of South African Trade Unions
CONSAS - Constellation of Southern African States
CRC - Constitutional Review Commission

DCN - Democratic Coalition of Namibia
DFID - Department for International Development
DoD - Dept of Defence (SA)
DRC - Democratic Republic of Congo
DTA - Democratic Turnhalle Alliance of Namibia
DTI - Dept of Trade & Industry (SA)

ECOWAS - Economic Community of West African States
EDF - European Development Fund
EFZ - Evangelical Fellowship of Zambia
EPZ - Export Processing Zones
ESAA - Economic and Social Research Agenda (ESAA)
EU - European Union

FAA - Forcas Armadas Angolanas
FAP - Financial Assistance Policy (Botswana)
FASC - Foreign Affairs Select Committee
FCN - Federal Convention of Namibia
FCO - Foreign and Commonwealth Office
FDI - Foreign Direct Investment
FLS - Front Line States
FNLA - Frente Nacional de Libertacao de Angola
FPC - Foreign Policy Centre
FRELIMO - Frente de Libertacao de Mocambique

GATT - General Agreement on Trade and Tariffs
GEAR - Growth, Employment and Redistribution (SA)
GNU - Government of National Unit (SA)
GNUR - Government of National Unity and Reconstruction
GSTP - Generalised System of Trade Preferences

HCT - High Commission Territories
HIP - Highly Indebted Poor Countries
HLCC - High Level Consultative Committee

IBRD - International Bank for Reconstruction and Development
ICC - International Criminal Court
ICCPR - International Covenant on Civil and Political Rights
ICJ - International Court of Justice
IFAD - International Fund for Agriculture Development
IFC - International Finance Corporation
ILO - International Labour Organization
IMF - International Monetary Fund
IOR - Indian Ocean Rim
IOR-ARC - Indian Ocean Rim - Association for Regional Cooperation
ISA - Initiative for Southern Africa
ISDSC - Inter-State Defence and Security Committee

JCS - Joint Chiefs of Staff
JCTE - Joint Combined Training Exercises

LAZ - Law Association of Zambia
LCP - Liseli Conservative Party
LDF - Lesotho Defence Force
LHWP - Lesotho Highlands Water Project
LLA - Land Acquisition Act
LSDI - Lubombo Spatial Development Initiative

MAG - Monitor Action Group
MANU - Mocambique African National Union
MC - Mwanakatwe Commission
MCG - Mauritian Court General
MCI - Ministry of Commerce and Industry (Botswana)
MCP - Malawi Congress Party
MDC (Zimbabwe) - Movement for Democratic Change
MDCs - More Developed Countries
MFA - Ministry of Foreign Affairs
MFP - Marema-Tlou Freedom Party
MIA - Military Intelligence Agency
MIGA - Multilateral Investment Guarantee Agency
MLP - Mauritian Labour Party
MMD - Movement for the Multiparty Democracy
MMM - Mauritian Militant Movement
MoD - Ministry of Defence (Britain)
MPLA - Movement for the Popular Liberation of Angola
MSM - Mauritian Socialist Movement
MUZ - Mineworkers Union of Zambia

NAFTA - North American Free Trade Agreement
NAM - Non-Aligned Movement
NATO - North Atlantic Treaty Organization
NCA - National Constitutional Assembly
NCACC - National Convention Arms Control Committee

NDB - National Development Bank
NDPJ - National Democratic Party for Justice
NEC - National Economic Council
NFLA - National Front for the Liberation of Angola
NGOs - Non-governmental Organizations
NIC - National Intelligence Council
NICOC - National Intelligence Coordinating Commission
NNDP - Namibia National Democratic Party
NNF - Namibia National Front
NPT - Nuclear Non-Proliferation Treaty
NRC - National Redemption Council
NRDP - National Rural Development Programme
NSC - National Security Council
NSHR - National Society for Human Rights
NSIA - National State Intelligence Agency
NUNN - National Union of Namibian Workers

OAU - Organisation of African Unity
OB - Operation Boleas
OBA - Operation Born Again
OBC - Operation Blue Crane
ODA - Overseas Development Administration
OPDS - Organ for Politics, Defence and Security

PAO - Public Affairs Office
PF - Patriotic Front
PMSD - Parti Mauricien Socialiste Democratic
PRC - People's Republic of China
PRP - People's Revolutionary Army

RDP - Reconstruction and Development Programme (SA)
RENAMO - Resistance Nationale de Mocambique
RF - Rhodesian Front
RMA - Rand Monetary Area

SACP - South African Communist Party
SACU - South African Customs Union
SADC - Southern African Development Community
SADCC - Southern African Development Coordination Conference
SADF - South African Defence Force
SAFTA - Southern Africa Free Trade Area
SAPs - Structural Adjustment Programmes
SAREP - Southern Africa Regional Program

SASS - South African Secret Service
SCU - Sector Coordination Unit (SADC)

SDR - Strategic Defence Review
SFE - Swaziland Federation of Employers
SFL - Swaziland Federation of Labour
SFTU - Swaziland Federation of Trade Unions
SIPA - Swaziland Investment Promotion Authority
SNCSC - Swazi National Council Standing Committee
SSA - Swazi Sugar Association
SSC - State Security Council (SA)
SSN - Swazi Solidarity Network
SWANU - South West African National Union
SWAPO - South West African People's Organisation

TANU - Tanzania African National Union
TAZARA - Tanzania-Zambia Railway Authority
TDCA - Trade and Development Cooperation Agreement
TIPA - Trade and Investment Promotion Agency (Botswana)

UDENAMO - Uniao Democratic Nacional de Mocambique
UDF - United Democratic Front
UDHR - Universal Declaration of Human Rights
UDI - Unilateral Declaration of Independence
UN - United Nations
UNAMI - Uniao Nacional Africana de Mocambique
UNAMIR - United Nations Assistance Mission for Rwanda
UNAVEM - United Nations Angola Verification Mission
UNDP - United Nations Development Programme
UNHCR - United Nations High Commission for Refugees
UNIP - United National Independence Party
UNITA - Uniao Nacional para Independencia Total de Angola
UNOMOSIL - United Nations Observer Mission in Sierra Leone
UNSC - United Nations Security Council
UNTAG - United Nations Transition Assistance Group
USAID - United States Agency for International Development
USDF - Umbutfo Swaziland Defence Force

WB - World Bank
WHO - World Health Organization
WRP - Workers Revolutionary Party
WTO - World Trade Organization

ZADECO - Zambia Democracy Congress
ZANU-PF - Zimbabwe African National Union-Patriotic Front
ZAPU - Zimbabwe African People's Union
ZCTU - Zambia Congress of Trade Unions
ZCTU - Zimbabwe Congress of Trade Unions
ZDI - Zimbabwe Defence Industries
ZEC - Zambia Episcopal Conference
ZHRC - Zambian Human Rights Commission
ZIMCOM - Zimbabwe Industrial Commercial Association

1 Southern African States' Foreign Policy and Foreign Policy-Making Process: An Introductory Contextualisation

KORWA G. ADAR AND ROK AJULU

The transformation taking place in Africa following the collapse of the Cold War provides compelling reasons for students, scholars, and practitioners to re-evaluate the methodological, theoretical, and conceptual underpinnings of African States' foreign policy and foreign policy-making process. The concept of foreign policy describes the involvement of a state abroad. It refers to actions taken by a state towards the external environment as viewed from the perspective of the state in the pursuit of its national interests. On the other hand, the foreign policy-making process can be defined as meaning the formulation and implementation of policies by various actors, traditionally sovereign states and their agents. Specifically, the foreign policy-making process is centred upon how policy is made by the employment of foreign policy instruments and institutions at the disposal of the nation-state.

Most studies in this area have focussed largely on the determinants of African States' foreign policy (Wright 1999; Shaw and Okolo 1994; Aluko 1977).[1] These can be divided into two broad categories. First, there are those who focus attention on the fact that the African States' foreign policies are influenced mainly by the global political economy (Mazrui 1977; Shaw and Okolo 1994; Shaw and Aluko 1984). These conceptualize African States' foreign policies within the contexts of a *dependence– dependency* paradigm. The incorporation of Africa into the global political economy over the centuries, it is argued, continues to perpetuate neo-colonial and post neo-colonial structural core–periphery relations between the African States and the industrialised countries. Within this structural systemic paradigm, African States' foreign policies exhibit two main features. In the global context compliance constitutes their main *modus operandi vis-à-vis* the donor countries. The idea that 'big brother is watching' — with its inherent concepts of compliance — on issues considered salient to the donors in the United Nations, for example, is offered as an example in some of the studies. At another level, the African élite class — sharing similar global socio-economic and political views with the élites of the donor countries — continues to promote the neo-colonial core-periphery relations.

Secondly, some studies correlate African States' foreign policies with African presidents. According to this school of thought, the post-independence African 'big men' became the 'original ancestors' of the state because they not only politicized the state, but also personalised state institutional functions to the extent that there can be no clear distinction between the state and the ruler. In other words, African foreign policies derive from the president and the presidency (Mckay 1966; Thiam 1963; Zartman 1966; Anda 2000, 45). In what is commonly referred to as the idiosyncratic big man **hypotheses, or better still, the** *psychological–perceptual* **school**, it is assumed that the state's and the 'big man's' interests are intertwined. In other words, it is the 'big man's' personal idiosyncrasy — replete with undemocratic cultural values and beliefs — which carries the day. Parliaments and other foreign policy actors have, in the process, become inert or mere rubber stamps since independence. According to the psychological reductionist perspective, this relationship was perpetuated by the ideological competition of the Cold War era. The psychological–perceptual school conceptualizes the state as a unitary value-maximizing actor, with the 'big man' at the helm.

These studies, however, fail to appreciate the impact of other variables which may influence African States' foreign policies. The psychological–perceptual points of departure discount the relevance of the bureaucratic–organizational school, particularly as it relates to foreign policy-making. The *bureaucratic–organizational* school focusses our attention on the role of foreign policy-making actors in decision output. In other words, foreign policy output is a function of the interplay of numerous actors (Allison 1971; Colebatch 1998). This perspective stresses that it is important to take cognizance of the plurality of actors and their interlocking and conflicting interests even in the African states' contexts.

Legislative bodies, governmental bureaucracies, political parties, the church, civil society in general, and interest groups, among others, have been and are increasingly directly involved in the domain of African States' foreign policy-making processes (Adar 1994; Korany 1986; Gambari 1989). Churches in South Africa, for example, though not united in the cause of systemic change in the country, played important roles in influencing the apartheid regime's foreign policies (SACC 1974; Rothe 1989; WCC 1980). In his analysis of Senegal's foreign policy-making, Schraeder, for example, argues that "even during the Cold War period, Senegal's foreign policy could not be explained simply by reference to the foreign actions of the superpowers, or by the personal beliefs of the two Senegalese presidents" (Schraeder 1996 and 1997). Similarly, in his analysis of Tanzanian foreign policy-making, Mushi argues that apart from the Party, known first as the Tanzania African National Union (TANU) — later re-named Chama Cha Mapinduzi (CCM) or People's Revolutionary Party in 1977 — and President Nyerere, "the bureaucracy (both ministerial and parastatal) has been more directly responsible for the maintenance and expansion of external relations, often with little party control or supervision" (Mushi 1981, 5). Thus the level of the involvement of foreign policy-making players or actors varies in every country and according to the regime in power, as well as with respect to the issues at stake. For example, whereas Angola, Namibia, and Zimbabwe, for various reasons, got involved militarily in the civil war in the Democratic Republic of Congo (DRC), the other members of the Southern African Development Community (SADC) view the regional body as the best viable instrument for conflict resolution in the DRC. It is important to emphasize here that the policy decisions taken by the members of the SADC, either to become militarily involved in the DRC or not, were made by a variety of decision units. These are the state and non-state actors who take part in the decision-making process at different stages.

Globalization

More recently however, the increasing marginalisation of African states appears to have dramatically shifted the locus of African states' foreign policies and policy-making processes.

At the very heart of this African marginalisation is the contemporary form of globalization — the march of capital all over the world in search of consumers and markets. Globalization has become a catchword associated with the 'compression' of the world into new patterns of production, integrated financial spheres, homogenization of cultures etc. (Robertson 1992). But as Nabudere (2000) points out, contemporary understanding of globalization is also about growing structural differentiation. In other words, globalization should be seen as a process which is propelled by contradictory tendencies. On the one hand, economic globalization has unleashed productive forces throughout the world leading to the expansion of markets, the insertion of technology into the processes of production, and hence the improvement of productive capacities, and massive increases in profits for multinational corporations. On the other, it has also manifested a tendency to fragment, differentiate, and marginalise social forces and countries incapable of catching up with its processes. Uneven development, long associated with capitalist expansion, is probably the most visible trade mark of globalization in its contemporary form.

Not surprisingly, the unevenness of globalization has been at it most intense in the countries of the third world. The accelerated globalization of the world economy has had a negative influence on African states. While global restructuring has no doubt had some positive spin-offs — the collapse of undemocratic and repressive regimes, and, of course, the acceleration of the so-called democratisation process in Africa — the predominant tendency, however, has been the increasing marginalisation of the continent. A declining resource base and continued peripheralization has more or less redefined the global playing field for the weak and the poor. Marginalization and declining access to resources have triggered new struggles and intensified old contests over resources, engendering conflicts and wars of annihilation throughout the continent. Not surprisingly, globalization has been marked by fratricidal wars in all corners of the continent: Somalia, Liberia, Sierra Leone, Rwanda, Burundi, and more recently, the ongoing conflict in the Great Lakes region of Central and Eastern Africa.

More significantly however, contemporary globalization has rendered the classical notion of the nation-state all but meaningless. The traditional understanding of the nation-state, associated with the theories of realists and neo-realists, based on the assumption that the traditional nation-state had comprehensive control over its territory and population, and a capacity to operate as a unitary, autonomous actor in an anarchic international system (Stubbs and Underhill 1994), can no longer hold true for the majority of the African states. These countries have been collectively subordinated to a world-wide 'market totalitarianism' to which no exception is tolerated. In other words, contemporary globalization has imposed the unprecedented power of a few overwhelmingly wealthy and powerful countries upon the many weaker states in the international system. As Tandon puts it, "the strong can now extract what they will and the weak must surrender what they cannot protect" (Tandon 2000).

Globalization has equally rendered the nation state 'borderless.' Research and development of technology have facilitated the free flow of information across international borders on an unprecedented scale. Capital, particularly financial capital, now flows freely across borders with devastating consequences for the so-called emerging economies. And since the establishment of the World Trade Organisation (WTO), the rich and powerful states have sought to secure the free movement of commodities, done away with protectionist regimes, and generally decreased the powers of states to control multinational corporations and foreign investments.

This process of rolling back the state has been facilitated by the International Financial Institutions (IFIs). The two Bretton Woods institutions, the International Bank of Reconstruction and Development (IBRD) (the World Bank) and the International Monetary Fund (IMF), have become the most important instruments for streamlining and downsizing the postcolonial state. There has been a discernible shift from the post-war consensus on the role of the state-in-development process to the neo-liberal position which increasingly views the state as a hindrance to the free functioning of the 'market economy.' Thus the African states have been increasingly compelled by the Bretton Woods institutions to retreat and abide by the logic of the market. Furthermore, these institutions have increasingly been politicised, manifestly pursuing the political agenda of the most economically powerful states — the G7 or is it the G8?[2]

Furthermore, the use of aid to impose compliance or punish non-compliance with the 'market economy' has now become the *sine qua non* of the operations of these financial institutions. The consequences of these kinds of intervention have been far reaching: the dismantling of the institutions of the African states, with concomitant loss of sovereignty in a number of areas. As one author put it, policies which until recently were the exclusive reserve of the nation-state, are now largely determined by the International Financial Institutions.[3]

Finally, the completion of the Uruguay Round and the establishment of the World Trade Organisation (WTO) has produced stringent new regulations and rules for global economic engagement, with devastating consequences to the good old notion of national sovereignty. The WTO has in fact emerged as the most important instrument of globalization. It has centralised within its ambit the most powerful instruments for regulating global trade, investment and production, and of course, capital flows, with negative implications for the poor and the weak. For instance, the WTO has introduced new rules that make Trade Related Intellectual Property Rights central to the control of technology by the multinational corporations, and detrimental to developmental strategies of the third world. Furthermore, under the

Multilateral Agreement on Investments (MAI), multinational corporations will now increasingly be liberated from the regulatory control of national governments. Once more, the African countries are at their most vulnerable.

In the past, African states were able to exploit the Cold War to advance their own strategic objectives. Indeed this offered certain trade-offs and gave the impression that they were important actors in the international system. The advent of globalization would seem to have put an end to this. In fact, the last two decades have witnessed the weakening of the African state with an accompanying loss of sovereignty over a large area.

Case Studies

It is against this background that contributors to this volume have sought to analyse African states' foreign policies and their policy-making processes. Almost without exception there is a general consensus that developments over the last two decades have not only undermined the capacity of African states to play a meaningful role in the international system, but more critically, multilaterised foreign policy-making processes. No longer is the weak nation-state the sole captain of its fate, because an array of actors ranging from multinational corporations, non-government organisations (international and national), trade lobby etc., have become important actors in the sphere of foreign policy-making processes. Not surprisingly, the content and focus of foreign policy has shifted dramatically. African foreign policies, it would seem, are now more reactive, occupied with the new demands of global economic governance.

Contributing authors to this volume examine foreign policies as well as the impact of the interlocking interplay of the multiplicity of actors on foreign policy-making in Southern African countries in the era of globalization. The volume is not based on the members of the Southern African Development Community (SADC) *per se*, but on Southern Africa as a contiguous geographical region with socio-cultural and econo-political linkages. Not surprisingly, a couple of SADC member countries are missing from the volume. For example, Tanzania — though an active participant in the FLS deliberations during the apartheid era, and a member of SADC — is excluded.

One of the central arguments is that globalization not only reduces state sovereignty and its attendant sovereign authority, but also paves the way, slowly as it may seem, for the involvement of state and non-state actors in foreign policy-making (Shubin 2000, 75; Holton 1998). Presidential dominance in the area of foreign policy and foreign policy-making reminiscent of the Cold War era is facing challenges in southern Africa and Africa in general, with state and non-state actors taking centre stage.

In Chapter 2, Assis Malaquias argues that it is because of the civil war in Angola that the functions of the other foreign policy-making institutions became subordinated, with the presidency taking centre stage. He argues that though this has changed dramatically since the advent of multi-party politics in Angola, the combination of domestic, regional and international environments has contrived to restrict Angola's foreign policy options.

Focussing mainly on the economic aspects of foreign policy, Zaffiro, in Chapter 3, argues that since the 1990s, globalization has reshaped Botswana's foreign policy and influenced the structure of foreign-policy making. Ajulu, in his chapter on Lesotho, points out that during the Cold War era, Lesotho's foreign policy was influenced mainly by the élite's struggle for survival, and the preservation of the state. In the post-Cold War era, Lesotho finds itself unable to formulate an independent foreign policy. Instead, Lesotho is becoming what he calls a "colony of the newly established SADC." The continued subordination of the Legislature by the Executive on matters pertaining to foreign policy and foreign policy-making in Malawi is articulated by Kaunda in Chapter 5. Kaunda argues that the 1994 multiparty democratic electoral dispensation in Malawi has not altered the institutional frameworks for foreign policy-making.

In Chapter 6, Laville observes that the adoption of economic liberalism in Mauritius has not necessarily led to the transformation and democratization of the foreign policy-making process in that country. She argues that over the years, particularly since the 1970s, Mauritius has pursued a neutral foreign policy stance, with the Prime Minister as key actor. In his chapter on Mozambique, Mwangi argues that for two decades after her independence, Mozambique's foreign policy-making process was characterised by presidential dominance. The personalization and centralization of foreign policy-making within the Office of the President has been influenced mainly by three factors: the proactive role Mozambique played in the liberation struggles in southern Africa; the war efforts against RENAMO; and FRELIMO's lack of institutional capacity on matters pertaining to foreign affairs. Even though this trend is gradually being challenged in the post-Cold War era, the presidency still exhibits more power and influence *vis-à-vis* other institutions responsible for the formulation and implementation of foreign policy in Mozambique.

8   *Globalization and Emerging Trends*

In Chapter 8, Matanga argues that Namibia's foreign policy objectives are guided by two precepts, namely, the promotion of economic development and the maintenance of her territorial integrity. Namibia's membership of the Southern African Customs Union (SACU) and SADC are, therefore, viewed in these contexts. On the issue of foreign policy-making, Matanga states that, due to the prevailing authoritarian system of governance in Namibia, the presidency remains the key actor.

In Chapter 12, Adar demonstrates that apart from the presidency, other actors are increasingly becoming important players in Zambian foreign policy-making. Domson-Lindsey, in Chapter 11, provides a detailed analysis of the relationship between the King as the executive monarch and other foreign policy-making institutions in Swaziland.

In Chapter 13, Adar, Ajulu and Onyango argue that the 1988 merger of the Zimbabwe African People's Union (ZAPU) and Mugabe's Zimbabwe African National Union-Patriotic Front (ZANU-PF) laid the main foundation for the centralisation of power within the Office of the President. Over the years, the presidency became the dominant actor in foreign policy-making. The authors note that this trend is changing, particularly since the 2000 parliamentary multiparty electoral dispensation.

Whereas Philip Nel, in Chapter 9, focusses on the élite perceptions of South African foreign policy during the Mandela presidency, Le Pere and Van Nieuwkerk analyse the central underpinnings of the country's foreign policy and foreign policy-making process since the 1994 multiparty democratic electoral dispensation. They argue in Chapter 10 that even though Mandela's domestic and international stature tended to overshadow other foreign policy actors, the Cabinet and Parliament maintained checks and balances on the presidency. The authors also state that Mbeki's personal interest in foreign affairs dates back to the time when he was in exile, and afterwards, when he was the chief diplomat for the African National Congress (ANC). He remains the key figure in the South African foreign policy-making process.

In Chapter 14, Bischoff examines foreign policy-making trends in the SADC. Focussing on what they call the New Labour Party's 'third way' — that is the ethical dimension of foreign policy — Abrahamsen and Williams argue, in Chapter 15, that since taking over the leadership in Britain, the Labour Party has yet to translate its objectives into reality in southern Africa. In Chapter 16, Schraeder finds persistent inconsistencies in the Clinton administration's democracy enlargement policy in southern Africa and Africa in general.

Notes

1 See also, Vernon Mckay (1966); Timothy M. Shaw and Olajide Aluko (1984); and Doudou Thiam (1963).
2 For a detailed discussion of this see, for example, the excellent discussion on global restructuring in Cox (1994, 45-53) and Tandon (2000, 56-83); on the changing role of the Bretton Woods institutions see Szeftel (1987, 87-140).
3 See for example A. Hoogvelt (1997, 162-180); see also Baylies' excellent discussion of conditionality and democratisation (1995, 321-337).

References

Adar, Korwa G. (1994) *Kenyan Foreign Policy Behavior Towards Somalia, 1963-1983*. Lanham: University Press of America.
Allison, Graham T. (1971) *The Essence of Decision: Explaining the Cuban Missile Crisis*. Boston: Little, Brown.
Aluko, Olajide, ed. (1977) *The Foreign Policies of African States*. London: Hodder and Stoughton.
Anda, Michael O. (2000) *International Relations in Contemporary Africa*. Lanham: University Press of America.
Baylies, C. (1995) "Political Conditionality and Democratisation." *Review of African Political Economy* 65.22: 321-37.
Colebatch, H.K. (1998) *Policy*. Minneapolis: Minnesota University Press.
Cox, R.W. (1994) "Global Restructuring: Making Sense of the Changing International Political Economy." *Political Economy and the Changing Global Order*. Ed. R. Stubbs and G.R.D. Underhill. New York: St Martin's Press.
Gambari, Ibrahim. (1989) *Theory and Reality in Foreign Policy Making: Nigeria After the Second Republic*. Atlantic Highlands, N.J.: Humanities Press International.
Holton, Robert J. (1998) *Globalization and the Nation-State*. London: Macmillan.
Hoogvelt, A. (1977) *Globalization and the Post-colonial State: The New Political Economy of Development*. Basingstoke: Macmillan.
Korany, Bahgat. (1986) *How Foreign Policy Decisions are Made in the Third World*. Boulder: Westview.
———. (1976) *Social Change, Charisma and International Behaviour*. Leiden: Sijthoff.
Mazrui, Ali A. (1977) *Africa's International Relations: The Diplomacy of Dependency and Change*. London: Heinemann.
Mckay, Vernon. (1966) *African Diplomacy: Studies in the Determinants of Foreign Policy*. New York: Praeger.
Mushi, S.S. and K. Mathews, eds. (1981) *Foreign Policy of Tanzania, 1961-1981*. Dar-es-Salaam: Tanzania Publishing House.
Nabudere, D.W. (2000) *Globalisation and Post-Colonial African State*. Harare: AAPS Books.
Robertson, R. (1992) *Globalization: Social Theory and Global Culture*. London: Sage.
Rothe, Stefan. (1989) "The Churches and Sanctions: The SACC and the SACBC." *Sanctions Against Apartheid*. Ed. Mark Orkin. Cape Town: Catholic Institute for International Relations: 68-80.

Schraeder, Peter J. (1996) "African International Relations." *Understanding Contemporary Africa*. Ed. April A. Gordon and Donald L. Gordon. Boulder: Lynne Rienner: 129-165.

———. (1997) "Senegal's Foreign Policy Challenges of Democratization and Marginalization." *African Affairs* 96: 485-508.

Shaw, Timothy M. and Julius E. Okolo, eds. (1994) *The Political Economy of Foreign Policy in ECOWAS*. New York: St. Martin's Press.

Shaw, Timothy M. and Olajide Aluko, eds. (1984) *The Political Economy of African Foreign Policy*. New York: St. Martin's Press.

Shubin, Vladimir. (2000) "African Renaissance and African Unity in the Era of Globalisation." *Problematising the African Renaissance*. Ed. Eddy Maloka and Elizabeth le Roux. Pretoria: African Institute of South Africa: 68-80.

South African Council of Churches. (1974) *Report of the Director to National Conference of SACC, Division of Justice and Reconciliation*. Johannesburg: SACC.

Stubbs, R. and G.R.D. Underhill, eds. (1994) *Political Economy and the Changing Global Order*. New York: St Martin's Press.

Tandon, Y. (2000) "Globalization and Africa's Options." *Globalization and Post-colonial African State*. Ed. D. Nabudere. Harare: AAPS Books.

Thiam, Doudou. (1963) *The Foreign Policy of African States: Ideological Bases, Present Realities, Future Prospects*. London: Phoenix House.

World Council of Churches. (1980) *Programme to Combat Racism. WCC's Statements and Actions on Racism, 1948-1979*. Geneva: WCC.

Wright, Stephen ed. (1999) *African Foreign Policies*. Boulder: Westview.

Zartman, I. William. (1966) *International Relations in the New Africa*. Englewood Cliffs, N.J.: Prentice-Hall.

PART I
COUNTRY CASE STUDIES

2 Dysfunctional Foreign Policy: Angola's Unsuccessful Quest for Security since Independence

ASSIS MALAQUIAS

Foreign policy refers to the relationship between a state and its external environment. It focuses on the strategies employed by states to cope with the intrinsic instability of the international system in which they must operate. To successfully navigate this "turbulent" system, states must constantly seek to increase both power and wealth. Failure to do so can lead to loss of independence and, in Buzan's words, sometimes "loss of existence" (1991, 294). States seek power and wealth within two domains: domestic and international. The critical intersection between these two realms delineates a state's foreign policy. However, whereas some western states have been able to use domestic power and wealth to influence their external environments, other countries are involved in ongoing struggles to achieve domestic stability, let alone international relevance. The case of Angola illustrates this enduring struggle for survival, if not relevance, within the anarchic international system.

Angola has achieved a measure of international relevance since gaining independence from Portugal in 1975. This relevance, however, can be attributed to the peculiarly complex nature of its twenty-five year civil war. This conflict's various mutations — from a conflict between nationalist groups with opposing views about the country's post-colonial objectives, to proxy war, to resource war — has caused both extensive domestic devastation and regional instability. It has also generated international concern and intervention. The Angolan government's foreign policy since independence has been crafted primarily to help it respond to the various domestic, regional and international pressures resulting from the civil war's various mutations. Specifically, Angola's foreign policy has focused on enhancing the regime's ability to win the civil war. As a first step towards achieving this objective, Angola has sought to reshape its regional environment.

The regional dimension of Angola's foreign policy has produced important and positive results. Once surrounded by unfriendly governments, Angola now enjoys amicable relations with its neighbors. However, Angola has not yet been able to translate these regional successes into tangible benefits at home where, notwithstanding recent government victories on the battlefield, the war continues without an end in sight. Arguably, Angola's lamentable condition can be blamed on a quarter-century of civil war. However, this emphasis does not account for some important governmental shortcomings including the failure to establish a viable governance framework and pragmatic domestic and foreign policy agendas. This chapter deals with some of these shortcomings. It focuses on Angola's idiosyncratic and often dysfunctional foreign policy. The chapter also highlights the effects of the ideological choices made by the new regime upon gaining independence and suggests how they have affected foreign policy.

Foreign Policy-Making Process: The Single-Party Era

Angola's foreign policy-making process during the single-party era reflected the relationship between the ruling party, Movimento Popular de Libertacao de Angola (MPLA), and the executive. During the single-party regime, between 1975 and 1991, the party and government shared responsibilities regarding foreign policy. However, it was the party that set the main policy objectives. The MPLA's structure and ideology reflected its close relationship with the Soviet Union. Structurally, the MPLA consists of three main national decision-making bodies: the Political Bureau, Central Committee, and Party Congress — all headed by the party chairman who is also the country's president. In addition, the party comprises provincial, district, and local committees.

The MPLA Political Bureau, the most influential body within the party, is an elected body of the Central Committee entrusted with the responsibilities of overseeing the implementation of party policy. The Central Committee, in turn, is responsible for formulating party policy, including foreign policy, between Congresses. The Central Committee implements its actions through its Secretariat. The MPLA Central Committee Secretariat includes nine departments (Executive Personnel, Foreign Relations, Defense and Security, Organization, Administration and Finance, Economic and Social Policies, Ideology, State and Legal Agencies, and Productive Sector). The MPLA Party Congress — an assembly of party delegates, including local, district, and provincial representatives as well as members of the Central Committee, Political Bureau, and the army — meets every five years. The Congress is responsible for setting the party's overall policy direction. This structure affected the making and implementation of Angola's foreign policy in important ways, particularly during the one-party era. Specifically, the party, and not the executive, established the main foreign policy guidelines. The Ministry of External Relations, far from becoming a repository of technical expertise in international relations, was relegated to the mundane day-to-day implementation of foreign policy. The commanding position of the Party in all areas, including foreign policy, partly explains the high levels of dogmatism in Angola's foreign policy during the single-party era. The ruling party saw the external environment primarily through ideological lenses and, consequently, imparted doctrinaire ideological rectitude — not pragmatic expediency — to Angola's foreign policy. Even the President, as both the party chairman and head of government, was constrained by the policy guidelines set by the party Congress.

The Presidency: Setting the Tone Despite Party Constraints

Notwithstanding the constraints imposed by the party, the president — by virtue of his positions as both party chairman and head of government — had important opportunities to set the tone for the country's foreign policy while ensuring that its main goals and objectives were fulfilled through careful implementation. Angola's first president, Agostinho Neto, was particularly adept in infusing Angola's foreign policy with a 'non-aligned' rhetoric, if not substance, without appearing to stray too far from the party line. An intensely nationalist leader, Neto yearned to chart an independent foreign policy for Angola. According to Lucio Lara, Neto's long-time deputy and MPLA's former ideology chief, this independence caused some friction with the Soviet Union. As Lara explains,

> We had terrible problems with the Soviets, the MPLA, Neto, the leadership of the MPLA, we all did. We had problems every time the Russians tried to use their approach . . . to force our country to do something. We always reacted with outrage. The Soviets withdrew their support from the MPLA when we returned to Angola. We had no support from them! At this time we had managed to receive some weapons brought to Angola on a Yugoslav boat. The Portuguese were still here, there were rival freedom movements, and we had already been attacked by the South Africans in the south and from the north by the Portuguese and Zaireans. We managed to get hold of weapons from

Yugoslavia, not Russia . . . . It wasn't until later when we got the support of Cuba, which we asked for, that relations with Russia improved. We've always been very independent, even with regard to our allies. The Soviets had misgivings and wanted to impose their party line on us, and we never accepted it (Brittain 1996, 1).

There is additional evidence supporting Neto's desire to pursue a 'non-aligned' foreign policy. For example, Neto's government decided to allow Western enterprises, particularly American oil companies, to continue operations in Angola. Neto also made attempts to open diplomatic channels with the USA before his sudden death in 1979 in a Moscow hospital. With hindsight, however, Neto could afford this posture because Angola had not yet been pushed to the edge of the abyss by more aggressive foreign intervention and a revived domestic threat. His successor, Jose Eduardo dos Santos, was presented with a different set of domestic and foreign policy challenges: a revived UNITA (Uniao Nacional Para Independencia Total de Angola) at home and the external threats represented by the Reagan Doctrine. Therefore, Dos Santos had little choice but to reposition Angola firmly within the Soviet sphere. In December 1979, three months after assuming the presidency in Angola, Dos Santos travelled to the USSR to secure continuing Soviet assistance. He returned to Moscow in 1983, 1986, and 1988 at times when his government's position debilitated militarily by UNITA's advances in the centre of the country (Brittain, 1986). The increased military support acquired from the USSR was crucial for the Angolan government's survival in the years before the signing of the Bicesse Peace Accord in 1991 that ushered in the era of multi-party politics.

Multi-Party Politics and Foreign Policy

The foreign policy-making process in Angola was affected by the transition to multi-party politics in the early 1990s. The governing party could no longer claim sole control over the foreign policy-making process. However, in accordance with international law and practice, the presidency has been able to resist such pressures and exercises near-exclusive control over the foreign policy-making process. Nevertheless, although the presidential palace (Futungo de Belas) has become the main site for foreign policy-making, there are at least four other sources of input into this process: the governing party, the fledgling parliament, the ministry of external relations, and the armed forces.

The Governing MPLA

The governing party is able to influence the foreign policy-making process through its structural links with the government. For example, as mentioned above, the President's authority is derived both from his position as head of government and as chair of the ruling party. Also, senior MPLA officials head key government ministries, including the Ministry of External Relations. Equally important, under Secretary-General Joao Lourenco, the MPLA has assumed a more dynamic role in external affairs. Lourenco has visited several foreign countries including the USA, China, Portugal, France, Israel, and South Africa, to brief foreign leaders on developments in Angola and to strengthen bilateral relations. In January 2000, Lourenco held discussions with South African President Thabo Mbeki and expressed his country's dissatisfaction over the destabilizing actions perpetrated by certain South African elements against Angola (BBC, 2000). It was also Lourenco who, in May 2000, declared Angola's intention to boycott the 36th OAU summit in Lome, Republic of Togo due to that country's friendly relationship with UNITA (BBC, 2000a).

Parliament and the Ministry of Foreign Affairs

With the introduction of multi-party politics, Parliament was expected to emerge as an important player in domestic politics by occupying the space and carrying out the functions previously performed exclusively by the MPLA. However, in the aftermath of Angola's problematic first multi-party elections held in 1992 — when President Dos Santos won with 49.57% of the votes to Jonas Savimbi's 40%, and the governing MPLA won 129 seats to UNITA's 70 seats in the 220-seat Parliament — such expectations have not materialized. Parliament has yet to achieve relevance in domestic politics. UNITA initially refused to take its seats, claiming that the MPLA's majority was the result of electoral fraud. UNITA eventually took its seats after the signing of the Lusaka Peace Accord on 20 November 1994 between the MPLA and UNITA, establishing yet another peace framework.

However, since the signing of the Lusaka Accord, UNITA has split into two factions: Jonas Savimbi's UNITA and Eugenio Manuvakola's UNITA-Renovada. Created in September 1998 by Manuvakola (a former Secretary

General of Savimbi's UNITA), UNITA-Renovada has assumed control over UNITA's parliamentary seats and has replaced those UNITA parliamentarians still sympathetic to Savimbi. UNITA-Renovada has become the main interlocutor with the government since the resumption of full-scale war in December 1998. In sum, UNITA has not been able to coherently carry out its functions as the official opposition in Parliament.

The smaller political parties represented in Parliament are severely handicapped by lack of financial and organizational resources. Many must depend on the 'good will' of the government to disburse enough funds to carry out their functions. Predictably, therefore, with UNITA in disarray and the voices of the new parties seldom heard, Parliament is unable to play a significant role. Specifically, regarding foreign policy, Parliament has been unable to fulfill its 'checks and balances' potential.

As is the case with Parliament, the Ministry of External Relations has struggled to maintain its relevance. Several reasons help to explain this ministry's inability to take a dominant position *vis-à-vis* its other domestic competitors. First, its bureaucracy is alarmingly incompetent. The former colonial power made no attempt to create a bureaucracy competent enough to manage important state functions after independence. Cuba's attempts to help create a cadre of Angolan diplomats after independence did not produce significant results, especially in light of the fact that, after the collapse of the former Soviet Union, Angola realigned its foreign policy in favour of the West. Given the new circumstances, the skills and language aptitudes acquired in Cuba were not always relevant. Cronyism compounds the problem. For example, most Angolan diplomats have achieved their posts due to membership of the ruling party or service in the army, not their technical competency in international relations.

The lack of technical competence in the area of foreign relations has received attention from President Dos Santos. As far back as 1989, the Angolan head of state noted a number of shortcomings, "particularly diplomatic inoperativeness mainly due to a lack of a practical attitude and diplomatic ability by several cadres to the extent of ignoring the scientific principles of diplomacy." Dos Santos suggested that "the improvement of the system of external relations was a matter of urgency, particularly the training of cadres and labour organizations, in order to ensure the practical implementation of principles upon which our diplomacy is based" (BBC, 1989).

The Armed Forces

Bureaucratic incompetence in foreign affairs and, for that matter, elsewhere throughout the state apparatus is partly attributable to the civil war. Specifically, some of Angola's best and brightest serve in the armed forces. Moreover, since neither Neto nor Dos Santos were career military officers before ascending to the presidency, both have relied on the military as a vital source of inputs to both domestic and foreign policies.

At the domestic level, Angola's military has played an important role since independence by defending the government against invaders and insurgents. But the army has also been an executor of the government's foreign policy, particularly when it involves the use of force at the regional level. Therefore, besides aiding the liberation armies in southern Africa, the Angolan army has intervened several times in the region: in 1977, to prop up the regime of President Manuel Pinto da Costa in Sao Tome and Principe; in 1997, to help topple the Mobutu regime in Zaire and also to help topple the regime of Pascal Lissouba in Congo-Brazaville; and in 1998, to help save the Kabila regime in the Democratic Republic of Congo against an insurgency.

The significance of Angola's army as a national institution — comprising more than 100,000 troops and consuming an average of 25% of the government's budget — evidenced by its victories, both at the domestic and regional levels, has kept it firmly at the centre of the decision-making apparatus. Thus, for example, during the 1980s and 1990s, Angola's diplomatic initiatives to find paths to end the civil war have consistently involved senior military officers. In fact, two of the most prominent soldier-diplomats — former chief-of-staff Gen. Antonio Fanca 'Ndalu' and Interior Minister Gen. Alexandre Rodrigues 'Kito' — now hold ambassadorial positions in the United States and South Africa, respectively.

Notwithstanding the diversity of inputs, however, Angola's foreign policy-making process is still essentially centralized. No longer dominated by the governing party, it increasingly reflects the president's concept of the national interest and of how foreign policy can facilitate its achievement. For Angola, given the diminutive international stature of its current president, this new centralization of the foreign policy-making process has contributed to its staleness with the result that Angola continues to be relegated to the margins of the international stage. But, taken singly, party-state relations do not fully account for Angola's decaying foreign policy. Other important conditioning factors — national, regional, and international — must also be taken into account (Malaquias 1999, 24-31).

Conditioning Factors in Angola's Foreign Policy

The Domestic Environment

Protracted civil war: impacts on foreign policy Angola's current domestic condition and international position is particularly deplorable since the country was expected to achieve a measure of international relevance when it attained independence after a long anti-colonial struggle. This expectation was neither unfounded nor unrealistic given Angola's considerable natural resource endowment, including vast deposits of oil and diamonds. Unfortunately, such expectations were shattered in the process of decolonization and the civil war that followed.

Decolonization in Angola was precipitated by a military coup in Portugal that deposed the regime of Marcelo Caetano on 25 April 1974. Among other things, the coup leaders sought a quick and negotiated settlement to the colonial wars. Thus, Portugal placed its colonies on the fast track to political independence. The former Portuguese colonies of Guinea-Bissau and Cape Verde, Sao Tome and Principe, and Mozambique were granted independence without major problems. In Angola — where three armed liberation movements representing different ethnic and ideological constituencies were unable to find agreement on a common blueprint for post-colonial state building — decolonization was considerably more complex and eventually degenerated into civil war.

In the aftermath of Portugal's disorderly disengagement, external forces intervened in an attempt to install their respective clients in power. Zairian troops invaded Angola from the north in support of Holden Roberto's Frente Nacional de Libertacao de Angola (FNLA), while South African troops invaded from the south in support of Jonas Savimbi's Uniao Nacional para Independencia Total de Angola (UNITA). Agostinho Neto's MPLA received help from the former USSR and Cuba. This support — particularly Cuban troops — was essential for the MPLA to gain power and remain in control, albeit precariously, of the government. However, Cuban and Soviet assistance could keep MPLA in power but it could not help inflict a decisive military defeat over its main rival, UNITA. Instead, the civil war escalated and destroyed any prospect for a viable economy whilst seriously compromising the security of the citizenry and the regime's stability. In this context, survival became the most dominant aspect of political life, with implications for Angola's foreign policy. After twenty-five years of civil war, the MPLA regime continues to search for ways to destroy by military force, or politically coopt its main domestic adversary. UNITA, on the other hand, does not seem to have abandoned its goal of capturing power by bullets, if not ballots. More importantly, it continues to display an uncanny ability to survive and, sometimes, thrive.

Since its creation in 1966, UNITA has established regional and international links to ensure survival as a political and military force. These links have involved major global and regional powers such as communist China in the 1960s as well as the United States and South Africa in the 1970s and 1980s. Indeed, UNITA acted as a United States and South African proxy army from the mid-1970s until the collapse of the apartheid regime in 1994. This association with the former minority regime in South Africa sealed UNITA's fate as an international pariah.

The major global and regional changes which took place in the late 1980s and early 1990s — the end of the Cold War and the collapse of the minority regime in South Africa — relegated UNITA to irrelevance at international and regional levels, even if not domestically. Unfortunately, UNITA's loss of external benefactors in the early 1990s did not place it in mortal danger: Savimbi had found alternative means in the form of diamonds to pursue his goals. During the 1990s, UNITA controlled significant portions of Angola's diamond mining areas. The British non-governmental organization, Global Witness, estimates that, between 1992 and 1997, UNITA was able to mine diamonds worth US$ 3.7 billion (*Global Witness*, 1998).

Unsurprisingly, much to the chagrin of the Angolan government and the United Nations (UN), UNITA has used its newfound wealth and independence to remain a lethal player in domestic politics. The UN has responded to the Angolan government's appeals for international sanctions against UNITA with a determined effort to curtail the rebels' ability to sell Angolan diamonds on the international market. To this end, the UN Security Council has taken several significant steps. For example, in the aftermath of the resumption of Angola's civil war in 1992 — after UNITA rejected the results of the first multi-party election won by the MPLA — the UN Security Council (UNSC) adopted Resolution 864 (1993) of 15 September 1993 which "prohibit[s] all sale or supply to UNITA of arms and related materiel and military assistance, as well as petroleum and petroleum products . . . ." UNSC Resolution 864 (1993) also established a Committee of the Security Council "To promulgate guidelines that may be necessary to facilitate the implementation of the measures imposed" by the resolution. This would be one in a series of Security Council resolutions aimed at incrementally isolating UNITA.

Currently, the UN's sanction regime against UNITA is based on the Fowler Report (UNSC 2000), prepared by the panel of experts established under UNSC Resolution 1237 (1999). The report presents a detailed account of UNITA's activities in circumventing UN sanctions in the areas of acquisition of arms and military equipment, petroleum and petroleum products as well as the trade in diamonds. It establishes, for example, that UNITA uses several international arms brokers as well as connections in several African states — especially Burkina Faso and Togo — to facilitate delivery of large quantities of weapons (mainly small arms and light weapons) from Eastern Europe. However, the Fowler Report found evidence that UNITA also imported conventional weapons systems including "mechanized vehicles such as tanks and armoured personnel carriers, mines and explosives, a variety of small arms and light weapons, and anti-aircraft weapons, and a variety of artillery pieces" (UNSC 2000, para. 48). Even with the support of the international community, Angola seems to be far from achieving peace within its borders. Therefore its foreign policy will continue to seek avenues to enhance regime stability both regionally and internationally.

The Regional Environment

At independence, the MPLA's single regional ally was the People's Republic of Congo, a relatively small and weak state. On the other hand, it was literally surrounded by enemies, especially Zaire and South Africa.

Mobutu's Zaire and Kabila's Congo Mobutu's Zaire was openly aggressive toward the new regime. Unable to establish a friendly regime in Angola at independence, Zaire would become an important rear base for FNLA – much as it had been during the 1960s and early 1970s – and, later, for UNITA. Zaire also became the key conduit of American military support to Angolan rebels. Angola's foreign policy toward Zaire was often contradictory, lacking a coherent pattern of engagement.

Immediately after independence and in the aftermath of the ill-fated Zairian invasion by anti-Mobutu forces based in Angola, President Agostinho Neto attempted to normalize relations with Zaire. For Neto, normalization of relations with Zaire was a pragmatic goal, an essential first step to enhance Angola's security by altering the regional environment. As a first step to normalizing relations, Neto was prepared to expel the Zairian secessionist forces from Angola in return for a similar measure from Mobutu regarding FNLA. However, neither president fully kept his promises.

On the surface, Mobutu appeared to have fulfilled his commitments: FNLA leader Holden Roberto was expelled from Zaire, FNLA bases in Zairian territory were closed and the activities of FNLA sympathizers were curtailed. These actions, however, did not represent a fundamental shift in Zaire's bellicose policy toward Angola. Indeed, Mobutu was instrumental in the creation of a new insurgent movement — the Comite Militar de Resistencia de Angola (Military Committee for Angolan Resistance (COMIRA) — in August 1980 (BBC 1981; *The Economist* 1982, 32). Led by former FNLA members, COMIRA was based in Zaire and carried out attacks in northern Angola. By the mid-1980s, however, COMIRA was a spent force both militarily and politically. Unable to control any significant portion of territory, COMIRA could not sustain external support. Its leaders eventually took advantage of the governing MPLA's policy of clemency to surrender and accept reintegration into Angolan society.

Much like his Zairian counterpart, Neto was also unable, or unwilling, to deliver on his side of the bargain. Instead, Zaire's Shaba province (former Katanga) was invaded in March 1977 and May 1978 by remnants of the Katangese rebel force that had sought independence for that region shortly after independence. The two Shaba invasions, both from Angolan territory, quickly revealed the ineptitude of the Zairian army and exposed the fragility of Mobutu's regime. In both instances, foreign troops and American transport planes had to be called upon to save Mobutu. The Zairian dictator felt betrayed and held Neto personally responsible for the invasions.

Angola's relations with Mobutu's Zaire remained severely strained through the 1980s and 90s as Zaire became the most important conduit for American weapons and supplies to UNITA and a convenient transit port for UNITA's $5 billion per year diamond smuggling operations. In the 1990s, however, after the end of the Cold War, Mobutu became a liability to the United States. His kleptocratic and undemocratic practices were no longer tolerable. Without powerful external backing and with mounting internal problems, Mobutu was toppled in May 1997 by an internal rebellion organized and supported by regional actors including Rwanda, Uganda, and Angola.

Angola played a key role by providing political support and training as well as "commandos, money, airplanes and arms" to the anti-Mobutu rebels (McKinley 1997, 1). McKinley states that, in January and early February 1997, "several giant Russian-built cargo planes registered in Angola were seen flying soldiers and arms from Luanda to the Rwandan capital, Kigali," from where they were trucked into Zaire. These soldiers, making up as many as six battalions, were instrumental in the final push toward the capital, Kinshasa.

In 1997, Angola realized a goal it failed to achieve in 1977 and 1978: to help overthrow the overtly unfriendly regime in Zaire. For Angola, the overthrow of Mobutu's regime has everything to do with domestic politics. The Kabila regime was expected to reciprocate by denying UNITA a vital route for the inflow of weapons and outflow of diamonds. Finally, for the first time since independence, Angola had a friendly government in Zaire, now renamed the Congo.

Unfortunately for Angola, the toppling of Mobutu's regime did not fundamentally alter the MPLA regime's domestic security predicament. UNITA survived the loss of its major regional ally in much the same way as it had survived the previous regional changes like the collapse of settler regimes in southern Africa. Alas, as the Fowler Report suggests, UNITA has been able to find alternative means of purchasing weapons.

Relations with South Africa As mentioned above, South Africa also carried out a failed attempt to place a friendly regime in Angola at independence. Understandably, therefore, the Marxist regime that emerged in Angola after decolonization did not develop a cordial relationship with apartheid South Africa. Angola paid a high price for this antagonistic relationship, including frequent military invasions and the consequences of UNITA's transformation into a proxy army for South Africa's regional strategy and within a wider international context.

The new Angolan regime understood that its ability to establish a viable state depended, to a considerable degree, on its ability to help establish friendly regimes in both neighboring states. As far as Namibia and South Africa were concerned, Angola's foreign policy involved open and unconditional military and diplomatic support to the nationalist liberation movements in Namibia and South Africa. In the end, Angola achieved its foreign policy objectives, albeit at a devastating cost.

South Africa's response to this aggressive foreign policy by the new Angolan state came in the form of the so-called 'total strategy,' a desperate set of policies aimed at ensuring the survival of the apartheid system through a combination of reform and repression — both domestically and regionally. The main proponents of this 'total strategy' argued that the source of instability and conflict — both inside South Africa and in the region — was neither apartheid nor colonialism, but external intervention. Therefore, it was necessary to ensure that neighbouring states refrained from actively supporting the armed liberation struggle for South Africa and Namibia and that no communist power gained a political or military foothold in the region. Thus Angola posed a direct threat on three counts. Firstly, Angola was an important base for southern African liberation movements, including Namibia's South West African People's Organization (SWAPO) and South Africa's African National Congress (ANC). Secondly, in terms of ideological orientation, the MPLA regime was overtly and uncompromisingly Marxist–Leninist. Thirdly, about 50,000 Cuban troops were stationed in Angola to help the government face its internal and external enemies.

To counter Angola's threat, South Africa further expanded its security and military apparatus to both suppress opposition at home and destabilize the region. As South Africa's principal enemy in the region, Angola suffered the brunt of the apartheid regime's 'total strategy.' South Africa used two main instruments to threaten Angola's territorial integrity. Firstly, the South African Defence Dorce (SADF) carried out frequent and well-planned military invasions deep into Angolan territory. This strategy resulted in tremendous devastation both in terms of human lives lost and infrastructures destroyed. Between 1975 and 1988, South Africa mounted yearly, large-scale military invasions of Angola. These invasions, carried out under the pretext of responding to increased SWAPO attacks in northern Namibia from bases in southern Angola, usually involved several SADF infantry battalions, paratrooper units, tank battalions, long-range artillery groups, and military aircraft squadrons. The duration of each invasion varied according to the real objective of the mission. Thus, for example, missions to destroy SWAPO bases did not take as much time as missions which involved fighting alongside UNITA to prevent advances by Angolan government troops.

Secondly, South Africa transformed UNITA into a proxy in its regional destabilization policies. Although virtually destroyed by MPLA and Cuban troops in 1975-6, UNITA was reorganized into a significant military force by 1979. As a result, by the end of the 1970s — while the MPLA government and Cuban troops were preoccupied with building massive defensive systems to deter South African military aggression — UNITA's operations had moved northward from its bases in the arid Kuando-Kubango province (southeast Angola) into Angola's central plateau. This was significant for three reasons: i) this is a fertile, densely populated region inahibited by the Ovimbundo ethnic group — UNITA's traditional base of support; ii) military actions effectively rendered the vital Benguela Railway — one of the region's major transportation links to the Atlantic — inoperable; iii) UNITA could use its new bases in the central highlands to initiate military operations further north with the objective of disrupting both oil and diamond exploration — the main pillars of Angola's economy.

In combination, apartheid South Africa's twin strategies toward Angola — regular military invasions and support for UNITA — convinced the Angolan government that a regional settlement with South Africa was in its best interest. Thus, it accepted the Reagan Administration's policy of 'linkage,' tying the withdrawal of Cuban troops from Angola to Namibia's independence on the basis of UNSC Resolution 435 (1978) of 29 September 1978. This resolution reaffirmed "the legal responsibility of the United Nations over Namibia" and approved a UN Secretary-General report containing a proposal for a settlement of the issue based on "the withdrawal of South Africa's illegal administration from Namibia and the transfer of power to the people of Namibia." The resolution also established a United Nations Transition Assistance Group (UNTAG) with a mandate to "ensure the early independence of Namibia through free elections under the supervision and control of the United Nations" (UNSC 1978, paras 1, 2, 3).

Besides increasing international diplomatic pressure, as exemplified by Resolution 435 (1978), by the early 1980s South Africa had its own domestic and regional reasons to accept a negotiated regional settlement. At the domestic level, policies — like the setting up of 'Bantustans' — aimed at resolving crippling political, economic and social problems ran into successive dead-ends. Regionally, the idea of creating a 'constellation of states' where economic and political power — not necessarily military might — would ensure the promotion of South African interests, did not move much beyond the conceptual stage. Zimbabwe's independence on 18 April 1980 under the leadership of Robert Mugabe finally put an end to this idea.

Given their respective sets of internal and external pressures, both Angola and South Africa accepted American diplomatic involvement to help pave the way for a settlement of the interconnected regional conflicts. The New York Accord of 22 December 1988 was the culmination of this process. Signed by Angola, Cuba, and South Africa, the Accord provided for the removal of Cuban troops from Angola in exchange for a South African commitment to implement UNSC Resolution 435 (1978) regarding independence for Namibia.

The Angolan regime saw this accord as a major foreign policy victory in as much as it was expected to bring the MPLA closer to finally achieving a measure of domestic security. It was hoped that full implementation of UNSC Resolution 435 (1978) would benefit Angola in two important ways: it would remove the South African threat from its southern border, and secondly, it would lead to the collapse of UNITA as a military threat since its main supply routes via Namibia would be cut off by a SWAPO–led government (Timsar 1991, 1). This optimistic expectation partly explains the MPLA's refusal to accept a broader peace deal that would include a settlement of Angola's civil war. The government believed that, without South African support, UNITA guerrillas would accept the terms of President dos Santos' 'harmonization policy' which promised jobs and houses to rebels who laid down their arms. But military surrender would not assure political survival for UNITA because, by the late 1980s, the MPLA government still adhered to the principles of one-party politics, arguing that the stability Angola needed "to continue implementing a political model that upholds the interests of the people" could only exist on the basis of the single party system (BBC, 1989a).

In the event, UNITA did not 'disappear' due to discontinued support from apartheid South Africa. Similarly, the collapse of the apartheid regime did not lead to the end of UNITA as a major security threat to the Angolan government. As the Fowler Report suggests, UNITA continues to use South Africa as an important source of weapons. For example, this report states that "a high level UNITA delegation, led by the Vice-President of UNITA, General Antonio Dembo traveled to South Africa in August 1999, and that while in South Africa Dembo and Karrica were able to purchase a 35mm anti-aircraft battery" (United Nations Security Council 2000, para. 30). The report cites "information from the South African Government acknowledging that General Dembo had visited the country in 1999, but stating that this visit was not official business or as a guest of the Government" (UN Security Council 2000, para. 31). Still, the MPLA regime — as a major ally in the anti-apartheid struggle — had sufficient reasons to be annoyed by post-apartheid South Africa's apparent lack of solidarity.

The International Environment

At the international level, Angola became an important battleground of the Cold War. One of the United States' major foreign policy goals during the Cold War was to contain the spread of communism around the world. Since the Angolan government was perceived to be a communist regime due to its close ties with the former Soviet Union and Cuba, the United States was willing to support the rebel movement fighting to overthrow that regime. The Soviet Union, on the other hand, was ideologically committed to supporting the Angolan government. Thus, not even Angola's fiercely nationalistic first president, Agostinho Neto, could extricate the country from the East–West chessboard. Neto did not live long enough to chart an alternative foreign policy truly non-aligned. He died in September 1979, less than four years after taking office.

Neto was succeeded by Jose Eduardo Dos Santos, a Soviet trained petroleum engineer. Dos Santos favoured even closer ties with the USSR and Cuba due to a quickly deteriorating domestic situation. Unlike his predecessor, dos Santos was prepared to give greater latitude to the Soviets in determining the main guidelines of the new state's domestic and foreign policy. Previously frustrated with Neto's flirtation with nonalignment, the USSR welcomed this new foreign policy orientation because Angola provided an important base in Southern Africa from which to affect change during a period of great instability caused by both regional and Cold War dynamics. The USSR was particularly interested in influencing events in South Africa, the richest and most developed state in the subcontinent, and thus fulfil its self-proclaimed role as the vanguard of Third World liberation movements and oversee the implementation of the Soviet model of political, economic and social development. Cuba also agreed to provide additional support for Dos Santos. Despite its own serious domestic and international problems, Cuba was willing to provide various types of assistance to Angola and other Third World countries to further its own foreign policy objectives, including, primarily, an assertion of its leadership in the Non-aligned Movement (Macfarlane 1992, 87). However, given their own problems and limitations, neither the USSR nor Cuba could solve the MPLA's domestic problems. In particular, they could not help solve Angola's economic problems or prevent UNITA from becoming a growing threat with Zairian, South African and American assistance.

Angola's Problematic Relationship with the United States The USA, like other Western countries, has historically maintained a presence in southern Africa to safeguard its access to the region's vast deposits of minerals. During the Cold War, the containment of the perceived Soviet expansionist threat in the region provided the rationale for additional involvement (Ogunbadejo 1985, 3). However, the involvement of the USA in Angola has been problematic due to its intervention on the side of FNLA and UNITA during the chaotic transition to independence, the withholding of diplomatic recognition to the MPLA regime, and continuing support for UNITA. Consequently, USA–Angola relations never moved past mutually beneficial commercial interests, notably with American companies' exploration of the vast Angolan oil fields. Although this commercial relationship, initiated during the colonial period, continued uninterrupted when the MPLA assumed power, the USA preferred not to deal with the MPLA government at a political level until it held democratic elections in Angola. It was assumed in Washington that free and fair elections would bring UNITA to power since this party's main base of support was among Angola's largest ethnic group, the Ovimbundu.

In September 1975, during the early stage of Angola's civil war, the USA Secretary of State, Henry Kissinger, declared that events in Angola had taken a "distressing turn" and that the United States was "most" alarmed at the interference of extracontinental powers," i.e., the Soviet Union and Cuba (Howland 1989, 16). Soviet and Cuban "interference" had frustrated the United States' own, more circumspect intervention. In addition to providing financial and material support to the FNLA and UNITA, the USA encouraged its regional allies to intervene in Angola on the side of pro-Western forces. Thus, in October 1975, South Africa invaded Angola to aid the FNLA-UNITA alliance. The South African thrust north towards Luanda could not be completed before Angola achieved independence on 11 November 1975. The intervention of about 2,000 Cuban troops — who had been arriving in Angola to aid the MPLA since March 1975 — and a significant increase in Soviet arms shipments to the MPLA halted South Africa's advance a few kilometers south of Luanda.

Predictably, American reaction to MPLA control of Luanda at independence was overtly hostile. Secretary Kissinger said that the United States would not recognize the MPLA, which had managed to seize Luanda "through a very substantial inflow of communist arms" and that it favoured negotiations to attempt to create "a transitional government that would permit the popular will to be consulted" (Howland 1989, 16).

MPLA leader Agostinho Neto believed that, sooner rather than later, the United States would recognize his government and deepen mutually beneficial trade relations — especially in the oil industry — and to help solve the remaining problems affecting southern Africa, notably the transition to majority rule in Namibia, South Africa and Zimbabwe. Thus, on 21 July 1978, Angolan President Agostinho Neto publicly urged the United States to recognize his government. Speaking at a press conference in Luanda, Neto said that the Angolan government had "no reservations" about establishing diplomatic relations with Washington. However, he reiterated his government's intention not to ask Cuban troops in Angola to withdraw in exchange for relations with the USA. Neto demanded that the USA "take us as we are and no other way."

The USA's response was immediate and unequivocal. A day after Neto's overture, the USA State Department stated that two major barriers prevented normalization of diplomatic relations between the two countries. Firstly, the presence of Cuban troops in Angola was still a matter of concern; secondly, "the problem of internal reconciliation among the various factions in Angola" needed to be resolved before the USA would extend diplomatic recognition (*Facts on File* 1978, 562 F1). Both issues — removal of Cuban troops and a negotiated settlement of the civil war involving the creation of a coalition government with UNITA — would guide American policy toward Angola for nearly two decades. And the USA could claim victory when, on 1 February 1988, its State Department announced that "the Angolan delegation for the first time affirmed its acceptance of the necessity of the withdrawal of all Cuban troops from Angola, in the context of a settlement" (Sparks 1988). This led to the signing of the New York Accord of 22 December 1988 between Angola, Cuba, and South Africa. The accord included provisions for the implementation of Resolution 435 on Namibian independence and for the withdrawal of all Cuban troops from Angola.

By this date, American pressure — both diplomatic and military — had forced Angola to meet another main condition for normalizing relations with the USA, i.e., a negotiated end to the civil war and power-sharing with UNITA. Under Reagan, UNITA became a major recipient of sophisticated American weaponry, including 'Stinger' anti-aircraft missiles which, for the first time, upset the air supremacy enjoyed by the MPLA government. Consequently, all major military offensives mounted by the MPLA/Cuban/Soviet forces to dislodge the Angolan rebels from their bases in southern Angola ended in failure. Unable to defeat UNITA on the battlefield, the MPLA agreed to a negotiated settlement to end the civil war.

The Peace Accord signed by Angolan President Eduardo dos Santos and UNITA leader Jonas Savimbi on 31 May 1991 in Bicesse, Portugal was aimed at ending the civil war and created the framework for Angola's transition to elected government. However, this Peace Accord ended only the proxy war stage of the conflict. In November 1992, in the aftermath of a failed electoral process, the MPLA and UNITA initiated another round of fighting, this time using mostly the domestic resources — oil and diamonds —they controlled. Ironically, UNITA ultimately refused to accept one of the main goals of American policy toward Angola: national reconciliation through elections and power sharing. However, the United States, then under

President Bill Clinton, fulfilled its promise by extending diplomatic recognition to Angola after the electoral exercise (Holmes 1993, A9).

Conclusion

In combination, domestic, regional, and international environments have severely restricted Angola's foreign policy options since independence. In addition, the Angolan government was unable to fully capitalize on important changes which occurred at regional and international levels to improve Angola's domestic security. This chapter argues that Angola's inability to take full advantage of these momentous changes to achieve its major foreign policy goals highlights important flaws in the foreign policy-making process. Ironically, the inability to take advantage of changing external environments is not unconnected to Angola's unresolved domestic problems.

Peace will eventually triumph in Angola as it has elsewhere in Africa. This may finally enable Angola to achieve domestic stability as a first step to fulfilling its potential within the region and to attaining relevance internationally. Angola's foreign policy can accelerate the process of peaceful transformation, but this will necessitate a fundamental reordering of priorities. As this chapter shows, changing external environments have not facilitated military solutions to Angola's domestic problems. The solutions to Angola's civil war must be found domestically. In this context, Angola can learn from the experiences of important regional states like Mozambique and South Africa that have overcome the legacy of many years of internal conflict.

References

Allison, Graham T. (1971) *The Essence of Decision: Explaining the Cuban Missile Crisis.* Boston: Little, Brown and Co.

BBC. (1981) "Angola Reports New Zaire-based Rebel Organization." *BBC Summary of World Broadcasts*, 24 December.

———. (1989a) "Angolan Agency Comments on Government Peace Plan, Policy of Reintegration and Military Measures against 'Subversives.'" *BBC Summary of World Broadcasts*, 13 March.

———. (1989b) "Angola Dos Santos on 'Shortcomings' in Diplomacy, Prospects for Economic Development and Cooperation in the Region." *BBC Summary of World Broadcasts*, May 8.

———. (1990) "Angolan President Addresses Traditional Leaders on Peace, Economic Prospects." *BBC Summary of World Broadcasts*, September 24.

———. (1999) "President Dos Santos says Government, not UN, will Restore Peace." *BBC Summary of World Broadcasts*, 19 January.

———. (2000) "Angola to Boycott OAU Summit over Togo's Backing for UNITA." *BBC Summary of World Broadcasts*, 18 May.

———. (2000a) "MPLA Chief Criticizes South African 'Destabilizing' Circles." *BBC Summary of World Broadcasts*, 14 January.

Brittain, Victoria. (1986) "Beleaguered Angola Looks to Kremlin." *The Guardian* (London), 7 May.

———. (1996) "Eighteen years later — speaking to Lucio Lara." *African Communist* 143, First Quarter.

Buzan, Barry. (1991) *People, States and Fear: An Agenda for International Security Studies in the Post-Cold War Era*. Boulder: Lynne Rienner.

Facts on File. (1978) "Angola Requests U.S. Relations." *Facts on File World News Digest*, July 28: 562 F1.

Frankel, Glenn. (1985) "Angola Breaks Off Peace Talks With U.S.: Move Protests Congressional Vote Allowing Aid to Rebel Forces." *The Washington Post*, 14 July: A22.

Global Witness. (1998) *A Rough Trade: The Role of Companies and Governments in the Angolan Conflict*. London: Global Witness.

———. (2000) *Conflict Diamonds: Possibilities for the Identification, Certification and Control of Diamonds*. London: Global Witness.

Gordon, Chris. (1999) "Eastern Europe Aid Bolsters UNITA." *Mail and Guardian* (Johannesburg), January 15.

Holmes, Steven A. (1993) "Washington Recognizes Angola Government." *The New York Times*, May 20: A9.

Howland, Nina D. (1989) "The United States and Angola, 1974-88: A Chronology." *Department of State Bulletin*, February.

Kaiser, Robert G. and Don Oberdonfer. (1978) "Africa Turnabout; Concern Over Soviets, Cubans Transforms U.S. Africa Policy." *The Washington Post*, 4 June: A1.

Lentner, Howard H. (1974) *Foreign Policy Analysis: A Comparative and Conceptual Approach*. Columbus, Ohio: Charles E. Merril.

Macfarlane, S. Neil. (1992) "Soviet-Angolan Relations, 1975-90." *Soviet Policy in Africa*. Ed. George W. Breslauer. Berkeley: University of California Press.

MacKenzie, Ian. (1995) "S. African Visit Gives Boost to Angola's UNITA Chief." *Reuters World Service,* May 18.

Macridis, Roy C. (1976) *Foreign Policy in World Politics*. Englewood Cliffs, NJ: Prentice Hall.

Malaquias, Assis. (1999) "Angola: The Foreign Policy of a Decaying State." *African Foreign Policies*. Ed. Stephen Wright. Boulder: Westview Press.

McKinley, James C. Jr. (1997) "Congo's Neighbors Played Crucial Role in Civil War." *The New York Times*, 22 May: A1.

O'Brien, Tim. (1999) "The Worst Place on Earth to Live." *The Irish Times*, September 18: 10.

Ogunbadejo, Oye. (1985) *The International Politics of Africa's Strategic Minerals*. Westport, Conn: Greenwood Press.

Ottaway, David B. (1978) "Lance Seeks Post at Area Bank Firm; Brzezinski's Strategists Confront Young's 'Africanists' in Policy Row." *The Washington Post*, 14 February: A1.

———. (1978) "Angolan Shakeup Signals Waning Soviet Influence." *The Washington Post*, 15 December: A44.

Pincus, Walter and Robert G. Kaiser. (1978) "U.S. Envoy Dispatched to Angola." *The Washington Post*, 22 June: A1.
Sparks, Samantha. (1988) "Angola: U.S. Sees Progress in Talks." *Inter Press Service*, 1 February.
The Economist. (1982) "Angola; the Detail that Matters." 7 August.
Timsar, Richard. (1981) "Marxist Angola Backs West's Namibia Blueprint." *The Christian Science Monitor*, 29 October:1.
United Nations Security Council. (1978) Resolution 435.
United Nations Security Council. (1993) Resolution 864.
United Nations Security Council. (1997) Resolution 1127.
United Nations Security Council. (1998) Resolution 1173.
United Nations Security Council. (2000) *Report of the Panel of Experts on Violations of Security Council Sanctions Against UNITA*. S/2000/203, 10 March.
World Bank. (1991) *Angola: An Introductory Economic Review*. Washington, DC: World Bank.
Xingzeng, Ye. (1995) "UNITA Wishes to Benefit from Mandela's Experience: Savimbi." *Xinhua News Agency*, October 14.
Xinhua News Agency. (1983) "U.S. Vice-President Meets Angolan Interior Minister." *Xinhua News Agency*, 15 April.

3 Globalization and Foreign Economic Policy-Making in Botswana

JAMES J. ZAFFIRO

Why is the Government of the Republic of Botswana — a landlocked, southern African state — opening costly new overseas missions in Tokyo and Beijing and posting more commercial attachés abroad? Why is it hosting international investment conferences and trade fairs, nurturing private enterprise and launching a country-wide push to upgrade the teaching of English? And why is it investing millions in human resource development whilst computerizing government ministries and departments? The answer is globalization. Without much official questioning of the wisdom of embracing neo-liberalism, or consideration of possible alternative strategies, the Government of Botswana is currently engaged in a fully-fledged effort to re-align key domestic and foreign economic policies to globalization. President Festus Mogae's 1998 Budget Speech lays down the challenge:

> We are facing a much more competitive regional and international environment, which rewards those countries which adapt to the dictates of market discipline and marginalise those that fail to do so. Our timely and adequate response to the opportunities and challenges of globalization, will, to a very large extent, determine our future prosperity as a nation (Mogae 1998, 1).

Globalization is re-shaping Botswana's foreign economic policy and influencing the structure and process of foreign policy-making; it is changing priorities, authority, and responsibility for decision-making and implementation. Who are the key decision-makers in this process? How is foreign economic policy conducted, coordinated and evaluated?

Heightened exposure to global markets magnifies and multiplies domestic inequalities. Botswana has an extremely open economy. Does Botswana have the institutional capacity to regulate markets and financial flows, manage domestic dislocations and compensate losers? Not yet.

Globalization is not an entirely new phenomenon for Botswana. Demand for Botswana's primary source of income, diamonds, depends upon the health of overseas markets and the economic prosperity of citizens in North America, Europe, and the Far East (Legwaila 1993, 617, 619). Never having had to sacrifice economic sovereignty to Bretton Woods bodies and without crushing external debt, globalization looms less threateningly for Botswana's leaders than it does for most other African decision-makers.

A decade before IMF–imposed Structural Adjustment took hold in Africa, Botswana was voluntarily adapting key macroeconomic policies for wider participation in global commerce. Today, many instruments required for expanded international trade, investment, and economic diversification are in place.

The theme of Botswana's National Development Plan 8 (1997–2002) (NDP 8) is "Sustainable Economic Diversification." One implication is that significant development has already occurred. Indeed, per capita income has risen substantially, from about $35 at Independence in 1966, to $4,800 in 1995/96 (NDP 8, 1997, xix). Some of the groundwork for the creation of competitive export industries and a more inviting investment environment for foreign capital was laid during NDP 7. The basic assumption was, and remains, that what Botswana needs is the establishment of "a small number of internationally integrated, anchor firms." Other smaller firms, both domestic and foreign, "will then follow as supplier firms" (NDP 8, 1997, 164). The key to NDP 8 success is attracting these anchor firms.

Government has made a major effort to promote economic diversification via employment-generating industrialization, investment and trade and comprehensively revised its 1984 Industrial Development Policy (IDP) in November 1997. Major emphasis is on development of competitive manufacturing and services, linkage of small and medium-sized firms with larger foreign firms, and aggressive export promotion (Siwawa-Ndai 1997, 342).

The country has worked hard in recent years to sweeten incentives to potential investors, setting up a new foreign investment fund to assist companies and removing foreign exchange controls in February 1999 (*DN*, February 11, 1999, 2). Botswana now has the lowest corporate tax regime in the SADC region, having reduced rates from 40% to 25%, with a special 15% rate for manufacturing enterprises (Mpabanga 1997, 385). Botswana has also worked to improve its national road and rail transport infrastructure, while moving to privatize parastatals, and deregulate. Major constraints remain, including higher production costs — especially utility costs — low labour productivity, and off-putting bureaucratic tendencies (Ndzinge 1998,

462), in addition to a small domestic market, lack of serviced industrial sites and factory space, lack of entrepreneurial and technical skills, and Botswana's landlocked position (Mpabanga 1997, 372). Botswana has a shortage of skilled manpower in all sectors. Access to credit and export pre-financing remains extremely limited for small to medium-scale manufacturing concerns operating in the country.

Capacity-Building: Responding to Globalization at Home

Botswana's leaders are pinning their hopes for employment creation and poverty alleviation on globalization. Rural poverty is especially problematic, as formal sector employment opportunities are almost totally urban-based (Jefferis 1997, 497). A revised national policy on education commits Government to overcoming human resource constraints to industrialization, with programmes designed to emphasize technical, science and business skills, along with knowledge of modern industrial technology (Mpabanga 1997, 378). Government spending on health, education and training is among the highest in Africa, comparable with Malaysia and South Korea.

Information technology is yet another area where government has made significant moves to develop a coordinated policy in support of global competitiveness. Botswana has invested heavily in a new telecommunications infrastructure. Rural areas are included in the upgrading and expansion of service. With the completion of the Ghanzi-Mamuno microwave radio link in 1998, Botswana had direct connections with all of its neighbours. Cellular phone service began in 1998–99 (Mogae 1998, 13).

There has been an explosion of new computing resources coming into the country. Government spending on computing rose from $22 million in 1994 to $33 million in 1996. The Government Computer Bureau is working closely with the private sector to develop efficient national networks. Over 5,000 PCs have already been installed in Government offices country-wide and plans call for full connectivity of all Government offices, including embassies and missions abroad, by the end of NDP 8 (99).

Post-Independence Foreign Policy-Making

For Botswana, as is the case in most developing countries, there has never really been a significant distinction between 'foreign' and 'domestic' policy concerns. A significant change today, however, is that this fusion is more clearly reflected in structures and processes of foreign policy-making. New foreign policy actors include not only new ministries and state institutions but also parastatals and private sector NGOs. Policy coordination with major regional and global IGOs is also a more central objective of Botswana foreign policy today than ever before.

Pre-1990s foreign policy-making strongly reflected the inherited British colonial administrative legacy (Zaffiro 1993). The President was the country's top foreign policy decision-maker and diplomat. Policy control was narrowly concentrated in the Office of the President (OP), a "super-ministry" encompassing foreign affairs, defence, mass media, police, public service, even Parliament. This pattern was steadily eroded during the 1990s. Other ministries have become increasingly sophisticated and successful at involving themselves in foreign policy-making and implementation.

Even before the discovery of massive diamond deposits within its territory, foreign mining interests dictated a foreign economic policy based on expanding pre-existing regional linkages with the global economy. During the 1980s, remittances from Batswana mine labour migrants were gradually replaced by diamond export revenues. Between 1967–84 and from 1990–92, Botswana had a negative balance of trade. In the late 1980s, terms of trade improved. Trade surpluses were recorded for 1985–89 and 1993–95 (NDP 8, 20). The state's revenue base grew and became more secure. Yet, as a 'rentier state,' working of necessity with, and dependent upon, a foreign multinational corporation (DeBeers) through a cartel (CSO) and a parastatal (Debswana), Botswana's foreign economic policy-makers never had full control. Economic success gradually enabled the state to buy into DeBeers and gain greater representation and economic policy-making sovereignty.

Debswana cheques to the Botswana state have financed the lion's share of social and infrastructural improvements and with them a degree of popular political support (Clapham 1996, 70). While economic decline was directly and negatively affecting most African states' external relations, Botswana's leaders became increasingly able to conduct "a foreign policy of economic success" setting them apart from virtually every other African state.

Foreign Policy Responses to Globalization

Botswana's most pressing foreign policy problem today is to effectively convey its successes and economic potential to foreign investors, trade partners, and tourists who still lump the country together with those economic and political failures which constitute the external image of Africa.[1]

Bilateral Economic Relations: South Africa Looms Large

For Botswana, effectively managing globalization depends upon improved bilateral economic relations with South Africa. Prospects for economic growth and diversification are also intimately linked to economic policies in South Africa. Botswana's need for food, fuel, and manufactured goods has been well-exploited by South African producers, investors, and exporters, Botswana's main source and suppliers.

Since independence, Botswana has been working to reduce economic dependence on South Africa, without much success (Tsie 1995, 8). Under President Mandela, South Africa pursued closer economic ties with its neighbours, including Botswana, on the basis of "equity, mutual benefit, and non-domination," realizing that it needs to reassure its own private investors in these states while ensuring stable export markets for its manufactured goods. South Africa continues to employ a range of non-tariff barriers to discourage Botswana goods from entering its markets. Examples include Hyundai vehicles assembled in Botswana, clothing and textiles, soda ash, and beef. Botswana would benefit from a bilateral trade agreement with Pretoria. Botswana has bilateral trade agreements with three fellow SADC member states: Malawi (1956), Zambia (1971) and Zimbabwe (1956, revised 1988) (Siwawa-Ndai 1997, 339). During the 1990s, several Botswana firms were reporting increased exports to South Africa. Success in breaking into local markets, long-dominated by South African imports, has been extremely limited (Mpabanga 1997, 371, 376).

Tensions over trade imbalances have flared on a number of occasions.[2] A major obstacle is the Southern African Customs Union Agreement (SACU). It has been a longstanding position of Botswana that SACU gives South Africa too much power and that renegotiation was necessary. In joining the GATT, Botswana signalled its embrace of globalization over a protectionist SACU. With the coming to power of the African National Congress (ANC), renegotiation with SACU rose to the top of Botswana's foreign economic policy agenda.[3] In 1996, President Masire made prospects for improved relations contingent upon successful renegotiation to decrease the South African customs and excise revenue policy-making monopoly.[4] With South Africa pressing for admission to the World Trade Organization (WTO) prospects for a more liberal regional trade regime are good.[5]

Expanding Relations with East Asia

The shifting geopolitics of globalization in Botswana's foreign policy are most dramatically illustrated by the rapid growth of economic and diplomatic ties with East Asia, in particular China and Japan, but also South Korea, Singapore, and Malaysia. Other than relations with the People's Republic of China (PRC), which date from 1975, and limited diplomatic contacts with Asian Commonwealth States, this activity mainly happened during the decade of the 1990s.

Significant budget increases for foreign affairs during the early 1990s resulted in the opening of a new embassy in the PRC and a consulate in Hong Kong, "to take care of trade and commercial interests in the Far East" (*DN* August 19, 1991, 1). As early as a decade before, Botswana was looking east, in search of new economic partners, sources of foreign aid, trade, and technology (Zaffiro 1999, 77). Official fascination with "Asian productivity" and presidential admonitions to "learn the secrets of Asia's rapid economic success" seemed at times to approach the mystical level.

Embracing Globalization in Trade and Investment Policy

Botswana is struggling to diminish its high dependence on diamond exports (70% of total exports and 40% of GDP in 1995), seeking new markets for its copper-nickel (5-8%), beef (4%), textiles (3%), and assembled vehicles (15%). South Africa remains Botswana's largest market for non-diamond exports. The result is major asymmetric dependence: heavy reliance on the global market to absorb exports and heavy reliance on South Africa for consumption and capital goods imports. How Botswana fares economically in the decades ahead will depend greatly on the interaction between the global economy and the South African economy. Changes and uncertainties in both make Botswana's foreign economic policy-making task more complicated and unpredictable than ever before. Botswana needs to develop and promote exports which are not dependent upon protected foreign markets (Hermans 1996, 120-21).

Pushing Regional Economic Integration: Botswana in SADC

For two decades, Botswana has actively promoted the benefits of regional economic cooperation, free trade and economic integration via the Southern African Development Community (SADC). In Botswana's eyes, the end of apartheid may have altered the original political motives for regional coordination, but it has not diminished the strength of economic arguments. The key issue today is competition for foreign investment. Botswana, like most SADC states, sees it as key to successful economic development.

Optimistic talk of a SADC Free Trade Area encompassing a market of over 190 million people and a combined GDP of more than $US160 billion ignores or underplays significant limitations. Member state economies suffer from a lack of diversity and complementarity of tradable products and services. Significant barriers to the creation of a successful free trade area remain, including non-alignment of regional currencies, forex shortages, lack of trade credit and insurance facilities, and a weak commercial banking and finance infrastructure. Despite consensus on an extended implementation period, realization seems far off. Intra–SADC trade has been growing, from about 5% of member states' total trade in 1990 to 17.4% in 1996 and 20% in 1998, fueled largely by the admission of South Africa (*DN* Nov. 19, 1997, 1). A goal of 35% by 2000 seems unattainable (*DN* August 19, 1998, 3).

Key Foreign Economic Policy Players

Ministry of Commerce and Industry (MCI)

Given the challenging public relations and marketing tasks underpinning Botswana's embrace of globalization, perhaps the most important 'new' foreign policy player is Commerce and Industry. MCI is the key 'line-ministry' responsible for the diversification of foreign economic relations via trade, investment, and tourism, key elements of a policy framework "to facilitate diversification of Botswana in a productive and competitive direction" (NDP 8, 150). In 1996, commercial attachés were posted to Botswana's new consulates in Johannesburg and Cape Town, where most new investment is expected to originate.

Tourism and manufacturing are slated to become the "third and fourth pillars of Botswana's economy" beyond beef and diamonds, creating thousands of badly-needed new jobs (*DN* February 3, 1997, 1). With EU assistance, a strategic plan for the development of the tourism industry was launched in 1997, and statistics indicate rapid growth of this sector (*DN* May 3, 1999, 1). Financial services is another growth area which MCI is currently promoting, along with diamond polishing, glass and chemicals, and leather products (*Vision 2016*, 1997, 47).

Commerce and Industry is responsible for administering and disbursing funds under the Financial Assistance Policy (FAP), an investment subsidy programme intended to promote diversification of the economy and employment creation (NDP 8, 95). New units have been created under its authority to do so. Trade financing, export credit insurance and trade information services are being provided to citizen entrepreneurs for the first time via the Botswana Export Credit Insurance and Guarantee (BECI) scheme (NDP 8, 139), and Trade and Investment Promotion Agency (TIPA) (Siwawa-Ndai 1997, 353).

MCI coordinates the parastatal Botswana Development Corporation (BDC) the main financial institution for industrial development. The 1997/98 Budget allocated $36 million to the BDC for equity finance for local investors and the construction of factory shells (*DN* February 11, 1997, 5). MCI also works closely with the National Development Bank (NDB), Botswana Technology Centre (BTC), Botswana National Productivity Centre (BNTC), and trade and industry NGOs, especially the Botswana Chamber of Commerce, and the Botswana Confederation of Commerce, Industry, and Manpower (BOCCIM).

The Trade and Investment Promotion Agency (TIPA)

TIPA is responsible for promoting foreign and domestic investment in Botswana and is in charge of export promotion. TIPA also runs investors facilitation services, undertakes marketing studies for Botswana businesses wishing to export, and administers the Selebi-Phikwe Regional Development Programme (NDP 8, 151).

Working with MCI's Commercial attachés in Botswana's foreign missions, TIPA initially suggests investment opportunities, emphasizing manufacturing projects which generate empoyment, then works to provide potential investors with information and services by liaising with senior officials in ministries and parastatals. Between 1995 and early 1996, more than 29 foreign companies worked with TIPA, including a South African textile company and USA pharmaceutical and plastics firms (*Mmegi* 12-18 April, 1996, 9).

In 1998 TIPA was restructured and turned into an independent statutory body, the Botswana Export Development and Investment Authority (BEDIA) with full autonomy to undertake investment and export promotion initiatives and to determine where to post its personnel abroad, separate from commercial attachés assigned by MCI to Botswana's foreign embassies and missions (*Mogae* 1998, 10; NDP 8, 1997, 165). Attachés will continue to carry out MCI–designed Publicity and Information Services in accredited countries. There is some confusion over lines of responsibility between BEDIA representatives and attachés. BEDIA will soon open a new Investor Service Centre, to expedite the provision of pre-investment support services, including industrial land, factory space, permits, grants, and utilities.

The Botswana Private Sector Development Project (BPED), begun in 1992 as an initiative to strengthen the private business sector's capacity, provides technical assistance to small entrepreneurs, and encourages international investment through sponsorship of investment delegations. Most of BPSDP's early efforts were directed at helping to launch the independent Botswana Confederation of Commerce, Industry, and Manpower (BOCCIM) as an economic policy advocacy body (Maipose 1997, 29). BOCCIM's former Director, George Kgoroba, is Minister of Commerce and Industry.

Botswana established a formal stock exchange in 1994, as part of a push to promote the country as a centre for international investment, as a step towards establishing an international financial services centre (IFSC) in Gaborone, and to increase international awareness of Botswana as a growing market-based economy. By late 1996, there were 12 listed companies with a market capitalization of P1.2 billion (NDP 8, 134, 137).

Private Sector Actors

Most policy contours of Botswana's embrace of globalization have been supported by key private sector actors. However, if these groups are to eventually play a leading role in economic development, they must be empowered to do so. USA and Swedish aid has helped to create and organize business and commercial lobbies where none existed prior to the 1990s. Sweden supported entrepreneurial development via the Botswana Enterprise Development Unit (BEDU) and helped create a Botswana Management Assistance Programme (BMAP) (*DN* February 2, 1998, 2).

With support from the USA, BOCCIM has become a significant foreign economic policy lobby, communicating private sector interests and concerns to government. Established in the early 1990s in support of privatization, BOCCIM had an American advisor, Dr. Millard Arnold, between 1992–94. Arnold helped BOCCIM gain a higher profile in government planning and budgeting (*Mmegi* 15-21 April 1994, 14). BOCCIM officials are now included in government trade and investment delegations (*DN* April 30, 1997, 1) and Deputy Director Elias Dewah has the ear of key foreign economic policy-makers. BOCCIM's reports and studies, such as "Privatization in Botswana" and "Cost-Benefit Study of Liberalising Foreign Exchange Controls," have served as important inputs in policy formation (NDP 8, 88).

Government is increasingly consulting and responding to the advice and concerns of private sector organizations as it formulaates foreign economic policy. Recent examples include the creation of the Botswana National Productivity Centre (BNPC), Bureau of Standards, Export Credit Insurance and Guarantee Corporation, and special rebate programmes on raw materials for exporters (*DN* March 24, 1997, 1).

Ministry of Foreign Affairs (MFA)

Foreign Affairs (MFA) is responsible for the "formulation, management and implementation of Botswana's foreign policy" (NDP 8, 1997, 483). Foreign Affairs is very much a "line ministry", charged with implementing decisions taken elsewhere. Officers coordinate and implement policies through the country's fifteen foreign missions. From headquarters, MFA facilitates communication across government ministries and departments, while managing bilateral relations with over seventy countries maintaining resident and non-resident missions with Botswana.

Foreign service officers have been told that the promotion of Botswana's vital interests in the areas of trade, investment, and tourism is now their primary responsibility, in addition to protecting the interests and serving the needs of citizens abroad (*DN* August 5, 1997, 1). From its foreign missions, the MFA is increasingly promoting trade, investment, and tourism ties. In the words of Minister Merafhe, the MFA "plays the role of a salesman" in advancing Botswana's interests abroad (*DN* April 2, 1997, 2). The MFA also coordinates the efforts of the MCI, BEDIA, and others exploring new export markets, sources of trade and investment, and technology transfers (NDP 8, 1997, 497). The Minister regularly leads trade and investment delegations to EU destinations, the USA and Japan.

Organizationally, the MFA continues to suffer from chronic staff shortages, frequent reshuffling of key people, and lack of training and development. Steps have been taken to address these issues since 1994 (Republic of Botswana, 1994). Existing accreditation portfolios among the Botswana Missions has been reviewed and rationalized with a view to improving representation and coverage. Some locations, such as Sweden, which were once key development aid sources, may be dropped, in favor of more trade and market-centered on-site representation locations. A new embassy in Addis

Ababa, the OAU headquarters, opened in November 1999. During NDP 8, two additional missions will be established. Some argue for Geneva, headquarters of the World Trade Organization (WTO).

A major restructuring at Headquarters has been undertaken based on the recommendations of a comprehensive Organization and Methods (O+M) Review, approved by Cabinet. The MFA now has four divisions: i) Management; ii) International Relations; iii) Protocol and Consular Services; and iv) Foreign Missions. Besides a Permanent Secretary and Deputy, a new post, that of Resident Ambassador, was created to facilitate coordination between Foreign Affairs and other ministries and departments, and to improve communications with foreign missions (Sebele 1996).

The IR Division is divided into three sections: i) Bilateral Relations; ii) Multilateral Relations; and iii) Research and Information. Bilateral Relations is further divided by region-based 'desks': Africa/Middle East; Europe and the Americas; and Asia/Australia. Multilateral Relations has similar 'desks' for UN, NAM, and WTO (Manyuela 1996).

The most serious internal problem facing Foreign Affairs is vacant posts (Kalake 1996). Under NDP 7, occupied posts grew from 76 to 116, out of 301 established posts. NDP 8 authorizes only 20 additional posts, compared with the MCI, authorized for 207 new posts. Staff shortages combined with a lack of adequately-trained, experienced officers make any reorganization, let alone expansion, more of a paper exercise than a tangible improvement in operations. A major study of training needs was undertaken in 1991 (Blunden 1991). With the help of the Commonwealth Secretariat, Foreign Affairs expanded in-house training and increased the number of officers sent abroad, mostly to Britain and Australia, for middle and senior-level diplomatic training. Computerization of the MFA continues. When complete, all foreign missions will be linked via internet to Headquarters and, eventually, to all government ministries and departments (NDP 8, 497).

Foreign Affairs received less than 1 percent of the budget, while the Botswana Defence Force (BDF) claimed close to 10 percent several years running (NDP 8, 102). The MFA was allocated $28 million for FY 1995/6 (*DN* April 3, 1995, 3), and $34 million for FY 1997/98, despite high costs associated with maintaining a growing number of foreign embassies and missions (*DN* April 2, 1997, 4) and computerization. Funding must be significantly increased, along with personnel allocations. FY 1998/99 allocation grew only slightly, to $40.1 million, despite plans to proceed with the opening of the Addis mission and another in Tokyo. This level of finance was called "grossly inadequate" by Minister Merafhe, who also complained of "inadequate manpower" and "overstretching" (*DN* March 27, 1998, 3).

The President and Ministry of Presidential Affairs

Under the Constitution, the President is the top foreign policy-maker in Botswana. The Office of the President (OP) functions as a ministry of Presidential Affairs, with a Minister and Permanent Secretaries. Current Minister, Lt. Gen. Ian Khama, son of Botswana's deceased first President Seretse Khama, is also Vice-President. Until 1998, when President Mogae designated it as a separate ministry, Foreign Affairs was a department within OP. There has been a separate Minister since 1974.

Cabinet involvement in foreign policy decision-making is a Presidential prerogative. The Economic Committee of Cabinet, chaired by the President and composed of key Ministers and Permanent Secretaries, wields significant advisory influence on any major foreign economic policy proposal in need of a Presidential decision. In addition, the President chairs the High Level Consultative Committee (HLCC). Established in 1995, it brings together Economic Committee members, key chief executives of major parastatals, and other executives from the private sector for policy discussions (NDP 8, 88).

No one else in Botswana today is as experienced and well-placed to preside over the momentous economic policy deliberations and changes associated with Botswana's embrace of neo-liberalism as is current President, Festus Mogae. At age 60, Mogae has been one of the key players in national economic policy planning and finance matters since the 1970s. He holds a MA degree in Development Economics from Sussex University (1970). Before becoming Minister of Finance and Development, Mogae served as Planning Officer at MFDP, Director of Economic Affairs, Permanent Secretary, Alternate Governor for Botswana at the IMF and African Development Bank (ADB), Director of the Botswana Development Corporation, and Permanent Secretary to former President Masire.

As Minister, Mogae accumulated valuable experience negotiating with South Africa and with key regional and international financial organizations. He was the key Botswana negotiator of SACU reform leading to the removal of all remaining trade barriers in preparation for a Southern African Free Trade Area. He also served as Chair of the SADC Council of Ministers from 1992–96, and represented 22 African central bank governors and finance ministers to the IMF and World Bank from 1992–94 (*DN* March 31, 1998,

2). Few, if any, heads of state travel so extensively in support of economic development. Mogae maintains the exhausting pace set by his predecessor. Almost every major trip includes a determined push to attract foreign investment, promote trade, and raise the economic and commercial profile of Botswana abroad, particularly by inviting foreign business delegations to visit Botswana.

In 1998 alone, Mogae personally extended Botswana's economic reach into Francophone Africa addressing the annual France-Africa Summit. He also attended the annual Southern African Trade and Investment Summit (Cape Town) and second Tokyo International Conference on African Development (TICAD II). While he was officially in New York to address the 53rd UN General Assembly in October 1998, the *Botswana Daily News* headline was, "Mogae Meets US Business Chiefs," and the story included prominent reference to Botswana's abolition of exchange controls. Accompanying the President on all of these trips was the Minister of Commerce and Industry as well as the Director of the Trade and Investment Promotion Association (TIPA).

Ministry of Finance and Development Planning (MFDP)

The Ministry of Finance and Development Planning (MFDP) has always been the most powerful Government ministry, because of its fusion of planning and budget authority, expertise and experience under the same roof. As the place where 'domestic' and 'foreign' policy issues most fundamentally merge in the decision-making structures of government, the MFDP is the central, cross-sectoral coordinating mechanism for foreign economic policy-planning and management, a national equivalent of the IMF or World Bank. The President and Cabinet depend upon information and advice supplied by the MFDP and usually accept its policy recommendations on key economic issues.

Much of the credit for the success of Botswana's foreign economic policy to date belongs to the MFDP. Moving the country towards financial viability was the MFDP's first and greatest post-independence task. For over two decades, this meant attracting and managing foreign aid in support of national development plans. Effective aid management allowed the country to develop much of its physical and social infrastructure. Economic growth and opportunities meant that nearly all Batswana who trained overseas returned home (Maipose 1997, 17, 19).

No other African state so effectively integrates aid into national development plans and budgets. Botswana has now 'graduated' from most aid programmes. Foreign aid today revolves around economic challenges associated with embracing globalization. Traditional donors, particularly the USA and EU, provide finance and technical assistance in support of industrial development, training of local entrepreneurs, diversification of export products, credit and loan guarantees to small and medium-scale entrepreneurs. The MFDP's experience in aid-management is now being applied to the formulation and coordination of new foreign economic policies based on state support of private sector growth, trade, and foreign investment. Future national development plans could be used by the MFDP as a detailed prospectus for potential investors and trading partners.

Bank of Botswana (BoB)

Almost as important as the MFDP, and even less visible, is the foreign economic policy-making support role of the Central Bank of Botswana. Established in 1975, working closely with the MFDP and well-connected to major global monetary and fiscal institutions, the BoB has also been a central player in macroeconomic policy planning.

A national currency, the Pula, was issued in 1976, to replace the South African Rand, making the BoB the key locus of monetary policy. The BoB is responsible for promoting monetary stability, a sound domestic financial system, and management of the country's substantial foreign exchange reserves (NDP 8, 132,140). The BoB also supervises domestic financial institutions and the Botswana Development Corporation (BDC), a parastatal, established in 1971, which provides loans and equity finance for projects to create employment opportunities and facilitate foreign investment (NDP 8, 23). The BDC has the most diversified loan portfolio in the country and is the leading provider of finance (NDP 8, 142).

In 1995, in an effort to attract foreign investment and encourage domestic investment, Botswana acceded to IMF Article VIII status. Commercial banks now offer foreign currency accounts and foreign exchange controls were progressively eliminated by 1998. The BoB closely monitors and analyzes forecasts by the IMF and World Bank, interpreting their significance for Botswana's economy and global trade position. This information is then provided in the form of reports and advice to the MFDP, the Cabinet and others.

During his tenure as BoB Governor, Quill Hermans was influential in calling for increased privatization. The BoB was instrumental in helping the MFDP make a case for the abolition of exchange controls and other economic liberalization initiatives now in NDP 8. The BoB urges, i) export-led economic growth; ii) taking measures to enhance Botswana's global economic competitiveness; iii) promoting higher economic efficiency; iv) developing human capital; and v) transforming some traditional values (*Mmegi* 30 June-6 July 1995, 14-15).

BoB analysis of the economic growth rates of countries of particular economic significance for Botswana as new or expanding export markets is highly valued by policy-makers. South Africa, Japan, EU countries, the USA and Canada receive regular attention. A 1996 report identified China as "a valuable new market for diamonds at some stage" (Hermans 1996, 121). The decision to re-locate the Botswana mission from Hong Kong to Beijing partly reflects the impact of BoB advice on the MFDP, the Cabinet and the President.

The BoB has been warning government policy-makers that high rates of inflation and violence in South Africa are major threats to Botswana's future economic health. The former reduces living standards by increasing the price of imports while the latter frightens foreign investment away from the SADC region, including Botswana. BoB monetary policy adjustments to maintain stability between the Pula and the South African rand are a major form of foreign economic policy-making, strongly affecting the viability of Botswana's exports and prices of imports.

Conclusion

Until the 1990s, Botswana's economic development was almost totally state-planned, financed and directed. The country's foreign economic policies have been characterized by underlying fiscal discipline, firm macro-economic management, centralized planning and budgeting. Unlike virtually all other African states, Botswana's stable political and economic environment enabled this approach to at least partially succeed.

Since 1994, Botswana has been in a period of major political and economic transition. Foreign policy is changing to reflect new realities. Mineral-led, state-directed development is giving way to increasing emphasis on private sector-led economic diversification. Privatization has been embraced. Foreign economic policy-making is now envisioned as a shared enterprise. President Mogae argues that primary responsibility for responding to the opportunities and challenges of globalization "will have to come primarily from our business people and entrepreneurs." Government's role will be to continue to provide a physical and institutional infrastructure, including an educated, healthy, skilled work force, domestic peace and security, regional economic cooperation and integration, and "an ever vigilant [macroeconomic] management to maintain the economy on an even keel" (*Mogae* 1998, 19). A productive, competitive export manufacturing sector for goods and services within the SADC region and beyond remains to be achieved. Foreign investment is slow to appear. Failure will mean increased economic instability, greater unemployment and underemployment, decreased ability of government to fund social welfare programs, and, eventually, political instability.

With so many government ministries and departments now directly involved in the formulation and implementation of foreign economic policy, chronic gaps in staffing, training, and support services must be addressed. Diplomatic recruitment and training is insufficient. Computerization needs, language training, and housing and support needs of officials serving abroad must be swiftly and adequately addressed. With plans to add even more new foreign missions, high numbers of chronically vacant posts in Gaborone ministries and the institutionalization of "skeletal staffing" (*DN* August 17, 1993, 1) abroad must be faced now, or the potential economic benefits of new on-site representation in Asia, and elsewhere, will not be realized. Botswana's eager embrace of globalization may ultimately hurt a majority of citizens.

Notes

1   "Why Treat Africa as One Country?" *Daily News*. Gaborone: 28 April, 1999: 1; hereafter *DN*.
2   "Tensions Over SA's Regional Trade Policy Boil Over." *Mmegi*. Gaborone: 14-20 June 1996: 12.
3   "SACU Gives RSA Too Much Power." *Botswana Guardian*. Gaborone: 7 July 1995: 10.
4   "Botswana Watching Dev. in South Africa." *DN*. Gaborone: 26 April 1996: 2.
5   "WTO Commends SACU." *DN* Gaborone: 12 May 1998: 2.

References

Blunden, M. (1991) *Diplomatic Training in Botswana*. London: Polytechnic of Central London.
Clapham, C. (1996) *Africa and the International System, The Politics of State Survival.* Cambridge: Cambridge University Press.
Daily News. Gaborone. (Government daily newspaper).
Hermans, Q. (1994) "Botswana in the 21st Century: Impact of External Political and Economic Changes on Botswana." *Botswana in the 21st Century.* Gaborone: The Botswana Society. 117-31.
Jefferis, K. (1997) "Poverty in Botswana." *Aspects of the Botswana Economy.* Ed. J. S. Salkin. Gaborone: Lentswe La Lesedi. 473-499.
Kalake, M. (1996) Interview with author. Ministry of Foreign Affairs, Gaborone, July 11.
Legwaila, E. (1993) "Botswana — Coherence With a Strong Central Government." *International Review of Administrative Sciences* 59: 617-628.
Maipose, G.G. Somolekae and T. Johnston. (1997) "Effective Aid Management: The Case of Botswana." *Foreign Aid in Africa*. Uppsala: Nordic Africa Institute. 16-35.
Manyuela, C. (1966) Interview with author. Ministry of Foreign Affairs. Gaborone, July 11.
Mmegi. Gaborone. (A private weekly newspaper).
Mogae, Hon. F. (1998) Budget Speech 1998. Gaborone, 17 February. http,//www.bizafrica.co...na/busbul/budgethi.html.
Mpabanga, D. (1997) "Constraints To Industrial Development." *Aspects of the Botswana Economy*. Ed. J. S. Salkin. Gaborone: Lentswe La Lesedi. 369-387.
Ndzinge, S. (1998) "Trade: Botswana in the Post-Apartheid Era." *Botswana, Politics and Society*. Ed. W.A. Edge and M.H. Lekorwe. Pretoria: J.L. van Schaik. 461-476.
Republic of Botswana. (1994) O And M Review. Department of Foreign Affairs. Gaborone: Management Services Division, Directorate Of Public Service Management. Ref. No. DP.20/15/15.
Republic of Botswana. (1997) *National Development Plan 8*. Gaborone: Ministry of Finance and Development Planning.
Siwawa-Ndai, P.O. (1997) "Industrialization in Botswana." *Aspects of the Botswana Economy*. Ed. J.S. Salkin. Gaborone: Lentswe La Lesedi. 335-367.
Tsie, B. (1995) *The Political Economy of Botswana in SADCC*. Harare: SAPES Books.
Vision 2016. (1997) *Report of the Presidential Task Group for a Long-Term Vision for Botswana*. Gaborone.
Zaffiro, J. (1993) "Foreign Policy-Making in Botswana, Structure and Process." *The Political Economy of Botswana*. Ed. S.J. Stedman. Boulder: Lynne Reinner. 139-160.
———. (1999) "Exceptionality in External Affairs: Botswana in the African and Global Arenas." *African Foreign Policies*. Ed. S. Wright. Boulder: Westview Press. 68-83.

4 Survival in a Rough Neighbourhood: Lesotho's Foreign Policy in the Era of Globalization

ROK AJULU

For much of the period of apartheid, Lesotho existed largely as a hostage state. Structurally integrated as a dependency of South Africa, its political and economic survival has historically been caught between the goodwill of its powerful neighbour, and its desire to project itself as an independent sovereign state. These considerations have also been historically compounded by the character of post-colonial Lesotho and the character of its ruling class.

Broadly speaking, Lesotho has been a dependent neo-colonial state presided over by authoritarian and parasitic non-hegemonic classes, which have consistently lacked the capacity to establish their legitimacy and produce some semblance of hegemonic ideology. Thus the pursuit of domestic legitimacy has also been an important aspect of Lesotho's foreign policy, more particularly since Leabua Jonathan's 1970 para-military coup when the Basutoland National Party (BNP) usurped power after losing democratically conducted elections.

Lesotho's foreign policy since independence has reflected a constant preoccupation with two sets of issues: dependence on South Africa, and its inability to establish political legitimacy domestically. In other words, it is a policy which has perpetually been concerned with survival in a 'rough neighbourhood.' And not surprisingly, the country's foreign policy has swung from one extreme to the other, beginning with the collaborative policy of the 1966–71 period; followed by the assertive foreign policy of the 1972–86 period; and finally the submissive foreign policy of the military regime of the generals, Lekhanya and Ramaema. More recently, Lesotho has manifested a lack of foreign policy initiative and direction, engendered by a shift in the balance of forces in the region, and a global politico-economic environment which seems to have severely limited the country's options for independent policy formulation.

This chapter examines the regional, domestic, political and economic developments which have informed Lesotho's foreign policy of survival in a 'rough neigbhourhood.' The central thrust of the argument here is that historically, successive phases of Lesotho foreign policy have been informed by considerations of survival, of the ruling élite and the preservation of the Sotho state, which they have historically depended upon for the accumulation of wealth, property and power. It is further argued that the end of the Cold War, and the advent of globalization have all but rendered small states like Lesotho irrelevant within the international political system. We will demonstrate that in the circumstances of shifts in the global balance of power, the end of apartheid in South Africa, and the advent of democratisation in the region, Lesotho has found its ability to formulate independent foreign policy severely constrained; rather, it has been transformed into a small colony of the newly established Southern African Development Community (SADC). Globalization, with its tendency towards the marginalization of small countries in a world increasingly dominated by a few overwhelmingly wealthy and powerful countries, has compounded the situation.

The chapter first provides a brief historical background to the emergence of Lesotho as an independent sovereign state in the belly of South Africa — a backdrop against which the subsequent analysis takes place. The second part looks at the changing nature of independent Lesotho's foreign policy; the chapter concludes with a consideration of the impact of globalization and recent regional changes on Lesotho's capacity for foreign policy formulation.

The Lesotho State in Historical Perspective

Lesotho, a tiny mountainous kingdom completely surrounded by South Africa, is the most dependent on South Africa of the three former High Commission Territories (HCTs) – Botswana, Lesotho and Swaziland. With a population of 2.2 million (1998 est.), only 13% of the country's 30.335 square km. is suitable for agriculture, making it densely populated by African standards. The country remains predominantly a remittance economy. An exporter of labour from the 1870s when gold was discovered in South Africa, labour migration to that country has recently been replaced by water as the main export to South Africa, the first phase of the Lesotho Highland Water Project having been completed. Since the end of apartheid,

Lesotho has also become one of the major exporters of skilled personnel to South Africa. Because these migrants are free agents, their contribution to the national economy is not readily quantifiable, but South Africa remains the most important labour market for Lesotho and a generator of national income.

Its membership of the South Africa Customs Union (SACU), its landlocked status, its total reliance on fuel imports through South Africa and dependence on electricity from that country, coupled with the domination of the commercial sector by South African capital, renders Lesotho a semi-colony of successive South African regimes. Furthermore, Lesotho relies on the South African rail and road infrastructure for transportation of goods in and out of the country.

This acute dependence on its powerful neighbour is the outcome of a historical process which dates back to the first half of the 19th century. The modern Sotho state emerged in the immediate aftermath of the *lifaqane* wars.[1] Through assiduous deployment of the pre-capitalist institutions of *matsema, mafisa* and *bohali* (an indigenous ruling élite), the *Mokoteli* of the *Koena* clan, had by the 1830s, secured the compliance of the subordinate classes and emerged as the custodians of the pre-colonial Lesotho state (Kimble 1982). At that time the country of Lesotho covered the present Free State areas in the confluence of the Caledon and Orange rivers and northwards to Excelsior, Clocolan, Fouriesberg and Clarens, historically claimed by successive Lesotho regimes as part of the "conquered territory."

Predictably, there was bound to be tension between the embryonic Sotho state and the new Afrikaner (Boer) settlers following the Boer (Great) trek from the Cape Colony. The migration of Afrikaner farmers and the establishment of the Orange Free State marked the beginning of border conflicts between the Sotho and the Boers. At the heart of these conflicts was the struggle for ownership of land and cattle between two groups of people who had competing concepts of land ownership — communitarian and individual rights to private property. Initially, Lesotho's ability to assemble a standing army and secure arms in the open market ensured that the embryonic Sotho state could not be overrun by the equally embryonic Afrikaner state, and it took nearly thirty years before these running battles could be decisively concluded in favour of the Afrikaners. The penultimate confrontation came in 1865 during the Basotho-Boer War which led to Lesotho's annexation by the British and the settlement of the country's present borders.

The breaking of the balance of power between the African and the Afrikaner was obviously the responsibility of the British. Article 2 of the Bloemfontein Convention of 1854 had forbidden the supply of guns from

British controlled sources to those "natives of surrounding states" in favour of the Boers of the Orange Free State (Machobane 1990). Not surprisingly, the Basotho were vanquished in the 1865 war. Pinned down in his mountain fortress of Thaba Bosiu, the Sotho King, Moshoeshoe, had no alternative but to look to the very same British for protection against the Orange Free State. Lesotho thus became a colony of the British very much against the wishes of the indigenous ruling class who would obviously have preferred a different arrangement (Machobane 1990, 43).

Ultimately, Lesotho's boundaries were reconfigured to reflect the interests of the Afrikaner and British victors. The country lost large tracts of arable land to the Orange Free State and was left with a territory two thirds of which consisted of mountains and only 13% of arable land along the Caledon river valley. Surrounded on all sides by South Africa, the syndrome of dependency set in, and the transformation of Lesotho from a granary to a labour reserve was already underway.

Independent Lesotho and Foreign Policy Influences

Lesotho's progress to independence has been the subject of a number of detailed studies, and need not detain us here.[2] My main concern in this section is to identify the salient features and the character of the post-colonial state with a view to examining key influences on Lesotho's foreign policy perspectives. One of the arguments proffered here is that its dependency on South Africa notwithstanding, Lesotho's foreign policy has equally been a response to domestic pressures, and to the crisis of political legitimation. To appreciate this point, an analysis of the class character of the state and its ruling élite is appropriate.

At independence, the new ruling élite inherited an extremely fragile post-colonial state. Indeed, this remains the case today. Completely surrounded by South Africa, and totally reliant on South Africa's communications and transport infrastructure both for the movement of its goods and links with the outside world, its dependence on South Africa is total. Moreover, in comparison with other African post-colonial states, it inherited neither a manufacturing, commercial base, nor a secure agricultural base. It was thus a dependent neo-colonial state par excellence.

In addition, the class forces which assumed control of the state at independence were equally weak. The Basutoland National Party (BNP) of Chief Leabua Jonathan which assumed state-power at independence in 1966 by a razor-thin majority, was avowedly a conservative nationalist party. Its social base lay mainly within the traditionalist elements (the rural peasantry), the lower levels of traditional chiefs, and the Roman Catholic Church (Nolutshungu 1975). Moreover, it is now generally acknowledged that the BNP was established mainly with the assistance of apartheid South Africa and the Catholic Church, as a counter to the perceived radicalism of the opposition Basutoland Congress Party. Nurtured in the right-wing, anti-communist ideological environment of the Catholic Church, Lesotho's ideological proximity to the apartheid regime was considered natural and consistent with its world outlook. This was confirmed in both the 1965 and the 1970 election manifestos — cooperation with South Africa was seen as being in the interests of the people of Lesotho.[3]

In contrast, the opposition Basutoland Congress Party (BCP) was perceived as a party of national anti-colonial struggle. It had a long tradition of political organisation. In terms of its political traditions and ideology, it could trace its political inheritance to Josiel Lefela's *Lekhotla la Bafo*, the Basutoland Progressive Association (BPA), and the Basutoland African Congress (BAC). Its social base lay within the Protestant church, migrant labourers, intelligentsia, the Protestant educated élite, and the indigenous proto-commercial classes (shopkeepers and taxi-owners) — precisely, the coalition of class forces which had the potential and capabilities to participate in the limited opportunities for indigenous capitalist accumulation offered by the newly independent state.

Right from independence it was fairly obvious that Leabua Jonathan's government would be faced with an uphill task in establishing its domestic legitimacy. As Hirshman (1979) correctly points out, the BNP had won thirty one of the sixty seats, but the opposition had taken the majority of the votes with considerable support from the influential urban population in the lowlands. The BNP thus was confronted with opposition from the King who had ambitions for executive power, BCP members who had occupied senior positions within the civil service, and more significantly, a large chunk of the migrant mine workers, traditionally the political constituency of the opposition. These factors rendered the legitimacy of the new independent state highly contestable, as was the legitimacy of the new ruling élite. The readiness of the BNP élite to collaborate with South Africa — expressed publicly in the run-up to the independence election, and put in practice soon after their inauguration — immediately became a major bone of political contention, and a key influence on foreign policy calculations.

It can therefore be argued that the internal balance of political power and the class character of the new ruling group, have been important factors in determining the shape and direction of Lesotho's foreign policy. The collaborationist policies of the 1966-71 period were largely informed by the attempts of a narrowly based ruling élite to consolidate its power base through external support. Faced with its inherent weaknesses, the BNP had no alternative but to seek to strengthen its position by close collaboration with the South African ruling class. The period of assertive foreign policy (1972-86), on the other hand, can similarly be seen as an attempt to achieve the same objectives by skillfully playing on Lesotho's geo-political and economic vulnerability to the apartheid regime. As Daniels (1984) correctly observes, its principle not withstanding, this policy stance earned the country considerable aid and support from the international community.

The submissive foreign policy of the 1986-93 period would appear to have been a return to the earlier policy of collaboration with apartheid South Africa. Once again, it is obvious that this was championed by a ruling élite representing a very narrow power base. The contemporary period of post-liberation, democratization and globalization would seem to me to have confronted the country with a completely different configuration of questions. The shift in the balance of forces in the region appears to have severely limited the country's options for independent policy formulation as can be seen by the lack of predictability, direction and consistency in Lesotho foreign policy since the collapse of apartheid.

The Changing Nature of Foreign Policy Postures, 1966-1993

The Collaborationist Period, 1966-72

For the first ten years of its independence, Lesotho pursued a policy of close collaboration with South Africa, a collaboration which was presented as being in the interests of the people of Lesotho, and defended in terms of the imperative survival of the Sotho nation. As we have indicated above, this was fairly consistent with the political outlook of the new ruling élite, a view which was confirmed by a joint communique issued on the occasion of Chief Leabua Jonathan's official visit to South Africa in 1967:

> On fundamental issues we found ourselves in complete accord, more specifically on the fact that differences in political philosophy are no bar to fruitful

cooperation. We both firmly believe in peaceful coexistence on the basis of equality, mutual respect, and non-interference in another's domestic affairs (cit. in Swatuk, 1988).

At an ideological level, this policy of 'good neighbourliness' was presented as a strategy of survival. "Economic cooperation and interracial consultations," was seen as a recipe for bringing about political détente inside South Africa (Kotsokoane 1969). At a practical level, the policy was a response to far more complex internal and regional issues.

Soon after independence, the Prime Minister replaced the outgoing colonial bureaucracy with one which was recruited almost exclusively from the ranks of the National Party in South Africa. These included the Chief Justice, Judges of the Appeal Court, the Electoral Officer, and the higher echelons of the military apparatus, the Paramilitary Unit, the PMU. Similarly, the Lesotho National Development Corporation was not only set up with the assistance of Afrikaner capital, but until the early seventies, its senior personnel were recruited from the Anglo-American and Rembrandt conglomerates in South Africa (Hanlon 1986). All this served largely to exclude the educated and commercial classes of the BCP from the bureaucracy, as well as from parastatal enterprises. Concurrently, this led to the domination of the economy by South African commercial capital, and the exclusion of indigenous classes of property from the fruits of independence.

Through these policies, the ruling BNP was able, in the short-term, to achieve two objectives. First, it was able to keep the more educated BCP members from control of the state bureaucracy. Secondly, it managed to buy enough time to recruit and train a bureaucracy from within its own ranks, but it was a move, nonetheless, which was pregnant with its own contradictions. As Hirschman (1979) has pointed out, South African technical assistance was not only dysfunctional, and insensitive to the psychological and political needs of a newly independent African state, more fundamentally, it was to prove a political embarrassment both internally and externally.

At the economic level, the expectation in Maseru was that South Africa would provide substantial financial assistance in return for the policy of good neighbourliness. The BNP expected Pretoria to underwrite the proposed Ox-Bow/Malibamatso Hydro-electric Scheme, and to purchase its water at terms advantageous to Lesotho. And finally, it was also expected that the close collaboration would translate into decent treatment of Basotho nationals in their daily interactions with South Africa. The petty humiliations suffered by Basotho crossing into South Africa were expected to be ameliorated to a visible degree.

It can thus be argued that the collaborationist policies of the first four years of independence cannot be explained by the fact of economic dependence on South Africa alone. The collaborationist policies pursued in the first decade of independence were no less the product of the struggles between the class forces of African nationalism in Lesotho than they were of the dependent nature of the Lesotho state. It would seem that the BNP opted for a collaborationist policy because it was perceived as the best way of enabling it to retain control of state power as well as reproducing itself as a political and social force.

Be that as it may, none of the objectives of the collaborationist policies were ever realised with any degree of satisfaction. As a number of scholars have correctly pointed out, it was precisely the frustration with the policy of collaboration which pointed Lesotho in the direction of a confrontational policy with South Africa in the period 1976 to 1985.[4]

Assertive Foreign Policy, 1973–1986

The policies followed between 1973–86 can be said to constitute an attempt by Lesotho to assert its independence despite the problems of economic and geo-political dependence on South Africa. The policies were characterised by verbal hostilities against the apartheid regime and a strong anti-South African diplomatic posture. They represented a complete reversal of the fundamentals upon which the earlier policy of collaboration — good neighbourliness — had been predicated. Rhetoric notwithstanding, this policy about-turn can essentially be seen as an attempt to achieve the same objectives, (a strategy of survival of a ruling élite), only this time by skillfully exploiting its geo-political and economic vulnerability to the apartheid regime. As a number of observers have pointed out, this policy stance earned Lesotho considerable aid and support from the international community (Daniels 1984; Hanlon 1986; Swatuk, 1988).

But why the change in strategy? In his seminal paper on changes in Lesotho foreign policy towards South Africa, Hirschman (1979) suggests a number of interlinked and mutually reinforcing possible explanations for the change of policy. This has been done most ably and need not be repeated here. For the purposes of the central thrust of our argument, I only wish to elaborate on one aspect, and that is the political consequences of the earlier policy on the Sotho state and their implications for the hegemonic stability of the BNP and its élite. By 1970, the collaborationist policy, despite maintaining the BNP in government, had not yielded sufficient economic resources to enable the party to enlarge its social base. Moreover, the pro-South African policy was very unpopular with the majority of the Basotho. The anti-Boer sentiment — very much a historical tradition of the Sotho — was further fuelled by the fact that there was not much to show for five years of close collaboration with South Africa.

Thus despite considerable funding from its Pretoria masters, the BNP was unable to retain its razor-thin majority in Parliament. The traditional Basotho hostility to South Africa (should have) swept it from office. It lost the elections to the BCP by 12 seats, winning only 23 seats to the BCP's 35 and one for the royalist Marema-Tlou Freedom Party (MFP). But Chief Jonathan would not relinquish power. He pronounced the elections null and void, declared a state of emergency and suspended the constitution. The political violence which accompanied the BNP's usurpation of constitutional power undermined its base even further, confronting the state with an intractable political crisis.

In addition, the popular resistance which had followed the BNP's seizure of power in 1970, and the unmitigated state repression which followed it, had telling consequences for the cohesion of the Sotho social formation. The ruling class was therefore increasingly confronted with a legitimation crisis. At the same time there was also a shift in the balance of forces regionally, the collapse of the Caetano regime in Portugal, the initial liberation of Angola and Mozambique, the growing isolation of South Africa, and mounting global pressure upon the apartheid regime for meaningful changes internally. All this confronted Jonathan and those around him with a serious political dilemma.

The ruling BNP clearly needed to reconstitute its political constituency and base it more firmly within the domestic terrain. From the point of view of the BNP, the rapidly eroding social and political base, now exacerbated by the political crisis of the 1970s, had to be given serious attention. This largely defined the limits within which brute force could be relied upon as a central plank for retaining the cohesion of the social formation. In addition, Pretoria's reluctance to provide economic benefits in reward for the BNP's collaboration, meant that the aid so crucial to the economy had to be secured from elsewhere.

Thus the explanation for what was to emerge as a period of hostility and confrontation between the two countries must be sought within the economic and political predicament of the ruling class in Lesotho as it faced the changing balance of forces in the region, political and economic uncertainties resulting from its awkward relationship with South Africa, and more importantly, political crisis at home. It was in these circumstances that the regime decided to multilateralise the country's dependency. This implied adopting policies which would ingratiate Lesotho with international donors. Chief Jonathan therefore had to try to distance himself from his Pretoria patrons.

This policy turnabout opened the way for cordial relations with the African National Congress (ANC), the establishment of diplomatic relations with Mozambique, and ultimately Maseru's commitment to adhere to the United Nations (UN) protocol regarding the treatment of South African refugees in Lesotho.

This shift was to reach its nadir with the establishment of diplomatic relations with the socialist countries in the early eighties. More significantly, this assertive foreign policy struck a favourable chord especially amongst European social democratic regimes (notably in Scandinavia). Such governments were particularly sympathetic to those countries in the region which were perceived to be resisting Pretoria's pressure, providing succour to refugees from apartheid and supporting liberation movements in South Africa and Namibia. Predictably, Chief Jonathan was able to draw on the strong anti-South African sentiment in the country, and even temporarily overcome the divisions within his ruling party. As Daniels (1984) points out, it was a policy stance that earned Lesotho considerable aid and support from the international community.

However, the political implications of the multilateralisation of Lesotho's dependency were to prove unacceptable to Pretoria. Faced with a growing crisis internally and regionally, the departure of Lesotho from the ranks of its surrogates represented a serious political blow to South Africa, the psychological impact of which would further undermine the apartheid regime's hegemony. It was in these circumstances that, at the end of the 1970s, Pretoria launched a policy of destabilization pursued through the exiled opposition Basutoland Congress Party's military wing, the Lesotho Liberation Army (LLA) — actually a creation of South Africa defence and security apparatuses. The objective of this destabilization was to shepherd Chief Jonathan back into the fold, but as O'Meara (1986) suggests, South Africa's destabilization only served to strengthen Chief Jonathan's resolve to drift further away from Pretoria. He strengthened his ties with various Eastern bloc countries and reinforced his relationship with the ANC, a fact which earned him substantial support from a wide section of the population.

Pretoria now considered Lesotho a troublesomely independent neighbour which had to be replaced with a malleable regime. Initially Pretoria reasoned that some measure of pressure could bring Chief Jonathan to his senses. When Jonathan refused to be intimidated, destabilisation turned into an undeclared war with the intention of toppling the Chief's faction of the BNP. From the 'Maseru Raid' in 1982, it was to take another three years before South Africa's objectives were achieved. General Lekhanya's bloodless putsch which ousted the undemocratic regime of Chief Leabua Jonathan was widely regarded as a South African-orchestrated coup. As Edgar (1987) points out, the Lesotho coup was seen as a major triumph for South Africa's policy of regional destabilization. Unfortunately for the coup makers, the BNP faction which joined General Lekhanya in toppling Chief Jonathan was unlikely to provide political stability, and like the previous regime, it remained caught in a crisis of legitimation. This explains the foreign policy turnabout that occurred in the immediate aftermath of the *coup d'état*.

Submissive Foreign Policy, 1986-93

With the coup, it would seem that Lesotho's policy had come full circle. One of the first policy pronouncements from the coup makers was the restoration of the policy of good neighbourliness and non-interference in the affairs of other states (Lekhanya, cit. in Sejanamane 1986):

> It is our commitment to normalise relations with South Africa and we shall do all that is humanly possible to achieve this objective. We espouse the noble principle of peaceful coexistence and good neighbourliness and we are prepared to demonstrate our sincerity whenever called upon to do so.

This was soon followed by the removal of most, if not all, ANC refugees from Lesotho. In return, in October 1986, the South African Foreign Minister, Pik Botha, was in Maseru to sign the agreement for the Lesotho Highlands Water Project, a multi-million dollar project which would bring much needed water to South Africa's industrial hub of Johannesburg in return for the payment of royalties to the Lesotho government. The significance of this change in policy was probably best articulated by Colonel Thaabe Letsie, member of the Military Council responsible for Foreign Affairs, when he stated at the signing ceremony that: "In Lesotho we are particularly proud of the fact that we have realised that no price is too small for good neighbourly relations and that dialogue and negotiations are clearly demonstrating their superiority over disagreements and conflict."[5]

Quite obviously this was a complete reversal of the policies pursued throughout the 70s and the first half of the 1980s. Sejanamane attributes this drastic change of policy to parochial class interests on the part of the ruling élite which displaced the interests of the state. It seems clear that continued pressure from South Africa had engendered serious divisions within the BNP, not least because the protagonists were already looking ahead to a post-Jonathan era, but also primarily because fifteen years of political confrontation between the two main political groupings in the country, the seven years of hostilities and confrontations with South Africa, and finally the fratricidal factionalism within the BNP during the period 1983-85, had weakened the government and rendered it incapable of initiating policies to counter South African political manoeuvres.

However, this period of submission to South Africa was bound to be short-lived. First, the BNP faction which took over from Chief Jonathan was not only weak, but also a politically discredited force precisely because of its policy of submission to South Africa. The Basotho particularly resented the idea of the sovereignty of the country being compared to that of a South African Bantustan. As Daniels points out,

> . . . the bulk of the Basotho male electorate has at one time or another worked in South Africa where they have experienced at first hand the degradation of the apartheid system. Nowhere is this more the case than the experience of the underground miner. It is he who suffers . . . the indignity of working at the behest of perhaps the most racist elements in South Africa — the white miner . . . . the hostility acquires a political expression when he returns home (1984, 237).

Secondly, the BNP inherited a divided armed force, and more tellingly, a very narrow social and political base. In order to retain control of state power, it had to subordinate itself to South Africa more than the original BNP regime had done during the first post-independence decade. Finally, it assumed control of the Sotho state when the contradictions of apartheid in South Africa and in the region were at their most volatile. As events would soon prove, its patron — the Pretoria regime — had not much longer to go. Once its patron signalled that it could no longer rule in the same old way, it was just a matter of time before this new ruling élite would be compelled to relinquish political power.

Lesotho's experience up to 1993 thus provides valuable insights into foreign policy-making in small, landlocked states. Lesotho's unique position

— completely surrounded as it is by South Africa and structurally dependent on it for all its requirements — meant, predictably, that foreign policy-making in that country was largely affected by regional events over which it had no control. Moreover, the foreign policy of a landlocked state of this type — as the foregoing analysis indicates — was entirely about the survival of Lesotho as a sovereign independent state.

Having unsuccessfully experimented with a policy of collaboration with its powerful neighbour, Lesotho's foreign policy-makers opted for a policy of multilateralising their dependency, with the objective of drawing big power players into the regional scene. In fact it could be argued that it was the success of this policy that drew such a hostile reaction from South Africa, ultimately leading to the demise of the Jonathan regime and the reassertion of submission to its powerful neighbour, South Africa. But as a number of scholars have argued, it was the lack of a cooperative environment at home that ultimately led to the collapse of Chief Jonathan's regime (Swatuk 1988; Sejanamane 1988; Edgar 1987). A policy which was pursued to address the domestic problem of internal legitimacy collapsed precisely because of a lack of such legitimacy.

Be that as it may, there is a broad consensus that the period to 1993 represented some degree of certainty and predictability as far as foreign policy positions were concerned. The demise of apartheid, the end of the Cold War, and the advent of globalization appear to have rendered small states like Lesotho irrelevant within the international political system, and their foreign policy postures highly unpredictable. It is this situation that we now turn to.

Lesotho's Foreign Policy in the Era of Globalization

The formal return of democracy in Lesotho occurred against the background of a changing world order. First, the end of apartheid and the beginning of the emergence of democratic regimes in the region (Namibia, South Africa and Mozambique) at a stroke removed the geo-political environment that Lesotho had taken advantage of over the previous quarter of a century. Secondly, the collapse of the Soviet Union as a world power and the end of the Cold War in 1989 brought an end to a global dualistic system (the socialist sub-system) which had provided weaker and rebellious countries with a safe haven. Finally, and more significantly, the advent of globalization — the march of capital all over the world in search of consumers and markets coupled with a tendency towards the marginalisation of the classical notion of the nation state — threatened the survival of small states such as Lesotho.

'Globalization' has become a catchword associated with the 'compression' of the world into new patterns of production, integrated financial spheres, homogenization of cultures etc. (Robertson 1992). But as Nabudere (2000) points out, contemporary understanding of globalization is more than that. It is also about growing structural differentiation globally. In other words, globalization should be seen as a process which is propelled by contradictory tendencies. On the one hand, economic globalization has unleashed productive forces throughout the world leading to the expansion of markets, the insertion of technology into the processes of production, and hence the improvement of productive capacities leading to massive increases in profits for multinational corporations. On the other hand, it has also manifested a tendency to fragment, differentiate, and marginalise social forces and countries incapable of catching up with its processes. Uneven development, long associated with capitalist expansion, is probably the most visible trade mark of globalization in its contemporary form.

Not surprisingly, the unevenness of globalization is seen at its most intense in countries of the third world.[6] A declining resource base and the continued peripheralization of marginal states within the world economic system have redefined the global playing field for the weak and the poor. Marginalization and declining access to resources have triggered off new struggles and intensified old contests over resources, engendering conflicts and wars of anihilation for control of the state, the main institution through which accumulation has been mediated in these economies. As can be expected, the contemporary epoch of globalization has been marked by fratricidal wars in places as diverse as Bosnia, Chechnya, Somalia, Sierra Leone, Rwanda, Burundi, and more recently, the ongoing conflict in the Great lakes region of Central and Eastern Africa.

Lesotho has been no exception. As we have shown above, it is a typical example of a post-colonial state that has been contested rather uncompromisingly by a small stratum of property hunters over the entire period of its political independence. The formal return of democracy after the 1993 election does not appear to have changed the character of contestation over the state. On the contrary, it would seem that these struggles have intensified since the demise of apartheid and the beginning of formal democratisation in Lesotho. Understandably so, because the collaborationist ruling class we have discussed above has been primarily concerned to transform the state in its own interests and to use it as an organ for facilitating the demands of a narrow social class base.

This conflict has been further exacerbated by the continued economic decline of the Lesotho state. Recent figures suggest that migrant workers' remittances account for an average of 46.8% of income for all households, and 55.1% for rural households. Mineworkers' remittances, on the other hand, now account for an average of 44.7% of the income of all households and 52.7% of that of rural households (Ajulu 1995). Despite the recent shifts from the export of cheap labour to that of skilled labour, and more recently, water to South Africa, the state of the economy has hardly changed. The deteriorating nature of the economy no doubt contributes to the contestation of state-power in the period 1993 to 1999.

The period of the formal return to democracy, 1993 to 1998, has witnessed the continuation of the tussle for state-power between the three traditional rivals, the Royalists, the BNP and the BCP. The Lesotho state remains vulnerable and unstable precisely because the democratically elected ruling party is hardly in control of the institutions of the state, as was sadly demonstrated by the political events of 1998/9.[7] In 1993, the ruling Basutoland Congress Party (BCP) inherited a civil service, an army, police, and an intelligence service which had been recruited, and trained by the BNP and was fiercely loyal to it. The BCP then proceeded to make the mistake of assuming that its overwhelming electoral victory would nullify these alternative centers of power. On the other hand, having been accustomed to the exercise of power over the last 27 years, the BNP has demonstrated a remarkable reluctance to make way for a democratically elected regime and a political dispensation which would render it subject to democratic control mechanisms. The two groups appear uninterested in cooperating through negotiation to avoid disputes over resources.

After the 1993 election in which the BCP won all the contested sixty-five parliamentary seats, the BNP — stunned at being trounced by the BCP — questioned the legitimacy of the electoral process and by extension, of the elected BCP regime, and soon set about rendering the state ungovernable. In this the BNP was assisted by the royalist wing represented by the young King Letsie III. In August 1994, by combining the forces of the BNP, the army and the royalists, King Letsie overthrew the democratically elected government in a coup which very much mirrored the Lekhanya coup of 1986 in terms of the representation of its forces. The elected government was only restored thanks to the intervention of the SADC.

The BCP split in June 1997, with the majority retaining control of the government under the new name, Lesotho Congress for Democracy (LCD). Once again, in the wake of LCD electoral victory in 1998, the BNP was back to its old tricks. As before, the BNP mobilised the same forces: the breakaway BCP, the royalist Marema-Tlou Freedom Party, and of course, the armed forces. The pattern of events was, predictably similar: demonstrations at the Royal Palace accompanied by propaganda campaigns and pressure on the King to dissolve the supposedly undemocratically elected government. The role of the King in this last round was not quite clear, but the extent to which the King allowed the Palace to be used so partisanly against an elected regime lends credence to claims that he had hoped the ensuing lawlessness would strengthen the monarchy's ambition to assume political leadership. As before, the LCD-elected regime appeared to have survived thanks to the intervention of the SADC (Botswana and South Africa).

It is against this broad background that Lesotho's foreign policy in the era of globalization can be assessed. The important question then is: what is the content of this foreign policy? It would seem that the old preoccupation with apartheid and South Africa's regional destabilization has been replaced by an élite contest for control of post-colonial Lesotho. In other words, globalization and its attendant developments have peripheralized Lesotho and rendered it largely irrelevant within the global system. Thus, in the face of declining resources, and an inability to subordinate the new developments to the logic of its own sovereign policies, the élites have turned to contesting the most important source of resources, state power. Periodic conflict over state power in Lesotho has now become a common feature of the region and a threat to regional stability. Lesotho has progressively become the subject of regional diplomacy as SADC power brokers attempt to subordinate it to the wider regional logic of democratization.

As mentioned above, the first intervention by the SADC and the Organization of African Unity (OAU) occurred towards the end of 1993. This was in response to violent clashes between rival factions of the Lesotho Defence Force (LDF) which led to the murder of the Deputy Prime Minister, Selemetsi Baholo. The ensuing instability became a threat to regional stability and an issue of international concern. Paralysed by the army mutiny, the newly elected democratic regime of Ntsu Mokhehle could only appeal for international intervention. Attempted mediation by the United Nations and OAU envoys was initially unsuccessful, and unfortunately, South Africa was in no position to intervene militarily, preoccupied as it was with its own transition, and approaching its first democratic election. It was therefore left to the other SADC countries to play an active role in the resolution of the conflict. Even though South Africa had moved its security forces to the Lesotho border to monitor events, it was the Tripartite Task Force (TTF), comprising Botswana, Zimbabwe and South Africa, which was instrumental in brokering a temporary moratorium between the elected government and its defence force.

Hot on the heels of the military confrontation came the 'King's coup' in August 1994.[8] At the instigation of the BNP, a section of the principal chiefs and the royalist party (Marema-Tlou Freedom Party), King Letsie III suspended the constitution on 17th August 1994. He dissolved the government and appropriated all legislative powers to himself, whereupon he appointed an interim Provisional Council to run the country until a commission could be established to organize fresh elections on a proportional representation basis. The King's alliance with the opposition was informed by longstanding rivalry between the royalists and the opposition BCP, and especially its failure to address in a meaningful way, the reinstatement of the late Letsie II who had been deposed by the military junta of General Lekhanya.

Once again it took coordinated action by the regional power-brokers — South Africa, Zimbabwe and Botswana — and of course, non-state actors in Lesotho, (particularly the Lesotho Council of the NGOs whose mobilisation against the Provisional Council denied the King's coup any legitimacy) to end the Lesotho crisis. The negotiations were very protracted. Significantly, in the ultimate analysis, King Letsie was literally given an ultimatum to withdraw his Provisional Council and hand back power to the democratically elected government of Ntsu Mokhehle. The ultimatum, involving the immediate imposition of sanctions, was reportedly delivered by the foreign ministers of the three countries, South Africa, Zimbabwe and Botswana.

Following the election of 1998, Lesotho was once again consumed by a political crisis. The root cause of the crisis had to do with the electoral system. Lesotho operates according to the Westminster parliamentary system — the First Past the Post or 'winner-takes-all' electoral system. In the 1998 election, the LCD took 60% of the vote and 79 of the 80 parliamentary seats. The combined opposition with 40% of the vote gained only one seat. Thus, following the LCD victory, the BNP was up in arms. Once again the BNP mobilised the same forces as before, including the Marema-Tlou Freedom Party; even the BCP, its traditional rival, threw in its lot with them. The support of both the army and the monarchy also appeared to have been secured. As the crisis deepened, it became clear that the elected government of Prime Minister Palilitha Mosisili had been abandoned by his army, the police and other adjuncts of the security forces, and he could not prevent power from sliding gradually into the hands of his opponents. As happened before, the democratically elected regime appealed for external support, but this time — alarmed by the country's descent into chaos — SADC, through South Africa and Botswana, intervened militarily to restore the elected regime of the LCD.

The SADC (South Africa/Botswana) military intervention in South Africa has been the subject of great controversy.[9] It is not my intention to enter into the debate on the merits and demerits of the intervention. What we are concerned with here is its outcome, which was as follows:

- an agreement by the ruling LCD to an early election;
- an acceptance by the opposition alliance that the LCD would retain executive power until after the said elections;
- the establishment of an interim transitional authority, the Interim Political Authority (IPA), to oversee the preparations for the elections.

Given the history of failed agreements between the main players in Lesotho's political theatre, and the proven inability of the contending forces to cooperate so as to avoid disputes over resources, it is obvious that agreements such as the above can only work with continued intervention from external forces — in this case the SADC countries.

The foregoing analysis suggests that since 1993 the whole notion of Lesotho sovereignty has been greatly circumscribed. The country has increasingly proved incapable of managing its own affairs without the direct intervention of the regional powers. It would seem, therefore, that the demise of apartheid in South Africa, the advent of democratisation in the region, and more significantly, the forces of globalization have played havoc with the autonomy of the state of Lesotho. Indeed, its autonomy has been severely undermined and it has increasingly found itself severely constrained in its ability to formulate an independent foreign policy; rather, it has been transformed into a small colony of the newly established SADC.

Let me conclude by reasserting the central core of the main argument here. The case of Lesotho does provide us with valuable insights into the position of weak countries in an era of globalization. The experience of the last decade shows that Lesotho's autonomy has been so undermined as to render it almost irrelevant regionally and internationally. The preoccupation of its ruling party with fratricidal conflict over the state has further undermined the state's capacity to play any meaningful role in the region as a sovereign power. It is therefore worth asking if Lesotho can, in fact, maintain a viable foreign policy. While military intervention and a continued military presence in Lesotho have served to bring some semblance of order to this small mountain kingdom, a solution to its problems is far away. What the military intervention has accomplished so far is a temporary moratorium between the traditional rivals for state-power in Lesotho. The battle for power, however, continues in the background. It is almost certain that a general election within the next 18 months will not bring about a solution, since an outcome overwhelmingly in favour of the LCD is probable.

Lesotho's position does not appear sustainable on a long-term basis. The regional power brokers are unlikely to prop up this country indefinitely. As soon as another election is concluded, in all probability the barricades will be up again, and the contest for power will resume where it left off in 1998. In the long run it would seem that the most logical option is for South Africa to annex Lesotho, making it the tenth province, thereby subordinating it to the wider logic of democratization in South Africa. Yet as Southall (1999) suggests, those who argue for this option in Lesotho are in the minority. None of the major parties have demonstrated support for integration into South Africa. So long as the state remains the dominant institution for accumulation of wealth and in Lesotho, this situation is likely to remain the same.

Notes

1   For a detailed discussion of the Lificane (Mfecane) wars see Omer-Cooper 1966, p. 208.
2   See Khaketla 1971; Bardill and Cobbe 1985, and Machobane 1990.
3   1965 and 1970 Election Manifesto; see Hirschman 1978.
4   See Hirschman 1979; Daniels 1984; Swatuk 1988; and Ajulu 1985 and 1986.
5   *Lesotho Today*; see Sejanamane 1988.
6   For a more detailed discussion of the impact of globalization on the economies of the third world countries, see for example, Tandon, Y. "Globalisation and Africa's Options," in *Globalisation and the Post-Colonial State*. Ed. D. Nabudere. (Harare: AAPS Books, 2000).
7   For details of the post-1998 election crisis in Lesotho see Southall, R. "Is Lesotho South Africa's Tenth Province?" in *Crisis in Lesotho: The Challenge of Managing Conflict in Lesotho*. Ed. K. Lambrechts. IGD Monograph Series; see also Makoa, F. "The Challenges of the South African Military Intervention in Lesotho after the 1998 Election," in *Lesotho Social Science Review* 5.1.
8   For a detailed discussion of events leading to the 'King's coup,' see Matlosa, K. "The Military after the Election: Confronting the New Democracy," in *Democratisation and Demilitarisation in Lesotho: the General Election of 1993 and its Aftermath*. Ed. R. Southall and T. Petlane. (Pretoria: Africa Institute).
9   Makoa 1999; Molomo 1999, and Van Nieuwkerk, 1999.

References

Ajulu, R. (1995) "From Collaboration to Dilemma: A Historical Background to Lesotho's Election of 1993." *Democratisation and Demilitarisation in Lesotho: The General Election of 1993 and its Aftermath.* Ed. R. Southall and T. Petlane. Pretoria: Africa Institute. 3-17.

Ajulu R. and D. Cammack. (1988) "Lesotho, Botswana and Swaziland: Captive States." *Frontline Southern Africa: Destructive Engagement.* Ed. D. Martin and P. Johnson. New York: Four Walls, Eight Windows. 191-231.

Cobbe, J. (1988) "Economic Aspects of Lesotho's Relations with South Africa." *Journal of Modern African Studies* 21:2.

Daniel, J. (1984) "A Comparative Analysis of Lesotho and Swaziland's Relations with South Africa." *South African Review* 2: 228-238.

Edgar, B. (1987) "The Lesotho Coup of 1987." *South African Review* 4: 373-382.

Hanlon, J. (1986) *Beggar Your Neighbour: Apartheid Powers in Southern Africa.* London: Catholic Institute of International Relations.

Hirschman, D. (1979) "Changes in Lesotho's Policy Towards South Africa." *African Affairs* 78.31: 177-196.

Kimble, J. (1985) *Migrant Labour and Colonial Rule in Basutoland.* Grahamstown: Institute for Social and Economic Research, Rhodes University.

Kotsokoane, J.R.L. (1969) "Lesotho and her Neighbours." *African Affairs* 68. 271.

Machobane, L.B.B.J. (1990) *Government and Change in Lesotho, 1980—1966: A Study of Political Institutions.* Basingstoke: Macmillan.

Makoa, F. (1999) "The Challenges of South Africa's Military Intervention in Lesotho after the 1998 Election." *Lesotho Social Science* Review 5.1: 83-109.

Matlosa, K. (1995) "The Military after the Election: Confronting the New Democracy." *Democratisation and Demilitarisation in Lesotho: the General Election of 1993 and its Aftermath.* Ed. R. Southall and T. Petlane. Pretoria: Africa Institute. 118-139.

Molomo, M. (1999) "External Military Intervention in Lesotho's Recent Political Crisis." *Lesotho Social Science Review* 5.1.

Nabudere, D.W. (2000) *Globalisation and the Post-Colonial African State.* Harare: AAPS Books.

O'Meara, D. (1986) "The Coup d'Etat in Lesotho." *Southern Africa Report* 11.5.

Omer-Cooper, J.D. (1966) *The Zulu Aftermath: A Nineteenth Century Revolution in Bantu Africa.* London: Longmans.

Pule, N. (1999) "Power Struggles in the Basutoland Congress Party." *Lesotho Social Sciences Review* 5.1: 1-30.

Robertson, R. (1992) *Globalization, Social Theory and Global Culture.* London: Sage.

Sejanamane, M. (1988) "Lesotho in Southern Africa: From Assertive to a Submissive Foreign Policy." *Lesotho Law Journal* 4.2: 7-31.

Southall, R. (1999) "Is Lesotho South Africa's Tenth Province?" *Crisis in Lesotho: The Challenge of Managing Conflict in Southern Africa.* Ed.K. Lambrechts. IGD Monograph Series. 19-25.

Swatuk, L. (1988) "Lesotho: Walking the Highwire Between Rhetoric and Reality." *Foreign Policy in Small States: Botswana, Lesotho, Swaziland and South Africa..* Ed. D. R. Black *et al.* Centre for Foreign Policy Studies, Dalhousie University. Monograph Series. 32-53.

Tandon, Y. (2000) "Globalisation and Africa's Options." *Globalisation and the Post-Colonial African State.* Ed. D. Nabudere. Harare: AAPS Books. 56-82.

Van Nieuwkerk, A. (1999) "The Lesotho Crisis: Implications for South African Foreign Policy." *Crisis in Lesotho: The Challenge of Managing Conflict in Southern Africa.* Ed. K. Lambrechts. IGD Monograph Series. 13-17.

5 Continuity and Change in Malawi's Foreign Policy-Making

JONATHAN MAYUYUKA KAUNDA

Malawi is one of the least developed countries in the world. *The World Development Report, 1999-2000* (IBRD 1999) ranks it amongst the eight poorest countries in the world. By June 1999, the country had a population of approximately 10.5 million, growing at an average annual rate of 2.8 per cent. The population density of 1 046 persons per thousand hectares is high compared to the African average of 249. Life expectancy is only 43 years, compared with 51 for the sub-Saharan region. Similarly, the country's GNP of United States dollars (USD) 200 is far below the sub-Saharan average of USD 510.

In 1997, Malawi's real gross domestic product (at constant 1987 prices) was USD 1 701 million, of which agriculture contributed 36, industry 19, and manufacturing 14 per cent respectively. Of the agricultural output, tea, tobacco, cotton and sugar accounted for about 90 per cent of export earnings. Private consumption was 85 per cent of GDP in 1998, while gross domestic investment grew negatively at –27. The local currency, the kwacha, was devalued by 65 per cent in August 1999. At that time, the inflation rate was 52 per cent (IBRD Online 1999; RBM 1999, 91). The country has had recourse to structural adjustment lending since 1981.

In 1999, the United Nations Development Programme (UNDP) warned that the country's debt was unmanageable and likely to undermine economic growth (UNDP 1999). Hence, in late 1999, Malawi qualified for the Highly Indebted Poor Countries (HIPC) initiative, aimed at writing off the country's unsustainable debts, once certain conditions prescribed by the World Bank and the International Monetary Fund (IMF) had been met.

The Background

Malawi was initially called the Nyasaland Protectorate, which from 1953 to 1963, together with present-day Zambia and Zimbabwe, constituted the

Federation of Rhodesia and Nyasaland. Hastings Kamuzu Banda was the first Prime Minister from 1962, and led the country to political independence in 1964. Malawi became a republic within the British Commonwealth at the same time as it was declared a one-party state in 1966. In 1971 Banda became life president, remaining undisputed national leader until the reintroduction of a multiparty system in 1994.

Banda concentrated both political and economic power in his own hands, and exercised a firm grip on all aspects of Malawi society. Politics was non-participatory and conducted within the strict limits imposed by state centralisation. Policy decisions were the preserve of Banda, who was the head of state, head of government, supreme leader of the sole legal Malawi Congress Party (MCP), as well as minister of foreign affairs, agriculture, justice, works and supplies, and commander-in-chief of the armed forces.

The year 1994 witnessed a retreat from the overt state centralisation that had become a distinct characteristic of the one-party state. Events associated with domestic developments, together with the globalization of Western economic and political ideologies, triggered the transition from single-party rule to a multiparty system of government. Notably, there was internal opposition to Banda's authoritarian rule, which was backed by external pressure that favoured democracy and the liberalisation of political and economic relationships. The demise of the Banda regime may be explained in terms of its rigidity and unbending nature that appeared to defy both domestic and global trends, but which was ultimately overtaken by events.

Internal weariness with one-party authoritarian rule, and the three-decade long presence of Banda at the political helm, was the principal domestic gripe. The globalization of the international economy that was gathering momentum in the early 1990s was accompanied by the globalization of the ideology of liberal democracy, which called for more effective, participatory and accountable government. At the forefront of the global economic and political changes was the United States of America, which took advantage of the collapse of the Soviet bloc and the emergence of a unipolar world system to advance its own capitalist and liberal democratic ideologies through the international financial institutions and the United Nations.

The alteration in the nature and processes of the Malawi political economic system only actually began with the removal of Banda six years ago. But the one-party era provides a crucial background to understanding contemporary changes. This analysis of change in the country's foreign policy-making processes begins with the post-Banda era, a short period in which to determine definite trends in the political system's development. The new political and economic order which had promised democratic participation in governance and an overall improvement in the people's welfare has been characterised by uncertainty and lack of clear direction.

The chapter's basic assumption is that Malawi has historically operated in a world system that is characterised by specific economic and political interactions which affect the organisation of its economy, political processes, and social structures. It seeks to investigate the underlying features of Malawi's foreign policy and policy-making processes by placing the country within the context of the international system. It examines the manner in which national components articulate with the international political economy and suggests what the consequences of this articulation are.

As in many other southern African countries, domestic policies and foreign policy are inseparable and inextricably linked. Micro-level domestic politics and macro-level international relations are connected through the national policy-making processes. National leaders, state bureaucracies and institutions operate in the context of social, political, and economic formations which shape their decisions. But these decision-making units link the domestic spheres with the international political and economic system within which Malawi is incorporated. Thus these units that make up the decision-making apparatus — and their relationships with each other — should be studied to understand Malawi's foreign policy and policy-making processes (Light 1994, 93).

Malawi's economic underdevelopment has had a significant influence on its international relations; the country has always depended on foreign assistance. Its former colonial master, the United Kingdom, even financed Malawi's recurrent budget deficit during the first decade of independence, thus exercising a direct influence on its development strategy and foreign policy. Presently, the influence of aid donors, especially the multilateral aid agencies, is quite significant, and bears on both Malawi's development policies and external relations. But these agencies are the standard bearers for economic and political arrangements that promote the global dominance of the Western countries, led by the United States of America.

The chapter, therefore, addresses three central concerns. Firstly, it examines how underdevelopment and external economic dependence have constrained Malawi's capacity to determine autonomous foreign policies. Secondly, it explores the effects of domestic political and economic circumstances on foreign policy decisions. That is, it examines how, and to what extent, internal political structures and processes have influenced foreign policy decisions and actions. Thirdly, it investigates the impact of globalization on the foreign policy processes of Malawi and looks at the changes which have occurred in the light of the democratization and liberalization of the political process in that country. The chapter, therefore, seeks to determine the effects of domestic and international environments in shaping Malawi's foreign policy. It avoids the artificial and unsustainable distinction between the domestic and international arenas, but considers them as interactive and influential upon each other (Wright 1999, 1-2).

Executive-Legislative Relations in the Policymaking Institutions of the Single Party State, 1964–1994

As a protectorate, Nyasaland (Malawi) had no foreign policy, as that was the domain of the British government, but executive dominance, which has colonial roots, is a significant aspect of the evolution of the Malawian political system. This colonial system of governance was essentially rule by British civil servants who exercised centralised political control in furthering the interests of British imperialism. State centralisation was manifested by the territorial Governor's presidency of both the legislative and executive branches of government. These institutions were non-elected and composed mainly of appointed colonial administrators. African political representation was severely constrained. The majority of the territory's inhabitants had no say in the determination of the colony's public policy.

The subsequent one-party system in Malawi evolved from this form of political and administrative centralisation and exclusivity. The first general election of August 1961 ushered in popular representation in government. It led to internal self-government in February 1963 and independence in July 1964, under the leadership of Banda and the Malawi Congress Party. The cancellation of the pre-independence elections, which had been scheduled for April 1964, and the declaration of the one party state in July 1966, meant that electoral and representative politics remained dormant until 1994. Popular representation and influence in the public policy process was thus completely undermined.

The single-party political system also deepened state centralisation. The October 1965 convention of the MCP accepted a set of proposals that became the basis for the 1966 Republic of Malawi Constitution. Amongst these was the proposal that the functions of head of state and head of government should be combined in the office of the president. Although this was carried over from colonial rule, associated provisions further strengthened the president's role in the political system. The proposals urged the creation of a strong executive presidency without a deputy, ostensibly because this would enhance national unity and stability. These conditions were deemed essential for the processes of nation building and the promotion of economic development.

In relation to the legislative branch, it was stated that the task of the executive president was to ". . . decide the policies . . . and to carry those policies into effect . . ." (MG 1965a, 4), while the function of the legislature was:

> To provide . . . an opportunity for the elected representatives . . . to discuss the policies put forward by the executive, and on approving those policies to enact the necessary laws, levy sufficient taxes and authorise the appropriate expenditure of public money required to enable the policies to be put into operation (MG 1965a, 5).

The president appointed, at his own discretion, members of the cabinet from within or outside parliament, and any additional members of parliament to represent "minority interests." Cabinet ministers were required to resign if they failed to "co-operate in the fulfilment of the President's decision on any important issue" (MG 1965a, 11). Throughout the one-party period, the Legislature and the Cabinet would, therefore, play a secondary role to the executive presidency in the public policy processes. Moreover, the one party regime emphasised the paramountcy of the MCP and its leader over all aspects of political life. President Banda was the national leader of the MCP, which was the sole legal party. All members of parliament belonged to the party, whose constitution demanded their unconditional allegiance to it. They had to adhere to its four cornerstones of "Unity, Loyalty, Obedience and Discipline," subordinate their interests to those of the Party, and show complete solidarity with the Party Leader (MCP Constitution, Part 1, Article 2.2; Preamble).

The combination of the one-party system and the executive presidency relegated the legislature to a rubber-stamping role. There was no likelihood of the latter questioning the executive's policies. The concentration of decision-making power in the presidency meant that policymaking was the sole preserve of Banda.

Whereas policy-making was centralised, its implementation was delegated to the state bureaucracy, whose characteristics and operations were defined by the existing political realities. The state bureaucracy was subordinated to the presidency and the MCP. Its role was to implement centrally determined policies, and to ". . . serve the government . . . with fidelity and undivided loyalty" (MG 1965a, 11). The president appointed, on his own prerogative, the officers at the highest echelons of the public service, such as the principal (permanent) secretaries and their deputies. He was also minister responsible for the public service and the Public Service Commission was accountable to him. The state bureaucracy was, thus, directly under the control of the office of the president. On the other hand, the MCP constituted the government, and was superior to the bureaucracy. The state bureaucracy (as employees of the Malawi government) was, therefore, ultimately subordinated to the MCP.

The fusion of the offices of the head of state, head of government, and supreme party leader in the hands of one man indicated that the highest levels of state organisation were fused with and indistinguishable from Banda. He controlled both the political and administrative aspects of the state. The president formulated public policy and ensured its execution in a centralised, non-participatory political system. Malawi's foreign policy processes during the one-party era must, therefore, be examined in the context of this domestic political setting and how it interacted with the international political and economic system. At the centre of all foreign policy was Banda who, as mentioned earlier, was minister of foreign affairs throughout his reign. As demonstrated below, his own involvement in the domestic economy, and the conduct of Malawi's international relations were closely interrelated.

The Foreign Policy of the One-Party State

Colonialism was the foundation of Malawi's involvement in the international political and economic system. Nyasaland had been incorporated into the system primarily as a labour reserve for the mines of southern Africa and secondarily as a producer of tobacco and tea for the international markets The country is landlocked, having been carved out of mountainous land between Mozambique, Tanganyika and Northern Rhodesia. The territory was not economically viable since it lacked lucrative raw materials. The economic infrastructure was not developed. There was not even a central banking system. Additionally, a professional, technical and administrative cadre was non-existent. The only economic resources that were readily available were land and the people. In short, Malawi lacked resources, economic infrastructure and a framework for development. Consequently, at independence in 1964, the country inherited a huge recurrent budget deficit from the Federation of Rhodesia and Nyasaland, which had been dissolved the previous year. Malawi also had to take on a sizeable proportion of the federation's debts, and finance the provision of essential services within the country — services which had previously been provided by the federal government. However, government revenue could not be significantly increased because of widespread poverty and the subsistence nature of the economy. The country was actually on the verge of insolvency (Morton 1975, 12-13).

This limited resource base dictated a conservative development policy and considerable reliance on foreign aid. Domestically, Banda sought to preserve the limited capital that existed predominantly in the hands of the few Europeans and Asians. He also wanted to create favourable conditions for economic growth through the building of an economic infrastructure that would promote private entrepreneurship (Nyasaland Government 1962; 1965b; 1968; 1971). Hence Banda adopted a domestic policy of multi-racialism and economic nationalism: he tolerated the dominance of Asians in commerce and Europeans in the agricultural estates and manufacturing industry. Economic nationalism involved his encouragement of political and public officials to undertake commercial farming, to supplement white-owned estates with indigenous ownership. Banda himself became a principal participant in the economy as one of the largest owners of agricultural estates and other business enterprises.

At the international level Banda pursued a policy of "discretionary alignment and neutralism," which was pro-Western and anti-Communist, and confirmed the continuation of historic economic and political ties. Thus, in the context of the Cold War, Malawi aligned herself with the Western countries. There was also a heavy reliance on foreign aid to stimulate development, which led to a reasonable economic growth rate averaging six per cent in the 1970s, but did not result in significantly broad-based economic development (Kaunda 1998, 63). Aid was only sought from the United Kingdom, the United States of America, West Germany, and the United Nations. The aid that was offered by communist China was rejected out of hand.

Meanwhile, diplomatic relations were established with Taiwan, Israel, and South Africa, countries from which development assistance would also be sought. At the same time, a friendly policy towards the Portuguese colonialists in Mozambique was adopted, as a prelude to the extension of Malawi's rail network to the Indian Ocean port of Nacala in that territory.

Malawi's early foreign policy thus reflected reliance on Western economic assistance. All the countries that Malawi sought assistance from were those that had friendly relations with the United Kingdom. Likewise, countries regarded as unfriendly by the United Kingdom and the West were shunned. These included Tanzania and Zambia, Malawi's neighbours, whose regimes were considered supportive of the communist bloc. Malawi claimed territory along its common boundaries with both countries, and apparently used these border disputes as an excuse for avoiding trade and political cooperation with these countries.

What was particularly evident during Malawi's early years of independence was the economic and political influence of the former colonial master, the United Kingdom, in Malawi's affairs. The British government guaranteed the financing of Malawi's recurrent account budget deficit from independence up to 1973. During that time the United Kingdom was also the leading source of bilateral aid. The first decade of Malawi's independence was actually characterised by an obvious neo-colonial British role in the conduct of foreign relations and the choice of development partners. Technical assistance together with financial aid from the former colonial master was largely responsible for shaping the economic and administrative framework through which Banda's policies were executed (Morton 1975). Even the choice of development strategy reflected British influences. Malawi advocated development policies that emphasised a mixed economy, commercial agriculture, development of the infrastructure, and reliance on foreign aid. All these were suggested in the recommendations made in the Jack Report of 1960 (Nyasaland Protectorate 1960, 7-8). The report was commissioned by the colonial government to determine future policy options for the country.

Therefore, Malawi's foreign relations and development policies remained within the ambit of British influence. This was apparent in the refusal to recognise communist China and to accept its aid offer, and also in the setting up of diplomatic relations with Taiwan and Israel. Additionally, the maintenance of friendly relations with the Portuguese colonialists in Mozambique, the appeasement of the apartheid regime of South Africa and the tolerance of the minority regime of Ian Smith in Rhodesia, manifested a foreign policy orientation that was shaped by Western, in particular British interests.

It can be argued that Malawi's capacity to determine an autonomous foreign policy was enhanced by the ending of British aid. But this was not the case. In the late 1960s, Western aid donors (including the United

Kingdom) refused to fund two projects. One was the relocation of the capital from Zomba in southern Malawi to the centre of the country at Lilongwe. The other was the construction of a rail link from landlocked Malawi to Nacala on the Mozambican Indian Ocean coast. These projects were important for the wider distribution of the national infrastructure, and for long-term economic development. However, the traditional donors claimed that there were other more important projects that they would rather finance. This rebuff compelled Banda to seek financial assistance from South Africa and to establish diplomatic relations with the apartheid regime. The recourse to South Africa was a sign of desperation rather than the display of an autonomous foreign policy orientation. The unpopular liaison with the Portuguese in colonial Mozambique may also be explained in similar terms.

In 1978, Malawi embarked on the National Rural Development Programme (NRDP) that was to span twenty years and was at the time the country's largest single investment. The sources of aid were diversified. Nevertheless, the NRDP was entirely financed by Western donors. These were the British Overseas Development Administration (ODA), the United States Agency for International Development (USAID), the European Development Fund (EDF), and the Federal Republic of Germany. The multilateral donors were the International Fund for Agricultural Development (IFAD), the International Development Association (IDA), and the African Development Bank (ADB), all of which are in the realm of Western influence and control.

By 1980, West Germany had surpassed the United Kingdom as the principal bilateral aid donor. Japanese aid was also increasing. However, the diversification of aid sources did not alter Malawi's dependence on Western aid and the subsequent influence of these aid donors on the country's development and foreign policies.

The fact that Western governments and agencies financed the NRDP implied their general agreement with Malawi's development strategy. Banda's choice of national development strategy actually indicated his perception of what was regarded as acceptable practise by the Western donors. Therefore, Malawi under the leadership of Banda remained within the Western-dominated international economic order, and continued to be a subordinate actor in that system. This perpetuated Malawi's economic dependence as well as the influence of Western considerations in foreign policy.

Foreign Policy-Making in the Multiparty Era

In 1994 Banda was defeated in the first multiparty elections since 1961. The multiparty system of government heralded an attempt to re-orientate political practices and relationships amongst the presidency, the legislature, and the state bureaucracy and society. A new constitution had been drafted as the Banda era came to a close, and this was adopted just before the multiparty elections. This constitution reflected liberal democratic ideals, including periodic elections, a separation of powers, and a system of checks and balances in the operations of the principal state institutions.

The Republic of Malawi Constitution Act (No. 20 of 1994) stipulated that the president should be both the head of state and head of government. There would be a vice-president, and a cabinet selected by the president. The cabinet would provide advice to the president. The president retained the power to appoint state officials above the rank of deputy secretary, as well as the Attorney General and the Director of Public Prosecutions. It also introduced new provisions, such as the establishment of the Senate, the office of the Ombudsman, the Human Rights Commission, and the Law Commission. All these were to be independent of external interference. The Senate role would be to scrutinise government policy. The Ombudsman was to investigate (administrative) injustices suffered by persons. The Human Rights Commission was meant to protect human rights and investigate reports of abuse, the Law Commission, to review and recommend desirable changes to the law. In addition, a joint sitting of the Parliament and Senate (the National Assembly) was empowered to impeach the president or vice-president. Acts of Parliament were given primacy over other forms of law. All public official functions would be subject to the constitution rather than to the whims of any particular person or party. All these measures were designed to remove the exclusive, absolute and centralised governance that had prevailed during the one-party era.

Similarly, the role and function of the state bureaucracy was altered. The Public Service Act (No. 19 of 1994) prescribed that the bureaucracy's character would be ". . . impartial, independent and permanent . . . [and] guided only by concerns of public interest and the welfare of the public . . ." This implied that it would no longer be subservient to any political party or individual. Emphasised too was the primacy of the constitution, which embodied the public and national interest. The new political order was, therefore, expected to usher in a new form of public policy making. There was supposed to be public responsiveness, transparency, accountability, and generally the paramountcy of national interest over particularistic or sectional interests in the formulation and execution of public policies.

However, whereas the constitution advocated the separation of the executive branch of government from the legislature and the judiciary, it also laid down conditions for continued executive pre-eminence in the public policy-making process. Close scrutiny reveals that the president and cabinet are not answerable to parliament, but to the constitution and the electorate. Whereas the parliament is essential in passing legislation initiated by the executive, the legislature cannot challenge executive policy and action on a regular basis.

When President Bakili Muluzi took over in May 1994, it appeared that he wanted to strengthen regional ties. He made inaugural trips to Zambia, Zimbabwe and Botswana. However, the first two years of his regime were characterised by an apparent lack of clear direction or unanimity over foreign policy. This was partly a result of the president's leadership style as well as the difficulties of transition to the new democratic order.

Initially, it seemed that President Muluzi would adhere closely to the constitutional provisions, especially with regard to the separation of powers. He did not reserve any ministerial portfolio for himself, but distributed them widely amongst his cabinet. He more than doubled the size of the cabinet, thus apparently making it more inclusive. His leadership style was characteristically less directive or control-oriented than Banda's. It was one in which he performed a supervisory role, seeking input from the cabinet ministers before a decision was taken on any important issue. Rather than act as the supreme leader, he relied considerably on each minister to initiate and propose policies to be authorised and adopted by cabinet. Ministers had to report on the progress of their departmental activities. The conduct of cabinet business was thus more consultative, collegial, and involved more discussion than in the previous regime.

The problems of transition were the direct outcome of shifting alliances after the May 1994 general election. President Muluzi's ruling United Democratic Front (UDF) had won only 46 per cent of the popular vote, and needed the co-operation of the Alliance for Democracy (AFORD), which had obtained 19 per cent of the of the votes. The two parties had established a meaningful working relationship in their joint opposition to the Banda regime in the period running up to the establishment of the multiparty system. Together, they had won popular support because they had promised a new era of democracy and prosperity. But contrary to popular expectation, they could not co-operate with each other over the formation of a coalition government.

Their coalition negotiations collapsed. Subsequently AFORD signed a memorandum of understanding with their erstwhile enemy, the MCP, to work as a united, joint opposition to the minority UDF government. With a combined strength of 91 parliamentary seats compared to the UDF's 86, the opposition paralysed government business. The UDF government could not pass legislation and implement its policies. Hence the absence of new foreign policy initiatives during the first six months of multiparty democracy, when the foreign minister was Edward Bwanali.

This political confusion continued until December 1994 when Chakufwa Chihana joined the government and was made the second vice-president. He brought along with him five other AFORD members, who were immediately made ministers and deputy ministers in an UDF-AFORD coalition government. The cabinet was expanded to 37 members. The inclusion of AFORD parliamentarians meant that the government now had a working majority which would allow it to function normally.

Barely 18 months later, Chihana resigned, signalling the collapse of the coalition government and a return to the uncertainties of the first six months. However, the other AFORD members refused to quit the coalition government. The president was thus able to achieve a working majority in parliament, by retaining in cabinet members who had been elected on an opposition ticket.

The collapse of the coalition prompted a reshuffle of the cabinet, leading to the appointment of Mapopa Chipeta from AFORD, as the new minister of foreign affairs. Soon initiatives were taken to cultivate relations with countries with whom Banda's regime would never have dealt — Libya, Kuwait, Saudi Arabia, the United Arab Emirates, Egypt and Sudan. The exact rationale for the diversification of external relations is not immediately obvious. Muluzi's Moslem faith was perhaps the prime motivation for establishing relations with Arab Islamic states.

Chipeta, as minister of foreign affairs, had considerable clout within the cabinet. One of the most educated ministers in the cabinet and quite articulate, he had earned considerable respect amongst foreign governments. He is articulate and suggested the clustering of Malawi's foreign missions around core representative missions on every continent. This implied an increase in the number of diplomatic missions. Chipeta's influence on foreign policy issues may also have been strengthened by the support that emanated from Malawi's permanent representative to the United Nations, Professor David

Rubadiri. The professor's calm and reasonable demeanour is reputed to have brought international respect and recognition for Malawi even amongst counties that might have balked at Banda's rather eccentric foreign policy.

The first five years of Muluzi's regime, therefore, brought about a change in the determination of foreign policy. Foreign policy-making was no longer the sole preserve of the executive president, but became a ministerial and, by extension, cabinet responsibility. However, policy-making remained the prerogative of the executive branch of government, and the legislature had a negligible role in the process. Even with the replacement of Chipeta as foreign affairs minister by Brown Mpinganjira in 1999, ministerial influence prevailed. Mpinganjira is perceived as one of the most powerful ministers, with substantial influence within the UDF and the cabinet. He is also reputed to be a confidant of the president. As such, from 1999, foreign policy-making appears to have been concentrated in the core UDF leadership that is close to the presidency. This reinforces the centrality of the executive in the determination of foreign policy. The cabinet reshuffle of early March 2000 which brought in Lillian Patel as the new minister of foreign affairs did not seem to have altered the central role of the executive in foreign policy determination.

The legislature has not had a significant role in the foreign policy-making process. Apart from its Public Appointments Committee's vetting of nominations to diplomatic missions, parliament has not exhibited strong influence in the determination of foreign policy. Moreover, the senate, which was to be established for the function of policy review, has yet to be constituted. There are thus negligible countervailing mechanisms to check the power of the cabinet, and the executive branch in general, in making policy decisions. The predominance of the executive branch of government over the legislature continues, even though the extreme forms of state centralisation have been removed.

The state bureaucracy continues to perform its traditional role of policy execution, but its characteristics have changed so significantly that it is doubtful whether it performs its functions with the desired independence and commitment to the public interest. The state bureaucracy has become increasingly inept and even untrustworthy. Its composition in the upper echelons has drastically changed, especially after Muluzi won a second term as president in June 1999. The elections exacerbated political divisions that had been brought to the fore by the first multiparty elections five years earlier. AFORD and MCP co-operated during the 1999 elections, and are now a formidable allied parliamentary opposition. They are also challenging the validity of Muluzi's re-election, claiming that rigged the elections in his favour.

Officials who are perceived by the regime as being supporters of the opposition parties have been systematically dismissed and replaced by UDF supporters, without due regard to merit, qualifications and competence. These patronage appointments mean that even though the UDF (unlike the MCP in the previous regime) is not politically and institutionally supreme over the public service, it exercises significant leverage over it. The implication of this development is that the state bureaucracy has not lived up to its constitutional expectations. It is aligned with the ruling party and serves the interests of its leader.

The policy processes are thus characterised by executive dominance over the legislature, and by the subordination of the state bureaucracy to the chief executive. Foreign policy-making has tended to revolve around the interactions of the core UDF leadership, and is thus increasingly being re-centralised. This indicates continuity in institutional relationships involving the policy-making processes, in spite of the transition from a one party to a multiparty political system.

External Influences on Foreign Policy-Making

There are two other major aspects in which continuities in the pre- and post-Banda era may be observed. These are i) the significant dependence on foreign aid, and ii) the pro-Western foreign policy stance.

Malawi's multilateral aid donors are the International Bank for Reconstruction and Development (World Bank), the European Union, and the United Nations. Together, they provided USD 1 832 million (79 per cent) of the total of USD 2 328 million of foreign aid in 1998. In that year the World Bank group accounted for 64 per cent of the total multilateral lending. The principal bilateral aid donors are the United States of America, the United Kingdom, Canada, Japan, Germany and the Netherlands, who contributed about 13 per cent of aid in the same year (RBM, 1998, 26). The bilateral aid is for finance, infrastructure, agriculture, social services and poverty alleviation, and environmental protection. Although the list of aid donors has barely changed from what it was during the one-party era, the proportion of bilateral aid coming from these countries has grown. Whereas in 1992 the USA, United Kingdom, Japan, and Germany accounted for 64 per cent of total bilateral aid, they provided 80 per cent in 1996 (IBRD, 1998, 43).

Donor aid is systematically coordinated through consultative group meetings, the last one of which was in December 1998. The World Bank has assumed a central role as multilateral aid donor and principal advisor to Malawi, in contrast to the initial prevalence of the United Kingdom as bilateral aid donor and major influence on development strategy. Malawi has credits from the bank's International Development Association (IDA), for infrastructure and social sector development, public sector management, and the development of the financial sector. The International Finance Corporation (IFC), which is the bank's private sector lending arm, has commitments in the capital market, tourism, health and agribusiness. Malawi is also a member of the Multilateral Investment Guarantee Agency (MIGA), which positions the country favourably to attract foreign investment.

Furthermore, the bank has sponsored workshops and training programmes in institution-building, fiscal decentralisation, micro-finance, banking, etc. for senior government officials and technical personnel. It also provides technical assistance in the form of advice on the formulation of sector investment strategies, assessments, and expenditure review (World Bank 1999). Even though the United Kingdom is still significant as an aid donor (providing USD 31.7 million, or 32 per cent of bilateral aid in 1996) (IBRD 1998, 43), it has relinquished the role of principal economic advisor, as that is now the domain of the World Bank. But in the post-Cold War era, the bank is an instrument for disseminating Western policy prescriptions.

Malawi's pro-Western foreign policy stance has also not changed, even though recent overtures indicate the diversification of international relations. The continued pattern of international relationships is evident in the choice of trading partners. These include all the bilateral aid donors and Austria, Zimbabwe and South Africa. Historically South Africa has been Malawi's major trading partner and in 1996 it received 13 per cent of Malawi's exports and provided 44 per cent of the country's imports (IBRD, 1998, 40-41).

Malawi's relations with all its 'traditional' aid donors and trading partners remain cordial. The relationship with the United States of America is even warmer since the establishment of the multiparty system. For example, the new ambassador from Malawi to the United States, Tony Kandiero, had this to say when presenting his letters of credence in February 2000:

[The] Republic of Malawi ... convey[s] ... gratitude for the invaluable technical, financial and moral support you gave us during our fight against repression and one-party dictatorship in 1994; and during last year's Presidential and Parliamentary Election . . . now we need a push to assist us consolidate our young democracy . . . lift Malawi from abject poverty onto a platform of a prosperous nation . . . I will spare no effort . . . to further strengthen the warm and cordial relations which happily exist between our two countries . . . I look forward very much to support and guidance from you (USA Department of State, 7 February 2000).

To which President Bill Clinton replied:

There is no finer example of our two countries' mutually beneficial relationship than success of the Africa Crisis Response Initiative (ACRI) in Malawi . . . a US program to eventually train 12 000 military personnel . . . for peacekeeping and humanitarian assistance operations on the [African] continent. You can take pride that Malawian troops have excelled in ACRI field exercises and training sessions (USA Department of State, 7 February 2000).

What this diplomatic exchange exposes is the deepening of the relationship between Malawi and the USA after the end of the Cold War, and the submission of Malawi to the USA's agenda for political and economic change in Africa. Malawi has now been incorporated into the United States' foreign policy initiatives. As of December 1999, it was only one of seven African countries, including Senegal, Uganda, Tunisia, Mali, Ethiopia and Ghana which had participated in the Africa Crisis Response Initiative (ACRI), which was initiated in 1997 (Adair 1999). ACRI provides training and non-lethal equipment and preparation for a multinational force. It aims at capacity building for a rapid deployment peacekeeping force (*Africa Confidential*, 1997). In fact, ACRI establishes a military foothold for the USA in Africa, where direct military involvement is not possible due to the USA's own domestic politics.

Malawi/USA military co-operation dates from 1994 with Malawi's involvement in the Joint Combined Exchange Training (JCET) programme. Most senior army officers have also participated in the USA's International Military Education and Training (IMET) programmes that impart planning and resource management skills, and are aimed at strengthening civil-military relations and the rule of law (Adair 1999). The expanded version of IMET has involved not only the military but also government officials including the Speaker of Parliament and high court judges.

Thus, the level of co-operation between Malawi and the USA has expanded from the economic to include political and military aspects.

Malawi has become both economically and politically incorporated into the ambit of American foreign policy, in the USA's quest to predominate over the international economic and political system. This development is a direct result of the growing power and stature of the USA after the collapse of the Soviet Union and the creation of a uni-polar world order in which the USA's political and economic ideologies are being globalized. It is no secret that the major impetus for change from a one-party regime to the multiparty system in Malawi, and in Africa in general, emanated from pressure from the USA. That country has also used its policy dominance over the multilateral aid donors such as the World Bank to insist on the imposition of conditions that favour the democratization and liberalization of political and economic life as a prelude to the disbursement of foreign aid. As noted above, Malawi has been a recipient of structural adjustment loans since 1981. This explains why Malawi has edged closer to the USA, and further strengthened its subordination to Western interests.

Conclusion

The most significant change that has occurred in Malawi over the last decade is the transition from a centralised, authoritarian one-party state to a democratic, multiparty system. This change held the promise of transforming the country's internal political and economic characteristics and international relations. Although internal opposition drove the change, its major support was pressure from Western aid donors, led by the USA, to democratise and liberalise political and economic relations in African countries. The process of democratisation was closely related to the march of globalization. It was thus merely an extension of Western influence on the conduct of Malawi's domestic politics. This influence is perpetuated by the dependence of Malawi on foreign aid from and on trade relations with the West. It has been deepened by Malawi's extended co-operation with the USA in the political and military fields. The subordination of Malawi to Western interests has thus been continuous from the time the country was colonised, through the reign of Banda, up to the present. Globalization effectively strengthens this subordination.

The Banda era exhibited a close interrelationship between domestic material interests, political power and the determination of foreign policy. Banda's maintenance of close relations with the Western countries was apparently influenced by his desire to obtain aid for the promotion of economic development, as that was the basis of his legitimacy. But he used political power to concentrate economic power in his own hands. In his quest for personal wealth, he created friendly relations with the minority regimes in South Africa and Mozambique, which were in the sphere of Western influence.

The regime of president Muluzi has not altered Malawi's historical international relations. The dependent nature of the economy dictates that such relations be perpetuated. The current regime has, in fact, extended and deepened relations with the West, encouraged by the globalization of Western ideologies since the end of the Cold war; these global ideologies have been imposed on certain African countries such as Malawi which are so poor and dependent that they cannot afford to de-link from the exploitative ties they have with the West.

Nor has the democratically elected regime in Malawi changed the basic orientation of domestic institutional relationships. Centralisation of policy making persists, with the systematic subordination of the legislature and the manipulation of the public service. Even though the extreme forms of state centralisation were removed with the demise of the one-party state, the executive branch still monopolises policy decision-making. The elected parliament has limited involvement in the overall policy-making process. Elections have broadened representation, but this has not been matched by an extension of the influence of the people's representatives in the policy-making process. Furthermore, the divisions in Malawi's parliament have weakened the institution's capability to engage in meaningful policy debate.

Delays in establishing a senate also mean that the legislature has been denied the power to scrutinise government policy. Added to this is the absence of an elected local government system, which has increased the tendency to concentrate power in the hands of the executive (Kaunda 1999). The apparent concentration of decision-making within the cabinet has also strengthened the relative power of the chief executive. Meanwhile, the system of presidential patronage has reduced the role of the state bureaucracy to that of a tool to serve the whims and wishes of the incumbent president rather than being an impartial servant of the people.

What has been removed from the political system is the extreme form of state centralization; but once again, the narrow interests of the leadership appear to be taking precedence over the need for a genuine democratization of the political process. Democratization has not developed beyond the conduct of regular elections and has not significantly altered the basic orientation of the Malawian state. The state is still characterised by executive presidential dominance over the political process, the subordination of Malawi to underdevelopment. All this leads to a deeper and more comprehensive incorporation of the country into the inequitable international political and economic order that is dominated by the West. It does not enhance the country's autonomy to develop its domestic economy or to engage in beneficial international relations.

References

Adair, V. (1999) "Peacetime Engagement Programmes in Malawi Strengthen Democracy." *Africa News Online.* 16 December.
Africa Confidential. (1997) 38: 16. 1 August.
Allison, G.T. (1971) *The Essence of Decision: Explaining the Cuban Missile Crisis.* Boston: Little, Brown.
Cox, R.W. (1981) "Social Forces, States and World orders: Beyond International Relations Theory." *Millennium* 10.2: 126–55. (Qtd. in M. Wright and T. Evans, 1993.)
Economist Intelligence Unit (EIU). (1995) *Malawi. Country Profile, 1994-95.* London.
Economist Intelligence Unit (EIU). (1998) *Malawi. Country Profile, 1998-99.* London.
Groom, A.J.R. and M. Light, eds. (1994) *Contemporary International Relations: A Guide to Theory.* London: Pinter Publishers.
Harrigan, J. (1994) "Malawi." *Aid and Power: The World Bank and Policy-based Lending.* Ed. P. Moseley *et al.* London: Routledge and Kegan Paul.
International Bank for Reconstruction and Development (IBRD). (1988) *Malawi. Industrial Sector Memorandum.* (Report No. 7402, 1988). Washington, DC.
International Bank for Reconstruction and Development (IBRD). (1999) *World Development Report, 1999-2000.* Washington, DC: IBRD.
International Bank for Reconstruction and Development (IBRD). (1999) *Online, 1999. Malawi. Country Overview; Malawi at a Glance; Various Indicators.* Washington, DC.
Kaunda, J.M. (1998) "The State and Society in Malawi." *Commonwealth and Comparative Politics* 36.1: 48–67.
———. (1999) "State Centralisation and the Decline of Local Government in Malawi." *International Review of Administrative Sciences* 65.4: 579–595.
Light, M. (1994) "Foreign Policy Analysis." *Contemporary International Relations: A Guide to Theory.* Ed. A.J.R. Groom and M. Light. London: Pinter Publishers.
Malawi Government (MG). (1965a) *Proposals for a Republican Constitution of Malawi.* Zomba: Government Printer.
———. (1965b) *Development Plan, 1965–69.* Zomba: Government Printer.
———. (1968) *Development Programme, 1968–70.* Zomba: Government Printer.
———. (1971) *Statement of Development Policies, 1971–80.* Zomba: Government Printer.
Malawi Congress Party (MCP). (Undated) *The Constitution of the MCP and Rules and Regulations Governing the Discipline of the Malawi Congress Party.*
Morton, K. (1975) *Aid and Dependence. British Aid to Malawi.* London: Croom Helm/ Overseas Development Institute.
Nyasaland Protectorate. (1960) *Report on an Economic Survey of Nyasaland, 1958-59.* (The Jack Report). Zomba: Government Printer.

Nyasaland Government. (1962) *Development Plan, 1962-1965*. Zomba: Government Printer.
Pan African News Agency (PANA). (1998) "SUCOMA Attacks CAMA's Report on Sugar." 23 April.
———. (1999) "Malawi Kwacha Weakening against the US Dollar." 2 November.
Press Trust Deed, 10 February 1982; 14 July 1993.
Republic of Malawi. (1994) Public Service Act (No. 19 of 1994).
Republic of Malawi. (1994) (Constitution) Act (No. 20 of 1994).
Reserve Bank of Malawi (RBM). (1998) *Financial and Economic Review* XXX: 4.
———. (1999) *Financial and Economic Review* XXXI: 2.
Shaw, T. and O. Aluko. (1984) "Introduction: Towards a Political Economy of African Foreign Policy." *The Political Economy of African Foreign Policy. Comparative Analysis*. Ed. T. Shaw and O. Aluko. New York: St. Martin's Press.
Smith, H. (1994) "Marxism and International Relations Theory." *Contemporary International Relations: A Guide to Theory*. Ed. A.J.R. Groom and M. Light. London: Pinter Publishers.
Snyder, R.C., H.W. Bruck and B. Supin. (1962) *Foreign Policy Decision-Making*. New York: Macmillan.
Sylvan, D.A. and S. Chan. (1984) *Foreign Policy Decision-making: Perception, Cognition and Artificial Intelligence*. New York: Praeger.
United Nations Development Programme (UNDP). (1999) *Human Development Report*.
USA Department of State (Office Of International Information Programs).(2000) "Malawi Ambassador Kandiero Presents Credentials at White House." 7 February 2000.
Williams H., M. Wright and T. Evans, eds. (1993) *A Reader in International Relations and Political Theory*. Buckingham: Open University Press.
Wright, S. (1999) "The Changing Context of African Foreign Policies." *African Foreign Policies*. Ed. S. Wright. Boulder: Westview Press.

6 From Ramgoolam to Ramgoolam: An Analysis of the Mauritian Foreign Policy-Making Process

ROSABELLE LAVILLE

Mauritius is often hailed as an "island of success" (Dommen and Dommen 1999, xiii). In the space of a single generation, the population has managed to improve its economy, increase human development and maintain peace. These important achievements have come about through the island's maintenance of judicious relationships with foreign states. However, these have not benefited all Mauritians, nor have they always contributed to the deepening of democracy on the island.

This chapter focuses on the foreign policy-making process in Mauritius and suggests that in the pursuit of macroeconomic growth and development, the successive governments of Mauritius have (since independence in 1968), largely failed to facilitate the successful political and economic integration of many Mauritians. The argument presented in this chapter contradicts various analyses of economic development in Mauritius, especially those emphasising the presence of economic liberalism and efficient political institutions on the island (Dommen and Dommen 1999; Srebnik 2000). Rather, it is argued that the current foreign policy-making process in Mauritius does not necessarily lead to the furthering of democracy in that country. This situation is a result of various factors which include the island's history of slavery; the control of trade by a predominantly white oligarchy; and the vulnerability of Mauritius as a small island developing state that is largely dependent on external assistance for its economic prosperity. In view of these factors, the Mauritian state has maintained strong ties with its former colonial powers, namely Britain and France. Throughout the Cold War period for example, Mauritius preserved its links with Britain and the United States (USA) for both ideological and security purposes. In the post-Cold War era, it is still evident that the foreign policy-making process in Mauritius is influenced by Britain, France and the USA. These relations have fostered a form of dependence, which is specifically conditioned by internal cultural and economic needs. Thus, while many Southern African states subscribe to both independent political and economic development, they continue to be pressured to accept the terms and conditions set by influential states in their participation in an increasingly globalized international society.

Thus Mauritius maintains a dependent relationship with Britain, France and the USA and this state of affairs has a profound influence on its foreign policies and policy-making process. At one level, the dependency of Mauritius on economically influential states, like Britain and France, may be due to an emotional response from Mauritian policy-makers that is not always discernable to the public eye: fear. This response promotes cooperation rather than conflict with those who are perceived as being powerful. Beyond the dependency model, Mauritius has managed to emerge from colonial rule to establish its identity as a sovereign state. However, its decision-making ability is still conditioned by the cultural and social reality within the nation-state. For example, since independence Mauritius has cultivated diplomatic and economic relations with India, France and Britain. Generally, these relationships have been promoted in the interests of the various ruling parties' constituencies. More important, these ties have been strengthened for economic reasons. In the last decade, the government of Mauritius has increased its focus on regionalism and greater cooperation with the Southern African Development Community (SADC).

This newfound cooperation indicates the Mauritian government's need for new spheres of collective security in a multipolar world (where a greater number of players have more bargaining power and greater access to dangerous weapons) as well as the country's need for new economic partners as its preferential trade agreements with Europe and America come to an end. The Mauritian government's involvement in the region has little to do with the interests of the island's African descendants, who are locally known as Creoles. Despite this apparent lack of concern (on the part of the state), a greater number of Creoles are turning to Africa and the African diaspora to reconstruct their cultural identity and they look to the present Mauritian government to assist in the facilitation of contact and cooperation with the African continent. In view of these new pressures and demands, it is possible that Mauritian foreign policy-makers will have to consider building stronger links between Africa and Mauritius. However, given the apparent intractability of current social and economic disparities in Mauritius, it appears that this process will take considerable time. Finally, both the interests and identity of the Mauritian state, affects, and is affected by, social practices and norms which it constructs and which are constructed in its domestic and international environment. Furthermore, its foreign policy-makers are not necessarily rational and independent decision-makers — their decisions are informed by many variables, such as the country's location, colonial past, domestic politics, economic imperatives, and cultures.

The Population of Mauritius

The foreign-policy making process in Mauritius is profoundly influenced by the country's diverse population. In 1997, the estimated population of the island was 1.2 million. Mauritius is a country of immigrants and each ethnic and/or religious group has contributed to the island's rich tapestry of cultures. Approximately 60% of the Mauritian population consists of people of Indian descent, 27% of African and Malagasy descent, 2% of European descent, 1% of Chinese descent and 10% of people of mixed ancestry. Until 1982, Mauritians were required to declare their ethnic status in national censuses. However, the abolition of this practice after 1982 did not necessarily lead to the declining importance of ethnicity in all aspects of social and political life. In fact, ethnicity continues to play a crucial role in domestic and international relations.

Examples of ethnicity abound. Mauritians of Indian descent tend to promote political and trade links with the Indian sub-continent. Members of the Sino-Mauritian community continue to foster important trade bonds with Hong Kong, Japan and Singapore. Historical connections with Britain and France have been maintained by European business people on the island. Naturally, there is significant overlapping where international partnerships are concerned but it is possible to note how (since independence) successive Mauritian governments have promoted formal relations with Europe, Asia and (to a lesser extent) Africa, in line with the interests of its voters.

There has been less intensive exchange between Mauritius and the African continent. This situation is largely due to the marginalised position of African and Malagasy descendants, who are locally known as Creoles in Mauritius. The Creoles of Mauritian descent are themselves part of a broader, residual political category known as the General Population and, for various reasons are considered racially and socially inferior (Laville 2000, 279). Historically, it has been the white Franco-Mauritian community that has assumed leadership positions for this group as they had access to education and continue to enjoy the support of powerful patrons and are generally perceived as being racially superior to non-whites. As a result, there are few Creole descendants who presently feature as members of parliament. This means that they rarely obtain the opportunity to contribute to foreign policy-making processes.

A Historical Overview

In the last decade, Mauritius has been likened to an enterprise (Dommen and Dommen 1999, 69). From as early as the 18th century it obtained hub status as its capital, Port Louis, provided a stopover for ships between Asia, Africa and Europe. These trading links meant that the islanders developed a strong sense of international trade and diplomacy from an early stage in Mauritian history. Furthermore, the island's ethnically diverse population (made up entirely of immigrant communities and families from Asia, Africa and Europe), was, from the start compelled to forge a plural society where there was some form of social cooperation and peace. In addition, the general geographical isolation of the island encouraged social interaction and cultural diffusion among the population, resulting in concessions for religious and social freedom, such that, on the eve of independence, Mauritius had the highest number of public holidays in the world. Despite such conciliatory methods, Mauritius did not always manage to avoid domestic conflict.

In 1965, 1968 and 1999, Mauritius experienced ethnic riots. The riots of 1965 were associated with the rise of a socially and politically significant Hindu élite, which led many to fear the possibility of Hindu domination. The late Sir Gaetan Duval, known as 'King Creole', warned the population of the possibility of ethnic majority domination in Mauritius.[1] A referendum was called for by Duval's Parti Mauricien Socialiste Democrate (Mauritius Social Democratic Party) (PMSD) to fight against Mauritian independence from colonial rule. The Anglo-Mauritian agreement of 1965 ensured that no referendum took place before the first Mauritian elections in 1968. As a result, the Mauritius Labour Party (MLP) gained 54.5% of the vote and the PMSD 43.5%. According to Mannink:

> This was the first time in British colonial history that so many people had voted against independence. Had the issue been settled by referendum instead of an election, it is possible that voters would have decided against independence (1989, 23).

Independence from colonial rule was ideologically and politically appealing for the new Mauritian government. In the early 1960s, many states were on the path to independence and it was ideologically fashionable and economically rewarding to be independent of colonial rule.[2] 'Liberated' states received some economic concessions and aid from multinational corporations and banks (the United Nations and the World Bank) to assist them on the path to economic and social development. This aid was partially designed to compensate for the terrible toll European colonialism had inflicted on previously colonised states and their inhabitants. European assistance was further supported by various forms of economic investment. Britain maintained important businesses on the island, it established preferential trade agreements between Mauritius and the UK and it maintained a diplomatic presence in the country.

Fabian socialism was a prominent doctrine of Mauritius' first prime minister, Seewoosagur Ramgoolam, and it guided both domestic and foreign policy. Thus, it was up to the state to provide security and development for the nation and to make decisions on its behalf. This was to be achieved through a variety of social and economic development programmes, implemented with approval of appropriate scientists and technocrats. To achieve the goals set in these programmes, Mauritius depended on former colonial powers to offer technical assistance. For example, several technical experts and researchers were recruited to assist in the setting up of the Family Planning Programme in the Ministry of Health and others were employed to set up Mauritius' first Economic Planning Unit.

In the 1980s, according to Brautigan, "policymaking became at times exceptionally open." For example, in 1983 the new minister of finance took the unprecedented step of publishing his letters to the International Monetary Fund (IMF) and the World Bank outlining their agreements with the government. The World Bank noted that in Mauritius, "many economic policies are decided by polling and party alignment, rather than by technocratic professionals" (1997, 54). This suggests that by the 1980s, a measure of negotiation and democracy existed in decisions regarding foreign-policy. In the 1990s, however, one needs to consider factors beyond macro-political structure. Ethnicity for example, continues to play a crucial role in Mauritian politics and one finds that certain ethnic groups are scarce in government and business circles. Thus, while policy-making became exceptionally open in the 1980s, it is likely that Creoles, who constitute almost 20 percent of the population (200,000 people) did not really contribute to decisions concerning their livelihood.

96 *Globalization and Emerging Trends*

As a small island state, with particular vulnerabilities, the Mauritian government appears to have been compelled to compromise on domestic issues.[3] Bennett and Lepgold provide an overview of this new state of affairs, suggesting that these circumstances have been urged on by the "widespread sense that a new world order requires new institutional mechanisms to replace those made obsolescent by the end of the Cold War"; and that the breakup of the Soviet Union (and the subsequent preoccupation of its successor states with internal reform), have facilitated liberal cooperation between Eurasian powers, Japan and the United States (1993, 1). Furthermore, the authors argue that nuclear and ballistic missile technologies have spread to seventeen Third World countries, each of which have ballistic missiles with ranges of over 100 miles. Nine of these countries have access to missiles with ranges of over 500 miles. In this scenario, it has become increasingly problematic to enforce collective security, and it is difficult for small island states such as Mauritius, to bank on the form of collective security provided by powerful countries like America. To this end, Mauritius, in common with a number of developing states in Southern Africa, has been compelled to stand on its own and to forge new international links in its political and economic interest. The Mauritian quest for political and economic independence was apparent from 1968 and is currently evident in the structure of the Mauritian government.

Structure of Government

According to Chapin Metz, "the 1968 constitution proclaims that Mauritius is a 'democratic state' and that the constitution is the supreme law of the land. It guarantees the fundamental rights and freedoms of the people, including the right to hold private property and to be free from racial or other discrimination. Fundamental rights can only be suspended during wars or states of emergency, which must be duly declared by the parliament and reviewed every six months" (1994, 3). The political structure of Mauritius is modelled on the British system. Those who obtain support from the majority in government choose the prime minister. It is the prime minister, along with members of the cabinet, who hold political power. There are numerous political parties. The government presently consists of a coalition of the Mauritian Militant Movement (MMM), Militant Socialist Movement (MSM), Mauritian Labor Party (MLP) and the Mauritian Social Democratic Party (PMSD). Chapin Metz states that:

The National Assembly (Assemblée Nationale or parliament), the country's prime law-making body, consists of representatives elected from twenty three-member constituencies and one two member district on Rodrigues. In addition, unlike the British system, eight assembly seats are apportioned to the 'best losers' among the non-elected candidates, according to their ethno-religious affiliation — two each for Hindus, Muslims, Chinese, and the general population. An attempt must be made to distribute these seats proportionally to the major political parties, which are expressly referred to in the constitution (1994, 3).

Democracy is encouraged in Mauritius through the constitutional provision of specific commissions. These include the Judicial and Legal Service Commission, the Public Services Commission, the Police Service Commission and an ombudsman. The role of these commissions involves the appointment of government officials; the ombudsman investigates official misconduct. However, the Best Loser system has been subject to criticism. In seeking to promote ethnic representation, it has (in several instances) promoted ethnic discrimination. What Metz does not tell us is that in submitting their candidature, participants in the Best Loser system must declare their ethnic group. This rule has a number of implications — a Muslim candidate cannot submit his/her candidature for a best-loser seat that is to be allocated to a member of the Sino-Mauritian community. Creoles (who experience social stigmatisation and form a part of the General Population category), are rarely elected as candidates for the General Population seats.[4]

The country's legal system reflects Mauritius' colonial history. It is based on the Napoleonic Code and English common law. The Supreme Court heads the judicial system and has the power to interpret the constitution and to judge the constitutionality of legislation brought to its attention. Appointed by the prime minister and president, the chief justice helps to select five other judges for the court. The Supreme Court also serves as the Court of Criminal Appeal and the Court of Civil Appeal. Mauritius continues to refer legal and constitutional matters of indeterminable jurisdiction to Britain's Privy Council. Lower courts having original jurisdiction over various kinds of cases include the Intermediate Court, the Industrial Court, and ten district courts (Metz 1994, 1). However, the constitution does not specify the form of local government. Each village and town has its village or municipal council. While local governments depend on the central government for more than 70 percent of their revenues, only the municipal councils have the power to levy their own taxes. The existence of political institutions and access to the vote does not necessarily amount to democracy

(Laville, 291). Despite the strides in human and economic development made in Mauritius in the last 30 years, it seems that old social cleavages (especially ethnicity) and historical practices (mercantilism) still play an important role in both domestic and international relations. Most political power is vested in the prime minister of Mauritius and little (if any at all) is vested in the Mauritian military.

The Military

According to Metz, Mauritius has not had an established army since 1968, largely because of the cost of maintaining such a force. This reasoning is compatible with the Mauritian state's concern with economic growth and development. Instead, the security establishment includes the Mauritian Police Force which consists of a regular armed police of about 4,000 personnel, the paramilitary 1,200-member SMF, and the 240-member Special Support Unit (SSU), all of which are responsible for internal security. In 1965, ethnic riots between Hindu and Creole communities compelled the **governor to declare a state of emergency. A company of 2nd Battalion,** Coldstream Guards flew from Aden to Mauritius to re-establish peace. Military assistance was further required from Britain in 1968, when violence broke out between rival Muslim and Creole gangs in Port Louis. Troops **from B Company of 1st Battalion, The King's Shropshire Light Infantry were** deployed from Malaysia to assist the Special Mobile Force.

Mauritius also has a Special Constabulary and a small Anti-Drug and Smuggling Unit under police jurisdiction. Expenditures for the various police services from 1991 to 1992 amounted to 167.3 million Mauritian Rupees (6.692 million United States dollars) or about 1.4 percent of total central government spending. According the United States Department of Arms Control and Disarmament (ACDA) the Mauritian state's military expenditure has increased steadily since 1985, from approximately 3 million United States dollars to 14 million US dollars. It is unclear whether the increase in military expenditure is due to the purchase of more hardware and expertise, or whether increased expenditure is related to the devaluation of the Mauritian Rupee in the 1990s.

Recruitment to the Mauritian police force and other security units is by voluntary enlistment from all ethnic communities. Training is usually conducted in Mauritius; however, Metz suggests that some officers have received training in foreign military academies such as the Royal Military

Academy at Sandhurst in Britain. In 1982 the Mauritian government established the National Investigation Unit (NIU), which had been known as the State Service, to monitor internal security developments and the activities of foreign embassies and certain foreign visitors. This organization includes up to 200 full-time agents, all of whom are recruited from the regular police force, and 3,000 informers scattered throughout the country. In 1989, after an unsuccessful attempt on the life of the prime minister, Aneerood Jugnauth, a 100-member Very Important Persons Security Unit was established.

Mauritius also has a coast guard (Mauritian Coast Guard (MCG)) comprised of 350 members, designed to ensure the safety of Mauritian fisher-men, prevent smuggling, and protect the marine environment. In 1994, an Indian naval officer commanded the MCG; an unknown number of MCG personnel have received training from Indian naval instructors. With regard to foreign relations, it is evident that Mauritius has made use of its international connections to provide training and assistance to the Mauritian military. The military has a limited role to play in the foreign policy-making process. It is in parliament that most foreign policy decisions are debated and formulated.

Parliament

As noted above, the Constitution of Mauritius provides for the representation of minority communities at the National Assembly through an indirect electoral process known as the 'Best Loser' system, a system designed in the 1960s to safeguard the rights of minority communities on the island from the ills of majority rule. 'Best Losers' may only be represented at the national level through 'community'-defined candidates who are elected to the National Assembly. The electoral process of Mauritius is divided into two distinctive parts. The first part consists of direct elections to the National Assembly where there are seventy seats to be allocated. A total of twenty-one constituencies exist and each constituency elects three representatives, with the exception of Rodrigues island, which is a single constituency that elects two representatives to the National Assembly. The direct elections supply seats for sixty-two candidates. The second part of the electoral process consists of indirect elections that seek to fill what are known the eight 'Best Loser' seats. According to Mathur:

> The Best Loser seats are categorized into two sets of four seats. The first four seats are awarded on a community basis regardless of party affiliation, provided

100   *Globalization and Emerging Trends*

> the candidates belong to a party . . . . To ascertain the under represented community or communities, the breakdown for each community is used. For that purpose the official population census of 1972 is employed. [the classification] in descending order [is as follows] Muslim, General Population, Sino-Mauritians and Hindu (1997, 63).

Given that there is significant controversy in Mauritius as to whether people vote for candidates who represent them in ethnic terms, it would seem that for the Creoles, this means that their interests may only be represented if a candidate from the General Population is directly or indirectly (through the Best Loser system) elected to the National Assembly. With the exception of representatives from Rodrigues, there are few Creoles in parliament. According to Chapin Metz:

> Parliament may remain in office for a maximum of five years, unless it is dissolved by a vote of no-confidence or an act of the prime minister. A constitutional amendment, however, provided that the first assembly reckon its term from 1971, a de facto term of eight years. The assembly is responsible for all legislation and appropriations and may amend the constitution by either a two thirds or three-quarters majority, depending on the part of the constitution in question. A largely titular governor general presided over parliament in the name of the British monarch from independence in 1968 until March 12, 1992, when Mauritius declared itself a republic. Since then a president, appointed by the prime minister and ratified by the parliament, has assumed the role of the governor general (1994, 4).

Parliamentary Promises and Ethnic Exclusion

The quietist approach of Navin Ramgoolam's government to issues of sovereignty that involve France (regarding Tromelin island) and Britain (regarding Diego Garcia), may be linked to past approaches of the Mauritian government to foreign policy and international relations.[5] According to Mukonoweshuro, "at the level of foreign policy formulation," the coalition government in Mauritius (from 1971–1976) "was marked by dualism . . . Prime Minister Seewoosagur Ramgoolam preferred a neutralist stance in international affairs" (1991, 206). It is also possible to argue that the same neutralist stance adopted by the Mauritius Labour Party (MLP) in the 1970s, is being followed by Ramgoolam's son in the 1990s. The neutralist stance appears to have won Mauritius many important benefactors on the economic and political front. In an account of his political career and of politics in Mauritius, Sir Satcam Boolell attests to the vacillation of the late Ramgoolam over the Diego Garcia affair: "He was sincerely in favour of demilitarisation of the Indian Ocean and, in the same breath, he would insist Diego was a fortress for the advancement of peace" (Boolell 1996, 29).

Continuity in the Mauritian Foreign Policy-Making Process

Economic support from Britain (and essentially the world market) was especially important in the years following Mauritian independence as the island was heavily dependent on the profitable export of its major cash crop, sugar.[6] Furthermore, the island was experiencing significant population growth, at over 4 percent per annum. Unemployment was high and ethnic riots prior to and during the first elections were threatening to tear the nation apart. At this point in the political history of Mauritius, it became imperative for Seewoosagur Ramgoolam's newly elected governement to pursue rapid economic growth and employment in order to stabilize the economy and society. The fragile economy and society of Mauritius called for the intervention of the International Monetary Fund (IMF). The IMF and the World Bank proposed the introduction of export industrialisation and structural adjustment. It was argued that these changes would allow the Mauritian government to deal with local pressure to create employment and to resuscitate the economy.

In 1970, the implementation of the Export Processing Zones (EPZ) Act, paved the way for export-led industrialisation in Mauritius. The EPZ created employment for many Mauritians in the textile, food and other manufacturing industries. Shortly after the implementation of the EPZ Act, Mauritius experienced significant economic problems due to the 1973 Opec Oil Crisis. To neutralize the adverse effects of the economic depression on Mauritius, the government increased social welfare services and wages. This led to a massive drop in exports from the EPZ and according to Brautigam, unemployment rose by 20 percent. Nevertheless, this was a bright period in the social development of Mauritians (Brautigam 1997, 50). Citizens had increased support from government in the form of food subsidies (of rice and flour) and structures were created to provide financial assistance to families severely affected by the loss of employment and income. For example, a government employment programme entitled *Travail pour Tous* (Work For All) was implemented. The state made an effort to obtain jobs for those who could not find employment on their own (Mukonoweshuri 1991, 204). By

1999, 90,000 (out of a total number of 496,900 people employed in Mauritius) were employed in the EPZ sector.[7] A significant number of people (200,000) are also employed in the tertiary sector (trade, restaurants, hotels and services), and, judging by the previous years' figures, it appears that employment is on the increase in the tertiary sector.[8] In contrast, employment in certain sectors of the EPZ has fallen. A comparison of March 1999 and March 2000 figures show that employment in the 'wearing apparel' group fell by 1,177; — in the 'pullovers and other knitted garments' and 'other garments' sectors, there was a decline of 858 and 319 respectively.[9] It seems that this decrease is partly due to the relocation of some industries to Madagascar, where labour is less expensive.

Prior to the first national elections, the foreign policy process was guided primarily by the Prime Minister and the Ministry of Foreign Affairs. Shortly after independence in 1968, foreign policy actors in Mauritius, included the Prime Minister, Ministry of Foreign Affairs, Commerce and Industry and to a certain extent, Parliament. (Members of Parliament are encouraged to discuss issues that have a bearing on the foreign policy-making process, yet they are not involved in the final decisions.) At this time, foreign policy making in Mauritius was extended to other sectors of government, in particular, that of commerce and industry.

The empowerment of this ministry to contribute to the foreign policy-making process appears to have been particularly influenced by the country's trade requirements and its geographical isolation in the Indian Ocean. Its isolation, lack of natural resources and manpower, necessitated cooperation "with all friendly countries, East or West, in the interests of the prosperity of the people" (Mannick 1989, 142). Initially, this approach led to the establishment of various agreements between Mauritius and the Soviet Union. In 1970 for example, the government announced that it would grant harbour facilities to Soviet trawlers. However, the government stopped short of permitting the Soviets to build a naval base in Mauritius and made its position on this issue very clear in London, on 16 July 1970. The statements of the Prime Minister, Seewoosagur Ramgoolam, were supported by the Foreign Affairs Minister, Gaetan Duval. The latter explained to the British, that a technical agreement (partly for the supply of trawlers), did not "imply a reorientation of his country's foreign policy" (Mannick, 144). An initial lack of direction in the Mauritian foreign policy-making process was later said to be due to contradictions between domestic policy/political rhetoric and foreign policies. This contradiction became evident in the Mauritian government's foreign policy, especially with the entry of the Parti Mauricien Socialiste Democrate (PMSD) into the coalition government in 1969.[10]

The Ministry of Foreign Affairs and the Apartheid Question

As the representative of mostly white and coloured voters in Mauritius (in the 1960s), Gaetan Duval, the Minister of Foreign Affairs, cultivated links with the apartheid regime in South Africa in line with the needs of his electorate.[11] According to Monique Dinan, approximately 17,000 Mauritians (mostly of white and coloured descent) emigrated to South Africa before and shortly after, 1968 (1985, 210). Some had taken Duval's speeches about the threat of Hindu domination seriously. But the cultivation of ties with South Africa was inconsistent with Duval's politics in Mauritius. He sought to obtain Creole voters by claiming to promote an appreciation of black power and Negritude among those who had descended from the slaves. At the same time, he entered into trade negotiations with the South African government. In his essay, "An Overcrowded Barracoon," the author V. S. Naipaul, relates Duval's foreign policy tactics. His disregard for issues of human rights in favour of economic profit is described as follows:

> Mr. Duval, the Black Power man, has his own *Projet Cochon*, Operation Pig. He distributes piglets to potential minders and hopes in this way to create a pig-rearing industry . . . he was especially pleased, when I met him, with his 'Black is Beautiful' campaign. "In these few weeks I have created a psychological revolution in the mind of the black man in this country." But he was also advocating trade with South Africa. How was that linked to Black Power? "They're not! That is the point." And he roared with laughter. . . But the South Africans were slow. "They're slower than the old Boers." When he came back he said, "the consul has just had a telephone call from South Africa. They've offered a gift of fifty sows and two boars and free food for them for one year" (Naipaul 1971, 304).

The Minister of Foreign Affairs also established close links with the French government, and secured financial aid from the French for the development of the Mauritian private sector. Ties with the French government were also fostered by Duval, who represented the white Franco-Mauritians. Eventually, "given the great wealth of the West as well as Mauritius' own past, it was predictable that Mauritius' foreign policy would inevitably become more pro-Western . . . Mauritius has cultural as well as economic links with the UK and France" (Mannik 1989, 145). Traditionally, France has been Mauritius' largest customer, especially for textile products. (In 1994 France provided Mauritius with its largest source of financial aid.) The French have contributed to the computerization of the island's government ministries; they have performed a variety of road feasibility studies, and have contributed to the maintenance of the island's highways. France has also contributed to other economic activities such as undertaking livestock services and constructing a cannery. In the western part of Mauritius, France contributed US$60 million to construct a large diesel-electric power station, which was completed in 1992; and in January 1995, that country sponsored a five-year project to create a ninety-hectare free-port area and attendant facilities at Port Louis, the object of which is to attract African trade under the Preferential Trade Area for Eastern and Southern Africa.

Since approximately 60 per cent of the Mauritian population is of Indian descent, strong links are also maintained with India, and Mauritius therefore has many Indian politicians and businessmen who travel to the sub-continent on a regular basis. India is noted for its deep social and historical links with a large portion of the population of Mauritius and is Mauritius' second largest source of foreign assistance. Most notably, India has contributed substantial aid to Mauritius for cultural ventures such as the construction of the Mahatma Ghandi Institute — a library and language school inaugurated in 1976. In the 1990s, India entered into a number of cooperation agreements with Mauritius in the fields of agriculture, oceanography, maritime resources, science and technology, drug trafficking and sports and youth affairs. In recent years, India has provided Mauritius with technical expertise in computer and high sensing technology, radio and telecommunications, the further expansion of Mauritius' telephone system from 60, 000 to 100, 000 lines over a three year period beginning in 1991, and the creation of a science centre and planetarium.

In 1998, Mauritius had one of the highest ratios of trade of goods and services to GDP in the world, exceeding 133 percent. Total international trade (excluding activities in the freeport zone) approximated nearly 89 billion **Mauritian Rupees (3.56 billion US Dollars), an increase of over 12 per cent** compared to 1997. With regard to exports in particular, there were three main buyers — the United Kingdom, France and the United States — representing 34 per cent, 18 per cent and 14 per cent of total exports respectively.[12]

The Impact of Culture and Identity on the Foreign Policy-Making Process

In view of these cultural and business links, it is possible to argue that historical connections and economic imperatives have had in the past, and continue to have, an impact on the foreign relations of Mauritius. Throughout the 1990s, it was also evident that culture and identity are also important to the foreign policy-making process in Mauritius. This is particularly apparent in Mauritius' enduring cultural and economic contacts with India. Mauritius has benefited enormously by maintaining cultural links with the Indian sub-continent. By cultivating such links, the state has also catered for internal social and economic needs, especially the people of Indian descent. This type of cooperation is largely facilitated by the predominance of Indo-Mauritians (Mauritians of Indian descent) in the public sector and, by a substantial population of Indian business people in the private sector.

By contrast, the foreign relations between Mauritius and the African continent are relatively low key. It is possible to argue that this may be due to the fact that there are few individuals of African descent (i.e. Creoles) who feature in arenas where foreign policy decisions are made. This argument implies that foreign policy decisions are ethnically based, a situation that is evident in domestic politics, where those elected to parliament are often expected to cater for the needs of their ethnically based constituencies.[13]

In the post Cold War era, greater emphasis has been placed on the importance of culture and identity to foreign policy-making processes. According to Sagarika, "IR's fascination with sovereign statehood has greatly decreased its ability to confront complex issues of ethnic nationhood and political 'otherhood'. IR theorists have turned to culture and identity to better encompass, describe and explain novel issues of global heterogeneity and diversity" (1998, 411). This suggests that one looks beyond the state (as a political institution) to explain foreign policy-making processes. In the case of Mauritius, one has to analyse the impact of ethnicity in political life. It can be shown, for example, that the increasing level of cooperation between India and Mauritius appears to be creating tensions within the Mauritian population.

During my anthropological fieldwork, it became evident that among Creoles (and citizens of non-Indian descent), there is a certain level of resentment against the Mauritian state for encouraging India's cultural contribution to Mauritius. In 1999, some non-Indian interviewees explained that no space was left for the cultural expression of other ethnic groups in what is a multi cultural society. There seems to have been a similar situation in India, in the 1970s. In the aftermath of Nehru's death, there were various forces in favour of the centralization of the state. This led to much tension and conflict in the country, as India has long experienced social, economic and political tendencies toward pluralism, regionalism and decentralization. During Nehru's time, central government favored pluralist approaches to policy formulation, but under Indira Gandhi's government, these pluralist approaches were reversed for short-term gain. In the Mauritian context, one finds that politicians are not only influenced by the prospect of immediate political gain, their actions are also deeply motivated by personal cultural identity.

Thus, to understand the foreign-policy making process in Mauritius, it is helpful to refer to conventional constructivist theory concerning the politics of identity. According to Sagarika (1998), nationalism, ethnicity, race, gender, religion, and sexuality, and other inter-subjectively understood communities, are each involved in an account of global politics. With regard to Mauritius, it is not only important to know how the country's political institutions and actors function, it is imperative that one understands how identities are constructed and what norms and practices accompany their reproduction. These processes shed light on the constitutive practices of the state, and as a result, they contribute to an understanding of domestic and foreign politics. Thus the constructivist approach helps to explain the cultural context in which Mauritian foreign policy-making processes occur. Accordingly, ethnicity in Mauritius assumes an important dimension in the social, political and economic life of that country and therefore affects foreign relations with other countries.

The author's anthropological research conducted in 1999 confirms that different ethnic segments of the population express a particular interest in maintaining foreign relations with the countries of their ancestors. This is especially evident in the influence of East Asia on the EPZ. It required a Sino-Mauritian academic, Edward Lim Fat to urge Chinese business people in Hong Kong to set up factories in Mauritius' EPZ. Dommen explains how "the British made no attempt to understand the inner workings of Chinese culture in Mauritius, preferring to deal with it through a recognized spokesman." In 1998, EPZ exports to Hong Kong totalled 87 million Mauritian Rupees (3.48 million US dollars), exports to Singapore totalled 20 million Mauritian Rupees (0.8 million US dollars) and exports to Japan totalled 146 million Mauritian Rupees (5.84 million US dollars).[14]

The release of Nelson Mandela in 1990, altered the traditional orientation of Mauritian foreign policy-makers. The emergence of South Africa as the economic powerhouse of the Southern African Development Community (SADC) has encouraged the Mauritian government to re-establish commercial and political links with the country. Even though the orientation of Mauritian foreign policy-makers to Africa began in the mid-1970s, this bearing was largely due to Mauritius' concern with non-alignment in a divided global political environment. In the last decade, more attention is being paid to regional economic integration.

Regional Politics and Discontinuity in the Foreign Policy-Making Process of Mauritius

The economic imperative of the Mauritian state can also be perceived in its cultivation of foreign partnerships with countries in the southern African and south west Indian Ocean region. In this instance, the principle objective of integration is to achieve the necessary economies of scale to attract foreign direct investment. Mauritius is currently a member of the Indian Ocean Commission (IOC), the Common Market for Eastern and Southern Africa (COMESA), the SADC and the Indian Ocean Rim Association for Regional Cooperation (IOR-ARC). Its joining of COMESA, for example, indicates that the Mauritian state is eager to participate in an expanded economic zone by contributing to the reduction of trade barriers and tariffs in the eastern and southern African regions. To achieve this, the government plans to introduce a Regional Development Certificate Scheme that will partly enable members to participate in the island's expanding economic zone of influence. The recent concern with regional integration is also due to Mauritius' reduced prospect of trade (especially within the preferential agreements framework) with markets in the European Union. According to McDougall (1997, 53):

> . . . increased attention has been given to developing economic links with southern Africa. As well as having some potential for expanding Mauritius' trade, southern Africa is also important because of the role it plays in relation to Mauritius' objective of developing itself into an economic platform for the region. That is Mauritius sees itself as becoming an offshore centre providing financial services and channelling investment into southern Africa. There is also some potential for Mauritius to develop into a transportation centre for the region. From this perspective SADC is seen as the most important regional organization at the moment.

Since the mid-1970s, Mauritius has also been compelled to consider regional politics in its foreign policy making process. The island hosted the 13th Summit meeting of the Organisation for African Unity (OAU), in June 1976. At this meeting, the Prime Minister condemned apartheid and the persistence of colonial regimes in Africa. In April 1977, Ramgoolam attended the fourth Franco-African Summit meeting held in Dakar. There he supported the French president's call for the setting up of a development fund to help Africa's poorer countries (Mannik 1989, 146). In 1979, at a meeting of the OAU in Freetown, Sierra Leone, members called for the demilitarization of Diego Garcia and the declaration of the region as a 'Zone of Peace'; this call was furthered by Seewoosagur Ramgoolam at the 1980 summit of the OAU, where members demanded that Diego Garcia be returned to Mauritius.

In the 1990s, the Mauritian government established new ties with post-apartheid South Africa. A South African trade bureau was set up in 1990 and a health cooperation agreement was concluded in 1991 where, Mauritians requiring specialised medical attention could obtain such care in South Africa. In March 1992, diplomatic relations were established between the two countries and trade links (especially in terms of tourism), have facilitated greater economic cooperation between the two countries.[15] The deeper level of cooperation between Mauritians and the new democratic government of South Africa, was evident during anthropological fieldwork in 1999, when I attended a gathering of Creoles in a village on the eastern coast of the island. The guest of honour was the South African High Commissioner (a black man), who pledged to help the Creoles of Mauritius in their bid to deal with social and economic exclusion. Thus, indirectly, greater cooperation between the Mauritian and South African state appears to be having a major impact on the island's black population. Although this is not demonstrable in a statistical format, anthropological observation and interviews in 1999 indicate that beyond formal bilateral relations between the two countries, Creoles have created various subconscious connections between themselves and the African continent. This is enabling them to regain social and political confidence in themselves and they are beginning to assert their democratic rights.

Thus, over and above a state-centric approach to the analysis of the Mauritian foreign policy-making process, it is possible to identify non-state actors who are eager to foster productive foreign relations in a bid to advance democratic rule. For the Creoles of Mauritius, it appears that these exchanges are contributing to a rise in Creole political consciousness.

This is not to say that a form of political consciousness did not exist among Creoles before this time. Part of the work done by Sylvio Michel and his associates in the *Organisation Fraternel* (OF) was aimed at empowering Creoles by raising political and social awareness of their situation in Mauritian society (Michel 1998). In recent years, Creole concerns with political and macro-economic issues appears to have increased as Mauritius has become wealthier and socio-economic disparities have become more apparent.[16] According to Burton Benedict (1962), such economic disparities were not easily perceived shortly after 1968. The general economic situation in Mauritius was very poor, such that most Mauritians, were focussed on issues of economic survival. The situation of Mauritius in the 1960s, led Benedict to forecast that Mauritius would disintegrate in the wake of ethnic conflict, overpopulation and poverty.

Rational or Irrational Foreign Policy-Makers?

One of the factors rarely considered in foreign policy-making processes is emotion. Foreign policy-makers are often portrayed as rational decision-makers who are not guided by their personal or group feeling in the decision-making process. Psychological analyses of international conflict suggest that there is often a strong element of emotion in the foreign policy-making process:

> ... where studying emotion seems most appropriate, analysis of foreign policy decision making has emphasized cognition. This focus is understandable given the interesting insights psychology has mined in the analysis of "cold" cognitive processes, especially in highlighting the effects of cognitive heuristics and information processing limits. Only more recently has psychology begun to untangle emotion in a way that may be useful to scholars of world politics (Crawford 2000, 1).

The usefulness of psychological analysis to international relations has been demonstrated in studies of war and suggests that states will go to war not only because their sovereignty has been challenged, but also because politicians encourage emotional support for war by arguing (for example) that national honour has been besmirched. With regard to the foreign policy-making process in Mauritius, perhaps the most appropriate and (possibly the least discernable) emotion that guides the foreign policy-making process is fear — especially the fear of losing significant international economic support.

It seems as though among Mauritian foreign policy-makers, fear has translated into a belief in the fact of insecurity. This insecurity appears to be compensated for by concerted efforts to maintain good relations with those who have the ability to support and protect Mauritius — economically and politically influential states such as Britain, France and the United States.

Nel and McGowan's analysis of the Allison models shed some light on the contradictions within the Mauritian foreign policy-making process. In their analysis of foreign policy-making processes in South Africa, the authors attempt to explain the extent to which elements of choice, routine and contest influence foreign policy decisions. With regard to Mauritius, it is difficult to argue that the rational actor model applies to Mauritian foreign policy-makers. It is more apparent that the bureaucratic politics model is in operation —

> ... this approach begins by assuming that the government is not a unitary actor in the making of foreign policy. The central focus is on conflict and cooperation between departments charged with decision-making and the administration of foreign policy, and suggests that the outcome of this dynamic is more important than the issue (1999, 212).

As a multi-ethnic state that promotes ethnic representation at the parliamentary level, foreign policy actors in Mauritius are not merely rational actors. Their decisions appear to be informed by cultural and social factors. Thus, they are, as Nel and McGowan tell us, "players [who] compete for resources, attention and the right to frame the policy question. The result is conflict, although it can, and often is, about the building of coalitions between competitors. The outcome of these political struggles affects policy output" (1999, 212).

Foreign Direct Investment versus Human Rights

Some Mauritian social analysts argue that shortly before independence, the MLP was hungry for power and that it considered the displacement of a few descendants of slaves (that is, the Ilois of the Chagos islands) as a small sacrifice for the achievement of statehood (Mukonoweshuro 1991; Houbert 1992). Since the 1980s, the government of Mauritius has not found it so easy to ignore the Ilois and it appears to be avoiding direct confrontation with the British government regarding Mauritius' rights to the Chagos Islands. It can be argued that this is largely due to the Mauritian government's fear of alienating

British (and Euro-American) investment. The government's cautiousness is particularly warranted when we consider the precarious position occupied by Mauritius as a small island state, one which is attempting to ride the crest of globalization whilst trying to sustain economic development on the domestic front.

In 1995, the new Foreign Minister, Paul Berenger (also the leader of main opposition party MMM), suggested that "priority was to be given to the protection and advancement of Mauritius' economic interests" (McDougall 1997, 55). Such a comment suggests that issues of basic human rights in Mauritius (especially with regard to the island's descendants of African and Malagasy slaves) are not a priority of the state. The forms of economic advancement evident in Mauritius thus far, often involve a privileged few; economic upliftment programmes such as the government's recent *A Nou Diboute Ensam* (Let us Stand Together), do not appear to be filtering down to those in need.

As a developing state, Mauritius is largely dependent on Foreign Direct Investment (FDI). In the last decade much foreign investment has come from the Far East, particularly Hong Kong and Japan. The country has also developed close relations with China.[17] Presently however, the USA tops the list as the most important FDI contributor.[18] In view of the recent (1998) economic turmoil in Singapore, Japan and other Far East states, Mauritius is looking to reduce its economic vulnerability by soliciting development assistance from other investors.[19] This is especially important for its Export Processing Zone (EPZ), which is reliant on sound investment and a profitable export market.

Mauritius' dependence on the EPZ is evidenced by the fact that much of the EPZ's manufactured products are sold in the profitable markets of Europe, and, to a lesser extent, the USA. Of the total EPZ exports during the period January–March 1999, 66 per cent went to countries of the European Union whilst exports to the USA showed a 37 per cent increase [from 1998]. From January to March 1999, EPZ exports amounted to Rs5,888 million, an increase of 17 per cent compared with the same period last year.[20] It is possible to argue then, that the present Mauritian government is once more not in a politically and economically advantageous position to call for its repossession of the Chagos Islands (from the USA) or the Tromelin Islands (from France).

The Power to Negotiate: Lobby Politics in Mauritius

Recently, potent allegations of corruption and communalism have surfaced in the Mauritian press.[21] These allegations have retained the attention of the population since the occurrence of nationwide riots in February 1999, when a well-known black Creole singer died in custody, an event which seems to contradict the image of Mauritius as a democratic and peaceful society. The promotion of peace and cooperation between Mauritians has not been an easy task for the population to achieve, as Mauritius is very heterogenous, and many of its inhabitants continue to nurture strong ethnic and cultural identities. These cultural and ethnic affiliations appear in both community interaction and party politics, and they continue to impinge on democratic processes.[22] For example, the combination of democratic structures and ethno-cultural forces, often results in the use of democratic means (such as lobby groups) to obliquely advance specific community rights.[23]

The ancestors of the Creoles left Africa and Madagascar more than 150 years ago. Their present bid to transform their identity and situation in a positive manner has resulted in accusations of ethnocentrism and the incitement of social conflict. In the analysis of foreign policy-making processes, it is possible to forget that foreign policies have an important effect on local reality. Such omissions are often apparent in studies of Mauritius that tend to emphasise the island's economic success, but ignore the salience of the achievement of human rights. For almost 200,000 Creoles, important foreign relations and prosperous international trade have not done much to improve their livelihood; nor have these furthered their experience of democratic rule. Many continue to live in the most impoverished sections of the island and to occupy the least desirable jobs.

Thus one can say that, in Mauritius, foreign policy-making does not promote democracy. Foreign policy decisions are still the preserve of parliamentarians, and ethnicity continues to play a very important role in the allocation of seats in the National Assembly. The participation of Mauritians in these important decision-making processes is, in fact limited by the country's ethnically based electoral institution. Foreign policy decisions based on general economic needs have, however, benefited many Mauritians. In 1999 for example, it was noted that the per capita income of Mauritians stood at 3,300 US Dollars — nearly ten times that of Madagascar (Oliver 1999, 1). Economic growth and development however, does not always guarantee democracy and, in some instances (as is the case in Mauritius), it does not contribute to the improvement of human rights.

Conclusion

This chapter has attempted to show the extent to which a state that is considered to be one of the most developed in the Southern African Development Community (SADC), is unable to formulate foreign policies that address the social and economic needs of a considerable section of its population. It is argued that the Mauritian state has invested greatly in its potential for economic growth and that despite the existence of democratic structures and systems in the country, the political will of its statesmen is directed at a form of liberal economic development that tends to exclude many of the country's impoverished people. As a geographically isolated country, Mauritius has had to cultivate important economic and political ties with prosperous countries in order to survive.

However, at the end of the 1990s, it has become difficult to consider Mauritius as a country which is geographically and economically isolated. The introduction of new technology, the diversification of the economy and new regional relations, have ensured that Mauritius is in contact with the rest of the world, but it remains a small island and a developing state which means that it is vulnerable to economic and ecological vagaries. For this reason, the country is still compelled to maintain precious economic and political links with the USA and Britain, and — for economic and political reasons — these ties appear to be more important to Mauritius than its links with the other member countries of the SADC.

In conclusion, the Mauritian experience of globalization is profoundly influenced by its historical and cultural alliances. In the 1990s, it is evident that the country's foreign policy is largely determined by the population's cultural links. This has encouraged Mauritius to cultivate relationships with states that are both powerful economic players and historical allies, rather than with a variety of economic and political partners in an increasingly globalized world.

Notes

The data presented in this chapter is the result of the author's Doctoral research in Mauritius from July to December 1999. The author wishes to acknowledge the financial and institutional support of the following sponsors for her ethnographic research: The Council for the Development of Social Research in Africa (CODESRIA) in Senegal; The Netherlands Foundation for the Advancement of Tropical Research (WOTRO); and Rhodes University.

114 *Globalization and Emerging Trends*

1 It is interesting to note that at the time this chapter was written, Duval's son (Xavier Duval) had entered politics under the banner of the PMSD. He has now joined the son of the founder of the nation (Navin Ramgoolam) in the campaign for the by-elections for the Beau-Petite-Riviere region, one of the poorer regions of the country.
2 Ideologically fashionable in the sense that many colonised countries were advocating the benefits of western style democracy and economic development. Furthermore, it was an exciting era for the emerging politician as the 1960s heralded the birth of many powerful 'indigenous' statesmen in neighbouring Africa and Asia.
3 Especially on the issue of the forced removal of the Ilois from the Chagos Islands and in particular, Diego Garcia.
4 The implications of the Best Loser system are discussed at length in Nave (1998) and Laville(2000).
5 While Mauritius supports the Indian Ocean Zone of Peace, it has tense relations with France over its claim to Tromelin Island and there is tension with USA and Britain because of the USA's military base on Diego Garcia island.
6 At independence in 1968, sugar accounted for 93% of Mauritius' domestic exports and employed about 30% of the population. "Until 1974, 60% of the Mauritian sugar crop was sold to the United Kingdom under the Commonwealth Sugar Agreement of 1951" (Mannick 1989, 97). In the African, Caribbean and Pacific Protocol on sugar (ACP Protocol) of 1974, Mauritius secured the highest sugar quota of 500,000 tonnes per annum (Boolell 1996, 55). The British price for Mauritian sugar was set at 260 per tonne.
7 The exact numbers of Creoles employed in these sectors is not clear. However, my fieldwork and observations in Mauritius from 1998 to 1999 suggest that whilst some Creoles are employed in these sectors, they are rarely found in supervisory, middle management or management posts.
8 The Central Statistical Office at: http://ncb.intnet.mu.
9 The Central Statistical Office at: http://ncb.intnet.mu/medrc/epz/epz1q00.htm.
10 The Social Democratic Party of Mauritius was initially led by Gaetan Duval, who eventually became S.S.R. Ramgoolam's Minister of Foreign Affairs.
11 As the date of independence drew nearer, Duval looked for support in a broader section of the Mauritian population, especially among the black Creoles. He became a strong advocate of black power and Negritude in Mauritius.
12 http://ncb.intnet.mu/mobaa/intro.htm#Business.
13 See the sub-section on Parliament in this chapter.
14 http://ncb.intnet.mu/medrc/epz/table112.htm.
15 "Of 422 500 tourists arriving in Mauritius in 1995, 10.1 per cent [came] from South Africa. At about US$920 per tourist in 1995, the average tourist expenditure was relatively high" (McDougall 1997, 53).
16 According to Olivier (1999), "... the last 20 years have been a golden age for Mauritius. Thanks to the success of its textile and tourism industries, the island has grown into one of the most prosperous countries in Africa. Since 1980, per capita income has risen more than 300%, and now stands at $3,300, over ten times that of its nearest neighbor, Madagascar."
17 http://lcweb2.loc.gove/cgi-bin/query/r?frd/cstd:@field (DOCID+mu0040).
18 Exact figures for USA FDI were not available at the time of going to press, but Mauritius exported Rs7006m worth of goods to the USA in 1999, Rs13, 156m to Britain and Rs7,234m to France. Mauritius' total international trade for the 4th quarter of 1999 totalled Rs26,898 million (Ministry of Economic Planning and Development, 1999).

19 In his opening speech at the 1999 Indian Trade Exposition (INDEX099), the Mauritian Prime Minister welcomed the increased investment made by India in Mauritius. He noted that to date the sum of 4 billion Mauritian Rupees had been injected into the Mauritian economy by India.
20 *News on Sunday*, July 25-31, 1999: 3.
21 The term 'Communalism' has been used in Mauritian politics and academia to describe the tendency to promote specific ethnic/religious group rights in Mauritius. Communalism has, in certain instances, led to riots and the social marginalisation of people stigmatised within the cultural and political framework of the island.
22 This phenomenom is considered in greater detail elsewhere — suffice it to mention that the expression of sentiments about ethnicity in Mauritius tends to occur in private and that subtle representations of the self are necessary to avoid ethnic conflict on a daily basis.
23 This is a particularly relevant strategy for Creole organizations in Mauritius. Many Creole families have suffered economically and socially in the hierarchical societies of Mauritius. In the bid to rehabilitate Creole culture and identity, groups compatible with Mauritian civil society have been created to repair the social and economic damage done by centuries of oppression and prejudice.

References

Adar, K. (1985) "The Indian Ocean as a Zone of Peace." *Strategic Studies* VIII.2: 70-86.
Bennett, A. and J. Lepgold. (1993) "Reinventing Collective Security after the Cold War and Gulf Conflict." *Political Science Quarterly* 108.2: 213-238.
Boolell, S. (1996) *Untold Stories, A Collection of Socio-Political Essays 1950-1995*. Mauritius: Edition de l'Ocean Indien.
Brautigam, D. (1997) "Institutions, Economic Reform and Democratic Consolidation in Mauritius." *Comparative Politics* 30.1: 45-62.
Briguglio, L. (1995) "Small Island Developing States and Their Economic Vulnerabilities." *World Development* 23.9: 1615-1632.
Crawford, N. (2000) "The Passion of World Politics." *International Security* 24.4: 116-157.
Dinan, M. (1985) *Une Ile Eclatée: Analyse de l'Emigration Mauricienne 1960-1982*. Mauritius: Best Graphics.
Dommen E. and B. Dommen. (1999) *Mauritius: An Island of Success. A Retrospective Study 1960-1993*. Wellington: Pacific Press; Oxford: James Currey.
Houbert, J. (1992) "The Indian Ocean Islands: Geopolitics and Decolonisation." *The Journal of Modern African Studies* 30.3: 465-484.
Laville, R. (2000) "In the Politics of the Rainbow: Creoles and Civil Society in Mauritius." *Journal of Contemporary African Studies* 18.2: 277-294.
McDougall, D. (1997) "Indian Ocean Regionalism: Perspectives from Mauritius, The Seychelles and Reunion." *Round Table* 341: 53-67.
Mannick, A.R. (1989) *Mauritius, The Politics of Change*. Mayfield, East Sussex: Dodo Books.
Mathur, R. (1997) "Parliamentary Representation of Minority Communities: The Mauritian Experience." *Africa Today* 44.1: 62-82.

Metz, Chapin H. (1999) *Indian Ocean — Mauritius.* Federal Research Division, Library of Congress. http://lcweb2.loc.gov/cgi-bin/query/r?frd.

Mukonoweshuro, E.G. (1991) "Containing Political Instability in a Poly-Ethnic Society: The Case of Mauritius." *Ethnic and Racial Studies* 14.2: 199-223.

Naipaul, V.S. (1972) *The Overcrowded Barracoon and Other Articles.* Harmondsworth: Penguin.

Nel, P. and P.J. McGowan. (1999) *Power, Wealth and Global Order: An International Relations Textbook for Africa.* Cape Town: University of Cape Town Press.

News on Sunday. July 25-31, 1999.

Powe, E. (1982) *The Lore & Lure of the British Indian Ocean Territory.* The Herskovitz Collection. Evanston: Northwestern University.

Sagarika, D. (1998) "Identities and the Indian State: An Overview." *Third World Quarterly* 19.3: 411-435.

Srebnik, H. (2000) "Can Ethnically-based Civil Society Succeed? The Case for Mauritius." *Journal of Contemporary African Studies* 18.1: 7-20.

US State Department, Arms Control and Disarmament Agency (ACDA) Main Statistical Tables p. 82.

7 Mozambique's Foreign Policy: From Ideological Conflict to Pragmatic Cooperation

OSCAR GAKUO MWANGI

Mozambique as a country was a creation and expansion of Portuguese interests, and it was territorially configured by countries such as Portugal and Great Britain. Its colonial history dates back to 1498, with the settlement of a few Portuguese traders (Schultz 1995, 112). Despite the Berlin Conference of 1884-1885, which sought to partition Africa between European colonial powers, it was only more than twenty-five years later that Portugal managed to assert political and military control over Mozambique.

Mozambique is a country which has been characterized by several natural, economic and political calamities. The civil war, apartheid South Africa's destabilization campaigns during the Cold War period, and prolonged drought severely affected the country's political stability and economy. An adverse combination of circumstances forced it to initiate and implement a series of economic and political reforms in its domestic and foreign policies aimed at resuscitating economic development and political stability. The pace of implementation was initially slow, but accelerated following the end of the Cold War due to the dynamics of domestic, regional and international economic and political changes. As the country's economic and political situation continued to deteriorate, ideological considerations were increasingly replaced by pragmatic considerations in foreign policy-making.

This chapter traces foreign policy and foreign policy-making processes in Mozambique from its independence in 1975 up to the post-Cold War period. Foreign policy during the Cold War is examined within the context of the civil war in Mozambique, South Africa's destabilization campaigns against it, and the country's declining economic performance.

The post-Cold War period is addressed against the background of liberalization and democratization processes in Mozambique, the end of apartheid in South Africa, and regional cooperation. The chapter argues that as

Mozambique's economy and political situation continued to decline over the years as a result of civil war and natural calamities, its foreign policy-makers increasingly became more pragmatic in a bid to end the economic and political crisis.

The Background

The assumption by Atonio Salazar of the post of prime minister of Portugal in the late 1920s, heralded a legacy of fascism and fascist policies, where colonies were to remain under the control of Lisbon; and where human and natural resources in Mozambique had to be more effectively and directly exploited for the benefit of the metropole and the emerging Portuguese class (Isaacman 1985, 133; Hall and Young 1997, 3-11). Over the years, these policies began encountering opposition from white Mozambicans who were struggling to establish their own economic dominance in Mozambique. Policy changes to rectify this came too late, as a radicalized anti-colonial opposition had emerged and was totally behind the *Frente de Libertacao de Mozambique* / Freedom for the Liberation of Mozambique (FRELIMO) (Abrahamsson and Nilsson, 21).

FRELIMO was created in September 1962 out of a merger of three Mozambican nationalist groups: the Uniao Nacional Africana de Mocambique Independente (UNAMI), the Uniao Democratia Nacionale de Mocambique (UDENAMO), and the Mozambique African National Union (MANU). Eduardo Chivane Mondlane was its first president (Hoile 1989, 16). The formation of FRELIMO and its commencement of the armed struggle two years later, forced the Salazar regime in Portugal to reassess its policies in order to finance its military operations against FRELIMO, and other liberation movements in Angola and Guinea-Bissau (Isaacman, 134). The Salazar regime, however, soon began to receive mounting and widespread criticism for its fascist and colonial policies. There were also demands for democratization in Portugal as a means of improving and strengthening its economy in Europe. Portugal, however, continued to be of strategic importance to the West, since its presence in Mozambique and Angola was a guarantee that the oil route from the Persian Gulf to the Western countries would not be disrupted from the African continent; therefore Portugal continued to receive extensive support, despite its authoritarian domestic and colonial policies. This angered FRELIMO'S leadership, forcing the organization to turn to Eastern countries and to China for military assistance. FRELIMO became more ideologically Marxist-Leninist in 1968, following the death of its founding leader, Mondlane (Schultz, 114).

In April 1974, the Armed Forces Movement in Portugal launched a successful coup which ended forty years of fascism, thereby raising the possibility of Mozambique's independence. This became actualized in the Lusaka Agreement of September 1974, when the new Portuguese government reluctantly agreed to FRELIMO's demand for independence after a nine month transitional phase. During this transitional period, FRELIMO devoted most of its time to the consolidation of power. Mozambique gained its independence on 25 June, 1975.

Following independence, FRELIMO established a one party Marxist-Leninist state and outlawed political activity. Over time, it adopted radical Marxist-Leninist policies, reshaping the country's social, economic and political landscape. These policies were, however, initially hindered by natural calamities, opposition from Portuguese settlers and the exodus of skilled human resources. This left Mozambique's fragile economy crippled, leading to discontent (Schultz, 114; Isaacman, 137).

In response to these crises, a civil war between FRELIMO and the *Resistance Nationale de Mocambique* / Mozambique National Resistance (RENAMO) erupted in 1976. Initially, RENAMO was a creation of the Ian Smith regime in Rhodesia aimed at destabilizing the Mozambican government which was supporting Zimbabwean and South African liberation movements. Between 1976 and 1979, Mozambique suffered more than 350 RENAMO and Rhodesian attacks. By 1979, however, the tide had turned against RENAMO and its sponsors. The Lancaster House Agreement, signed in 1979, guaranteeing the end of white minority rule in Rhodesia, forced RENAMO to abandon its Rhodesian sanctuaries and bases. With the granting of independence to Rhodesia as Zimbabwe in 1980, the South African government took over the sponsorship of RENAMO and began providing RENAMO with logistical support and training. At the same time, Mozambique turned its energy to national reconstruction. It was during this period that Mozambique played a crucial role in transforming the loose political alliance of frontline states into an integrated regional alliance, the Southern African Development Coordination Conference (SADCC).[1]

RENAMO's strength, however, did not decline. Despite its brutal methods and human rights abuses, it was able to garner some support among local populations. Apartheid South Africa's strategy in backing RENAMO was to ensure that the movement's activities discouraged Zimbabwe and Botswana from exporting their commodities through Maputo, thereby further crippling the Mozambican economy. Between 1981 and 1983, South Africa increased its military attacks in Mozambique in a bid to discourage FRELIMO from harbouring the African National Congress (ANC) within its territory. By 1982, FRELIMO had realized that unless it reached some agreement with South Africa, peace would not be possible. At the end of the year, Mozambique raised the possibility of a non-aggression pact with South Africa and after a series of difficult negotiations, South Africa finally accepted the idea. This culminated in the Nkomati Accord of 16 March 1984, which committed both countries to cease hostilities against each other. Mozambique honoured its part and severely restricted ANC activities within its borders, while South Africa officially reduced, but covertly continued its support for RENAMO.[2]

In 1986, Samora Machel, Mozambique's first president was killed in an air crash near South Africa's border with Mozambique. He was succeeded by the then Foreign Minister, Joaquim Chissano. Despite Machel's death, the FRELIMO government continued with various economic and political reforms, introduced in 1983, aimed at strengthening the economy and transforming Mozambique into a more pluralistic society. Peace talks between FRELIMO and RENAMO, initiated earlier, also continued. The first proposals for amendments to the Mozambican constitution were presented in 1988 and consisted of only minor changes within the framework of the existing political system. A comprehensive proposal for meaningful change was presented in January 1990. The new constitution was enacted in November 1990 and it simultaneously introduced a multiparty system. In December the same year, FRELIMO and RENAMO agreed to a partial cease-fire which continued through mid 1992. Though the negotiations progressed slowly during 1991 and 1992, the concerned parties, nonetheless, agreed on three protocols regarding the electoral system, political parties, and the structure of the talks (US Govt. 1996, 3-4; Abrahamsson and Nilsson, 166; Isaacman, 148-155).

The General Peace Accord was signed in October 1992. The United Nations Operation in Mozambique (UNOMOZ) peace-keeping force was deployed and successfully oversaw the ceasefire and the two year transition to multiparty elections. The first multiparty democratic elections were held in October 1994. Fourteen parties contested seats in the National Assembly and 12 candidates ran for President. Chissano was elected president by a margin of 53-34 percent over Alfonso Dhlakama, the RENAMO leader, and FRELIMO gained a narrow majority in the National Assembly by winning 129 of the 250 seats (US Govt. 1996, 4).

Mozambique's Foreign Policy and Foreign Policy-making Institutions

The foreign policies of contemporary African states are currently being shaped by the rapidly changing international and domestic environments to the extent that it is becoming increasingly difficult to isolate purely 'foreign policies.' These changes have had both adverse and positive effects on policy options and particularly affect intra-African diplomacy. During the 1980s, the main factors that shaped foreign policy were said to be the impact of colonialism, the role of resources, membership of international governmental organizations (IGOs), non-alignment, security and sovereignty, unity against apartheid, economic development and centralized decision making. Following the end of the Cold War, however, foreign policy in the 1990s has, arguably, been shaped by new factors. These include, the end of the Cold War itself, the pressures of liberalization and democratization, globalization, and the debate over what is termed as an 'African agenda.' African foreign policies in the 1990s are, nonetheless, characterized by continuity and change (Wright 1999, 1-10).

The 1970s and 1980s

It is important to consider three points with respect to foreign policy-making in southern African states during the 1970s and 1980s. Firstly, other than in Zimbabwe, there were no foreign policy establishments with official or unofficial sectors in southern African states. Foreign ministries executed policy, rather than formulating it. There were no independent inputs into the systems, and there were no structures designed to solicit and incorporate such inputs. Consequently, expertise was lacking, even at the élite levels. Party secretariats which existed to brief senior party officials had rudimentary research sections and hence policy making élites could consider foreign policy, but not make it (Chan, 31; Abrahamsson and Nilsson, 77).

Secondly, there was the militarization of policy, since among the few high élite-level inputs, the military contribution was substantial. This was natural in those countries under military siege, or military threat and those with military leaders having vast experience in military matters. Mozambique was a case in point. Finally, southern African foreign policies were not in practice greatly influenced by the onging liberation struggle in the region.

Mozambique's foreign policy was formulated in plain language during the third FRELIMO party congress in 1977. Non-alignment was emphasized as an integral part of the foreign policy. The policy was clearly anti-imperialist, placing Mozambique amongst the more radical countries within the non-aligned movement. During the congress, the importance of regional independence from South Africa was stressed, as was support for black majority rule in neighboring countries. The need for regional cooperation also came to dominate the agenda, and for this to succeed, Mozambique believed that free market capitalism and racism in the region would have to be combated. The liberation of neighboring states was also perceived to be a precondition for the country's economic development (Abrahamsson and Nilsson, 45). The country's foreign policy is currently enshrined in Articles 62 to 65 of Chapter Six of the Constitution of Mozambique.

During the first two decades, Mozambique's foreign policy was inextricably linked to the struggles for majority rule in Rhodesia and South Africa. Mozambique's military threat primarily came from Rhodesia and South Africa, due to FRELIMO's support for the Zimbabwe African National Union (ZANU) and ANC liberation movements. The decision by Mozambique to enforce United Nations sanctions against Rhodesia and deny that landlocked country access to the sea, led Ian Smith's regime to undertake covert actions to destabilize the country. However, the end of minority rule in Zimbabwe in 1980 removed this threat. On the other hand, the apartheid regime in South Africa continued to exert pressure on Mozambique. The 1984 Nkomati Accord, which provided the beginnings of a political and economic accommodation with South Africa, marked a watershed in Mozambique's history (USA Govt. 1996, 6; Abrahamsson and Nilsson, 45).

Mozambique's foreign policy position was that only a black majority-ruled South Africa could lead to long-term stability in the region. This irked the South African government. South Africa also felt threatened by Mozambique's development strategy and ideological image, since the country's transformation would be a source of inspiration for the blacks' struggle within South Africa. FRELIMO's Marxist-Leninism was also seen as an ideological threat. This coupled with the Soviet presence in Mozambique, provided apartheid South Africa with justification for its destabilization campaign in that country (Abrahamsson and Nilsson, 45-47).

From 1975 to the late 1980s, Mozambique's foreign policy-making process was largely influenced by three actors, namely the presidency, RENAMO and an external actor, South Africa. The internal conflict between FRELIMO and South African-backed RENAMO, saw the presidency assume a leading role in an apparent effort to end the civil war and promote a policy of good neighbourliness and cooperation in the region.

The Role of RENAMO and South Africa, 1975–1980s

Mozambique's first distinct act of foreign policy took place in March 1976, when it closed its border with Rhodesia. Rhodesia, thereafter, had to divert all its imports and exports from Mozambique to South Africa, prompting it to retaliate by waging an undeclared war against Mozambique by backing RENAMO. It is estimated that Mozambique lost approximately $550 million by applying sanctions against Rhodesia (Chan, 48-49). This loss in revenue, combined with civil war, drought and the mass exodus of skilled human resources, soon forced Mozambique to seek a lasting solution to the Rhodesian crisis. To Mozambique, stability in the region, at that time, could only be achieved through a negotiated settlement in Rhodesia. It is against this background that Mozambique threw its weight behind Robert Mugabe in the 1979 Lancaster House negotiations and the follow-up elections in Rhodesia. Meanwhile, when it became apparently clear that ZANU was going to win the elections, South Africa decided to reconsider its regional policy, and on the eve of the 1980 elections in Rhodesia, a number of high-level meetings were held in Mozambique with high-ranking South Africans participating. South Africa was reassessing its regional policy, with regard to either *detente* or tolerance. Informal diplomacy, however, continued to be a component of its foreign policy. Mugabe's election victory closed the first chapter of Mozambique's regional policy. It was no longer concerned about a minority regime in Zimbabwe, but the minority regime in South Africa (Chan 48; Chingono 1996, 29-33).

Rhodesia was renamed Zimbabwe following the end of white minority rule. The end of this rule initially ushered in a relative period of tranquility in Mozambique. RENAMO lost its support from Rhodesia and was soon riven by internal rivalry which weakened it. Mozambican government forces captured the RENAMO Sitantonga base in June 1980, marking what appeared to be RENAMO's defeat. The SADCC, through Mozambique's support, was formally inaugurated and in November 1980 a top-level SADCC meeting was held in Maputo, indicating that regional cooperation was also becoming an integral part of its foreign policy. Towards the end of 1980, South Africa set about reconstituting and re-arming RENAMO, and in January 1981, the South African military attacked ANC targets in Mozambique, an act of aggression which indicated that South Africa's 'total strategy' was being expanded into the region. Mozambique, thereafter, became a military and economic target for South Africa (Davies and O'Meara 1990, 195-211; Chan, 49).

RENAMO, backed by South Africa, was solely a destabilizing force. It was primarily meant to be used as a military instrument against economic targets, particularly transport routes. Initially, RENAMO had no political programme and was not intended to act as an alternative to FRELIMO. Though it managed to control and threaten considerable areas, it never became a popular movement nor did it resemble a government. By early 1983, RENAMO had suffered serious military defeats at the hands of the Mozambican forces. At the same time, Machel was devoting much energy to an international diplomatic campaign aimed at discrediting RENAMO and South Africa. In October 1983, Machel toured several western countries for the first time in a bid to discredit South Africa's destabilization policies; a further aim was to seek aid for Mozambique's constructive development programme as a country and in the regional context of SADCC. The assistance offered to him was, however, inadequate. Meanwhile, the economic situation in Mozambique continued to deteriorate, forcing the country to reassess its regional policy. For Mozambique, peace and stability could only be achieved through negotiated settlements with South Africa. Despite differences and difficulties, in December 1983 and February 1984, a series of preliminary meetings was held, which culminated in the signing of the Nkomati Accord in March 1984, by Presidents Machel and Botha on behalf of Mozambique and South Africa respectively.

Part of Article 3 of the Accord stated that the contracting parties would not allow their territories, territorial waters or air spaces to be used as bases, thoroughfares, or in any other ways by other states, governments, foreign military forces, organizations or individuals to commit acts of violence or aggression against the territorial integrity or sovereignty of the other or threaten the security of its inhabitants (Jaster 1992, 28-30; Jaster *et al* 1992, 162). In short, Mozambique was meant to stop providing sanctuary for the ANC, and South Africa would reciprocate by withdrawing its support for RENAMO and its military attacks in Mozambique. Mozambique honoured its side of the agreement, by expelling the ANC. South Africa did not honour its side of the Accord — it continued to back RENAMO.[3]

The Role of the Presidency, 1975–1980s

In Mozambique, the actual formulation of foreign policy rested within the élites, at the highest levels around the president. Sometimes the foreign policy process was personalized in the thought of the president alone. In Mozambique, FRELIMO, as a party, was weak in terms of its institutional capacity and capability as a policy-making body because it was overshadowed by the presidency. The party, government and state never managed to shed the work methods of the liberation war and enter into an organized administrative and political system that could function normally in day-to-day tasks. Normal routine and methodological work came to be replaced by continuous *ad hoc* solutions, built on personal relationships, political bonds and lines of command that the political leadership brought from the war to the state apparatus (Chan, 31; Abrahamsson and Nilsson, 77).

The presidency played a leading role in the foreign policy-making process particularly in the 1980s, as exemplified in the Nkomati Accord and thereafter. South Africa's noncommital posture toward the Nkomati Accord led to a significant and historic point in southern African policy. In June 1985, Machel — determined to neutralize RENAMO — met Mugabe and President Julius Nyerere of Tanzania in Harare. It was a significant meeting in that, for the first time, three African states decided upon a joint military action against a military agent of South Africa. In the beginning, this joint military initiative proved to be effective when Zimbabwean troops captured the strategic Casa Banana RENAMO base. Zimbabwean and Tanzanian troops were, however, not meant to eradicate RENAMO, but to safeguard transport routes. The neutralization of RENAMO was the responsibility of Mozambican government forces who were by this time, weary, demoralized and poorly equipped for sustained war. Subsequently, by early 1986, RENAMO had recaptured Casa Banana. Machel was killed in an air crash later in the same year.

During the last year of his presidency and life, Machel appeared to be following three major directions in his foreign policy. According to Chan, he relied heavily on Zimbabwean military strength to protect transport corridors in Mozambique as Zimbabwe was in a position to supply fresh troops. Secondly, he continued to solicit assistance from the west hoping that the west would provide economic relief and at the same time impress upon South Africa the need for it to stop its regional destabilization policies. This, however, proved ineffective, as the economic and military assistance offered to Mozambique was inadequate and, moreover, the west was not willing to discourage South Africa's policy toward Mozambique.

Thirdly, Machel also continued to rely on the Soviet Union, as it was Mozambique's principal supplier of petroleum and other essentials. These were not free and the weak Mozambique economy had to pay for these supplies. There was a relative degree of success, but a larger degree of failure in all three areas (Chan, 52).

Machel was replaced by Chissano, who was then the foreign minister. Chissano continued to undertake the socioeconomic and political policies initiated by his predecessor Machel. Mozambique's economy, under Chissano, continued to perform poorly due to weather vagaries and the civil war. Like Machel, Chissano turned to the west for further economic assistance, an act which was to affect his country's foreign policy. By the time he visited Washington in October 1987, Chissano had already realized that the civil war could not be solved by military action. In Washington, Chissano outlined to President Bush and Secretary of State George Schultz, his government's plans to introduce social, economic and political reforms in Mozambique, in particular to implement political liberalization and to restore religious freedom. The following year, proposals for minor amendments to the constitution of Mozambique were presented to the National Assembly. In January 1990, a more comprehensive proposal with meaningful changes was introduced and by November the same year, a new constitution was enacted in Mozambique.[4]

Towards a Pluralist Foreign Policy-Making Process in the 1990s

Mozambique's foreign policy has become increasingly pragmatic; the twin pillars of the country's foreign policy are its desire for good relations with its neighbours and the need to maintain and expand ties with current and potential donors. Since the Nkomati Accord in 1984, and the country's membership of the International Monetary Fund (IMF) and the World Bank, comprehensive changes in foreign and domestic policies have been initiated. In the late 1980s, Mozambique's radical foreign policy stance, which found expression within, among others, the United Nations, was toned down. The country began to play an important intermediary role between the west and the Front Line States on several important matters, such as conditions for the independence of Namibia and the withdrawal of Cuban troops from Angola. Relations with the United States were also further improved (USA Govt. 1996, 6; Abrahamsson and Nilsson, 110).

During the 1990s, Mozambique's foreign policy and foreign policy-making processes were shaped by three key factors: the end of the Cold War; liberalization and democratization in the country; and the end of apartheid in South Africa. The end of the Cold War signified the end of an era of superpower competition in Africa. The internal disintegration of the Soviet Union and its subsequent breakup in 1991 removed the possibility of the apartheid regime to encourage its white minority population to continue their support for the 'total strategy' through invoking the threat of communism. Communism no longer posed an ideological threat to the apartheid regime in South Africa. In any case, FRELIMO, had abandoned its role as a Marxist-Leninist party and had already embarked on transforming Mozambique from a centrally controlled economy to a more liberal market economy (Wright 1999, 7; Abrahamsson and Nilsson, 109-110).

Liberalization and democratization processes in Mozambique have also influenced the country's foreign policy and foreign policy-making processes, which, as Stephen Wright has emphasized, is also the case in some other African states. Wright argues that where reforms have taken meaningful root, the framework for foreign policy has been expanded, with various state institutions and civil society groups becoming factors in the foreign policy equation, attempting to shift decision-making away from a purely centralized command post, usually the presidency. He further argues, that due to these reforms, the quality of political leadership becomes important, as numerous and competing foreign policies emerge through which different factions pursue or articulate their own goals (Wright, 1999, 8).

The post-1990 economic and political reforms have ushered in new actors in the country's foreign policy-making process. These are illustrated in Figure 7.1 on page 128.

The Presidency

At the helm of the foreign policy-making process is the presidency. In as much as it is becoming decentralized, the presidency largely remains a central and key actor in the process. According to Article 123 of the Constitution of Mozambique, the President has, in matters of international relations, the powers to guide foreign policy (Govt. of Moz. 1990). Many foreign policy issues mainly concerning interstate relations continue to revolve around the presidency. Added to this constitutional and positional attribute, is the personal factor, namely, the charismatic leadership qualities of President Chissano. Chissano is a moderate pragmatist and possess a sharp, cautious sense of the practical. He has many valuable attributes and believes in and practises effective delegation of authority. Chissano is a superb conciliator, both within FRELIMO and in Mozambique's regional and international relations. FRELIMO remains a salient actor on the international level, largely due to him (Schultz, 121).

Figure 7.1 The Structure of Foreign Policy-making in Mozambique

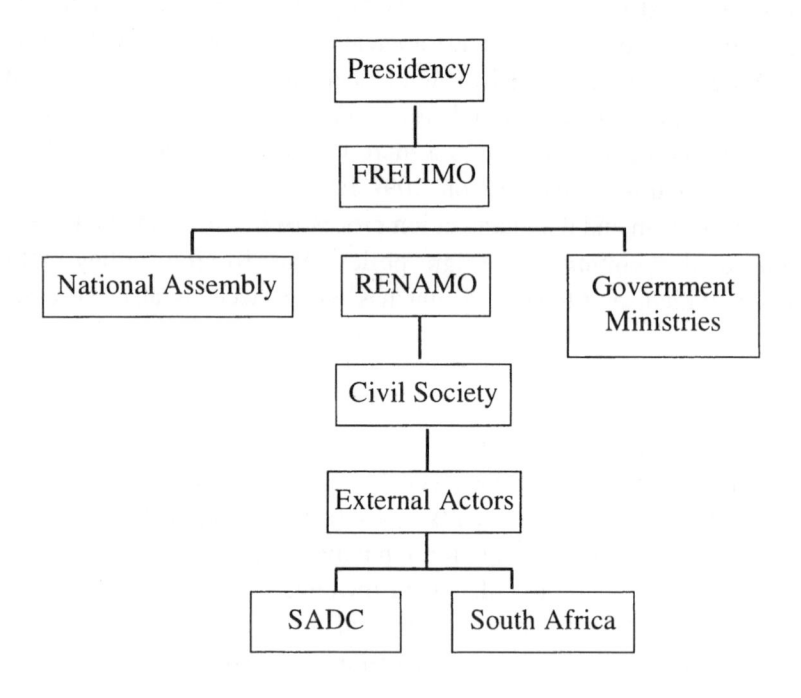

```
                    Presidency
                        |
                    FRELIMO
         _____|_____
        |           |          |
National Assembly  RENAMO   Government
                    |       Ministries
                Civil Society
                    |
              External Actors
                ____|____
               |         |
              SADC   South Africa
```

Political Parties and the National Assembly

Political parties, both ruling and opposition parties, as well as the National Assembly are also increasingly becoming important actors in the foreign policy-making process, more so due to the legitimacy they have acquired following the enactment of the November 1990 constitution. The new constitution provides for a multiparty state, a market-based economy and free elections, thereby creating an environment conducive to a pluralistic society. Consequently, in 1991 FRELIMO party activities and government responsibilities were officially separated, and mass organizations created by FRELIMO declared themselves independent, autonomous entities (Schultz, 119).

FRELIMO plays a key role in the process as the legitimate ruling party and its policies are implemented by government. The party's legitimacy, at the domestic and international level, has also been enhanced by the post-1990 electoral processes and elections. In October 1994, FRELIMO passed the legitimacy test in the internationally supervised democratic multiparty elections, with President Chissano winning the election and FRELIMO forming the majority in the National Assembly. The international donor community played a major role in financing and supervising the elections, which were held under the formal supervision of an independent National Elections Commission. The polls were monitored and pronounced generally free and fair by the UN and other international organizations. Opposition parties — including RENAMO — accepted the results, despite their complaints of irregularities. The international community legitimized the electoral process, elections and the election outcomes. Schultz, however, argues that effective legitimacy emerges only when a second successful election occurs, thus confirming the legitimacy of the constitutional process rather than a specific government. This was the case, five years later, when FRELIMO once again successfully won the 1999 multiparty elections. Chissano obtained 53.3 per cent of the votes against Dhlakama's 47.7 per cent of the votes cast. FRELIMO captured 133 of the 250 National Assembly seats. The National Assembly, according to Article 135 of the country's Constitution, has the powers to legislate on basic questions of the country's domestic and foreign policy. Legitimate electoral systems and outcomes, enhance political stability which in turn shapes the parameters for foreign policy.[5]

Likewise, the tentative, Italian-led process of peace talks begun between the Chissano government and the RENAMO leadership, impacted on Mozambique's foreign policy by ushering in a period of peace and tranquillity. The peace talks in Rome (under the auspices of Italy and the Roman Catholic Church) initially began in the 1980s, but it was not until December 1990 that FRELIMO and RENAMO agreed to a partial ceasefire, covering two of the country's main transport corridors. This partial ceasefire continued through mid-1992. FRELIMO had realized by then that it was not in a position to militarily defeat RENAMO, and was at the same time seeking a successful outcome to the peace process in order to compete for legitimate popular support in the general elections. To seek legitimacy, FRELIMO first needed to seek peace. According to Schultz, FRELIMO therefore needed to take four distinct steps towards achieving that peaceful end. First of all, it was necessary to conclude the war. The agreement of 4 October 1992 signed by both FRELIMO and RENAMO, did precisely this. It terminated all armed hostilities. Secondly, RENAMO had to be neutralized and coopted into the emerging political system. This objective was achieved with RENAMO's acknowledgment of the October 1994 election results, thereby reducing its justification for the resumption of armed hostilities. Thirdly, the military on both sides had to be reformed and reduced in size. Part of the Rome Accord allocated 30 percent of the positions inside the military to RENAMO. RENAMO's acceptance of the election results and its participation in the legislative process legitimizes its role as an actor in the policy-making process of the country (Schultz 1995, 119; Crocker 1992, 488; USA Govt. 1996, 3-4; Dhlakama 1994, 19-21).

State and Civil Society Institutions

Following the 1991 official separation of FRELIMO party activities, government responsibilities and the subsequent declaration of autonomy by mass organizations initially created by FRELIMO, state and civil society institutions began influencing the foreign policy-making process in Mozambique. Government ministries have been entrusted with implementing various foreign policy issues in pursuit of the country's attempts to establish mutual relations of friendship, economic and regional cooperation with other states. Recent foreign policy issues include the need to assist other states in the establishment of a just economic and equitable international order, the pursuit of a policy of peace, the support for disarmament and advocating the transformation of the Indian Ocean into a nuclear free zone of peace. Government ministries have been given the responsibility of formulating and drafting international treaties which will be used to guide the foreign policy-making process. In a bid to attract economic assistance from Western countries, as well as to expand links with current and potential donors, various government ministries also encourage the country's foreign policy stance to become more pragmatic, by implementing various donor-initiated economic and political reforms.[6]

Civil Society institutions also influence the foreign policy-making process. Non-governmental organizations (NGOs) involved in the repatriation, resettlement and rehabilitation of refugees have had a significant influence in the post mid-1990 period. The pacification of the countryside appears to be relatively successful as is evident by the return of a steady number of refugees. By mid-1995, more than 1.7 million refugees who had sought asylum in neighbouring Malawi, Zimbabwe, Swaziland, Zambia, Tanzania, and South Africa as a result of war and drought had returned to Mozambique as part of the largest repatriation witnessed in sub-Saharan Africa. Additionally, a further estimated four million internally displaced persons have returned to their areas of origin. The refugee crisis and repatriation programme has largely been financed by Western countries, IGOs and non-governmental organizations (NGOs), a fact acknowledged by the Mozambican government. This has impacted on the country's foreign policy as it strives to ensure that the refugee crises is resolved in a bid to reduce the possibility of domestic and interstate conflicts (SAPEM Sept. 1993, 22; Hall and Young 1997, 205-216).

External Actors

Mozambique's foreign policy-making process is also influenced by regional external actors, namely South Africa and the South African Development Community (SADC). The end of apartheid also marked a turning point in Mozambique's foreign policy. This was significant in that South Africa was no longer perceived as a military threat and instead was seen as a new partner in regional cooperation. The end of the Cold War, coupled with the assumption of FW de Klerk as South Africa President in 1989, had positive effects in South Africa. He had come to grips with the reality that the regime could no longer sustain apartheid, due to domestic and international political pressures from liberation movements and the international community. In 1990, De Klerk began initiating a series of reforms aimed at dismantling apartheid. These included, among others, the unbanning of political organizations such as the ANC and the release of political prisoners such as Nelson Mandela. The implementation of internal reforms in South Africa led to improved relations with Mozambique, which eventually culminated in the establishment of full diplomatic relations in October 1993.

In April 1994, South Africa held its first non-racial democratic multi-party elections which ushered in black majority rule under the hegemony of the ANC. South Africa was no longer the military enemy. Mozambique's foreign policy had always been clear that stability in the region would only be achieved when all countries in the region were under black majority rule. For South Africa, Mozambique, was no longer perceived as an ideological threat (USA Govt. 1996, 6; Abrahamsson and Nilsson, 109). South Africa's good neighborliness policy with respect to Mozambique was also witnessed when President Mandela of South Africa, declined an invitation to Britain in July 1994 for a ceremony marking South Africa's return to the Commonwealth and instead chose to go to Mozambique for his first overseas visit as a head of state. During his Mozambique tour, Mandela made a point of visiting Dhlakama, in the spirit of reconciliation, despite pressure from Chissano not to do so. The democratization of South Africa with the demise of apartheid signalled the end of that country's role as a destabilizing military threat.[7]

It is in this new post-apartheid context, and in its continued desire for good relations with its neighbours, that Mozambique's foreign policy became more focused on regional cooperation. South Africa was welcomed by Mozambique in regional cooperation and this became evident, and is still evident, in the relations between the two states with regard to the SADC. In the past, trends in the region have indicated and continue to indicate that a number of member states of the SADC — an organization that is increasingly assuming a political as well as an economic role — have established an early warning and monitoring system to prevent emerging conflicts within the region and the unravelling of positive developments such as those in Mozambique. A case in point happened when Dhlakama and RENAMO threatened to pull out of Mozambique's first multiparty elections in October 1994, arguing that the FRELIMO government was planning to rig the elections. This was to be a nightmare for Mozambique and the UN, which had spent two years and millions of dollars trying to prevent just such an allegation. Within eight hours, President Mugabe of Zimbabwe and Deputy President Thabo Mbeki of South Africa played significant roles in reversing RENAMO's withdrawal. Mozambique's foreign policy — which rests on encouraging good neighbourliness — has increased regional economic cooperation and bilateral initiatives, the result of which has been an increase in trade and South African investments in Mozambique. Mozambique is now also a member of several regional and international organizations.[8]

Conclusion

In as much as FRELIMO's leaders may have been sincere in introducing Marxism–Leninism with the hope of creating a socialist society in Mozambique, the economic and political consequences were disastrous. The existing economic and political situation in Mozambique, as is the case in many other African states, was not ripe for socialism. The Portuguese had left behind a relatively undeveloped economy and fragile and weak administrative and political institutions. From the very outset Mozambique's institutions were weak in terms of their capacity to effectively formulate and implement policies. Marxism-Leninism complicated the problem as there was no clear distinction between the party and the government.

Mozambique's ideological position was also a contributing factor to its own internal political problems as it posed an ideological threat to South Africa. The apartheid government in South Africa not only feared a total communist onslaught but also feared the fact that the regime in Mozambique had, at some point, provided sanctuary for liberation movements such as ZANU and the ANC. In response, the apartheid regime set out to cripple Mozambique's economy through various overt and covert destabilization methods.

Mozambique's initial foreign policy posture centred on issues of self preservation with regard to the military threat emanating from Rhodesia, and later from RENAMO and South Africa. However, when it became clear that it could not neutralize the military threats posed by RENAMO and South Africa because of its weak economy, Mozambique adopted a pragmatic position in its policies and approach. Its foreign policy was no longer conflictual in the ideological sense. It became one of accommodation and cooperation. Regional cooperation has now become an integral part of Mozambique's foreign policy in the post-Cold War period.

The democratization process in Mozambique is likely to impact positively on its foreign policy and policy-making process in the future, as the country sets out to construct democratic and democracy-promoting institutions. The creation of pluralism and a pluralistic society will see the emergence of many vibrant actors in state and civil society which is likely to have an influence on the policy-making process. Given its history, lessons from past experiences and the current economic and political situation, Mozambique's foreign policy is likely to be based on pragmatism.

Notes

1   See Winter 1989, 545-547; US Govt. 1996, 3; Isaacman 1985, 140-141; Abrahamsson and Nilsson 1995, 59-61 and Hanlon 1984, 213-218.
2   See Jaster 1992, 28-30; Chan 1990, 26-27 and Isaacman 1985, 150-151.
3   See Clough 1992, 121; Chan 1990, 50; Hall and Young 1997, 192-194.
4   See Crocker 1990, 247; Mbeki and Nkosi 1992, 82-87; Abrahamsson and Nilsson 1995, 166.
5   See Schultz 1995, 119; US Govt. 1996, 4; EISA 2000b, 28-30; Govt. of Moz. 1990 and Wright 1999, 8.
6   Govt. of Moz. 1990. Also see USA Govt. 1996, 4; Abrahamsson and Nilsson 1995, 166 and Schultz 1995, 121.
7   See *The Economist* 13-19 August 1994, 40-41 and 5-11 November 1994, 46.
8   See Schultz 1995, 120; Abrahamsson and Nillson 1995, 182-196; *The Economist* 13-19 August 1994, 40-1 and 5-11 November 1994, 46; USA Govt. 1996, 5.

References

Abrahamsson, H. and A. Nilsson. (1995) *Mozambique: the Troubled Transition. From Socialist Construction to Free Market Capitalism.* London: Zed Books.

Bender, G. et al, eds. (1985) *African Crisis Areas and United States Foreign Policy.* Berkeley: University of California Press.

Chan, S. (1990) "Foreign Policies in Southern Africa: The History of an Epoch, 1978-88." *Exporting Apartheid: Foreign Policies in Southern Africa.* Ed. Stephen Chan. London: Macmillan.

Chingono, M.F. (1996) *The State, Violence and Development: The Political Economy of War in Mozambique.* Aldershot: Avebury.

Clough, M. (1992) "The Superpowers in Southern Africa: From Confrontation to Cooperation." *Changing Fortunes: War, Diplomacy, and Economics in Southern Africa.* Ed. Robert Jaster et al. USA: Ford Foundation.

Crocker, C.A. (1992) *High Noon in Southern Africa: Making Peace in a Rough Neighborhood.* New York: W W Norton.

Davis, R. and D. O'Meara. (1990) "Total Strategy in Southern Africa: An Analysis of South African Regional Policy Since 1978." *Exporting Apartheid: Foreign Policies in Southern Africa.* Ed. Stephen Chan. London: Macmillan.

Dhlakama, A. (1994) "We will never go back to the bush." *SAPEM* **7.8.**

The Economist (1994) August 13-19; November 5-11.

Electoral Institute of South Africa (EISA). *Mozambique Election Update 1999* No. 2 October 1999; No. 4 March 2000.

Government of Mozambique. *Constitution of Mozambique.* http:// www.urich.edu/moz.htm

Hall, M. and T. Young. (1997) *Confronting Leviathan: Mozambique since Independence.* Athens, Ohio: Ohio University Press.

Hanlon, J. (1984) *Mozambique: The Revolution Under Fire.* London: Zed Books.

Hoile, D. (1989) *Mozambique: A Nation in Crisis.* London: The Claridge Press.

Isaacman, A.F. (1985) "Mozambique: Tugging at the Chains of Dependency." *African Crisis Areas and United States Foreign Policy.* Ed. G. Bender. Berkeley: University of California Press.

Jaster, R.S. et al, eds. (1992) *Changing Fortunes: War, Diplomacy, and Economics in Southern Africa.* USA: Ford Foundation.

Mbeki, M. and M. Nkosi. (1992) "Economic Rivalry and Interdependence in Southern Africa." *Changing Fortunes: War, Diplomacy, and Economics in Southern Africa.* Ed. Robert S. Jaster. USA: Ford Foundation.

SAPEM (1993) 6.12: 22.

Schultz, B. (1995) "The Heritage of Revolution and the Struggle for Governmental Legitimacy in Mozambique." *Collapsed States: The Disintegration and Restoration of Legitimate Authority.* Ed. I.W. Zartman. Boulder: Lynne Rienner.

United States Government. "Background Notes: Mozambique, July 1996." http://dosfan.lib.uic.edu/ERC/bgnotes/af/mozambique9607.html

Wright, S. (1999) "The Changing Context of African Foreign Policies." *African Foreign Policies.* Ed. S. Wright. Boulder: Westview Press.

Zartman, I.W., ed. (1995) *Collapsed States: The Disintegration and Restoration of Legitimate Authority.* Boulder: Lynne Rienner.

8 Towards an Understanding of the Foreign Policy-Making Process of a New State: The Case of Namibia

FRANK KHACHINA MATANGA

The timing and recency of Namibia's political independence give it somehow a unique status in African and global politics. Globally, it coincided with the coming to an end of a fundamental era: the Cold War. Continentally, it marked the end of the 20th century colonial experiment in Africa. In view of these significant changes, poignant questions revolve around the character of the newly emerging Namibian foreign policy. For instance, is it taking a radical departure from the traditional foreign policy determinants of the relatively older African states? What actors are emerging as key determiners in her foreign policy-making process?

Past analyses of the foreign policies of African states have tended to argue that these policies, in large measure, have been dependent on both domestic and external factors. Some of these factors have included: African states' colonial experiences, since their policies have been much shaped by their relations with their past colonial powers; the level of resource endowment by these states and therefore the capacity to formulate and pursue certain policies; the issue of securing and maintaining their states' security and sovereignty especially in relation to territorial boundaries and overall external interference; the need to achieve socio-economic development in the fastest possible period; the desire to end colonialism and apartheid on the continent; and, among many others, the need to consolidate nation-building in an attempt to thwart internal threats to the integrity of the state (Aluko 1977, 1-18; Wright 1999, 2-6).

In as much as some of these felt needs have been achieved and even surpassed — for example the eradication of colonialism and apartheid — it is our contention that the rest of them remain relevant to the African states in relation to the focus of their respective foreign policies. Namibia's foreign policy, in spite of the recency of her political independence, is very much a product of these variables.

Namibia: The Road to Independence

1990 was Namibia's golden year. It marked her liberation from varied colonial forces ranging from Germany to South Africa, the last colonizing power. Namibia, then called South West Africa, fwas first drawn into the web of German colonialism in 1884 following the 'scramble for Africa.' German rule, however, was short lived, coming to an end in 1914. In spite of its brief duration, German colonialism was just as brutal as any other in Africa. It was characterised by excessive use of force in occupying the territory and the rape of Namibian resources through the confiscation of the most fertile lands while instituting forced labour policies for the indigenous peoples (Koroma 1985, 141).

The defeat of Germany at the end of World War I by the allied forces marked the end of the first phase of the colonization of Namibia. Forced to evacuate from Namibia, Germany literally handed the territory to the League of Nations in 1919 as a mandate to be administered by South Africa. The terms of the mandate were made very clear: the administering power (i.e. South Africa), was to give first priority to the interests of the indigenous peoples while making annual reports to the League of Nations on its developmental obligations; but more importantly, the administering power had no right whatsoever to annex the mandated territory. South Africa, while largely keeping to the terms of the mandate, had in some significant ways already begun to have her own plans for Namibia; these included, for example, constituting a Legislative Assembly of whites only, thereby excluding the African population from participating in the important task of legislation and the making of ordinances pertaining to the running of the country (Koroma 1985, 143).

However, it can be argued that it was the aftermath of World War II that gave South Africa the clear opportunity to annex and colonise Namibia, thereby effectively contravening the terms of the mandate and later trusteeship. While refusing to hand over Namibia to the new United Nations Trusteeship Council (which was charged with preparing the territories for eventual decolonization), South Africa — without the blessing of the United Nations — incorporated Namibia into the South African Union, thereby making her virtually a fifth province (Koroma 1985; Cliffe 1994; Dreyer

1994). This incorporation from the mid-1940s, constituted Namibia's second colonization. Even more so than Germany, South Africa was thorough in the exploitation of Namibia with respect to the supply of African labour to the mines and white ranches, thus servicing the South African capitalist economy. Racist and apartheid policies along the lines of those in place in South Africa were put in operation to check the rise of the Africans and to ensure that they remained in a perpetual state of servitude (Cliffe 1994, 16-17).

The struggle against South African colonialism saw the birth of liberation movements such as the South West African People's Organization (SWAPO) and the South West Africa National Union (SWANU). Namibia's history, in the period from the mid-1940s to the years leading to independence in the late 1980s, was largely characterised by South Africa's refusal to decolonize. The many international meetings convened, and resolutions adopted under the auspices of the UN in an attempt to find a peaceful solution to the Namibian crisis, were either ignored, or simply refuted by South Africa with the passage of time. However, the final stretch towards Namibian independence was fast approaching when Cuba and Angola — in talks with the USA in 1988 — agreed to formally withdraw Cuban forces from Angola as demanded by South Africa in exchange for Namibian independence. Supervised by a multinational UN observer force — the UN Transition Assistance Group (UNTAG) — Namibia eventually became independent in March 1990 under Nujoma's SWAPO.[1]

The Evolution of Namibia's Foreign Policy in the Post-Colonial Period

Namibia's foreign policy has been tailored around the twin issues of economic development and territorial integrity within the context of southern Africa. To this extent then, Namibia's responses to economic and political challenges since her independence in 1990 are of crucial interest. It has been argued that the economic situation in Namibia differs substantially from that of most African states: the forging of a dualistic economy that, due to apartheid, produced a privileged white minority and a marginalised black majority; the inheritance of a little debt from South Africa, her former colonizing power; and, among other things, not being subject to any international commitments in the form of the International Finance Institutions' (IFIs) structural adjustment conditions (Melber 1997, 6). Credited with a relatively strong economy in the early years of independence, recent performance has not been impressive, with a gradual drop in Gross Domestic Product (GDP) rates. From a record 6 per cent growth rate in GDP in 1994, this dropped to a paltry 2.5 per cent by 1996 and an even lower 1.8 per cent in 1997 (Melber 1997, 6; RSW 1999, 779).

Namibia's economy is fairly dependent on the mining sector with agriculture playing a secondary role. Minerals accounted for approximately 59.9 per cent of total exports in 1997 with diamonds constituting the main element with a contribution of 70.1 per cent of the sector's GDP. Other minerals have included uranium and salt (RSW 1999, 780-781). Agriculture and fishing contributed only 10.5 per cent to the GDP in 1997. The major agricultural activity is livestock production. Like other settler economies in Africa, the agricultural sector of Namibia is characterised by inequitable land distribution in favour of the minority white population. There are about 4,000 large commercial ranches owned by whites, 20,000 African stock-raising households squeezed into the central and southern reserves, and 120,000 black families tied to only five per cent of the arable farmland in the north of the country (RSW 1999, 781). Other sectors of the Namibian economy include the manu- facturing sector which provided 13.7 per cent of GDP in 1997. The manufacturing sector consists mainly of fish-processing, as well as the processing of meat and minerals (RSW 1999, 782). In addition to the fact that Namibia's economy is not yet particularly diversified, it is overtly vulnerable in the sense that it largely relies on South Africa for trade. It is estimated that 80 per cent of Namibia's imports come from South Africa whilst its exports are also mainly directed to that country. These close economic relations between Namibia and South Africa have been acknowledged by both the Namibian government and South Africa. Eksteen (1991, 18), South Africa's representative to Namibia, could thus confidently declare that:

> Because of the close geographical proximity of Namibia and South Africa to each other and their long association in respect to trade, the trade relations between the two countries are so intertwined that Namibia will find it difficult to break away from South Africa and to stand on its own.

These ties have occasionally become stormy with Namibia on the offensive, accusing South Africa of undermining and undercutting her development efforts. Having inherited a debt of $250 million from the years of South African administration, Nujoma insisted that South Africa clear the debt. These demands by Namibia were largely resisted by South Africa which argued that the loans incurred at the time were used to improve Namibia's infrastructure (social and physical) for the benefit of Namibians (Eksteen, 20). However, with the take-over of power in South Africa by Mandela's

African National Congress (ANC), this dispute was smoothed out by his government's move to cancel Namibia's debt to South Africa, estimated at $240 million rand (Republic of Namibia n.d.).

However, Namibia continues to be uncomfortable with South Africa as a trading partner. In an interview in 1997, Namibia's Trade and Industry Minister, Hidipo Hamutenya accused South Africa of hampering industrial development in the neighbouring states by deliberately pursuing policies that sabotage industrial production plants in these states, and sticking to a protectionist industrial policy that made it difficult for these countries to penetrate her market. At the same time, South Africa is seen as being bent on dumping her manufactured goods in Namibia using ill practices, including the selling of goods at "unfair price advantages, often ignoring profit, transport and other costs in order to conquer and dominate the Namibian market".[2]

Attempts to check South Africa's economic monopoly in the region have included Namibia's efforts to join regional economic organizations — most notably the Southern African Development Community (SADC) and the Southern African Customs Union (SACU). Joining the SADC in 1990/1991, Namibia had hoped to benefit from an expanded market in the region, thereby reducing her dependency on South Africa. SADC member states, including Namibia, aim to remove trade barriers in order to facilitate cross-border trade and general investment with improved regional links (Melber 1997, 64). However, the ability of the SADC to break South Africa's trade dominance in the region has been minimal. In 1995 for instance, SADC countries purchased 89.5 per cent of South Africa's exports to the rest of Africa, and South Africa had a trade balance in her favour of $5,381 million within the community (Ahwireng-Obeng and McGowan 1998, 8).

Yet another attempt at regional integration in southern Africa has been made through the founding of SACU. SACU was formed in 1969 and its members include South Africa, Botswana, Lesotho, Namibia and Swaziland. The last four form what has popularly become known as BLNS. As a customs union, it has favoured mainly the interests of South Africa in terms of providing a rich market for her goods at the expense of BLNS. South Africa, for example, exported to the rest of SACU some 5.7 times the value of the goods and services that it imported from its partners in 1993. This trend does not seem likely to improve for BLNS in the near future. In Ahwireng-Obeng's and McGowan's realistic judgement:

> Thus Botswana, Lesotho, Namibia and Swaziland may be juridically independent, sovereign states; but from the point of view of regional trade they are totally dependent on South Africa. And this relationship is very unequal (10).

140 *Globalization and Emerging Trends*

The Namibian Trade Minister has admitted that SACU is overtly favouring South Africa in terms of its policies in relation to BNLS, which have called for a renegotiation of the SACU agreement. As reported in the *Mail and Guardian:*

> Another shortcoming of the 1996 SACU Agreement was the lack of democratic decision-making structures as reflected in the structure of the Common External Tariff set by the Board on Tariffs and Trade . . . These countries (BNLS) have made concrete proposals to renegotiate the agreement in order for it to provide for democratic decision-making, and the administration of the agreement through truly multi-lateral, not unilateral South Africa governance . . . However, South Africa to date has not shown a clear disposition to accept these proposals in good faith.[3]

The issue of Namibia's economy as it relates to her southern African neighbours — in particular South Africa — has become of central concern in her foreign relations, with Namibia more often than not taking a confrontational approach in an attempt to force South Africa to take BNLS interests into consideration. As we have noted, however, South Africa's enormous political and economic power make it almost impossible for BNLS to secure meaningful changes and reforms in the southern Africa economic structure. Appreciating the need for diversification in her economic relations, Namibia embarked on an ambitious infrastructural programme in an attempt to link her road network to that of her southern Africa neighbours. This involved the construction of the Trans-Kalahari Highway and the Trans-Caprivi Highway linking Namibia, Botswana, Zambia and Zimbabwe. Namibia has also been aggressive in the signing of bilateral agreements on various issues beneficial to her economy. Beyond the region, Namibia has forged economic links with other African countries as well as with European states, especially Sweden and Germany. In 1997/1998, Germany was the leading provider of aid to Namibia. In addition, Namibia imports an assortment of manufactured goods from Germany while exporting agricultural products and beef.[4] Sweden also has been closely associated with Namibia, especially as an aid donor (Melber 1997).

Political Issues and Namibia's Foreign Policy

Political issues that have contributed largely to the shaping Namibia's foreign policy have had to do with the need to secure her territorial boundaries.

This has involved boundary conflicts with her neighbours, most of which have been resolved diplomatically. Emerging from colonialism, Namibia's first boundary dispute concerned the ownership of Walvis Bay which South Africa had continued to occupy, in spite of UN recognition of the bay as Namibian. Being the only deep water port on the Namibian coast, Walvis Bay is of great strategic significance to Namibia and this explains that country's concerted efforts to reoccupy it (Cliffe 1994, 118-120). Interviewed in 1991, Eksteen, South Africa's representative to Namibia, clearly indicated South Africa's indecisiveness on the future of Walvis Bay.

> This is a matter that is being discussed at bilateral level between the two countries (South Africa and Namibia). South Africa will not be dictated to by other countries or institutions about Walvis Bay . . . South Africa and Namibia will decide on a date to discuss the Walvis Bay question.

In a further comment that clearly revealed the overall hostile relations between the new government of Namibia and South Africa, Eksteen, when asked about Nujoma's refusal to establish full diplomatic relations with his country, remarked rather harshly that,

> In view of the changes that have already been made in the political field, South Africa will not go out of its way to beg understanding for its situation from foreign countries. South Africa can not dance to anybody's tune (1991, 17).

However, possibly due to international pressure combined with the need to prove to the world that the 'new' South Africa was in favour of peaceful change in the region, the De Klerk government eventually agreed to transfer the Walvis Bay administration back to Namibia in 1994, thereby participating in the conflict's peaceful resolution.

A more recent conflict with South Africa has concerned the 1000 km-long border on the Orange River. Prior to 1990, South Africa claimed sovereignty over the whole river and the minerals therein. In as much as South Africa later agreed to move the border to the middle of the river, she has been reluctant to give up the mineral claims over the whole river. This dispute, which began in 1990, has also involved the grazing rights on the river's islands and fishing vessels.[5]

Namibia, too, has recently been locked in a boundary dispute with Botswana over the 3.5 square km Kasikili-Sedudu Island and the 91 square km island of Situngu on the Linyati-Chobe River. The situation deteriorated to such an extent that both countries stationed troops on both islands, threatening a military confrontation.[6] An attempt to resolve the crisis in a non-military fashion in May 1998 through a bilateral accord between the two countries, did not seem to fare well, prompting the two states to take the case to the International Court of Justice (ICJ) both promising to abide by the ICJ judgement.[7]

In addition to boundary conflicts, Namibia's foreign policy has focussed on the continuing civil wars in the region. This, of course, is because Namibia's security in the region is very much linked to the stability of her neighbours. Nujoma's past experiences as a revolutionary leader who fought as a guerrilla to win the Namibian independence has tended to influence his policy choices in these wars.

Relations between Namibia and Angola — one of the countries experiencing a horrific civil war — date back to the early days of the liberation struggle against South Africa. These relations were forged between the two countries' liberation movements. Reasons suggested to account for the close working relationship between the Namibian and Angolan liberation forces have included the fact that the two states share ethnic kinship in Namibia's Ovambo (the key supporters of SWAPO) and Angola's Kwanyama. Secondly, since the early 1920s, Angolan migrant workers, for various reasons, worked in Namibian mines under South African rule which exposed them to a militant worker-consciousness long developed among the Namibians (Dreyer, 1994, 44).

SWAPO initially cooperated with Angola's Holden Roberto's National Front for the Liberation of Angola (FNLA). This movement is said to have developed out of the Bakongo peasant uprising against the Portuguese in the north of Angola in 1961. Facing similar colonial problems, the two liberation movements called for military action against the Portuguese in Angola and the South Africans in Namibia. At one point, the FNLA and SWAPO signed a joint declaration which called for a Federation of Independent States of Angola, Botswana and South West Africa under a central government to become part of the 'Federal States of Africa' (Dreyer, 47). But SWAPO, too, forged working relations with other Angolan liberation forces, notably, the National Union for the Total Independence of Angola (UNITA) and the Popular Movement for the Liberation of Angola (MPLA) in the 1960s. However, from 1976, following Angolan independence, SWAPO became a very close partner of the MPLA. The MPLA government promised SWAPO material assistance and military bases in Angola to assist in its fight against South Africa. In return, Nujoma of SWAPO, besides publicly paying tribute to the seeming victory of the MPLA in the Angolan civil war, pledged to act militarily alongside the MPLA and its Cuban allies in the war against South African forces in Angola (Cliffe 1994; Dreyer 1994). It has been argued that the MPLA's support for SWAPO in its colonial war with South Africa was fundamental to making SWAPO's military influence felt in Namibia (Dreyer, 105).

Namibia's current involvement in the continuing Angolan civil war between the Angolan MPLA government and UNITA, can thus be traced to Nujoma's long standing military and political relations with Angola. His intervention on behalf of the MPLA government in December 1999 was at the behest of the MPLA leadership, which requested bases in Namibia for the purpose of attacking UNITA rebels in the far south-east of Angola. So far it has been reported that Namibian assistance to its long-time ally, the MPLA, is not just the provision of military bases, but also of soldiers and weapons.[8]

Due to the heavy strain on the Namibian economy arising from its involvement in the Angolan civil war — as well as increased insecurity and destabilisation in Namibia and the region as a whole — there has been pressure on Nujoma to pull out of the war. However, President Nujoma, who has just won a third five year term as president of Namibia, has vowed to keep up Namibian involvement in the Angolan civil war in support of the MPLA government. He was quoted by the *Mail & Guardian* (15th Feb. 2000) as saying:

> The Republic of Namibia would like to reaffirm its position to fully support the Angolan government in its efforts against UNITA bandits in order to restore peace in Angola.

President Nujoma's obsession with an interventionist policy has not stopped with Angola. Around mid-1998, Namibia joined Zimbabwe and Angola in defending the beleaguered regime of Laurent Kabila of the Democratic Republic of Congo (DRC) against rebels backed up by Uganda and Rwanda (*CNN* 24th February, 2000). The ongoing civil war in the DRC is far from being resolved, with Namibia being deeply involved in supplying human and material resources.

Continentally, Namibia's impact has not yet been fully realized. Being a member of the Organization of African Unity (OAU), Namibia's key contribution has been in the direction of pressurising the establishment of a pan-African peace-keeping force. Beyond the forum provided by the OAU for inter-state relations, Namibia has established diplomatic relations with a number of other African states.

Namibia's Foreign Policy-Making Process: the Actors

The Presidency

The most active actors in foreign policy-making in Namibia have tended to be limited to institutions and processes influencing inter-state affairs. In this, the roles of the Presidency, the Government Ministries, the political parties and civil society are important (see Figure 8.1, below).

Figure 8.1 Foreign Policy-making Process: the Actors

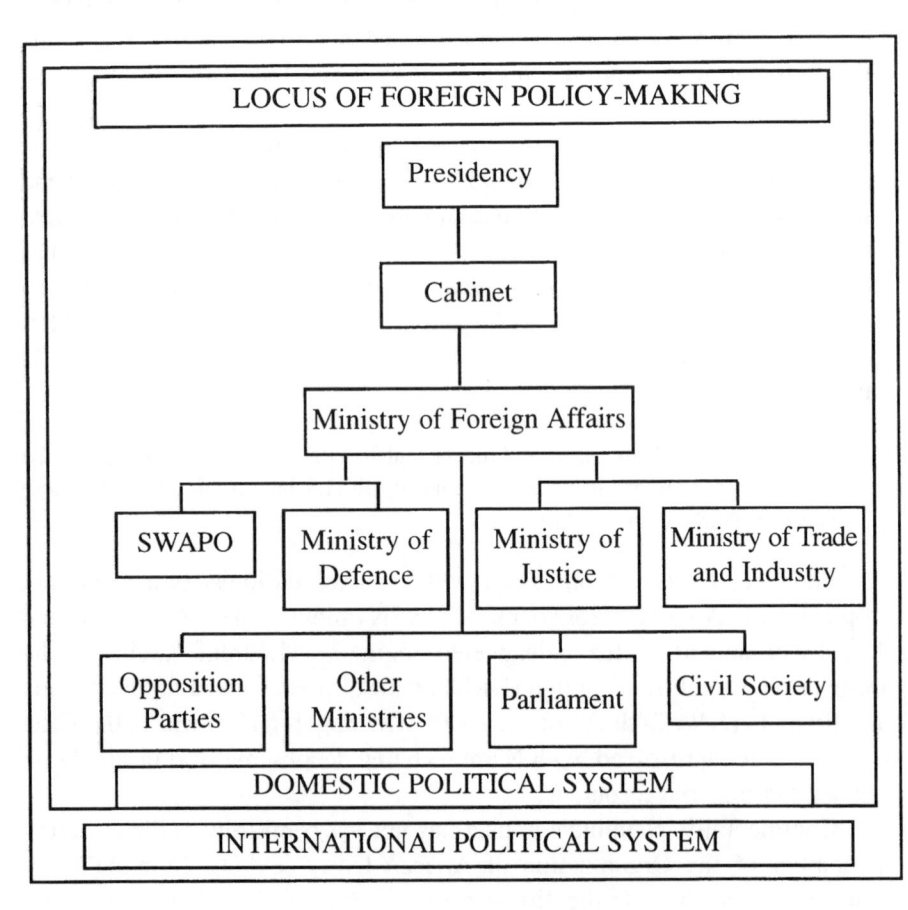

```
LOCUS OF FOREIGN POLICY-MAKING
            │
       Presidency
            │
        Cabinet
            │
   Ministry of Foreign Affairs
   ┌────────┬────────┬────────┐
 SWAPO  Ministry of  Ministry of  Ministry of Trade
        Defence      Justice      and Industry
 ┌──────────┬──────────┬──────────┐
Opposition  Other      Parliament  Civil Society
Parties     Ministries

DOMESTIC POLITICAL SYSTEM
INTERNATIONAL POLITICAL SYSTEM
```

As is the case in most African states, Namibia's Presidency — consisting mainly of the President and to some extent the Prime Minister — has been the most powerful actor in the foreign policy-making process. If the Presidency has monopolised the process, it is essentially tied to the authoritarian system of rule which has also been characterised by a personalization of power. Much evidence from the political observers of Namibia reinforces an image of a fast emerging dictatorship. As has happened before in Africa, a country that began on a promising democratic path is sinking rapidly into authoritarianism. Kevin Toolis's description in the *Mail & Guardian* of Nujoma's personal and public life since he became president is significant:

> In power, Nujoma is not much different than in exile. Probably because of his insecurity, he travels in a cavalcade of four black armoured Mercedes with screaming sirens and motorcycle outriders, regardless of how short the journey. He is fond of presenting himself as an important African potentate . . . And fond, too, of expensive presidential jets that his impoverished country can ill-afford. A squad of goons clad in Hawaiian shirts, with guns in their waistbands, follow his every move (*M&G*, 15th August, 1997).

The decision to send Namibian forces to the DRC seems to have been Nujoma's personal decision, without any consultation with the relevant government organs. Furthermore, information on Namibia's involvement in the DRC only came to light as a result of Zimbabwe's disclosure and the death of some Namibian soldiers on the war front in Kinshasa. Commenting on the decision to involve Namibia in the DRC, John Grobler noted in the *Mail & Guardian* of 4th September 1998 that:

> Informed sources this week said that at no stage had Nujoma informed either his cabinet or parliament of his intentions to become embroiled in the Central Africa conflict . . . . The presence of Namibian troops in Kinshasa was secret until disclosed by Zimbabwe, but evidence now points to early preparations by the NDF (Namibian Defence Force).

With the benefit of hindsight, observers of the Namibian political scene could now tie to the DRC crisis Nujoma's decision to increase the National State Intelligence Agency's (NSIA) portion of the 1998\1999 budget to a massive 40 per cent without any explanation to parliament. Like NSIA, the National Defence Force is said to be directly under Nujoma and operating from his State House. An analysis of Namibia's involvement in the Angolan civil war also clearly points to the heavy influence of the presidency under Sam Nujoma. As already argued, Nujoma's involvement in the civil war in support of the MPLA can only be meaningfully explained in the context of their long-term relationship forged during the struggle for political independence in both Angola and Namibia.

The Government Ministries

Namibia had approximately 22 Government Ministries by the close of 1999 (*Regional Surveys of the World-RSW* 1999, 789). Out of these, a few were quite active in Namibia's foreign policy-making process. These included the Ministry of Foreign Affairs, the Ministry of Justice, the Ministry of Trade and Industry, and the Ministry of Defence. The Ministry of Foreign Affairs is officially the locus of the foreign policy-making process in Namibia since it ought to have expertise in the field. In view of this role, the Ministry of Foreign Affairs set the following as its objectives in 1994:

- to promote Namibia's security and territorial integrity;
- to promote Namibia's national identity;
- to enhance Namibia's economic interests by securing better trade terms;
- to enhance peace on the country's borders by supporting the peace process;
- to promote world peace and security through its role in international organizations;

The Ministry of Foreign Affairs was instrumental in various bilateral negotiations which contributed to resolving the many territorial and boundary disputes discussed above. Of first importance in this regard was the Walvis Bay dispute with South Africa. The Ministry, through fairly quiet diplomacy, succeeded in having its administration taken over by Namibia. Initially, a Walvis Bay Joint Administration Authority (JAA) was formed in November 1992 comprising officials from both South Africa and Namibia. The work of the JAA was completed in February 1994 leading to the transfer of Walvis Bay to Namibia in March 1994. The Ministry of Foreign Affairs also played a fundamental role in the border dispute with Botswana involving among things, Kasikili Island on the Linyati-Chobe river. This dispute which was eventually forwarded to the ICJ in 1998, involved negotiations and agreements between Namibian and Botswana officials.

Besides the Ministries of Foreign Affairs and Justice, the Ministry of Trade and Industry has been active in shaping and promoting Namibia's economic interests in the region. This has happened particularly in the context of the SADC and SACU which are monopolised by South Africa. The crux of the matter has concerned South Africa's protectionist policies which have turned the balance of trade in her favour at the expense of her neighbours. Spearheaded by Namibia, the BLNS countries have been fighting to renegotiate the SACU Agreement. Other ministries which have been instrumental in Namibia's foreign policy include the Ministry of Defence which has, to some extent, shaped Namibia's policies towards the DRC and Angolan civil wars. This has been done through the activities of the National Defence Force.

The Political Parties

Today Namibia is a multi-party state with several political parties. These include the Christian Democratic Action for Social Justice, Congress of Democrats, Democratic Coalition of Namibia, Democratic Turnhalle Alliance of Namibia (DTA), Federal Convention of Namibia, Monitor Action Group, Namibia Movement for Independent Candidate, Namibia National Democratic Party, Namibia National Front, National Democratic Party for Justice, South West Africa People's Organization (SWAPO), South West African National Union (SWANU), United Democratic Front and Workers' Revolutionary Party (RSW 1999, 789-790). However, out of all these, only SWAPO and DTA have had an influential role in Namibia's post-colonial period.

SWAPO, in particular, as already discussed, became recognised by the international community as Namibia's national voice during the long struggle for political independence. As a liberation movement, SWAPO formed a government in exile which campaigned on three fronts. These were: an armed struggle along the border of Angola; an international political campaign focussing on the UN, the OAU, and Western and African capitals; and internal mobilization of peoples at the grassroots in Namibia (Legum 1992, 622). In Namibia's first-ever elections as an independent state, SWAPO emerged victorious with 57.3 per cent of the total votes cast. The leading opposition parties by then were the Democratic Turnhalle Alliance (which won 28.6 per cent of the votes), and the United Democratic Front (with 5.6 per cent of the votes). It is important to note that, even with this victory, SWAPO failed to achieve the two-thirds majority that would have given it control of the Constituent Assembly (Cliffe 1994, 183-185; Dreyer 1994, 192-193). Since then, however, Namibia has had two other national elections all won by SWAPO under the leadership of Sam Nujoma. These later elections served to make SWAPO a dominant political party, for having secured a two-thirds majority in parliament, it could now influence the changing of the constitution to suit its interests (Simon 1995; Bauer 1999, 432).

SWAPO's role as a dominant party has indeed translated into the manipulation of the constitution in favour of Nujoma, enabling him to stay in power. Whereas the constitution was clear on having a two-term limit for the head of state, this was recently changed by SWAPO's top brass, allowing the president to compete for a third term in 1999; he did so and won. Although fear of ethnic conflict amongst the Ovambo clans was the official reason for giving Nujoma a third term (in an attempt to avert an ethnic disaster by ensuring continuity in leadership), critical observers saw in it a push to make Nujoma life president, thus putting the country on a political path to authoritarianism and the personalization of power usual in Africans states. One observer succinctly noted, "They are launching Namibia on the road away from democracy and down the normal road in Africa, where power is claimed with the barrel of a gun".[9]

Symptoms of an ailing democracy have been further provided by the irregular conduct of the 1999 elections. It was alleged that representatives of opposition parties monitoring the polling were continuously turned away from the process by SWAPO officials. The National Society for Human Rights (NSHR) cited several irregularities in voting in various constituencies and declared that, "This state of affairs brings into serious question the transparency of the electoral process and consequently the credibility of the final results".[10]

The fact that SWAPO is Namibia's dominant party has also led to the blurring of the distinction between it and the Government. Many SWAPO policies have indeed become government policies, thereby influencing the direction of Namibia's foreign policy. For instance, SWAPO's ideology of a free market economy that calls for increased foreign investment (Bauer 1999, 440) has in fact become Namibia's foreign policy as she aggressively pushes for foreign investments and trade. Namibia's principal trade partners have included Britain, South Africa, Switzerland, Germany, Japan and the US. In the mining sector, Namibia has entered into several joint ventures with foreign companies. For instance, in April 1998, Nujoma signed an agreement with Russia providing for co-operation in mining and prospecting in which the Russian mining company, RAO Almazy Rossii-Sakha, was permitted to operate in Namibia (RSW 1999, 780). The Export Processing Zone policy has seen the establishment of several foreign multi-national corporations in Namibia that have included German owned Namibia Press and Tools vehicle components plant, a US $25m distillery owned by Rockwood-Heinz,

Global Textiles and Chinese Friendship Company, among others (RSW 1999, 782).

It can also be argued that SWAPO's influence on Namibian foreign policy has been most active in the area of relations with Angola. This is so especially in relation to the Namibian government's support for the MPLA government against the UNITA rebels. As discussed earlier, SWAPO's friendly relations with the MPLA go back to the period of the liberation struggle. The fact that SWAPO is a dominant party in Namibia has in turn meant that the opposition parties have a fairly insignificant influence on the direction of Namibia's foreign policy-making process. Equally important is the observation that Namibia's bicameral parliament, overshadowed by the presidency, has very little input into Namibia's foreign policy. The by-passing of parliament by the executive in matters of national importance to Namibia was clearly seen in the earlier example of Nujoma's unilateral decision to involve Namibia in the DRC conflict.

Civil Society

The role of civil society in influencing Namibia's foreign policy-making process has been minimal. This is mainly due to the weakness of the emerging nascent organizations and social movements. The inability of civil society to influence foreign policy-making in Namibia has been linked to attempts by SWAPO to co-opt the few vibrant organizations: SWAPO has officially co-opted the Namibian National Students Organization (NANSO) and the giant National Union of Namibian Workers (NUNW). So far the stiffest challenge the civil society has provided to the Government has been through the Caprivi Liberation Army (CLA). The CLA has its roots in Caprivi, a strip of land running across nothern Namibia, sharing borders with Angola, Botswana, Zambia and Zimbabwe. The Caprivi secessionists, seeking incorporation within a revived Barotseland of Zambia, have accused the Namibian Government of deliberately ignoring their development interests and thus their poverty.[11] The CLA has continued to receive extensive military support from Angola's UNITA. In addition, from 1998 Botswana agreed to accommodate the Caprivi refugees fleeing from Namibia, besides providing asylum status for leading CLA personalities (RSW 1999, 778).

It is precisely because of the CLA's attempt to internationalize the conflict that it has managed to impact on Namibia's foreign policy. In retaliation, the Namibian government undertook several measures. Firstly, it intensified its support for the MPLA Government in fighting UNITA (which supports the CLA). Secondly, it sought and received pledges of military support against the separatists from the governments of Zimbabwe and Zambia[12] (*Mail & Guardian* 10th August, 1999; RSW 1999, 778). Thirdly, in March 1999, Nujoma visited Botswana and agreed with Botswana's President Mogae that the secessionist leaders could be accorded refugee status on condition that they be resettled in a third country, an agreement which Botswana subsequently implemented (RSW 1999, 778). To this extent then, the Caprivi Liberation Movement (CLM) and its military wing, the CLA, have impacted on Namibia's foreign policy-making process.

Conclusion

This chapter has attempted to thread together different aspects of the young and still evolving Namibian foreign policy. Having acquired independence from South Africa only in 1990, Namibia is a relatively recent autonomous actor in the international system of states. However, as our analysis has shown, this has not precluded her from undergoing some experiences common to other African states. These experiences have, in a sense, constituted the salient variables around which Namibia's foreign policy has been formulated. First and foremost, South Africa's colonization of Namibia has established a legacy from which Namibia finds it extremely difficult to break free. Her foreign trade in terms of exports and imports is mainly with South Africa, South Africa being the senior partner, which obliges Namibia to dance to her tune. Namibia's joining of the SADC and SACU has not made matters substantially any better, for South Africa continues to dominate these organizations due to her political and economic might. Nevertheless, as argued in the text, Namibia has been making frantic efforts to diversify her economic relations in Africa, Europe and the United States.

Namibia's foreign policy has also been a response to a number of political issues. These issues have centred on Namibia's security and territorial integrity. It is within this context that Namibia's border disputes with South Africa and Botswana can be understood. Namibia's involvement in the Angolan civil war (on the side of the MPLA) seems to be driven by Nujoma's desire for stability and security for his regime. Indeed the continued power of the MPLA in Angola would seem to provide a better ally for Nujoma in the region as well as acting as a buffer against the Caprivi secessionist movement.

The ending of the Cold War does not promise to improve matters for African states since they are no longer able to take advantage of the

American–Soviet ideological rivalry. The developed world's focus is increasingly shifting to the former communist Eastern Europe. This, however, does not preclude the African states from also being sucked into the process of globalization on terms set and controlled by the industrialised North. To this extent, globalization as the newest tool of imperialism, will serve to consolidate and advance capitalism to the advantage of the developed world.

The role of Sam Nujoma, as a person, has had a fundamental influence on the formulation and practice of Namibia's foreign policy. With less emphasis on institutionalization, once again due to the recency of Namibia's independence, and the authoritarian nature of most African leadership, foreign policy-making in Namibia is more personalized than institutionalized. Indeed, the chapter has provided many examples to illustrate Nujoma's overwhelming role in Namibia's foreign policy. However, this is not to deny that other organizations and processes have also impacted on Namibia's foreign policy-making process. The government ministries such as those of Foreign Affairs, Justice, Trade and Industry, and Defence have made their contributions. Equally important has been the role of SWAPO as the dominant ruling party. Civil society's role has largely been limited to the Caprivi crisis through the CLM and its army, CLA.

Notes

1 See Dale 1991; Cliffe 1994; Dreyer 1994 and RSW 1999, 776.
2 *Mail & Guardian* 2 August 1997.
3 *Mail & Guardian* 2 August 1997.
4 NEPRU *Quarterly Review* Sept./Dec. 1998.
5 *Mail & Guardian* 27 April 1999.
6 *Mail & Guardian* 27 April 1999.
7 *Mail & Guardian* 6 January 1999.
8 *Mail & Guardian* 17 February 2000.
9 *Mail & Guardian* 5 May 1997, citing Katuutire Kaura of the Opposition Democratic Turnhalle Alliance.
10 NSHR, quoted in *Mail & Guardian* 2 December 1999.
11 *Mail & Guardian* 10 August 1999.
12 *Mail and Guardian* 10 August 1999; RSW 1999, 778.

References

Ahwireng-Obeng and P.J. McGowan. (1998) "Partner or Hegemon? South Africa in Africa." *Journal of Contemporary African Studies* 16.1: 5-38.

Aluko, O. (1977) "The Determinants of Foreign Policies of African States." *The Foreign Policies of African States*. Ed. O. Aluko. London: Hodder and Stoughton.
Bauer, G. (1999) "Challenges to Democratic Consolidation in Namibia." *State, Conflict, and Democracy in Africa*. Ed. R. Joseph. Boulder: Lynne Rienner.
Cliffe, L. (1994) *The Transition to Independence in Namibia*. Boulder: Lynne Rienner.
CNN. cnn.com/2000/world/africa/02/24/congo.un/
Dale, R. (1991) "The UN and African Decolonization: UNTAG in Namibia." *TransAfrican Forum* 8.3.
Dreyer, R. (1994) *Namibia and South Africa: Regional Dynamics of Decolonization 1945-1990*. London: Kegan Paul International.
Eksteen, R. (1991) "Namibia a Year Later." Interview. *RSA Policy Review* 4.3: 13-25.
Koroma, D.S.M. (1985) "Namibia: The Case of a Betrayal of Sacred Trust." *Journal of African Studies* 12.3: 141-153.
Legum, C., ed. (1990-1992) *Africa Contemporary Record* 23: 621-632.
Lindeke, W.A. (1995) "Democratisation in Namibia: Soft State, Hard Choices." *Studies in Comparative International Development* 30.1.
Mail & Guardian. http://www.mg.co.za/mg/news/
   97may/5may-nujoma.html,5th/5/1997, Johannesburg;
   97aug2/28aug-nam-trade.html, 28th/8/97;
   97aug2/15aug-namibia.html, 15th/8/97;
   98sep1/4sep-nam-congo.html, 4th/9/98;
   99jan1/6jan-nam-botswana.html, 6th/1/99;
   99apr2/27apr-namibia.html, 27th/4/99;
   98may1/7may-nam-botswana.html, 7th/5/98;
   99aug1/10aug-caprivi.html, 10th/8/99;.
   99dec1/2dec-namibia.html, 2nd/12/99;
   2000feb2/15feb-nam-angola.html, 15th/2/2000;
   2000feb2/17feb-namibia.html, 17th/2/2000;
Melber, H., ed. (1997) "Seven Years Independence: Current Developments and Future Prospects in Namibia: Some Topical Highlights." *Southern African Perspectives* 64. University of Western Cape: Centre for Southern African Studies.
Nel, P. and P.J. McGowan, eds. (1999) *Power, Wealth and Global Order: an International Relations Textbook for Africa*. Rondebosch: University of Cape Town Press.
Regional Surveys of the World (RSW). (1999) *Africa South of the Sahara 2000*. 29th Edition. London: Europa Publications.
Republic of Namibia. (1990) *The Constitution of the Republic of Namibia*. Windhoek.
Republic of Namibia. (1994) *Ministry of Foreign Affairs Official Document*. Windhoek.
Republic of Namibia. (nd) republicofnamibia.com/diplo.htm
Shaw, T.M. and O. Aluko, eds. (1984) *The Political Economy Of African Foreign Policy*. Aldershot: Gower Publishing.
Simon, D. (1995) "Namibia: SWAPO Wins Two-Thirds Majority." *Review of African Political Economy* 22.63.
Wright, S. (1999) "The Changing Context of African Foreign Policies." *African Foreign Policies*. Ed. S. Wright. Boulder: Westview Press.

9 Untangling the "Gamble on Investment": Élite Perceptions of Globalization and South Africa's Foreign Policy during the Mandela Era

PHILIP NEL

The Importance of a Cognitive Perspective

The first five years of the Government of National Unity's (GNU) foreign policy were characterised by two, seemingly unrelated tendencies. On the one hand, South Africa made quite a name for itself as an active, if not leading player in the field of multilateral diplomacy. In the process, it took on the leadership of, among others, the United Nations Conference on Trade and Development (UNCTAD), the Non-Aligned Movement (NAM), the Southern African Development Community (SADC), and the United Nations Human Rights Commission. It also played important roles in securing the renewal of the Nuclear Non-Proliferation Treaty (NPT), and in effecting two major normative innovations in international affairs: the Ottawa Treaty (1997) banning anti-personnel landmines, and the Rome Statute (1998), setting up an International Criminal Court. In many respects, the GNU has given South Africa a typical 'middle power' foreign policy profile of a 'good citizen,' committed to multilateral institutions, and promoting moderate normative reform in global affairs.

On the other hand, the GNU's foreign policy was characterised by a major attempt to open the country's markets to international competition, reduce the budget deficit, get inflation under control, and in general to make the country attractive for foreign investment. This also meant taking on board a very special relationship with the USA, institutionalised in the Bi-national Commission, overseen by the two deputy-presidents, Mbeki and

Gore. Despite some minor irritations on both sides, and an agreement to differ on the landmines ban, South Africa preferred not to oppose the USA on issues that are of central concern to Washington (such as the NPT, for instance). Most of this carefulness towards the USA, and the enthusiasm with which the GNU went into the Bi-national Commission, was predicated on the assumption that the 'new' South Africa would be a major recipient of foreign direct investment, particularly from the USA.[1]

What do this "gamble on investment" (Nattrass 1996) and the nature of South Africa's commitment to moderate middle-powermanship have to do with one another? It is the main thesis of this chapter that these two features of GNU foreign policy were closely connected during the Mandela era.[2] The specific mechanism that connects the two, I want to argue, is the conception and perception that the GNU policy élite during the first five years of the GNU had concerning globalization and its impact, both positive and negative. While factors such as the specific nature of the political-economic 'deal' that brought the GNU to power also need to be considered, the cognitive dimension pursued here is too often overlooked.

The concept of globalization, referring to the *"widening, deepening and speeding up of the processes of world-wide connectivity"* (McGrew 1998, 302), has become a central concept in public debates in South Africa. However, this debate suffers from a theoretical blind spot. In terms of the *structure-agency* divide in social science (see Desler 1989), most of the debate on globalization tends towards an almost exclusive institutional or structural interpretation of the nature and effects of globalization. Although structurally-induced constraints are indeed important variables, its credibility depends on the specification of a causal mechanism that makes structural constraints efficacious when it comes to the formulation of policy or other meaningful behaviour. Structurally-induced causality is only efficacious when it "passes through the minds of social actors," so to speak.[3] Structures only constrain to the extent that they determine the range of choices decision-makers have, and this range is defined by the way in which decision-makers perceive or evaluate the options they have. In turn, such perceptions (or evaluative conclusions — see Freedman, Sears and Carlsmith 1978) are based on the beliefs that decision-makers hold concerning the relevant set of issues, and their attitudes towards aspects of these issues.[4]

If we want to complement and rectify one-sided structural analyses in the globalization literature, it becomes crucial to generate some data on what decision-makers and other policy-relevant actors *believe* about globalization and macro-economic policy in general, what their *attitudes* towards the phenomenon of globalization are, and how they *evaluate* its effects on decision making. In a study on which this chapter is based (Nel et al. 1998), we concentrated on the beliefs, attitudes, and perceptions of both senior members of government and the opinion élite or opinion leaders. Such an élite can be defined *positionally* as "those persons who hold authoritative positions in powerful public and private organisations and influential movements, and who are therefore able to affect strategic decisions regularly" (Higley et al. 1991, 36; see also Kotzé 1992, 15). We use the term "policy élite" as an umbrella term for these two groups.[5] The beliefs and attitudes of senior members of government were traced by means of a content analysis of selected speeches and statements. In order to determine the views of the opinion élite in South Africa, use was made of a survey done through repeated waves of postal surveys in 1997 and 1998 aimed at a positional sample of the élite.[6]

The Élite's Beliefs about, and Attitudes towards, Globalization: A Fundamental Ambiguity

South African public responses to the various dimensions and impact of globalization cover the whole political spectrum, from right to left. On the one hand, there are commentators and interested parties who emphasise the sobering and efficiency-inducing effects of the exposure of the historically protected South African industries to global competition, and the potential that increased inward investment flows hold for growth and employment in the SA economy. On the other end of the spectrum, globalization has been roundly opposed by members of the trade unions, and by what has remained of the left in South Africa. Criticism from these circles has been strongly articulated and focuses on three basic themes. Firstly, it is argued that globalization is not simply a natural extension of the logic of the development of capitalist accumulation (although it is also that), but a deliberate strategy to promote the interests of powerful actors, predominantly transnational corporations and their political protector, the United States of America, supported by the G-7.

Secondly, globalization is said to be a contradictory process with very uneven effects. While it has had obvious benefits for the already privileged, it has not only contributed to a widening of the income gap on a global scale, but is also undermining the few positive redistributive steps that have been taken in South Africa in terms of the original Reconstruction and Development Programme (RDP) of the GNU. Thirdly, because globalization is a political project, it should and can be resisted on the political level. While almost all of the leftist critics agree that there is no way in which an extremely open and trade-dependent economy such as South Africa can escape the forces of globalization, the country should maintain a critical involvement in these global processes, buttressed by a strong and vibrant civil society and trade union movement. While the state should nationally and internationally instigate and support policies to rectify the negative consequences of globalization, a vibrant civil society is the only long-term political antidote to the growing power of transnational corporations.[7]

The understanding of the policy élite in South Africa about what globalization entails falls somewhere between these two ends of the spectrum, and there is some variation in their opinions and attitudes in this regard. For some that would be a sign of moderation and of tolerance for a variety of opinions. For others it may point to fundamental contradictions within the ideological bloc that constitutes the GNU.

Senior spokespersons of the GNU have, on a number of occasions, expressed views on globalization that echo some of the themes of the leftist critique. At the same time, members of the policy élite have also distanced themselves implicitly or explicitly from some aspects of the leftist position, and have emphasised that globalization also bring opportunities which South Africa can exploit.

The most notable treatment of the phenomenon of globalization on the part of the major partner in the GNU, the ANC, comes in the form of the extensive attention that President Mandela paid to the theme during his Political Report presented at the ANC's 50th National Conference in December 1997. Globalization, according to Mandela, refers to "the emergence of a global market represented by the movement of capital, goods and services to all parts of the world, unrestrained by national boundaries or differences in political systems." Acccording to Mandela, it is a process that is primarily driven by advances in science and technology; but he also attributes the emergence of the global market to the inherent dynamics of capitalism. In this context Mandela goes to some lengths to distance his conception from a view that evaluates globalization as the "invention of some reactionary cabal that sits somewhere in the world" (his words). Nevertheless, Mandela adds, globalization is clearly "led and dominated by the countries of the North." This is a crucial conceptual balancing act in the general conception of the GNU, we would argue, because it opens the way for a) accepting that engagement in globalization is inevitable, but b) that specific targets can be identified in a strategy of resistance against the unwelcome dimensions of globalization.

This dual response of accepting engagement on the one hand and resistance on the other, is a common theme in many of the other pronouncements of senior GNU decision makers. Thus, speaking at the annual Davos meeting of the World Economic Forum in 1997, Deputy President Mbeki described the process as inevitable and futile to resist.[8] This sentiment was endorsed by the then Minister of Labour, Tito Mboweni, when he addressed the International Labour Organisation in June 1997,[9] and also in the Political Report by the President in December 1997. In this respect the sentiment is also sometimes expressed that globalization should not only simply be tolerated, but that it should be exploited for the positive benefits that can accrue.[10]

For understandable reasons, the liberalisation of financial markets and the consequences it is having for macro-economic autonomy, feature very prominently in the minds of decision makers. Both Mandela and Mbeki have singled out this dimension of globalization as the most important source of concern, and have suggested ways in which this encroachment on the "freedom of smaller countries' governments to take totally independent decisions" should be countered.[11]

Are these concerns also foremost in the mind of other members of what we have called the policy élite in South Africa? To generate an answer to this question, we have to turn to the findings of the élite survey.

Firstly, supporters of the ANC clearly identify globalization as an economic process, and specifically as a process through which financial markets prescribe to governments what their national policies should look like. Although a clear majority of all the respondents preferred to think of globalization in fairly bland and unspecified terms, namely as a process in which "natural and national borders between people are disappearing and the world is becoming a global village," a majority of ANC supporters indicated that they prefer to think about globalization in terms of the growing power of financial markets. Of all the respondents who chose the latter interpretation of globalization, sixty-two per cent are ANC supporters. In addition, some eighty per cent of the respondents who hold senior positions in the Congress of South African Trade Unions (COSATU), a tri-partite alliance partner of the ANC, preferred the financial market interpretation of globalization.

There is a degree of ambiguity in the attitudes of the ANC-oriented opinion leaders towards globalization as they wished to define it, but in general

158   *Globalization and Emerging Trends*

the response pattern tends to echo that of the GNU decision makers. Globalization indeed elicits strong negative reactions among ANC élite supporters: some twenty-two per cent of all ANC supporters said that they *strongly* oppose globalization, compared to an average of thirteen per cent for the total sample. A further eighteen per cent of ANC supporters indicated that they oppose it (average for the whole sample = 16 per cent). COSATU members tend to be overwhelmingly opposed to globalization, and many have very strong negative feelings about it: eighty-six per cent indicated that they strongly oppose (60 per cent) or oppose it (26 per cent). Non-COSATU-affiliated ANC supporters are thus clearly more ambiguous about the phenomenon than are COSATU members. To the extent that ANC supporters (COSATU and non-COSATU) are opposed to globalization, the intensity of their opposition is quite strong.

Thus, the ambiguity detected in the statements by senior GNU members about globalization is also reflected in the beliefs and attitudes of ANC supporters. On the one hand, concern exists about the effects of globalization, specifically in terms of the impact of financial markets. On the other hand, globalization is also welcomed by a sizeable majority of ANC supporters (excluding COSATU members). The reasons why it is welcomed (only hesitantly, we may add) may be many, but one important reason is that the ANC supporters in our survey agree with the GNU's official view that globalization is inevitable and cannot be wished away. There may be another reason, namely that globalization implies a freer movement of capital across national boundaries and thus becomes a source of investment capital for the South African economy. Below we will see that there is indeed some evidence that this is a major factor in GNU macro-economic calculations. Before we get to that, it is important to look deeper into the one reason why the GNU's policy élite is also sceptical about the effects of globalization, namely the belief that the strength of financial markets robs the state of macro-economic sovereignty.

Losing their Voice: Perceptions of Loss of Sovereignty

"I've lost my voice." With these words Malaysian Prime Minister Mahathir Mohamad in March 1998 summed up his thoughts about the financial crisis that had beset Southeast Asia after the currency crash in Thailand in July 1997. Mahathir was clearly overdramatising the spat he personally had had with currency traders such as George Soros early in 1998. Nevertheless, many government leaders today see a link between these crises and the phenomenon of globalization. Like Mahathir, they also seem to stoically accept such crises as inescapable side-effects of globalization: "We are quite prepared to be poor for a long time," Mahathir said. "We were poor before. Because if this is what is meant by globalization, and because of it we are going to be poor, since we accept globalization, we must also accept being poor" (*Asiaweek* 27 March 1998).

There is no question that South African decision-makers are deeply concerned about what they perceive to be a significant loss of sovereignty to financial markets, not only as far as the South African state is concerned, but also with respect to what Mbeki calls "small states." These states, he warned the 1997 Meeting of the World Economic Forum at Davos, Switzerland, no longer have the freedom to take independent decisions. And although it would be foolish to try and resist this, it is something that has to be addressed, he added (*Business Day* 5 Feb. 1997).

The "loss of sovereignty" also became a major theme in the speeches of President Mandela during 1997 and 1998. Again, the Political Report that he delivered at the 1997 ANC Conference gives us insight into his, and the ANC's official thinking in this regard. In this report, Mandela repeatedly returns to the theme of "loss of sovereignty," but his comments can best be summarised in terms of two major points. The first is that the number of references to this theme in this Report, but also in his other speeches, is in itself an indication of how seriously the GNU feels affected by the impact of capital mobility. This impression is reinforced by looking at the qualifiers that he uses when he discusses the processes at play: he speaks about how these processes "make it *impossible* . . . to decide national economic policy without regard for the likely response of these markets" (emphasis added); that there is an "inevitability" to the loss of sovereignty; and that "a surrender (of society) to the economic processes" is at stake.

Secondly, Mandela identifies not only financial markets as the beneficiaries in this struggle for sovereignty, but he also claims that sovereignty of the state has been transferred, in crucial respects, to institutions of "international governance." Although he may also have had the IFIs in mind, it is significant that he does not single out the IMF and the World Bank for any criticism, something that the GNU did explicitly in the period 1994-1996.[12] Since 1996, however, the relationship between the GNU and the IFIs has markedly improved, especially following the visit by Michael Camdessus of the IMF to South Africa in late 1996, and because of the close alliance developing between South Africa and fifteen other African countries with the

160 *Globalization and Emerging Trends*

World Bank in the context of "The forum of development in Africa." This Forum met on 23 and 24 January 1998 in Kampala, Uganda, and was continued on 20-21 June 1998 in Dakar, Senegal. Notable was the consensus position which emerged from this Forum on the question of globalization. According to a document issued by the Deputy President's office (Mbeki has attended both meetings), the Forum noted "the irreversible nature of globalization" and said that it was up to Africa:

> to create the conditions for becoming part of the globalization process. This will essentially depend on the competitiveness of its economies and the adoption of successful industrialisation strategies.[13]

It comes as no surprise, therefore, that the GNU is becoming less and less inclined to single out the IFIs, and rather resort to general formulations such as "institutions of international governance." Nevertheless, the GNU saw such institutions, and also the WTO and the UN Security Council as candidates for reform to make them more democratically responsive.

In his Political Report Mandela alludes to the dialectic at play in the globalization process in this regard: globalization feeds a consciousness of the world as an interdependent place, with the result that "all major decisions that derive from the system of governance become subject to international review and become dependent for their success on approval and support from an international constituency." In this way, globalization feeds into demands for democratic control beyond the state, which in turn can counterbalance the loss of sovereignty, which ultimately boils down to a loss of democratic control by an electorate over their own destiny. Democratization of the institutions of international governance is thus an important recourse in making up for the loss of sovereignty, the GNU seems to believe.

Let us now turn to the survey results to see how much the perceptions of those members of the opinion élite closest to the GNU, coincide or differ from those of the decision makers. As it turns out, sixty per cent of the respondents did agree (47 per cent) or did strongly agree (13 per cent) that whatever redistributive intentions the GNU may have had, these have been curtailed by financial markets. When recoded into a two-point scale where 2.00 is the value for both agreeing and strongly agreeing, while 1.00 represents disagreeing and strongly disagreeing, the responses for this specific question have a mean of 1.727 for the entire sample, indicating a general tendency to agreement among the opinion élite that financial markets indeed impact on policy autonomy (see Table 9.1). While ANC supporters who are not members of COSATU tend to emphasise both the "amorphous financial markets" and the IFIs, COSATU members seem to be much more concerned specifically about the influence of the World Bank and the International Monetary Fund.

Table 9.1 Mean Scores for Two Questions (V217 & V218) by Party Support and by Positional Sector, 1997-1998

Party/Sector	Mean 217	Mean 218	St dev. V217	St dev. V218
ANC	1.642	1.628	.480	.484
NP	1.817	1.305	.388	.462
DP	1.825	1.516	.382	.503
Parliament	1.777	1.470	.418	.501
NCOP	1.846	1.375	.375	.500
Media	1.741	1.225	.444	.425
Prov. Gov.	1.666	1.272	.481	.455
Civil Service	1.685	1.561	.467	.499
SAPS	1.804	1.365	.401	.486
Business	1.810	1.610	.395	.491
SANDF	1.863	1.478	.351	.510
Trade Unions	1.418	1.702	.499	.462
Entire sample	**1.727**	**1.488**	**.446**	**.5004**

V217 = Question: agree or disagree with the statement that GEAR would have been more redistributive if it was not for the influence of markets. Values = 1.00 disagree and disagree strongly; 2.00 = agree and agree strongly.

V218 = Which group or institution has the biggest influence on GNU's economic policy? (1.00 = domestic, i.e. trade unions, academics, business; 2.00 = international, i.e. IFIs, and international financial markets.

The GNU policy élite tend to agree that some sovereignty has been lost to forces external to South Africa. In the case of GNU decision-makers, this perception leads to two policy initiatives. The one is a resolve to play a more active role in attempting to reform international institutions to offset the sovereignty deficit and some other negative features of globalization. On the other hand, this perception can also be taken to lie behind the shift of the GNU since 1996 to a macroeconomic profile which is more in line with the expectation of financial markets' actors. In this sense, the decrying of a loss of sovereignty reflects a discursive response to something that is both accepted as largely inevitable, but which is not altogether welcomed. Thus, again, we find evidence not only of a large variety of thinking in ANC circles, but also signs of a fundamental ambiguity in which globalization is both accepted but also resisted.

Re-defining the State, and 'Gambling' on Investment

There is at yet no consensus on what is the best way to describe the form of post-apartheid state that emerged after the 1994 elections. The programme of the GNU did originally display some prominent features of a state which saw its primary function, not in terms of international competition, but as focused on internal restructuring. In the self-conception of the new incumbents — expressed most clearly in the RDP programme — this state had the task of re-integrating South Africa rapidly into the global economy, without relinquishing domestic control over the economy. The RDP programme was thus hardly the socialist document some made it out to be, but neither was it impervious to the redistributive needs of the majority of South Africans (Le Roux 1997). It would be appropriate to see it as an example of the developmental compromise discussed above, that is, where vigorous engagement in the global markets via a strong export drive is the main modus of international involvement, but where additional external liabilities and exposure is limited, and domestically oriented infrastructural, redistributive, and human-resources programmes are instituted. All these elements were, in one way or another, present in the RDP programme.

By 1996, however, some of the emphases in the GNU programme had shifted, while one aspect that was very subdued in the RDP suddenly became of major importance. Growth, Employment and Redistribution (GEAR) places much more emphasis on regenerating the competitiveness of the South African economy as a primary vehicle for securing investment, domestic and Federal Direct Investment (FDI), to achieve the ambitious growth targets set by GEAR. While the RDP programme was still very careful about increasing the domestic economy's exposure to international finance, GEAR abandons this caution and envisages a whole series of measures, including cutting the budget deficit, to 'free' up capital for domestic investment,[14] and make South Africa a favourable place for investment.

Now, if this is indeed a significant shift, the question is, of course, what induced it? Again, we do not think this is the place to respond to the debate that is being conducted about the reasons for the presumed shift in emphasis and in substance between the RDP and GEAR (see Adelzadeh 1996, for instance). Nevertheless, it seems important to note that whatever external influences there may have been on the economic thinking of the GNU's decision-makers, there is sufficient evidence to conclude that GEAR is based on a fundamental calculated gamble induced, partly, at least, by the GNU's understanding of globalization and its effects.

The 'GEAR gamble' does not entail a trade-off between redistribution and growth, but rather a recalculation of what would ensure the necessary growth in order to achieve the redistributive goals to which the GNU is still committed, given the perceived constraints imposed by the globalization of financial markets. In terms of this recalculation, a rapid increase in domestic investment, fuelled by domestic capital that was previously 'crowded out' by state dissaving, and crucially, *by the inflow of foreign direct investment funds*,[15] could be secured if the GNU exploited the classification of South Africa as an emerging market — and one regarded as a big emerging market by the USA, to boot — and rapidly took the measures demanded by the neoliberal consensus to attract foreign investment in the extremely competitive global capital market.

Does this bargain amount to a transformation of the South African state into a competition state (Cerny, 1997)? On the basis of the data that we have available, our answer must be yes and no. Yes, because it is indeed clear that the GNU sees an internationally competitive South Africa as a pre-condition for any of its other, redistributively oriented policies. As a 1996 ANC discussion document on "The State and Social Transformation" states:

> The freer and more rapid movement of capital across national boundaries has been described as a process of globalization of the economy, one of whose effects is to reduce the sovereign capacity of states to take decisions without consideration of, and inserting such decisions within the context of the world situation as a whole. (At the same time) the democratic state has got a developmental and a transformative responsibility . . . . . This responsibility would be impossible without a similarly continuous process of increasing productive investment in the economy . . . Objectively, this places the process of investment, as an inalienable component part of development, formally among the historic driving forces of progressive social change and transformation (*African Communist*, 1st quarter 1997, 48-49).

Now, there is no way in which we can determine whether this somewhat laborious ideological justification of investment-friendly policies is shared by members of the GNU. What we can show, however, is that there is indeed moderate to strong support among ANC supporters in our élite sample for investment friendly policies. Table 9.2 contains a means summary of responses to a number of questions that we posed in terms of what we call an *investment-friendly liberalisation index*. Answers to these questions were recorded on a five-point scale with values ranging from –2.00 (strongly against investment friendly liberalisation) to 2.00 (strongly in favour). The value zero represents uncertain responses.

Table 9.2 Investor-friendly Liberalisation Index (S.A.)

		Ent[1]	Dev[2]	ANC	Dev[3]	TU	Bus
V73	'The government should play a smaller role in the regulation of the economy'	.340	1.29	-.639	1.10	-.938	1.03
V78	'The lowering of tariffs on imported goods should be done more rapidly'	.408	1.12	.032	1.23	-1.10	.640
V81	'The labour market must be made more flexible'	.962	.931	.516	1.10	-.40	1.48
V82	'The budget deficit must be reduced'	1.32	.732	1.17	.877	.740	1.35
V87	'Exchange controls must be done away with'	.377	1.13	-.152	1.13	-1.00	1.35
V102	'Incentives for foreign investors (should be provided)'	1.04	.971	.810	1.07	-.062	.899
V115	'More industries should be privatised	.664	1.26	-.07	1.22	-.920	1.32
Average investor-friendly index		**.730**	**1.06**	**.238**	**1.10**	**-.525**	**1.15**

Notes: 1 Entire sample; 2 Standard deviation for entire sample;
3 Standard deviation for ANC

What is notable is that the combined mean for ANC supporters on the index as a whole lies on the positive side of the spectrum, but is much lower than that of the business sector (regarded here as a benchmark of investor-friendly preferences). On the other hand, there is some distance between ANC and COSATU thinking.

However, when it comes to responses concerning question V102, namely whether there is agreement or not that incentives for foreign investors should be provided, there is very little to choose between the average responses from ANC supporters (mean = 0.81) and the business sector (mean = 0.89). The same applies to a question on reducing the budget deficit (V82), another issue which has featured centrally in the debate about investor-friendly measures. In other words, here we have some evidence that the belief-framework of the competition state has taken hold of a cross section of the GNU, with the exception of COSATU, who strongly resist investor friendly policy measures.

Over and against this evidence concerning the popularity of investor-friendly thinking in the GNU, stands evidence that the conceptual shift to the 'competition state' is neither total nor complete. Moreover, the degree of variation among ANC supporters is quite large compared to the standard deviation for the sample as a whole. ANC supporters seems to have widely divergent opinions on the lifting of exchange controls, the lowering of tariffs, and also on providing incentives for foreign investors. All of this confirms the general assumption that the ANC is a very broad church, even if one filters out the outlier effects caused by COSATU.

A second reason why it is premature to speak of a conceptual shift towards the competition state in the GNU is the fact that there is still a strong element of support for measures of redistributive state-intervention as was broadly foreseen by the RDP programme.

Table 9.3 contains a summary of the results obtained in terms of a *state-based redistributive index* used in our survey. The spectrum of values used is reversed in comparison with that used in Table 9.2, which means that a negative score in Table 9.3 corresponds with a positive score in Table 9.2. This reversal allows us to combine the two tables and come up with a set of means which then allows us to plot the thinking of groups of respondents on a liberalisation — regulation spectrum. In terms of this, ANC supporters occupy a very centrist position on the spectrum, with on average a slight predisposition against state-based regulation, but nevertheless with a moderate commitment to redistributive measures such as progressive taxation on wealth.

166 *Globalization and Emerging Trends*

Table 9.3 State-based Redistributive Index (S.A.)

		Ent[1]	Dev[2]	ANC	Dev[3]	TU	Bus
V69	'Banks should be nationalised'	1.16	1.15	.428	1.29	-.510	1.77
V74	'More private industries should be controlled by the state'	1.07	1.11	.407	.19	-.510	1.62
V89	'(There should be) a fixed minimum wage'	.11	1.31	-.588	1.19	-.958	1.04
V95	'(There should be) increased government control of the Reserve Bank' (reversed)	.42	1.35	-.583	1.20	1.58	1.42
V98	'(There should be) taxation of wealth'	.35	1.39	-.810	1.12	-1.52	1.30
V101	'(There should be) higher taxation of of corporate profits'	.06	1.32	-.833	1.14	-1.54	1.41
V103	'(There should be) progressive taxation of personal income'	-.36	1.06	-.683	.99	-.833	-.142
Totals		2.81	8.69	-2.66	7.12	-7.451	8.418
Averages for state-based redistributive index		0.40	1.24	-0.38	1.01	-1.06	1.20
Averages Table 4		.730	1.06	.238	1.10	-.525	1.15
Indices average = investor-friendly + 0.56			1.15	-0.071	1.05	-1.58	1.18
State-based redistributive index/2	5						

Notes: 1 Entire sample; 2 Standard deviation for entire sample;
       3 Standard deviation for ANC

Thus, what emerges from the discussion in this section is that the policy élite most closely identified with the GNU clearly has not taken leave of the redistributive goals of the RDP; at the same time they display a strong predilection in favour of investor-friendly policies as a means of building the material conditions to achieve those goals. This conclusion, we believe, sheds some new light on the specific policy initiatives taken by the GNU. In the concluding section, we set out some of the implications of our approach and our findings for some of the policy initiatives supported by the GNU.

Conclusions: Globalization and South African Middle-Powermanship

There is a close affinity between middle powers and multilateralism. "At its core," writes Cooper, "the concept of middle-power diplomacy signified a certain content of foreign policy based on an attachment to multilateral institutions and a collaborative world order" (1997a, 4). Keohane (1969, 296) also notes that "a middle power is a state whose leaders consider that it cannot act alone effectively but may be able to have a systematic impact in a small group or through an international institution." Accordingly, middle power activity is characterised by a tendency to pursue multilateral solutions to vexing international issues and a tendency to embrace compromise positions in international disputes (Cooper, Higgott and Nossal 1993, 19). Cox adds to this by asking: "how does the position of a purported middle power in the international political economy determine what it is doing?" He does not conceive of a middle power as "a fixed universal" but as something that "has to be rethought in the context of the changing state of the international system" (1989, 825). Moreover, the middle power's interest is "to support this process, whether in the context of a hegemonic order or — even more vitally — in the absence of hegemony" (Cox 1989, 825).

Three approaches have constituted the basis for the development of middle power internationalism since the Second World War. According to Cox, these are their interests in and approaches to the following: world order (i.e. the broader political environment); the sphere of production (i.e. the international political economy) including the economic and social forces it generates; and the nature or complexity of the dominant values, social forces and institutions embedded in their state-society complexes. The first two dimensions, the nature of the politico-strategic world order and international political economy, generated a fairly consistent interest among middle sized Western states in finding internationalist solutions through order-building and crisis-management mechanisms. Their own dominant values, material capabilities and interests created the will and capacity to actively pursue their internationalist interests (Black 1997, 139). It is important to note that internal societal forces may prompt engagement by middle powers and that "there is a potentially important role for capable middle powers with appropriate skills levels to build trans-governmental and transnational coalitions to facilitate policy co-ordination in important issue areas on the international agenda after hegemony" (Cooper, Higgott and Nossal 1993, 26).

Although these conditions also apply to 'emerging' middle powers — i.e. those in the developing world — there is a notable deficiency in the literature to distinguish between 'traditional' or 'established' middle powers in the industrialised Western world and 'emerging' middle powers in the South. The following are therefore preliminary suggestions:

- Past experience suggests that both the nature of the international system and the kind of internal pressures with which developing countries have to contend often dictate the nature of, and degree to which, emerging middle power activism can be sustained.
- The interests of middle powers of the South are often in conflict with those of the prevailing order because of the specific structural position that the middle power occupies in the global division of labour, and/or the specific values embedded in the state-society complex of that country. However, middle powers in the South are usually already incorporated into the specific division of labour and exit is not an option. Although this structural position, as we said before, does not of itself explain behaviour, it becomes an active motivational factor if internalised by a large enough group of the policy élite of a state. The result is that middle powers of the South are reformist (and not transformative) actors, also with respect to the procedures and rules of multilateral institutions themselves, because they believe that they have few other options. This is sometimes complemented by a tactical exploitation of the opportunities offered by multilateralism to advance specific interests. Such middle powers normally do not question the fundamental set of norms and values embodied in these institutions or regimes, but only try to achieve a better deal for themselves (and, on occasion, for the South as a whole) within these.
- What has been said above implies an ambiguous relationship between the emerging middle powers in the South and the USA as the main beneficiary and custodian of the current hegemonic world order. Because of its own societal interests, national goals, reformist ambitions, and/or desire to achieve credibility among its peers, the emerging middle powers may find it necessary to oppose the hegemon. Sometimes, the hegemon welcomes such 'independent behaviour' because it increases the legitimacy of the emerging middle powers, which is a resource that the hegemon can call on when it wants to use the middle powers to implement or support certain fundamental hegemonic system norms. Because of the relational and structural power of the hegemon, independent, reformist behaviour of the Southern middle powers can be sustained only if the issue at stake is not central to the relationship between

the middle powers and the hegemon. On this score, established middle powers of the North may have relatively more room for manoeuvre than emerging middle powers.
- Like middle powers in the North, those emerging in the South also focus on multilateral institutions as useful vehicles for their interests, because these institutions, dominated though they might be by the G-7 — and the USA in particular — do provide opportunities for refracting the hegemony of the big powers, and for forming and leading coalitions of states from the South in opposing the hegemon(s). Middle powers in the South therefore tend to play significant roles within the UN system, and because of that usually aspire to a higher level of representation within that body than is possible at present (viz. their support for reform of the Security Council). Middle powers in the Third World are also likely to be prominent members of the Non-Aligned Movement (NAM).
- Unlike traditional middle powers, those in the developing world tend to be regionally dominant. However, mere regional dominance does not suffice for middle power status, but rather involvement and leadership in both independent as well multilateral initiatives beyond its immediate regional domain.

South African foreign policy behaviour during the Mandela era (and beyond) fits the expectations of this deductive model very well. In terms of the explanation developed here, South Africa's commitment to multilateralism is qualified by the policy élite's conception of the country's position within a globalizing economy. One one hand, globalization is perceived as presenting options for attracting foreign investment, if only the main suppliers of such investment can be attracted in sufficient numbers. Proving itself to be a good citizen, and to be seen to endorse the fundamental (hegemonic) values of the current world order, were important steps for the new South Africa in its gamble on investment. With increasing exposure to investment-related thinking came an acceptance that a precondition for the exploitation of perceived opportunities is the introduction of investment-friendly macro-economic policies. Furthermore, the stated perception of loss of sovereignty served to rhetorically justify the inevitable departure from more 'populist' macro-economic policies proposed prior to GEAR in terms of the constraints that globalization places on decision makers.

On the other hand, globalization is perceived to be restricting the policy choices available, and, and to be at odds with some of the original redistributive intentions of the GNU. This perception, increasingly during the Mandela era, motivated the GNU policy élite to explore opportunities provided by multilateral institutions to push out the perceived limits. In addition, commitment to 'reformist' projects in international affairs — as long as they did not harm the central relationship with the main potential suppliers of investment capital — provided a means to both reflect and deflect the remaining redistributive goals within the policy élite and its allies.

Thus, the GNU also tried to balance the 'inevitable' investor-friendly measures by maintaining a core of redistributive goals, and by embarking on declaratory programmes of promoting change in the institutions of global governance. This latter commitment to reform of multilateral institutions was strongly expressed by Mandela during one of the most important policy speeches he has ever made, namely his Political Report at the 50th National Conference of the ANC in December 1997. It also formed the core of Mbeki's opening speech at the 12th NAM Summit on 31 August 1998. In terms of the argument presented here, such reformist commitments are a way of deflecting the perceived effects of globalization on the South African state, and of displaying a commitment to change for the sake of domestic coalition partners to the left. This also provides a way of critically engaging (at times de-legitimising) the USA and the hegemonic norms in the global political economy, without confronting the hegemon on issues fundamental to the bilateral relationship between the USA and South Africa.

Notes

1   This belief was actively promoted by the Clinton administration, and in particular by its Secretary of the Treasury, Rubin, whose main contribution to the first Clinton term was to open emerging markets for US investment.
2   During the first few months of the 'Mbeki era,' no fundamental change in the patterns described here could be identified, except that Mbeki is steadily developing into something of a spokesperson for the (presumed) benefits of globalization. See his address to the 35th Summit of the OAU in Algiers, July 1999.
3   This we take to be one of the fundamental legacies of Max Weber to the social sciences. For a general discussion of the social scientific debates about meaning, structure and subjectivity, see Hall (1993).
4   See Nel (1992) for a conceptual distinction between perceptions, beliefs, and attitudes, and for a model of how these cognitive dimensions are related.
5   As Kotzé has argued (1992, 1-16), the specific nature of the transition in South Africa makes the élite extremely important actors in the determining of public policy and no study of official responses can ignore the views of those who hold senior positions in the legislature and in the civil service. But the élite, inside and outside of government, also represents what can be called the first line of policy input and policy legitimisation (and de-legitimisation), and their views — wide-ranging and contradictory though they might be — provide crucial insights into the boader normative and ideological cohesion (or absence of it) in the ruling segments of society.

6 The sample was drawn using the positional approach. That is, individuals occupying the highest positions in key sectors of South African society were selected. Data gathering was done by means of structured questionnaires that were mailed to all the respondents, with the exception of the labour sector. Two follow-up waves of mailed questionnaires were sent in order to boost the response rate. The labour sector comprises COSATU and its affiliates. Markinor conducted face-to-face interviews with all the labour sector respondents.
7 See Vusi Mavimbela, "Be grateful unions are as strong as they are." *Sunday Times* 10.1.1997.
8 See "Report on the visit of Executive Deputy President T. M. Mbeki to Davos, Switzerland, 30 January to 2 February 1997," issued by the SA Communication Service. See also Jim Jones, "Other issues push Africa into background," *Business Day* 5.2.1997.
9 "Statement by South Africa's Minister of Labour, Tito Mboweni, to the 85th Session of the International Labour Conference in Geneva, 13.6.1997.
10 See "Signs of African recovery: Erwin." *The Citizen* 7.3.1997; and Opening Address by Deputy President Mbeki at the launch of the Information Society and Development Conference, 13-15.5.1996.
11 See Mbeki's speech at Davos, February 1997.
12 See Bond (1998) for a discussion of the evolution of the relationship between the GNU and the IFIs. See also the very guarded and apprehensive approach taken by the RDP programme document towards SA–IFI relations (para. 6.5.16).
13 ANC Daily Briefing, 24 June 1998 (www.anc.org.za/ancdocs/briefing).
14 For an analysis of the argument implicit in GEAR that the state is "crowding out" capital, see Adelzadeh (1996).
15 For the official GNU argument in favour of attracting foreign investment, see the budget-vote address of the Minister of Finance, Trevor Manuel, on 14.6.1996. This address launched GEAR as the official macro-economic policy of the GNU.

References

Adelzadeh, A. (1996) "From the RDP to GEAR: the Gradual Embracing of Neo-liberalism in Economic Policy." *Transformation* 31: 66-95.
Bond, P. (1998) *South Africa, the NAM and the Bretton Woods Institutions*. Paper delivered to a Foundation for Global Dialogue Workshop on "South Africa and the NAM in an Era of Regionalisation and Globalization," Pretoria, 30.4.1998.
Cerny, P. (1997) "Paradoxes of the Competition State: the Dynamics of Political Globalization." *Government and Opposition* 32.2: 251–274.
Cox, R. (1994) "Global Restructuring: Making Sense of the Changing International Political Economy." *Political Economy and the Changing Global Order.* Ed. R. Stubbs and R. Underhill. Toronto: McClelland & Stewart. 45-59.
Cronin, J. (no date) "Globalization – What Possibilities for a Counter-offensive? An SACP Perspective." Unpublished discussion document.
Debate Members (1997) "Resistance to Neoliberalism: a View from South Africa." *Debate: Voices from the South African Left* 1: 68–81.
Desler, D. (1989) "What is at Stake in the Agent-structure Debate?" *International Organization* 43.3: 441–473.
Freedman, J., D. Seras, and J. Carlsmith. (1978) *Social Psychology*. Englewood Cliffs: Prentice Hall.

GEAR. (1996) *Growth, Employment and Redistribution: a Macro-economic Strategy.*
Habib, A. (1997) "From Pluralism to Corporatism: South Africa's Labour Relations in Transition." *Politikon* 24.1: 57–75.
Habib, A., D. Pillay and A. Desai. (1998) "South Africa and the Global Order: the Structural Conditioning of a Transition to Democracy." *Journal of Contemporary African Studies* 16.1: 95–116.
Hall, J. (1993) "Ideas and the Social Sciences." *Ideas and Foreign Policy: Beliefs, Institutions, and Political Change.* Ed. J. Goldstein and R. Keohane. Ithaca: Cornell University Press. 31–54.
Harris, L. and J. Michie. (1998) "The Effects of Globalization on Policy Formation in South Africa." *Globalization and Progressive Economic Policy.* Ed. D. Baker, G. Epstein and R. Pollin. Cambridge: Cambridge University Press. 413–431.
Higley, J. et al. (1991) "Elite Integration in Stable Democracies: a Reconsideration." *European Sociological Review* 7.1.
Hirst, P. (1997) "The Global Economy: Myths and Realities." *International Affairs* 73.3: 409–425.
Hirst, P. and G. Thompson. (1996) *Globalization in Question.* Cambridge: Polity Press.
Hurrell, A. and N. Woods. (1995) "Globalization and Inequality." *Millennium: Journal of International Studies* 24.3: 447–470.
Jackson, R. (1990) *Quasi-States: Sovereignty, International Relations, and the Third World.* Cambridge: Cambridge University Press.
Kotzé, H. (1992) *Transitional Politics in South Africa: An Attitude Survey of Opinion Leaders.* Centre for International and Comparative Politics Research Report No. 3 of 1992.
Krasner, S. (1996) "Compromising Westphalia." *International Security* 20.3: 115–151.
Le Roux, P. (1997) "The Growth, Employment and Redistribution Strategy (GEAR): a Critical Discussion." *Africanus* 27.2:45–66.
Marais, H. (1998) *South Africa: Limits to Change.* Cape Town: University of Cape Town Press.
McGrew, A. (1998) "The Globalization Debate: Putting the Advanced Capitalist State in its Place." *Global Society* 12.3.
Nattrass, N. (1996) "Gambling on Investment: Competing Economic Strategies in South Africa." *Transformation* 31.
Nel, P. (1992) *Perception, Images and Stereotypes in Soviet-South African Relations — A Cognitive-Interpretive Perspective.* Annale van die Universiteit van Stellenbosch 4/1992.
Nel, P., J. Van der Westhuizen, J. Cornelissen, and B. Ratshilumela. (1998) "En route to the Competition State? The South African Policy Elite and Globalisation." Report prepared for the CSD (HSRC) programme on Global Trends and Social Transformation, Stellenbosch.
Pillay, D. (1998) "Globalization: a Terrain of Struggle." Paper given at a workshop on the Non-Aligned Movement by the Parliamentary Portfolio Committee on Foreign Affairs, Cape Town, 19.6.1998.
South Africa Foundation. (1996) *Growth For All — An Economic Strategy for South Africa.* Johannesburg: SA Foundation.
Sprout, M. and H. Sprout. (1957) "Environmental Factors in the Study of International Relations." *Journal of Conflict Resolution* 1: 309-328.
Stallings, B. (1992) "International Influence on Economic Policy: Debt, Stabilization, and Structural Reform." *The Politics of Structural Adjustment.* Ed. S. Haggard and R. Kaufman. Princeton: Princeton University Press: 41–88.
Strange, S. (1990) "The Name of the Game." *Sea Changes: American Foreign Policy in a World Transformed.* Ed. N. Rizopolous. New York: Council on Foreign Relations.
Strange, S. (1996) *The Retreat of the State: The Diffusion of Power in the World Economy.* Cambridge: Cambridge University Press.
Tilly, C. (1995) "Globalization Threatens Labor's Rights." *International Labor and Working-Class History* 47. 1–23.
UNCTAD. (1997) *Trade and Development Report, 1997.* New York: United Nations.

10 Facing the New Millennium: South Africa's Foreign Policy in a Globalizing World

GARTH LE PERE AND ANTHONI VAN NIEUWKERK

Post-apartheid South Africa has emerged in a changed and uncertain world, marked by contradictory tendencies and impulses. There is, on the one hand, "the grim prospect of a retribalisation of large swathes of humankind by war and bloodshed" and on the other, "a busy portrait of onrushing economic, technological and ecological forces that demand integration and uniformity" (Barber 1995, 4). In this struggle between the parochial and the universal, the classical notion of the nation-state is under siege. The grim imagery of fratricidal war in places as diverse as Bosnia, Chechnya, Somalia, Sierra Leone, Burundi, Sri Lanka and Kashmir demonstrates the potency of communities of blood and ethnicity rooted in exclusion and hatred. Besides having to contend with the centripetal tendencies associated with communal strife and ethnic persecution, there are globalizing capitalist forces trampling borders in search of consumers and profit. This has been hastened by rapid advances in communications and technological innovation.

It is against this backdrop that South Africa has to attempt to build its own democratic institutions and a new civic culture out of previously narrowly prescribed racial categories and communal memberships. The challenge since the first democratic elections of 1994 essentially comes down to constructing a new South African nation out of the tragic history of apartheid rule. It is a history informed by an oppressive state apparatus, waves of school, bus and local election boycotts, marches and civil disorders, murder of political activists, work stoppages and strikes, and direct confrontations with the police and the army. The country's nation-building challenges thus take place on the foundations of a bitter legacy. Successive apartheid regimes resorted to coercion and state violence in order to enforce what was universally condemned as illegitimate white minority rule (Magubane 1979, 323-30). Ethnic and racial communities were systematically disassociated into separate existential enclaves within a broad separatist statutory and discriminatory legal framework. Rather than being representative in nature, the apartheid state embodied the instrumental architecture of domination. For the excluded majority, political life had no real meaning—it was without rights, citizenship and inclusive civil institutions.

The plaudits hailing South Africa's negotiated political settlement and peaceful transition in 1994 are thus lyrical, to say the least. Given dour predictions of a racial civil war and harbingers of an apocalyptic future, its transition has been extolled as "one of the most extraordinary political transformations of the twentieth century".[1] The most liberal of constitutions replaces the narrow hegemony of apartheid and forms the backdrop against which the new African National Congress (ANC) leadership attempts to universalise the state, its institutions and civil society. New images are being advanced which stress the market, democratic institutions, individual liberties, human rights, rationality in public policy, inclusive norms and values and a common national identity (Marais 1998, 83-93). The struggle, however, is far from over. The evolution of an overarching and inclusive national identity must contend with potent forces of the country's past. Government strategies and policies aimed at promoting the new politics of non-racialism must do battle with particular visions and claims that reinforce old social and racial divisions.

The government's policies must also deal with a radically altered world order wherein it has to find appropriate niches and mould new foreign policy instruments to confront the challenges of globalization and its many manifestations. This chapter will examine the processes, institutions and actors which govern and determine the manner in which foreign policy has been made in South Africa since 1994.

Foreign Policy in the Mandela Years, 1994–1999

Once the ANC assumed power after April 1994, it had to come to terms with what amounted to a double transition. Firstly, there was the imperative to refocus philosophically and readjust politically from being 'first among equals' in the liberation movement to becoming the governing political party. The ANC–led Government of National Unity (GNU) had to register a decisive normative and moral break with the past and assume challenging new responsibilities relating to nation-building, democratic governance and institutional restructuring. Secondly, there was the imperative to understand the tectonic shifts in world order, following the collapse of the bipolar world and the end of the Cold War. This meant crafting a foreign policy which, while sensitive to the needs of internal transformation, would nevertheless reflect a recognition of the altered international relations terrain as well as adopting a 'pragmatic internationalism' towards engaging with a globalizing environment. As early as 1993, ANC president Nelson Mandela articulated several principles which would underpin South Africa's future foreign policy (1993, 87). These principles were further elaborated in March, 1994, when the ANC published a comprehensive foreign policy document entitled, "Foreign Policy Perspectives in a Democratic South Africa." This document advances seven principles which ought to guide the conduct of South Africa's new foreign policy:

- a belief in and preoccupation with human rights which extends beyond the political, embracing economic, social and environmental dimensions;
- a belief that just and lasting solutions to the problems of humankind can only come through the promotion of democracy world-wide;
- a belief that justice and international law should guide relations between nations;
- a belief that international peace is the goal towards which all nations should strive;
- a belief that South Africa's foreign policy should reflect the interests of Africa;
- a belief that South Africa's economic development depends on growing regional and international economic cooperation; and
- a belief that South Africa's foreign relations must mirror a deep commitment to the consolidation of its democracy.

For the ANC, the struggle for an apartheid-free South Africa was in many ways a struggle for fundamental human rights. It is no coincidence, therefore, that human rights are canonised as a cornerstone in its foreign policy. Furthermore, the emphasis on the promotion of democracy and adherence to international law embodies the values and norms enshrined in South Africa's new constitution. It is also worth noting that South Africa's neighbours suffered immeasurable harm in aiding and supporting the struggle for liberation. A range of African countries also provided the ANC with material support and formal diplomatic recognition while in exile. Much of the continent thus enjoyed a special relationship with the ANC and *vice versa* and Africa's elevation to a foreign policy priority is thus not surprising. There was a certain symmetry between the ethical and normative constructs of the ANC's domestic policies and the idealist foundations of its foreign policy in this period. The domestic public policy emphasis on democracy, justice and human rights was refracted in the above foreign policy principles. The government's initial economic framework, called the Reconstruction and Development Programme (RDP) for example, also referred to the importance of rebuilding the South African economy in partnership with its regional neighbours and the necessity for integrating trade and foreign policy as part of a broader strategic approach for strengthening South-South cooperation.

The *leitmotif* governing South Africa's foreign policy has been labelled 'universality,' essentially the opening of foreign and local doors in the same reconciliatory spirit that has characterised its own domestic transformation. The noble intentions and the affirmation of certain values in its foreign policy notwithstanding, their realisation and implementation in practice has proven to be an ongoing dilemma and a vexing problem. In the view of one analyst, South Africa's "... foreign relations could be said to be lacking the necessary broad orientation and strategic purpose" (Mills 1997, 19). In many respects the Department of Foreign Affairs (DFA) in the Mandela era was a prisoner of the past. The previous regime used and abused it to advance its apartheid policies. By the late 80s, the white, Afrikaner, male-dominated department became closely involved in the activities of the State Security Council, resulting in the department being relegated to an implementing instrument — whether in sanctions-busting operations, or ominously, in the security forces' regional destabilisation policies. By the time negotiations started on a new dispensation, between 1990 and 1994, the department was caught up in a complex process of restructuring. The challenge was twofold: absorbing the African National Congress's international affairs personnel, and integrating most of the 'foreign affairs' personnel of the previous four homelands (Evans 1995). Following the 1994 elections, the department then had to rationalise its size and structure in accordance with guidelines from the Public Service Commission.

There was also the political problem of how to deal with tensions between 'old-order' officials and the new cadres from the liberation movements. After 1994, white males continued to dominate top management. As one of the newcomers remarked in an interview, the ANC government "... took over the DFA and other departments as if nothing had changed. We expected Rusty Evans (the then director-general) to miraculously become a new person with new loyalties, but with what authority could he address the

Organisation of African Unity (OAU)?" By all accounts this problem persisted at the highest level and was only resolved in 1998 with the appointment of a new director-general, Jackie Selebi, a seasoned ANC diplomat and close confidant of President Thabo Mbeki.[2]

Currently, the top management of the DFA, the director-general and his deputies, are broadly from the same political school — that of the ANC — and are strategically linked to the real foreign policy power, President Thabo Mbeki. Alfred Nzo was suceeded by Nkosazana Zuma, the former Minister of Health and now one of only thirteen female foreign ministers in the world. She is a surprising choice and one that nobody had foreseen. Can someone with a forceful personality such as hers, and no obvious experience of global affairs and diplomacy, be an effective foreign minister? Two points are worth making. Firstly, as Cornish has argued, her appointment is not so much about diplomacy as it is about delivery: ". . . she has no intention of trying to reinvent the foreign policy wheel. Formulation of that policy is well advanced. It is now time to implement it" (1999). This focus on 'implementation' was emphasised by President Mbeki in his inauguration speech, as well as in his first 'state of the nation' address to Parliament in June 1999. It is further underscored by the recent restructuring of departmental and other aspects of the executive management of government. Secondly, Zuma is not unfamiliar with the international stage. She had extensive contact with the international community during her time as an ANC representative, and as health minister she interacted both bilaterally and multilaterally with organisations such as the World Health Organisation (WHO) and the South Africa-United States Bi-national Commission.

Because the ANC underestimated the scope and complexity of restructuring, coordinated policy-making and the identification of foreign policy priorities suffered in the early years of its government. This was exacerbated by at least two factors. Firstly, there was tense competition and conflict between different centres of foreign policy decision-making. These included, until 1999, the president and deputy president's office; other departments such as trade and industry and defence; and the partly restructured foreign ministry staffed by a significant number of senior 'old order' bureaucrats. Parliament and civil society generally felt marginalised in the process. As the foreign minister and his energetic but over-stretched deputy minister battled to develop an ANC–oriented foreign policy approach, they discovered that the department had to rely on old-order bureaucrats for foreign policy implementation. The telling illustration of this dilemma had to do with South Africa's seeming inability to resolve the so-called 'Two-

Chinas' dilemma. After 1994, many in the ANC alliance urged the government to confront what was seen as the folly of maintaining full diplomatic relations with Taiwan. However President Mandela relied on the then director-general of foreign affairs for advice on this matter, who strongly promoted the interests of Taiwan — an old friend of the Nationalist government, after all. It took the ANC a full three years to break the stranglehold of Evans over President Mandela.[3]

The second factor has to do with the quick separation of theorists and practitioners. Soon after taking power, the ANC's foreign policy-makers seemingly disengaged from their academic support base (primarily those responsible for developing the ANC's foreign policy template in 1994). What has happened in foreign policy circles may be related to a general post-1990s trend, namely, a marked shift to policy research in the post-1990 period which undermined the quantity and quality of critical radical scholarship. As Habib argues, ". . . post-apartheid South Africa has not taken kindly to critical scrutiny. Left-leaning scholars and activists are encouraged to raise criticisms in-house. Harsh responses to critics have discouraged most Congress-aligned scholars and activists from engaging in any form of public scrutiny (of the transition). Given this, criticism has become the preserve of mainsteam and conservative scholars" (1998). The implications of this fragmentation were perhaps felt mostly by the ANC's international relations department which, in the post-1994 period, appeared leaderless and adrift.

As a result of these and other factors, the South African government has made a number of foreign policy somersaults. In 1996, it was challenged to respond to the Abacha regime's violent excesses in Nigeria. It stumbled from one clumsy approach to another (Van Aardt 1996). It called for sanctions against the Abacha junta, only to discover that in Africa it stood alone. Stung by criticism that it was following Western agendas and being 'unAfrican' (meaning African brothers do not sort out differences on the world stage), a new approach was adopted: that of 'quiet diplomacy.' This enraged human rights activists in South Africa, Nigeria and elsewhere in the world. Dealing with Asia also proved problematic. The 'Two China' standoff has been described above. In the course of his state visit to Indonesia and East Timor in 1997, President Mandela courageously demanded to see and succeeded in visiting Xanana Gusmao (the jailed East Timor independence advocate). However, in a curious twist of logic, he awarded Indonesia's supreme autocrat, President Suharto, with South Africa's highest award for non-citizens. Foreign affairs personnel afterwards awkwardly tried to explain this away by insisting that this was how 'quiet diplomacy' was conducted; and that the government was in any case merely supporting efforts by the United Nations (UN) to resolve the East Timorese crisis (Lambert 1998, 6-13).

However, most of this paled in comparison to the government's apparent double standards on arms sales. Policy on China, Nigeria, East Timor and elsewhere might be described as 'honest mistakes,' and as awkward foreign policy responses to complex situations made by an inexperienced administration burdened by various internal processes of transformation. Selling deadly weapons to governing élites embroiled in civil war or in violent confrontation with their neighbours is another matter altogether. In such cases weapons are knowingly marketed and sold for profit only. Sadly, foreign policy considerations such as respect for human rights, regional stability and the like become relative values in concluding multi-million rand arms deals. As Minister Selebi once pointed out, foreign policy is about making choices, and for him the approach is to sell arms but not to use human rights as a conditionality for trade (Van Nieuwkerk 1999).

Indeed, during this phase it appeared as if the ANC's earlier *idealist* foreign policy was in the process of being challenged by another approach: so-called *neoliberalism*. This is an approach which advises foreign policy-makers firstly to listen to (and obey) the globalizing free market dogma and only then to pay attention to the issues of human rights and democracy (a useful neo-liberal policy guideline: 'do good — if it's cheap'). As a keen advocate of this approach, Mills has argued that because "the world does not know how to create democracies" and since "no country has been able to promote democracy and human rights values effectively," and given the lack of "human and political capital to expend on this issue at the expense of national imperatives," South Africa (the state and business) should rather work on developing a commercially-driven foreign policy strategy (1999). Thus, it would focus on economic growth and reducing unemployment. In this reading, South Africa should "take maximum advantage of its strength in the global and regional economies," by developing strategies which will produce better terms of trade, investment and aid. Such an approach leads to a straightforward, uncomplicated view of South Africa's relations with Africa, which is "about making the continent safe to do business." The DFA appears to have developed a more nuanced understanding of the dilemma. In its interpretation, neoliberalism demands the shifting of issues of human rights and democracy from the bilateral to the multilateral agendas of the South African Development Community (SADC), OAU, and the UN and perhaps also of the United Nations Conference on Trade and Development (UNCTAD) and the Non-Aligned Movement (NAM). Therefore, the active

Figure 10.1 South African Foreign Policy-making Environments

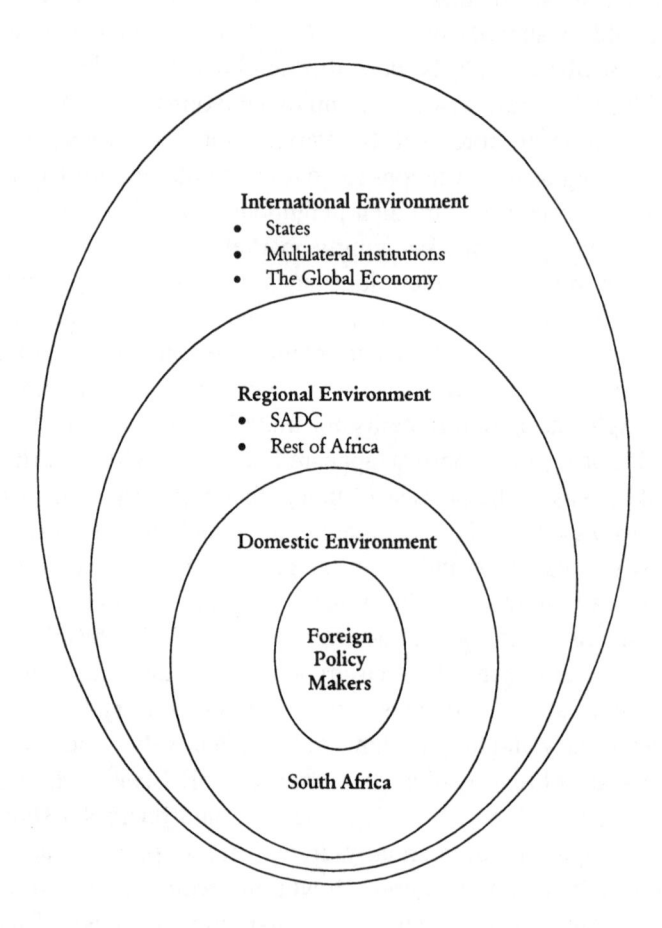

International Environment
- States
- Multilateral institutions
- The Global Economy

Regional Environment
- SADC
- Rest of Africa

Domestic Environment

Foreign Policy Makers

South Africa

and visible promotion of these issues will have to be judged against the question of whether it will advance or retard potential economic and other gains flowing from the promotion of the country's newly-defined national interest, namely 'wealth creation' and 'security.'

In summary, what does the record show of South Africa's conduct of foreign policy during the Mandela years? The demands of the so-called 'double transition' — managing internal domestic transformation in the context of a rapidly changing globalizing environment — revealed a range of policy-making and capacity (human and institutional) shortcomings. Besides a multiplicity of actors, there are distinct environments which have an impact and an influence on foreign policy making (see Figure 10.1 above). A treatment of these environments and actors now follows.

South African Foreign Policy-Making Environments

The Domestic Environment

The basic objectives of a country's foreign policy are determined within a domestic context. Seen through the prism of ensuring national security, welfare and economic growth, the means of achieving these reside increasingly in the external environment. There are several national factors which are important for a country's foreign policy and these include its history, geostrategic location, economic prowess, military power and resource endowments (Kegley and Wittkopf 1993, 60-70). These taken together permit and constrain a country's ability to act and interact with its external environment.

South Africa's domestic environment has been drastically altered since the formal demise of apartheid following the elections in April, 1994. The domestic imperatives of transforming the society and consolidating democratic gains have to do battle with the ethical and welfare concerns of addressing the historical legacies of apartheid, especially as these affect meeting very basic needs.

Although South Africa dominates the southern African region economically, in global terms it is a middle-income economy and maintains a medium human development ranking on the United Nations Development Programme's index, placing it below Cuba, next to the Dominican Republic and Sri Lanka. This is indicative of the troubling nature of its economic and social base. Its income inequality, which significantly divides the nation into a rich white minority and a poor black majority, is amongst the most severe in the world. South Africa experiences jobless growth, resulting from trade liberalisation and global competition, financial turmoil in emerging markets, a dearth of human resources, and structural deficiencies in its economy. These and other factors have exacerbated a number of negative social trends, such as worsening crime and corruption, as well as serious social disparities — not only between black and white, but also between the new black middle class and a poor uneducated mass, and between urban and rural households.

The South African government's response to the domestic socio-economic challenge was to adjust significantly its earlier Reconstruction and

Development Programme, which focused on poverty reduction. By adopting the neo-liberal macro-economic growth, employment and redistribution strategy, the focus has shifted to structural economic reforms. These include amongst others fiscal reforms, exchange control removal, monetary policy discipline, privatisation, labour market flexibility, tariff reductions and skills development deemed necessary to pursue a growth path which emphasises the systemic adaptability and efficiency of its manufacturing sector. This explains trade and industry minister Alec Erwin's emphasis on export capacity and competitiveness, because ". . . a country cannot industrialise in a global world if it cannot export." Consequently, South Africa has opted to negotiate free trade area agreements with the European Union (EU) and SADC — two of its largest trading partners.

In terms of the re-adjustment of the foreign policy-making machinery, there are at least three outstanding issues:

Firstly, concerning the structure of the department, it went through more-or-less ongoing adjustments until 1994 when it was forced to wrestle with South Africa's readmission into the global community in a more comprehensive manner. It had to open more missions in all major regions of the world, recruit personnel to represent the country at a number of international institutions it was previously barred from, and muster the resources to provide leadership of the SADC, Unctad and the NAM. As from 1999 South Africa now has diplomatic relations with 178 countries (there are 186 states world-wide). It maintains 94 missions abroad, and non-resident representation in 73 countries. Of the 53 countries in Africa, South Africa has official relations with 49 (with offices in 24 of these countries). It maintains 13 missions in Asia and a number of other non-residential accreditations. It has diplomatic relations with all the countries in the Middle East, the Americas and Europe, and maintains non-resident diplomatic relations with 11 of the 14 members states of the Caribbean Community. To undertake this enormous task of representation, the structure at the DFA's head office features five divisions or 'branches': Africa; Asia and the Middle East; Americas and Europe; Multilateral Affairs and Administration. The ongoing question before the department is whether South Africa ought to have missions in all countries, whether the taxpayer can afford it, and whether a more prudent utilisation of missions abroad cannot be achieved. There is also the question of prioritising South Africa's bilateral relations; it appears a process is already under way whereby a select group of countries is given preferential treatment via bi-national commissions. These include India, Japan, the United States, Germany and the United Kingdom. Another instrument in prioritising

South Africa's bilateral relations is what President Mbeki calls a coordinated strategic relationship with the South, involving influential countries such as Brazil and Chile, India, Malaysia, Singapore, the People's Republic of China, and so on.

Secondly, a more urgent question relates to the employment profile of the Department of Foreign Affairs. Perhaps not surprisingly, until 1994 South African ambassadors abroad were white and male. The first female ambassador, Cécile Schmidt, was appointed to Vienna in 1988. In the same year, Annette Joubert[4] became the first female consul-general and head of mission in Glasgow. However, after Cécile Schmidt's retirement in 1992, no female ambassadors were appointed until 1995. What has changed since 1994? Recent research indicates that despite some encouraging developments (the appointment of gender representatives and the establishment of a Women's Human Rights sub-directorate within the department's multilateral branch), gender equality in the DFA has not yet been achieved. The department still carries the label of 'boys' club' (Sadie 1998). Recent statistics (1999) point to a serious imbalance between the sexes at top and middle management levels: 81 percent male against 19 percent female. Current appointments such as Cheryl Carolus, Sheila Sisulu and Thuthukile Mazibuko-Sweyiya as ambassadors to London, Washington and Paris respectively, are good news indeed, but top management posts are still occupied by males. The racial balance also needs serious improvement. Although most of South Africa's career diplomats abroad are now black, the missions are composed of 40 percent black and 60 percent white staff. Matters at head office also need attention: despite the fact that the director-general and his deputies are black, 72 percent of top management (chief director and upwards) are white. There might be light at the end of the tunnel if one considers that at the level of middle management (director) 60 percent of staff are black. This means that over time the DFA will be able to draw the necessary people from this pool of human resources to address the racial imbalances at higher levels.

Thirdly, on the national level, there is departmental competition and contestation about who serves and promotes the interests of the country. In the areas of trade, investment and more generally re-integrating South Africa into the global economy, the departments of trade and industry and finance are leading the way. These challenges demand carefully coordinated, interdepartmental policy responses. However, as the complex negotiations around the Southern Africa Customs Union (SACU), the SADC trade protocol, the Lomé Agreement, and the free trade agreement between South

Africa and the EU demonstrate, the DFA sometimes appears to lack the required insight and influence to make a lasting contribution.[5] The thinly veiled tension between policymakers from the DFA and the Department of Trade and Industry (DTI) damages South Africa's performance in these areas. As a means of resolving this, serious attention should be given to a recent Presidential Review Commission recommendation that foreign affairs and the external trade directorate of DTI be grouped together in one department.

In other areas of South Africa's foreign affairs, the DFA often finds itself eclipsed as well. Consider the government's controversial arms sales record. Sales are regulated by a four-tier system, including a cabinet committee called the National Conventional Arms Control Committee (NCACC), headed by the Minister of Education, Kader Asmal. Some of the criteria to be considered during the decision-making process are the recipient country's record on human rights, as well as existing tension or armed conflicts and the security situation of the recipient country. It is the DFA's responsibility to supply the arms procurement process with such analysis and information. Yet, as recent research has suggested, the DFA's role in the system, although well defined, is regularly marginalised or undermined by the profit motive and the goal of maintaining South Africa's share in the world of the market (Shelton 1998). Consequently South Africa has the dubious record of supplying arms to countries such as Algeria, Rwanda, Congo, and Sudan — a record of which the South African public strongly disapproves (Van Nieuwkerk 1998).

Regarding the question of who makes and coordinates policy, several proposals are in circulation. One — drawn up by the DFA — suggested that the foreign trade promotion function of the Departments of Trade and Industry and Foreign Affairs be merged. Indeed, following a recent policy prioritisation exercise, the DFA wishes to elevate the promotion of trade, foreign direct investment, and science and technology transfer to one of two key foreign policy goals, the other being the promotion of security. It is clear that such reprioritisation — called 'wealth creation' — will impact deeply on departmental structures and activities. Key features of the new vision are the identification of thirteen themes that ought to underline the government's foreign relations, the development of strategies and actions to implement them, and the identification of performance criteria to measure progress. The wealth creation pillar includes: giving human rights their rightful place in international affairs; developing a coordinated approach to globalization; redefining South Africa's interface with international institutions; and attracting foreign direct investment. Security, which is the other central pillar, will be enhanced by promoting justice and compliance with international law; by combating the growth and spread of crime; by promoting stability and economic growth in the region; and by clarifying South Africa's role in conflict resolution and disarmament.

The Regional Environment

South Africa's regional relations have also benefited from its transition. In a rather ironic twist, South Africa has now become the main guarantor of regional security and by its example has strongly promoted regional norms of democracy and human rights. South Africa's destructive campaign of destabilisation and inter-state hostilities during the apartheid era have been replaced by a cooperative philosophy and a professed intention "to become part of a movement to create a new form of economic interaction in the region based on principles of mutual benefit and interdependence" (ANC 1994). The RDP White Paper further enjoined the new government to "negotiate with neighbouring countries to forge an equitable and mutually beneficial programme for increasing co-operation, co-ordination and integration" (RDP White Paper 1994). As a measure of its commitment to regional development, South Africa joined the SADC in 1994.

However, while policy-makers continue to be preoccupied with the demands of domestic restructuring, their stated commitment to regionalism and regional integration in southern Africa is fraught with differing and contradictory interpretations. On the one hand, a more welfarist approach stresses an affirmative action type of intervention by South Africa which will assist underdeveloped countries. At the other extreme are those who advocate an 'open' regionalism based on competition and comparative advantage. South Africa — whether the regional hegemon or partner — is forced to steer a middle path between regional and global pressures for promoting the region's development (Awhireng-Obeng and McGowan 1998). Whatever the case, South Africa's overwhelming economic superiority, and military and political dominance will be a focal point for the region's growth, and its own development, in turn, will prove decisive for the entire region.

The International Environment

South Africa's own transition more or less coincided with major shifts and changes in the global order. The most egregious of these was the disintegration of the Soviet empire and the unprecedented impact of globalization on the world economy. As commonly understood, globalization has resulted in a general decline of state sovereignty and the internationalisation of factors of production and consumption. Unfettered and uncontrollable market forces have become the principal agents and forces of change, further eroding the primacy of states in the world system (Hirst and Thompson, 1996). Anarchic market forces and a globalized world economy have proven to be insensitive to, and even disrespectful of, national development plans and macro-economic strategies.

Developing countries are particularly vulnerable to the pernicious effects of unbridled market forces and even South Africa as a semi-developed country has fallen prey to the 'Asian contagion' and has succumbed to speculative attacks on its currency. This has had dire consequences for its economic prospects. In the face of global market pressures, it has to continue to attract foreign investment, establish globally competitive credentials and commit the country to economic liberalisation by subscribing to the trade rules of the World Trade Organisation (WTO). The international environment forces a difficult set of economic and political circumstances and choices on South Africa such that it faces the spectre of a precipitous and inexorable decline in its position in the world economy. Indeed, according to McGowan (1993, 58), "South Africa will be fortunate to retain a place among the world's semi-peripheral powers over the next twenty years . . . . Rather more likely is a relative descent, so that South Africa will increasingly resemble a big Zimbabwe, at the border between the periphery and semi-periphery." To secure its democratic gains and to further make advances in welfare provision and poverty alleviation, South Africa's foreign policy tools and those who hone them will need to come to terms with these imponderable factors in the international environment. In so doing, an examination is now in order of who the main actors are in South Africa's evolving foreign policy drama.

Foreign Policy Actors

Traditionally, the most important persons involved in a country's foreign affairs are its head of government and the foreign minister. Whether the head of government be president, prime minister or autocrat, that person ". . . is formally the key figure in all foreign policy decisions. According to international law and practice, the head of government, as the political leader of the people, officially speaks for the state in international relations and exercises

Figure 10.2 South African Foreign Policy-making: the Actors

External Environment
States
International Organizations
Global civil society

Domestic Environment

Influences from other state sectors (see text)

Locus of decision-making
OP
DFA CABINET DTI
D&I

Influences from civil society (see text)

Regional Environment
SADC
rest of Africa

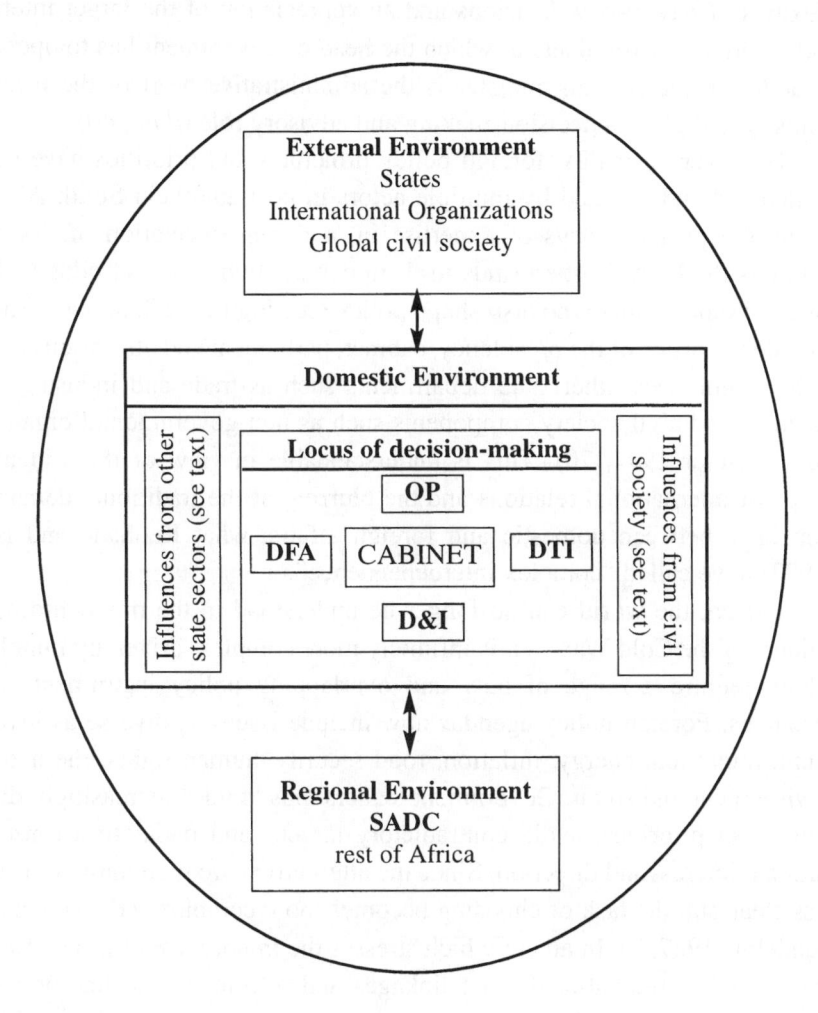

OP   Office of the Presidency
DFA Department of Foreign Affairs
DTI Department of Trade and Industry
D&I The Defence and Intelligence Community
SADC The Southern African Development Community

ultimate authority in the area of foreign policy" (Said *et al.*, 1995, 39). The foreign minister in turn is a specialist with a good technical grasp of the complexities of day-to-day decisions and an appreciation of the larger internal and external environments in which the head of government has to operate. In addition, the foreign minister is the administrative head of the foreign ministry and plays a decision-making and advisory role (*ibid.*, 40).

However, in reality, foreign policy principles and priorities have been formulated and planned by multiple actors in post-apartheid South Africa. While the primary locus of expertise in, and implementation of, foreign policy is the DFA, it often finds itself in competition, if not at odds with a range of other actors who also shape policy (see Figure 10.2, above). These include the office of the presidency, cabinet, parliament and its various oversight committees, other state departments such as trade and industry, and defence, and civil society components such as non-governmental organisations (Muller 1997, 70). This is understandable in view of the widening scope of international relations and the blurring of the traditional demarcation lines between domestic and foreign affairs, what Keohane and Nye (1977) have called "complex interdependence".

Indeed, the world can no longer be understood in the monochromatic colours of the Cold War — it is infinitely more complex, driven by impulses which require a range of new and overlapping policy instruments and resources. Foreign policy agendas now include issues as diverse as investment, migration, energy, inflation, food security, human rights, the natural environment and so on. Government leaders thus "find it increasingly difficult to set priorities, avoid contradictory targets, and maintain a sense of national interest and direction. Since the alternatives are more numerous and less clear-cut, the task of choosing becomes more complex" (Karvonen and Sundelius 1987, 7). In an era which stresses the importance of global financial markets, international trade linkages and information technology, the management of the foreign policy agenda becomes a task for multiple bureaucratic players.

The multiplicity of actors involved in policy formulation in South Africa encourages accusations of incoherence, inconsistency and opaqueness (Muller 1997, 69). Let us examine some of the actors in terms of their place in the policy-making process.

The Department of Foreign Affairs (DFA)

The DFA has been headed since 1999 by Minister Nkosazana Zuma with Aziz Pahad as her deputy. The department can be described as a bureaucratic labyrinth with four main branches: Africa, Asia and the Middle East, Europe and the Americas, and Multilateral Affairs. Of all state departments, its role as the new custodian of foreign policy has been mired in controversy and contestation. To begin with, it inherited a highly fragmented and ideologically polarised staff, and the integration of the old bureaucracy with the new government's corps of officials has not been a smooth process. One view holds that South Africa's foreign policy circles are divided between an 'internationalist' and a 'neo-mercantilist' camp. Officials representing the previous apartheid government belong to the latter group who ". . . consistent with the logic of neo-realism, emphasise the importance of trade and self interest over all else." The 'internationalists' are mainly those who returned from exile or "were in favour of a demonstrably greater degree of solidarity with the collective problems of the developing world . . . " (Van der Westhuizen 1998, 444).

An essential component in a country's foreign policy machinery is its diplomatic service. It is through this medium of communication that countries conduct their relations. Maintaining missions abroad is an expensive business. South Africa's missions vary in size and structure. Its largest embassy is in the United States with 55 staff members (including Consulates-General), followed by the United Kingdom with 40 staff members and Germany with 25. The expenditure priorities on foreign missions in developed countries has not matched South Africa's rhetoric about promoting South-South cooperation as a foreign policy goal. Former chairperson of the parliamentary portfolio committee on foreign affairs, Raymond Suttner, was led to complain in 1995 that "of R645 million budgeted for foreign missions only approximately R105 million was allocated to missions in Africa" (1996, 140).

The President

President Harry Truman, president of the USA from 1945–1952, once remarked that "the President makes foreign policy" (cited in Frankel 1968, 21). In South Africa's case, given President Mandela's towering personality, international prestige and stature, this would not be an inaccurate postulate, both during and after his presidency. His command and seeming domination of every major foreign policy decision and issue was so complete as to almost overshadow the role of the DFA, cabinet and parliament. However, cabinet and to a lesser extent, parliament, maintain checks and balances on presidential authority. Procedurally, the president has to consult and get the approval of cabinet on every major foreign policy decision. This notwithstanding, in the view of Mills, during the Mandela years "it has meant South Africa's image (and its foreign policy) tends largely to be equated with the President's profile. As a result, policy has often followed his public statements, rather than the other way around" (Mills 1997, 24).

President Mandela was a unique figure in South Africa's transition and international relations after 1994. His global statesmanship was primarily responsible for South Africa's rapid reintegration into global affairs. He thus leaves a rich legacy on which his successor, President Mbeki, can build.

The current president himself is also a very skilled diplomat and international statesperson. While in exile, Thabo Mbeki was the ANC's chief diplomat and his outlook is distinctly internationalist. Like President Mandela, he has had an influential hand in fashioning the contours of South Africa's foreign relations. He has, for example, been the prime architect of re-configuring South Africa's relations with the United States and Africa. With regard to the former, President Mbeki is co-chairman with US Vice President Albert Gore of the Bi-National Commission, which meets twice a year to enhance and consolidate the countries' bilateral relations. In Africa, he has articulated a visionary policy framework around the concept of an 'African Renaissance' which advocates a renewal of the continent by seeking African solutions to African problems (Mbeki 1999, 239-251). In addition, the Coordination and Implementation Unit (CIU) in the Office of the Presidency facilitates policy coordination across government. One of four professional units in the CIU is specifically concerned with international relations.

Parliament

Parliament in South Africa is made up of the National Assembly and the National Council of Provinces. The main function of the National Assembly as set out in the constitution is to represent the people by ". . . providing a national forum for public consideration of issues, by passing legislation and by scrutinizing and overseeing executive action." The National Council of Provinces, in turn, represents the interests of the nine provinces at national level and it does so ". . . by participating in the national legislative process and by providing a national forum for public consideration of issues affecting the provinces" (South African Constitution 1996, Article 42). Parliament thus has a distinct constitutional duty in the process of government and "is the pre-eminent institution through which the public expresses its views concerning foreign policy" (Suttner 1996, 136). The role of parliament in foreign policy is important for ratifying treaties and evaluating draft policy documents, for appropriating funds and approving departmental budgets. Furthermore, the parliamentary portfolio committee on foreign affairs is a specialist, activist multi-party body of representatives which must ensure that parliament's oversight and review function is properly executed and that democratic procedures and principles are observed (Calland 1999).

The Department of Trade and Industry (DTI)

Investment and foreign trade, especially gaining preferential access to developed countries' markets, has become an important instrument in South Africa's economic development, its export diversification and industrialisation strategy. As a consequence, since 1994, the DTI has emerged as the chief steward of South Africa's bilateral and multilateral trade diplomacy and it boasts a formidable team of negotiators. It is generally responsible for encouraging foreign direct investment, expanding transnational commerce, negotiating trade deals with countries and regional blocs, and representing the country in multilateral bodies such as the WTO and UNCTAD. It has, for example, developed South Africa's negotiating mandate for a free trade agreement with the 15-member EU which is its largest and most important trading partner (Davies 1997, 104-107). Closer to home, the DTI has been instrumental in the crafting and promotion of a free trade protocol in SADC. Its objective is to introduce a progressive reduction of tariff and non-tariff barriers to trade within the region such that all intra-regional trade is substantially free by 2006 (Mayer 1999, 10-13).

The Defence and Intelligence Community

The role of the military establishment has changed quite fundamentally since 1994. During the apartheid years when concerns about national security and "the total onslaught" were synonymous with defence, the military and its senior officials enjoyed unparalleled influence in shaping policy. Since 1994 the official discourse has embraced a widened, people-centred definition of security which incorporates political, economic, social and environmental dimensions (DoD 1996). The military and the Department of Defence (DoD) have become one of several important, actors in the decision-making process. For instance, as security matters and arms sales have become a more critical feature of South Africa's foreign relations, so has the profile of the DoD become more prominent. In regional security matters, the South African National Defence Force (SANDF) has played a key role in the operational planning of the SADC Organ for Politics, Defence and Security (OPDS) and although far from settled, an increasing role for the SANDF is contemplated in continental peace-keeping, peace-building and conflict prevention.[6]

With regard to arms sales, a cabinet committee was established to guide the terms of the sale and export of conventional arms. As already noted, the National Conventional Arms Control Committee is chaired by a cabinet minister; other members include the ministers of defence; trade and industry; arts, culture, science and technology; constitutional affairs; public enterprises; intelligence services; foreign affairs; and safety and security.

The DoD also represents South Africa where bilateral defence matters are concerned. Thus for example, the defence minister represents South Africa on a sub-committee dealing with defence and security at the US-South Africa Bi-national Commission.

Intelligence services acquire information which might be deemed important for a country's decision making processes and national security. Military intelligence tends to be highly centralised, concentrated as it is around its respective branches and it is a potential centre of power. A classic example is the United States Joint Chiefs of Staff. Civilian intelligence might have several arms which results in its decentralised and often uncoordinated nature. The two often vie for influence in policy. In South Africa there are various agencies charged with the intelligence function. The civilian bodies are the National Intelligence Agency (NIA) and the South African Secret Service (SASS). Their military counterpart is called the Military Intelligence Agency (MIA) and to obviate the struggle referred to above, all their work is centrally co-ordinated by the National Intelligence Co-ordinating Committee (NICOC). These agencies jointly and separately provide information on internal and external security and related matters to all important decision-makers in government. They are consequently in a position to substantially influence how a particular foreign policy problem is understood, conceptualised and resolved. This is particularly the case with regard to the 'new security' challenges confronting South Africa. The role of intelligence cannot be exaggerated in combating the scourge of international crime syndicates, drug cartels, illicit arms trade, money laundering schemes and illegal migration (Landsberg and Masiza 1996, 28-33).

Other Departments

It should be clear by now that there are a wide array of departments which, in one way or another, are involved in foreign affairs. In South Africa's case, examples would include the following departments (see *South African Yearbook 1998*):

- Arts, Culture, Science and Technology — negotiating the transfer and exchange of scientific and technological knowledge from other countries;
- Environmental Affairs and Tourism — responsible for the implementation and monitoring of international environmental agreements;
- Finance — representing South Africa in international financial institutions such as the World Bank, and International Monetary Fund (IMF);
- Justice — representing South Africa at international forums such as the International Court of Justice, and implementing international legal treaties;
- Sport and Recreation — supporting South Africa's participation in international sporting bodies such as the Olympic Games, the World Rugby Union and the International Football Federation; and
- Home Affairs — developing a policy framework for legal and other forms of immigration to South Africa based on international conventions.

Civil Society

While (as realists would have it) states remain the dominant actors in international politics, new participants now include non-state actors such as business, transnational interest groups and non-governmental organizations (NGOs) such as trade unions and churches. South Africa is no exception in the number of non-state actors which exert an influence on foreign policy, or at least, attempt to do so. The business community, constantly in search of new opportunities especially in Africa, has made ample use of the offices of the DTI and DFA in facilitating contact or promoting trade missions.

When in June 1996, the DFA released its equivalent of a foreign policy White Paper, the "South African Foreign Policy Discussion Document," it invited a cross-section of academic and other NGO interests to a forum where they significantly and critically influenced the prioritising of the goals set out in the document. To some extent the views of civil society on questions of South Africa's foreign relations are known. During the apartheid years regular but limited (whites only) opinion surveys were conducted which attempted to capture the public mood. More recently a comprehensive survey found that the South African public was not very concerned with global problems, but rather focused on domestic concerns (Van Nieuwkerk 1998). Respondents also held the view that South Africa should interact with the world mainly to the extent that this maximises trade relations with Africa, Europe and the United States. Finally, the survey suggested that South Africans had a mixed assessment of the government's handling of foreign policy. For example, the decision to switch diplomatic relations from Taiwan to the People's Republic of China was met with a healthy dose of scepticism.

There are several examples where organised civil society in South Africa has made an impact on foreign policy. The most dramatic case is that of the banning of antipersonnel landmines, due to the successful activities of the international campaign to ban landmines. Although difficult to measure, there is evidence which indicates that concerned NGOs have made important contributions in shaping South Africa's negotiating position in the South Africa–EU free trade talks. Furthermore, they have also assisted in prioritising issues on the agendas of NAM, UNCTAD and the Commonwealth.[7] On the other hand, despite a robust NGO opposition, South Africa has continued to pursue a vigorous arms sales policy.

It is important, therefore, to note that between 1990 and 1994 a comprehensive regime change occurred in South Africa, with a deep impact on political values, norms and decision-making structures and styles. This impact was also felt within foreign policy-making circles. Three features can be highlighted. Firstly, the influence of the military and intelligence has been balanced by civilian input. Secondly, the context of decision-making has altered significantly. The international isolation of the apartheid regime and the external context of the Cold War have been replaced by democracy in South Africa and a globalizing world. Thirdly, the locus of decision-making has shifted from a highly centralised circle of militarists to an open and interactive relationship between key individual decision-makers. These include the president, the ministers of foreign affairs, trade and industry, defence and finance, the National Executive Committee members of the ANC, and senior civil servants in the DFA and other departments. Complementing this dynamic relationship is the role of civil society or the non-state sector: the business community, organised labour, academics and the concerned public.

Finally, in light of South Africa's reintegration into the global community, bilateral and multilateral relations have become an important pillar of foreign policy. Key countries include South Africa's traditional trading partners in the North (Europe, North America, Japan) and, increasingly, trading partners in the South (India, Brazil, Indonesia, China) whilst key multilateral and regional institutions include the UN family, NAM and the Commonwealth, the SADC and the OAU, and the international financial institutions.

Facing the New Millennium: Foreign Policy in the Mbeki Years, 1999-2004

This phase represents the foreign policy of South Africa under the ANC government following the second democratic election. It is headed by a new President, Thabo Mbeki, and a new Foreign Minister, Nkosazana Zuma. As will become apparent below, these key individuals wrought changes in South Africa's foreign policy which built on preceding policy, yet introduced subtle new shifts.

As described above, the orientation of the South African government's post-1994 foreign policy can be described as vacillating between 'realist' and 'moral' internationalism. Indeed, in the early post-apartheid period, there was a palpable tension between prioritising its perceived commercial, trade, and political interests and its role as a moral crusader in the promotion of global human rights and democracy. However, following the second post-apartheid election in 1999 which saw overwhelming political control secured in the hands of the ANC, with President Mbeki and a close circle of colleagues at the centre of policy-making, this ambiguity and hesitancy was replaced by a strong sense of identity. The driving forces behind current official foreign policy appear to be two-fold. Firstly, a reformulated mission statement now places domestic economic and security concerns at the top of the priority list. Secondly, President Mbeki has articulated a powerful commitment to assisting the African continent and its revival as well as championing the cause of the global South through his government's leadership role in various multilateral institutions. This section examines various dimensions of South Africa's foreign policy conduct thus far and suggests what these might portend for the future.

Table 10.1 Decision-making Styles: a Comparison of the Old and New

OLD (Pre–1994)	NEW (Post–1994)
Locus of decision-making: State Security Council President Ministers of Foreign Affairs and Defence	**Locus of decision-making:** Cabinet The Office of the Presidency Department of Foreign Affairs, Trade and Industry, Defence
Marginalised Sectors Parliament Public opinion and the media Political parties Most external actors except fellow pariah states	**Involved Sectors** Parliament and the portfolio committee system Public opinion and the media The ruling party and alliance partners (ANC, SACP, COSATU) Extensive interaction with states, multilateral institutions, and the global economy
Ideological Orientation Apartheid mentality, racism Anti-communist — defence against the 'total onslaught'	**Ideological Orientation** Ongoing contest between idealist and 'neoliberal schools'
Decision-making Authoritative Secretive Reactive	**Decision-making** More democratic, open and transparent More inclusive and consultative However, still plagued by intra-state competition and conflict

Efficient Foreign Policy-making

As illustrated in Table 10.1, foreign policy-making under the democratically-elected ANC government is dramatically different from the process under apartheid. Gone are the days of excessive secrecy, the promotion of narrow sectional interests, the overbearing and cynical influence of the military and the myopic worldview. Despite a difficult transitional period, the current approach to foreign policy-making is refreshingly open and participative. Complementing this approach is an apparent broad societal consensus on the three broad objectives of foreign policy, namely the promotion of wealth creation and security for South Africans, prioritising southern Africa and the continent, and leading the global South on issues of democracy and sustainable, people-centred development. Officials regularly consult with specialists outside government when developing policy positions on issues such as the global landmine problem, South African participation in peace missions, or preparation for multilateral conferences or negotiations. However, there are sharp differences too. Some civil society interest groups are at loggerheads with the government over its continued arms trade, its reluctance to push harder for debt forgiveness, its seeming reluctance to be more outspoken on questions of human rights violations in neighbouring countries, and perhaps most critically, its apparent enthusiastic embrace of the global neo-liberal economic agenda. Regardless of the appropriateness of the criticism, the important point is that these debates take place and often impact on decision-makers. There is one caveat, though: the willingness of foreign policy-makers (politicians and officials) to listen to debates and alternative visions should never become the prerogative of individuals; rather, democratic exchanges such as the country currently experiences should continue to be channeled through institutions such as parliament, political parties, the media, and the often-mocked, but important NGO conference circuit.

A Responsible Regional Partner

Arguably, one of the most visible shifts in the new South African government's foreign policy orientation after 1994 has been its commitment to become a true partner in southern Africa and where possible, support regional economic development processes. This approach is not only driven by economic logic, but also political solidarity — many peoples and governments in this region have supported the South African liberation movement during the apartheid years, with their mutual support going back even further to the earliest independence struggles in southern Africa.

Why, then, do some governments and people in southern Africa still have misgivings about the regional intentions of the new South African government? Has it not made some serious inroads in starting to address the severe developmental, economic, and even political problems that are in many ways structural to the most marginalised group of countries in the world? Politically, especially in multilateral fora, South African representatives do not set South Africa apart from southern Africa. In fact, they have often laboured to insert the needs and interests of the southern African region as a priority on the agendas of fora such as UNCTAD NAM, and the WTO (Selebi 1999, 207-16).

Significantly, the South African government has been negotiating an 'asymmetrical' free trade agreement with the rest of the SADC for the past two years in terms of which South Africa will eliminate existing tariffs on imports from the rest of the SADC much faster than they are required to do in return. This is in recognition of the severe imbalance of the regional economy, with South Africa accounting for three-quarters in the region's total gross domestic product and manufactured production. South Africa also exports seven times more goods and services to the region than it imports from the region (Nkuhlu 1997, 78-85).

When it joined the SADC in 1994, many expected South Africa to become the economic and scientific engine in the region and, as a relatively stable and consolidating democracy, assist in building a peaceful region. How can it best fulfil this role? Some of the South African government's responses to these expectations have been listed above. But what are the remaining challenges? The current emphasis on dismantling tariffs on goods that are traded among SADC members is understandable. It follows in the wake of the consolidation of large regional free trade groupings such as the North American Free Trade Agreement (NAFTA), the EU, and even Mercosur, which have been erecting tariff walls against imports from the rest of the world. Intra-regional trade liberalisation also carries the theoretical promise of trade creation, which means that more efficient regional products (for example from Zimbabwe) replace less efficient home products (for example in South Africa) once they can enter a market free from import taxes.

It is common knowledge that the preconditions for reaping the benefits from free trade areas do not yet exist in southern Africa. The bulk of the region's trade is still with the EU, and intra-SADC trade (excluding SACU) hardly amounts to 6 per cent of total trade in the region. Paradoxically, South Africa has one of the most closed economies in the region, partly because it has never had to liberalise tariffs before under a structural adjustment programme (SAP) unlike most other members of the SADC. The real impediments to intra-regional trade are not high tariffs however. Only 5 per cent of products currently traded among SADC countries face tariffs higher than 40 per cent. Rather, the lack of potential products to trade among countries other than between South Africa (the hub), and the rest of SADC (the spokes), the lack of transport and communication networks among countries of the region, as well as problems with payment systems and customs procedures, are hampering trade (*ibid*).

In view of the above, it seems that SADC governments should rather focus their energies and resources on negotiating the joint management of 'regional public goods' such as telecommunications and transport networks, regional power grids, public health provision, water distribution, agricultural research and production, and food security than on free trade agreements. Many of these are covered by regional protocols. However, in view of the almost total dependency on donor money of the SADC sectoral co-ordinating units to implement their projects, it is difficult to see how these protocols will be implemented in a global environment of declining aid. One solution would be for South Africa to provide resources for this purpose proportional to its share of the regional economy.

Trade liberalisation will also not necessarily lead to more investment in the region, or by implication, to the creation of more jobs. To stimulate investment, trade liberalisation needs to be accompanied by a comprehensive regional industrialisation strategy. Such a strategy should encourage regional production in sectors where southern African countries share a comparative world advantage, especially those sectors that can benefit from economies of scale such as machinery and some agro-processing industries. However, the only current activity in this area is the construction or exploration of regional development corridors, driven by South Africa, and funded by the (South African) private sector. This is a very limited strategy.

South Africa's Trade and Development Cooperation Agreement (TDCA) with the EU, which stipulates that South Africa will eliminate tariffs on 86 per cent of its current imports from the EU over the next twelve years, could lead to severe hardship in the other member countries of SACU. Not only will they lose a significant share of government revenue as the SACU common revenue pool shrinks once tariffs on EU imports into the customs union fall away, but industries in these countries might also need to close down as they face increased competition from cheap EU products on the South African market or in their own domestic markets. Before ratifying this Agreement, the South African parliament should ensure that the EU and where necessary the South African government, explore remedial measures to prevent a scenario of increased unemployment coupled with less social spending, especially in the smaller and poorer Lesotho and Swaziland (Goodison 1999, 48-49).

The time is also ripe for the negotiation of a regional investment agreement, a process that will be driven by the South African government. This should not only serve to create regional incentives for foreign investors — SADC governments seem desperate to attract foreign investment, offering lucrative incentives to compete with one another — but also as a regulating instrument for foreign investment. This would include codes of conduct and rules that also apply to South African investors, many of whom are causing burgeoning local manufacturing or service industries in other SADC countries to close down; or are exploiting lax enforcement of labour standards or cheaper wages in these countries.

Another challenge is to strengthen the institutions supposed to implement and monitor regional projects, be it by grouping the existing country-based sectoral coordinating units into regional directorates, or by providing the poorer member states of the SADC with funding and the capacity to carry out their responsibilities. Expectations are that South Africa, which is in charge of the health sector in the SADC, will be able to drive a regional strategy to deal with the HIV/AIDS pandemic (given, of course, that it has the political will to do so). But what can one expect from a highly indebted poor country such as Tanzania, which has to drive the regional trade and industrial strategy?

Finally, it is common cause that no regional development strategy can take off if groups within states, or states among themselves, engage in violent conflict over a long period of time. The socio-economic destruction and misery evident in the Democratic Republic of Congo (DRC) and Angola, and even Mozambique until recently, testifies to the need for a regional consensus on the collective security needs of southern Africa. Only on this basis can leaders revive and review existing regional political structures such as the SADC Organ for Politics, Defence and Security (OPDS), or formalise a common security framework for the region (Tapfumaneyi 1999, 7). Structures without substance or political will, no matter how well designed, will only serve to perpetuate seemingly intractable conflicts in the region (Breytenbach 2000, 94-95).

Facilitating Peace on the African Continent

The African continent remains a theatre of many unmanageable and enduring conflicts. These range from those inspired by religious and sectarian strife such as in the Sudan, lawless banditry and warlordism such as in Somalia, the breakdown and collapse of government institutions such as in Sierra Leone, Lesotho and the DRC, to border disputes such as between Ethiopia and Eritrea. The glaring lack of continental and sub-regional institutional mechanisms and a common security infrastructure make prevention and resolution of conflict a difficult task. Inadequate human and material resources required for timely intervention in conflict and the absence of established doctrines and approaches to security issues further bedevil efforts to secure peace in areas of conflict.

Amid such seemingly insurmountable obstacles and despite its manifest imperfections, the 1999 Lusaka Agreement does offer a ray of hope that peace in the DRC can be achieved. The Agreement was brokered by regional actors acting in concert and with a common purpose to bring the protagonists in the conflict together to sign a cease-fire and create an atmosphere in which political settlement is possible.[8] Very soon after being installed as South Africa's new Foreign Minister, Nkosazana Zuma became involved in the Lusaka peace initiative and thanks in part to her catalytic role, the fractious rebels became signatories to the Agreement, thus lending it the necessary stature and legitimacy. While it cannot guarantee an enduring peace, the agreement provides a tentative framework for the belligerents in the entire Great Lakes region to move away from military confrontation towards political dialogue.

More controversial was South Africa's military intervention in Lesotho. It is now common knowledge that Lesotho was in the throes of anarchic violence and its government on the brink of collapse (Matlosa 1999, 6-10). In response to Prime Minister Pakalitha Mosisili's desperate *cri de coeur* that "we have a coup on our hands," South Africa launched Operation Boleas in September, 1998; but its intelligence apparatus underestimated the robustness of resistance by the Lesotho Defence Force and both armies suffered casualties as a consequence. However muddled and messy its siege, South Africa managed to restore order and stability such that a political dialogue among warring parties and factions could be resumed.

Despite its commitment and stated intention to work through these, South Africa finds itself trapped and constrained by effete and lacklustre multilateral security arrangements in the region and the continent. Conflicts tend to take on a life of their own, often allowing warlords and élites to extract instrumental advantage and material gain from peoples' misery. South Africa, therefore, must assertively pursue a strategy of sharpening and improving the OAU and SADC instruments which exist for preventive diplomacy, conflict monitoring and early warning. Furthermore, its approach to conflict management and intervention must be more strategic, vigorous and proactive, even at the risk of flouting traditional channels and norms. This is especially the case where governments are in the grip of imminent collapse or where civil war threatens.

The continent needs a corps of honest brokers or patrons of peace. South Africa certainly qualifies and is well situated to provide its good offices, offer technical assistance to conflict areas, take the lead in establishing multilateral efforts to secure peace in conflict zones, and move warring parties towards consensual and binding agreements. It appears to have made a good start with former President Mandela replacing the late President Julius Nyerere of Tanzania in mediating the peace process in Burundi. South Africa should consider expanding this role to address other areas of instability in the region and beyond.

A Voice for the South

Since coming to power, the new South African government has emphasised in both word and deed its commitment to, and solidarity with, other developing countries, many of whom experience similar problems of marginalisation and increased poverty in the global system. During the first five years of its transition, it accepted the challenge of using its 'moral capital' in building bridges of understanding and cooperation between the North and the South. South Africa's chairing of UNCTAD, NAM, the SADC and the Commonwealth is symbolic of this thrust.

Government representatives have been active in developing positive trade agendas for the region, the continent and least developed countries in the run-up to the 1999 Seattle Ministerial Conference of the WTO. They and especially the Minister of Finance have also spoken out against the role of the IMF in perpetuating the debt crisis and the organisation's undemocratic structure and practices. The government has even on occasion criticised the 'anonymous' market dominated by currency speculators who were in large measure responsible for the Asian meltdown of 1997. These sentiments presumably informed its decision to take part in the initiative that saw the establishment of a 'Group of 22' emerging economies which would examine ways of restructuring the international financial architecture.

The recent encouraging political ferment and renewed hope for democracy in Africa has almost coincided with the continent's "rapidly increasing marginalisation from the key processes of change in the world economy"

(Hyslop 1999, 6). African countries, for example, are more than ever mired in crippling debt and suffer from capital flight to developed countries; their economic policies are increasingly being shaped by the structural adjustment prerogatives and reform conditionalities of the World Bank and IMF; they experience declining levels of concessional loans and development aid; their preferential access to markets of developed countries is being systematically eroded by new rules governing the international trading system; and more generally, there is a widespread perception that the continent is collapsing into imminent anarchy (Kaplan 1994, 44-76). It is under these conditions that social movements have emerged which bind people in solidarity across national, linguistic and cultural boundaries (Mathews 1997, 50-66). South African civil society is an active member of Jubilee 2000 which is a global movement campaigning for complete and unconditional debt cancellation. It is also part of other coalitions and networks of NGOs which concern themselves with transnational campaigns for fairer terms of trade and better regulation of financial flows; nuclear disarmament; and protection of human rights.

The question of equitable representation of UN members on the Security Council was raised almost twenty years ago in the General Assembly. However, it was only in 1992 that concrete work commenced in a UN working group on how to restructure the Security Council with a view to making it more democratic, and, in so doing, provide the space for full membership with veto powers for developing countries. Since the Security Council in its current form reflects neither the political nor the economic power balance in the UN system, it faces a crisis of legitimacy, paradoxically at a time when it has become even more active during the 1990s (Field 1998, 13-20). A so-called African position advocates that two African states should become permanent members of the Security Council on a rotating basis. This is a source of great contention and as chair of NAM, this is an issue on which the South African government will have to provide guidance and leadership.

Defining South Africa's International Role

In summary, how can one describe South Africa's international role? In global geo-political terms, South Africa is a rather small country. It has variously been labeled as insignificant at worst and at best, as a middle power or pivotal state (Chase *et al.* 1996, 44-46). A healthy dose of realism is therefore necessary to understand and situate South Africa's international role in perspective. A fundamental problem has been South Africa's discomfort in dealing with the problem of identity construction in the global arena (Le Pere, Lambrechts 1999, 24-32). Following a brief (post-1994) period of exceptional international treatment — largely enhanced by a near universal recognition of President Mandela's moral standing — the South African government was faced with the complex task of advancing some of the idealist underpinnings of its foreign policy. These included issues such as the promotion of human rights in a changed global environment where the objective imperatives of geo-economics, capital markets, trade regimes, and the information age formed part of a new *Zeitgeist*.

South Africa quickly had to settle down to a post-Mandela re-assessment of its global capabilities. Without losing its internationalist moorings, its hierarchy of priorities have been recast and are firmly embedded in an embryonic and emergent 'South' identity. Thus the region, Africa and its role in multilateral institutions now provide a more secure policy anchor and a more prudent guide to action. The quality of ordinariness has brought a large measure of sobriety to what South Africa can possibly achieve in a turbulent and uncertain world. The country has taken key leadership positions in institutions which advance the cause of the South in international relations. This includes NAM, UNCTAD, and most recently, the Commonwealth.

The great challenge for South Africa is to form a tactical alliance with like-minded countries, which stand ready to lead a debate on the restructuring and enlargement of the UN Security Council to include developing countries as permanent members. However, such activist multi-lateralism sits uneasily with the country's contradictory impulses on peace promotion and arm sales (Shelton 1998). Whilst a careful and rigorous procurement monitoring process has been set up, South Africa stands accused of selling arms to countries and governments which do not conform to standards of good governance, let alone the observance of basic human rights. The tortuous explanations which serve to justify such sales are hardly convincing to an increasingly sceptical public and ultimately do violence to the potential good that South Africa can do as a peace patron on the continent and elsewhere.[9]

Conclusion: The Challenges of the Future

South Africa's post-1994 foreign policy — its making and implememtation — has benefited enormously from a newfound vigour and focus, provided mostly by President Mbeki. However, the DFA needs to formulate foreign policy — setting out the options, risks and priorities — without always having to rely on advice from senior politicians. Therefore, a strong and confident department becomes an absolute requirement for conducting a more prudent and efficient foreign policy. In pursuing this mission, the DFA needs to consider a number of issues.

Firstly, the departmental mission should be the subject of national debate, especially on the question of whose wealth and security is to be promoted. Current understandings of 'national interest' are subject to dual and schizophrenic interpretations and the term should be avoided until there is greater clarity of definition. It is in the area of economic policy ('wealth creation') that these faultlines are most evident. Despite vigorous opposition from the left to the government's GEAR framework, a broad societal consensus appears to be developing around macro-economic policies. 'Wealth creation,' in the context of an unforgiving international trading environment, needs to be interrogated through healthy debate for a national consensus.

Secondly, not all civil servants are comfortable with the notion of democratising foreign policy. However, the practice of consulting with civil society in developing policy orientations and positions should be continued. Good examples include preparing for the UNCTAD and NAM conferences, the SA-EU TDCA and producing the white paper on South Africa's involvement in peace missions. It is recommended that the next issue for consultation should be that of operationalising the white paper on peace missions (given the developments in the DRC) and secondly preparing a national position on UN reform and Security Council restructuring.

Thirdly, the South African government is involved in a variety of initiatives meant to strengthen and promote regional co-operation and integration. However, it appears that leadership on regional issues emanates in the main from the departments of trade and industry and (increasingly) defence. The DFA should strengthen and be seen to take seriously its regional commitments. This can be accomplished by addressing three related challenges:

- appointing and developing the appropriate expertise in the SADC sub-directorate and hosting regular Foreign Service Institute and departmental roundtable discussions on developments in southern Africa to improve its own in-house analytical capability;
- contributing to the efficient and effective functioning of the SADC and proposed OPDS secretariats by seconding and/or sponsoring specialists and donating whatever equipment is needed;
- supporting and facilitating research on deep-seated causes of instability in southern Africa to enhance the domestic NGO sector's ability to contribute to policy debates.

Fourthly, confronting the economic problems, social malaise and political crises of the continent requires a broad African and international strategic front of which South Africa must form an integral part. However, its role must be carefully calibrated in terms of a means-ends calculus and its approach must be informed by a search for modest accomplishments and not the pursuit of grand designs. To this end, it should:

- seriously develop a reputation, culture and capacity as a patron of peace promotion which means continuing to invest political will and resources in mediation and facilitation efforts; and
- engage in a concerted campaign to improve the peace-keeping ability and security mechanisms of the OAU through a commitment of technical and human resources.

Finally, we have argued that the South African government has made a firm commitment to developing its role as a voice for the global South. As such and as chair of the premier institutions of the South, it should develop principled and strategic positions on three key global issues, namely:

- the convening of a debtors' forum which will allow countries of the South to collectively strategise before negotiating with their creditors in the Paris and London clubs;
- the establishment of forums and discussions among developing countries to advance concrete proposals for international financial restructuring; and
- assisting with the further refinement of a set of clear and unambiguous OAU and NAM proposals on the issues of UN reform and Security Council restructuring to do battle in the UN itself.

These challenges capture and are indicative of the momentous changes which have been inaugurated by South Africa's domestic transformation and the impact which the era of globalization has exercised on its foreign policy orientations.

Notes

The authors acknowledge the important contribution of Kato Lambrechts to part of the chapter's concluding section. The chapter also draws on earlier work by the authors Le Pere and Van Nieuwkerk 1999; and Le Pere, Lambrechts and Van Nieuwkerk 1999.

1. *Financial Times*, 18 July 1994.
2. Selebi has now been appointed as the chief commissioner of police and has been replaced by Sipho Pityana, the former director-general of the Department of Labour.
3. For an analysis of South Africa's diplomatic relations with China and Taiwan, see Le Pere and Van Nieuwkerk, 1999.
4. Joubert was the first South African woman ever appointed to a diplomatic post. In 1972, she was sent to London as third secretary.
5. The complex dynamics of these trade negotiations were recently examined in a series of IGD publications. On the Southern African Customs Union, see Goodison 1999; the SA-EU FTA, see Houghton 1997; the SADC FTA, see Mayer 1999; the post-Lomé dispensation, see Le Pere and Ngobeni 2000.
6. The official South African position on peace operations is guided by the recently adopted White Paper on South African Participation in International Peace Missions, as approved by cabinet in October 1998. For a general discussion, see Solomon and Van Aardt 1998; Cilliers 1999, and Malan 1999.
7. Many of these activities are captured by research conducted by the IGD and SAIIA. For a general overview, see the publications at HYPERLINK http:// www.igd.org.za. www.igd.org.za and HYPERLINK http://www.wits.ac.za www.wits.ac.za/saiia.
8. For a full draft of the cease-fire agreement, see SA Journal of International Affairs 7.1 (January 2000): 165-181.
9. A 1997 public opinion survey on South Africa's foreign relations found that 38 percent of respondents believed South Africa should not sell arms at all. A further 27 percent believed their country should sell arms only to countries with a good human rights record and that are not involved in war (see Nel and Van Nieuwkerk 1998).

References

Anderson, B. (1983) I*magined Communities: Reflections on the Origins and Spread of Nationalism*. London: Verso.

Awhireng-Obeng, F. and P. McGowan. (1998) "Partner or hegemon? South Africa in Africa." Part One. *Journal of Contemporary African Studies* 16.1.

Barber, B. (1995) *Jihad vs McWorld: How Globalization and Tribalism are Reshaping the World*. New York: Ballantine Books.

Barber, J. and J. Barratt. (1990) *South Africa's Foreign Policy: The Search for Status and Security, 1945-1988*. Johannesburg: Southern Book Publishers.

Breytenbach, W. (2000) "The Failure of Security Cooperation in SADC: The Suspension of the Organ for Politics, Defence and Security." *SA Journal of International Affairs* 7.1.

Calland, R. (1999) *The First Five Years: A Review of South Africa's Democratic Parliament*. Cape Town: David Philip.

Chase, R.S. et al. (1996) "Pivotal States and US Strategy." *Foreign Affairs* 75.1.

Cilliers, J. (1999) *Building Security in Southern Africa: an Update on the Evolving Architecture*. ISS Monograph Series 4. Pretoria.

Cornish, J.J. (1999) "Zuma's consistent concern is delivery on a wider stage." *The Star* 2 June.

Davies, R. (1997) "Analysis of the Negotiations Process: Critical Areas, Contradictions and Commonalities." Ed. R. Houghton. *Trading on Development: South Africa's Relations with the European Union*. FGD/FES.

Evans, L.H. (1995) "The Challenges of Restructuring." *Mission Imperfect: Redirecting South Africa's Foreign Policy.* Ed. C. Landsberg, G. le Pere and A. van Nieuwkerk. Johannesburg: Foundation for Global Dialogue and Centre for Policy Studies.

Field, S. (1998) "Leading from the Front: Developing a South African Position on UN Reform." *FGD Occasional Paper* 14.

Frankel, J. (1968) *The Making of Foreign Policy.* London: Oxford University Press.

Frankel, P. (1984) *Pretoria's Praetorians: Civil Military Relations in South Africa.* Cambridge: Cambridge University Press.

Geldenhuys, D.J. (1984) *The Diplomacy of Isolation: South Africa's Foreign Policy Making.* Johannesburg: Macmillan.

———. (1987) "South Africa's International Isolation." *International Affairs Bulletin* 11.1.

Goodison, P. (1999) "Marginalisation or Integration? Implications for South Africa's Customs Union Partners of the South Africa – European Union Trade Deal." *IGD Occasional Paper* 22.

Habib, A. (1998) Review article in *Transformation* 37.

Hirst, P. and G. Thompson. (1996) *Globalization in Question.* Cambridge: Polity Press.

Hyslop, J., ed. (1999) *African Democracy in the Era of Globalisation.* Johannesburg: Witwatersrand University Press.

Kaplan, R. (1994) "The Coming Anarchy." *Atlantic Monthly*, February.

Karvonen, L. and B. Sundelius. (1987) *Internationalization and Foreign Policy Management.* London: Gower Publishing.

Kegley, C. and E. Wittkopf. (1993) *World Politics: Trend and Transformation.* New York: The Macmillan Press.

Keohane, R. and J. Nye. (1977) *Power and Interdependence.* Boston: Little Brown.

Lambert, R. (1998) "Dancing with Dictators: South Africa and Indonesia." *South African Labour Bulletin* 22.1.

Landsberg, C. and Z. Masiza. (1996) The Anarchic Miracle: Global (Dis)order and Syndicated Crime in South Africa. *Centre for Policy Studies* 9.6.

Lodge, T. (1987) "State of Exile: The ANC of South Africa 1976-1986." *Third World Quarterly* 9.1.

Le Pere, G. and A. van Nieuwkerk. (1999) "Making Foreign Policy in South Africa." *Power, Wealth and Global Order: An International Relations Textbook for Africa.* Ed. P. Nel and P. McGowan. Cape Town: University of Cape Town Press.

Le Pere, G. and K. Lambrechts. (1999) "Globalisation and National Identity Construction: Nation Building in South Africa." *Identity? Theory, Politics, History.* Ed. S. Bekker and R. Prinsloo. Pretoria: HSRC, Vol.1.

Le Pere, G. and S. Ngobeni, eds. (2000) "Regionalism and a Post-Lomé Convention Trade Regime: Implications for Southern Africa." *IGD Occasional Paper* 24.

Le Pere, G., K. Lambrechts and A. van Nieuwkerk. (1999) "The Burden of the Future: South Africa's Foreign Policy Challenges in the New Millennium." *Global Dialogue* 4.3.

Magubane, B.M. (1979) *The Political Economy of Race and Class in South Africa.* New York: Monthly Review Press.

Malan, M. (1999) "Peacekeeping in Africa." *SA Yearbook of International Affairs.* Johannesburg: SAIIA.

Mandela, N. (1993) "South Africa's Future Foreign Policy." *Foreign Affairs* 72.5.

Marais, H. (1998) *South African Limits to Change: The Political Economy of Transition.* Cape Town: University of Cape Town Press

Mathews, J.T. (1999) " Power Shift." *Foreign Affairs* 76.1.

Matlosa, K. (1999) "The Lesotho Conflict: Major Causes and Management." *Crisis in Lesotho: The Challenge of Managing Conflict in Africa.* Ed. K Lambrechts. FGD Africa Dialogue Series 2.

Mayer, M. (1999) "The EU – South Africa Trade Deal: Implications for Southern Africa." *Global Dialogue* 4.2.

Mbeki, T. (1999) *Africa – The Time Has Come.* Cape Town: Tafelberg and Mafube Publishers.

McGowan, P.J. (1993) "The New South Africa: Ascent or Descent in the World System?" *South African Journal of International Affairs* 1.1.

Medhurst, R. (1995) "The Effect of Taiwan's Pressure on South African Foreign Policy." Pretoria: Foreign Service Institute.

Mills, G. (1997) "Leaning all over the place? The not-so-new South Africa's Foreign Policy." *Fairy Godmother, Hegemon or Partner: In Search of a South African Foreign Policy.* Ed. H. Solomon. ISS Monograph Series 13.

Mills, G. (1999) "South Africa's Foreign Policy after Mandela." *South African Yearbook of International Affairs.* Johannesburg: SAIIA.

Muller, M. (1997) "The Institutional Dimension: The Department of Foreign Affairs and Overseas Missions." *Change and South African External Relations.* Ed. W. Carlsnaes and M. Muller. Johannesburg: International Thomson Publishing.

Nel, P. and A. van Nieuwkerk. (1998) "Constructing the Nation's Foreign Policy Mood." HYPERLINK http://www.igd.org.za www.igd.org.za.

Nkuhlu, M. (1997) "South Africa's Trade Policy with the SADC and Africa." *Trading on Development: South Africa's Relations with the European Union.* Ed. R. Houghton. FES/FGD.

Sadie, Y. (1998) "Women in Foreign Affairs." *South Africa's Yearbook of International Affairs.* Johannesburg: SAIIA.

Said, A. et al. (1995) *Concepts of International Politics in Global Perspective.* Englewood Cliffs: Prentice-Hall.

Selebi, J. (1999) "South Africa's Foreign Policy: Setting New Goals and Strategies." *SA Journal of International Affairs* 6.2.

Shelton, G. (1998) "South African Arms Sales to North Africa and the Middle East – Promoting Peace or Fuelling the Arms Race?" *FGD Occasional Paper* 16.

Singh, S. (1997) "Sino–South African Relations: Coming Full Circle." *African Security Review* 6.2.

Sole, D. (1994) "South Africa's Foreign Policy Assumptions and Objectives: from Hertzog to De Klerk." *SA Journal of International Affairs* 11.1.

Solomon, H. and M. van Aardt, eds. (1998) "'*Caring' Security in Africa.*" ISS Monograph Series, 20.

Southall, R. (1995) "A Critical Reflection on the GNU's Foreign Policy Initiatives and Responses." *Mission Imperfect: Redirecting South Africa's Foreign Policy.* Ed. C. Landsberg, G. le Pere and A. van Nieuwkerk. Johannesburg: Foundation for Global Dialogue and Centre for Policy Studies.

Suttner, R. (1996) "Parliament and Foreign Policy Process." *South African Yearbook of International Affairs.* Johannesburg: SAIIA.

Tapfumaneyi, W. (1999) "The SADC Organ of Politics, Defence and Security: Interpreting the Decision of the Maputo 1997 SADC Summit." *Accord Occasional Paper* 9.

Thomas, S. (1996) *The Diplomacy of Liberation.* London: IB Taurus.

Van Aardt, M. (1996) "A Foreign Policy To Die For: South Africa's Response to the Nigerian Crisis." *Africa Insight* 26.2.

Van der Westhuizen, J. (1998) "South Africa's Emergence as a Middle Power." *Third World Quarterly* 19.3.
Van Nieuwkerk, A. (1996) "Unpacking the Foreign Policy Black Box." *Global Dialogue* 1.2.
———. (1998) "South Africa's Foreign Policy Mood: Moral Internationalism or Commercial Realism?" *Global Dialogue* 3.1.
———. (1999) "South African Foreign Policy for the New Millennium: Do the Architects have it Right?" Paper presented to SA Political Studies Association Congress, June 1999.
Walker, S. (1987) "Role Theory and the Origins of Foreign Policy." *New Directions in the Study of Foreign Policy*. Ed. C. Hermann. Boston: Allen and Unwin.

11 Contextualising Foreign Policy-Making in the Kingdom of Swaziland

ALBERT DOMSON-LINDSEY

This chapter surveys the content of Swaziland's foreign policy and external relations from the period of independence to the present. It focuses on the contexts within which foreign policies and external relationships are made and looks at the various actors whose activities impinge on the policy-formulation and implementation process. The author suggests that civil organizations such as the trade unions sometimes set the agenda for external engagement or foreign affairs, a case in point being the issue of the Kingdom's Industrial Relations Bill. The chapter attempts to demonstrate that the decision-making process in Swaziland shares some resemblance to the bureaucratic process models of decision-making as postulated by Allison (1969 and 1971).

The Content of Swaziland's Relations from Independence to the 1980s

Economic and ideological factors have always played a major role in shaping the Kingdom of Swaziland's relations with the outside world. The desire for survival, national security and economic well-being prompted this small Kingdom to craft a policy which, for all intent and purposes, was conservative, especially in the context of her relations with apartheid South Africa. However, this conservativism in some sense reveals the shrewdness of those who were in charge of policy formulation and implementation at the time.

Domestic conditions greatly shape a nation's external relations, and so it was in the case of Swaziland. Economically, the country was subordinated to apartheid South Africa. There was therefore a dependence on her which could be seen from the fact that South African capital was ubiquitous in the economic life of the country, financing such sectors as mining, manufacturing, mercantile trade, transportation, timber, citrus and tourist industries (Daniel and Vilane 1986, 59). These economic links were deepened by the formation of the South African Customs Union (SACU) and the Rand Monetary Area (RMA), which comprises South Africa, Swaziland, Botswana, Namibia and Lesotho. For instance, the RMA establishes a parity amongst the currencies of the member states. The custom union has a special revenue-sharing formula, from which Swaziland derives 50 per cent of its income.[1] Since Swaziland is a peripheral state in the world economy, South Africa provides a market for her primary products as well as a market for migrant labour. The supply of labour to the mining centres in South Africa was a source of revenue to the Swazi government. The government kept the capitation fees paid for the recruits and also taxed their earnings (Daniel and Vilane, 184). As a result of this economic relationship, Swaziland could not adopt the same radical policy towards South Africa as her neighbours and the Organization of African Unity (OAU) had.

Swaziland, therefore, did not support economic sanctions against South Africa and preferred to look for diplomatic solutions to the apartheid question. Her pacific stance on the question of apartheid was reflected in her being a signatory to the Lusaka Manifesto in 1969. This document stressed the need for the eventual liberation of Southern Africa from minority rule, and conceded that this could be achieved through peaceful means, so long as South Africa showed her preparedness to negotiate the dismantling of apartheid (Bischoff 1990, 437). It also reflected Swaziland's policy of non-interference in the internal affairs of other states. Her position against sanctions may, in part, have been due to her awareness that none of the African states could offer economic or material aid to her to counteract the consequences of giving unqualified support to the liberation movements within the Southern African region (Bischoff 1990, 442).

It was a position which revealed that Swaziland's priorities were centred on security and survival. Because of its geographical proximity to South Africa and Mozambique, any whole-hearted commitment to the liberation struggle was bound to be suicidal to the tiny kingdom. The then Prime Minister expressed his apprehension thus: "We are surrounded by powerful neighbours and no one will come to our rescue if these big powers decide to remove Swaziland" (Bischoff, 442). In essence, Swaziland's policy position on the volatile situation in southern Africa in the 70s reflected a rational balance of appeasement towards the minority regimes on the sub-continent and the forces against them. In this, Swaziland explained her vulnerable position *vis-à-vis* her powerful neighbours, whilst at the same time espousing a policy which affirmed in principle her desire to see the establishment of non-racial societies. For example, in 1974 Swaziland stated that her policy of non-interference in the internal affairs of other states was "irreconcilable with any form of denial of fundamental human rights and that racial and discriminatory policies militate against fundamental human rights and the establishment of fruitful and normal relations between them" (Bischoff, 437). Such a policy position earned her the sympathy of her neighbours and the OAU, thereby avoiding diplomatic isolation from the rest of Africa. The policy was reflected in concrete terms in Swaziland's rejection of the independence of Transkei. The government of Swaziland declined to recognise the 'bantustanization' of South Africa.[2]

The Southern Africa Customs Union and Rand Monetary Area created an optimism in post-independence Swaziland. It was a generally held belief within governmental circles that they would help foster the creation of a manufacturing base in the country which could produce for the larger South African market. However, South Africa discouraged such development as it served her interests to maintain the peripheral status of the kingdom. In reality, Swaziland and the other countries in SACU and the RMA were junior partners (apart from South Africa). South Africa made all the rules governing the organizations. Thus such organizations, in spite of the advantages they offered, produced frustrations (Bischoff 1990; Daniel and Vilane, 75). There was, for example, disappointment within government circles when the perceived manufacturing or industrial base could not materialise. Besides, it made it impossible for Swaziland to adopt independent tariff and fiscal policies.

The Drive to Seek Trade and Economic Partners

As a result of the unequal relationship between Mbabane and Pretoria, Swaziland felt the need to initiate policies that would make her more self-sufficient and less reliant on South Africa. It therefore embarked on economic and trade relationships with countries such as Taiwan, South Korea, and Israel. The country also sought to establish similar links with other African countries such as Zambia, Ghana, Kenya, Nigeria and Tanzania. There was, however, little to show for these trade and economic ties. This was partly because of the dependant nature of the economies of both Swaziland and the African countries she had entered into relationships with

— they were all peripheral states which could only have meaningful economic and trade ties with the core states. For example, in the case of Swaziland, the preponderance of South African capital and investment meant that such attempts at diversification were bound to have little success.

It could be asserted that Swaziland's desire to reduce economic dependence on South Africa may also have motivated her policy-makers to reject the South African government's invitation to join its Constellation of southern Africa states, conceived in 1979, a move which would have deepened South African's economic links and control over Swaziland and other Southern African States (Davies and O'Meara 1985, 196). Instead, Swaziland brought her policy in line with the 'front line' states. The visible or concrete expression of alignment of policy was her membership of the Southern African Development Coordination Conference (SADCC) officially established in April 1980. The principal objective of the SADCC was to reduce external dependence and, in particular, dependence on South Africa. The constitutive document of the organization identified three levels of transformation that would be needed to achieve the desired independence:

- a transformation of the economies of the individual member states;
- a transformation in the relations between SADCC member states;
- a transformation in the relationship between the member states as a group and the outside world.

To achieve such transformation the SADCC devised a multifaceted development initiative with emphasis on infrastructural development, food security, energy development, industrial cooperation and training (Davies and O'Meara 1985, 197). The *raison d'être* for the formation of the SADCC meshed in well with Swaziland's desire for considerable economic independence from Pretoria.

The Role of Ideology

Ideology, undoubtedly, played an important role in shaping the foreign policy position of Swaziland. During the ideological conflict between the west and east, typified by the Cold War, Swaziland's pro-western, anti-communist policies could well be understood within the context of the kingdom's cultural values, institutions and capitalist orientation which were counterpoised to the communist ideology. Policy-makers had described

Swaziland's foreign policy at this time as multi-racial — a policy, which, among other things, sought to maintain the links with western capital and investment both internally and externally (Bischoff 1990, 460-461). On the eve of independence, Prince Makhosini Dlamini, who became the first post-Independence Prime Minister, expressed the nation's hatred for communism in the following sentiments: "Swazis regard communists as their biggest potential enemy. Communism has no place in Swazi life. We would fight it hard if it ever found its way here".[3] When communist forces swept into power after the liberation struggles in Mozambique and Angola, Swaziland made a plea for the rejection of ideology in favour of unity. Therefore, at OAU fora, Swaziland argued for the formation of coalition governments (which transcended ideology) in those countries. Arguably, it was a position calculated to dilute communist influence in the governments of Angola and Mozambique (Bischoff, 449).

At the height of the disinvestment campaign by the international community against apartheid South Africa, the kingdom's anti-communist pro-western and relatively stable credentials made it a safe haven for western or capitalist investment, especially for 'sanction busters.' For that reason, some businesses relocated from South Africa to Swaziland.

Change in Ideological Perspectives

There was a brief re-alignment of Swaziland's policy with the neighbouring states, and by extension, the OAU, a process which began in the late 1970s (Daniel and Vilane 1986, 63). Swaziland joined the SADCC in 1979. She also had a change of relations with the African National Congress (ANC) and following the visit of Oliver Tambo in 1977, allowed the ANC a 'low-key' but official diplomatic presence in the country and often turned a blind eye to the infiltration through the kingdom of ANC 'guerrillas.' This afforded them opportunities to carry out sabotage attacks on industries and military installations in South Africa — a state of affairs which caused the South African military establishment to complain that South Africa's eastern front "was leaking like a sieve" (Daniel and Vilane, 62). There was also at this time a good relationship between Swaziland and Mozambique. Samora Machel was reputed to have visited Swaziland in 1980; thereafter Swaziland detained a number of Mozambican National Resistance members and expelled the anti-Frente de Libertacao de Mozambique (FRELIMO) recruiting agents who had been enlisting Mozambican workers in Swaziland for military training in South Africa. In April 1981, the Prime Minister of Swaziland played host to Samora Machel (Mozambique), Quett Masire (Botswana) and Leabua Jonathan of Lesotho. At the end of the summit a communiqué was issued which was critical of attempts by South Africa to destabilise black-ruled states. In fact Swaziland herself came under attack from South Africa in that country's attempts to flush out the 'refugees' residing on her territory (Daniel and Vilane, 66).

Some political commentators have argued that the change in policy was a response to a perceived geo-political shift of power within southern Africa. The 'progressives' were on the rise, especially since the independence of Zimbabwe in 1980. The balance of power was tilting in favour of socialist forces; therefore, it was seen as rational and prudential for Swaziland to be aligned closely with them.

However, by 1982 Swaziland was collaborating closely with South Africa, and the relationship was intensified with the signing of the Nkomati Accord between South Africa and Mozambique. Among other things, the accord committed both states to prohibit the use of their respective territories by any state, government or foreign military forces, organizations or individuals who plan to commit acts of violence, terrorism or aggression against the territorial integrity or political independence of the other or may threaten the security of its inhabitants (Daniel and O'Meara, 207). Bischoff (1990) and Daniel and Vilane (1986) contend that the re-establishment of cordial relations between Swaziland and South Africa may have been due to the following: Pretoria at this time had expressed her willingness to cede back to Swaziland parcels of land which Swaziland had lost to South Africa, namely Ka-Ngwane which was in the Transvaal (now Mpumalanga) and Kwavuma in KwaZulu-Natal. The issue of the lost land was indeed an emotive one within the kingdom. Swazi nationalism centres on the land lost to South Africa. It expresses itself in an undying desire to retrieve lands lost during the colonial period and to unite with the Swazis residing on the lost lands in South Africa. It was the ambition of King Sobhuza II to see the restoration of this land. In the end, what stood in the way of an eventual transfer of those parcels of land to Swaziland was opposition from the leadership of the Ka-Ngwane and Kwavuma homelands. Finally, the South African government declared that any talks or negotiations on border adjustments had to happen between Swaziland and representatives from the two homelands (Matsebula, 1988).

Other incentives offered by South Africa included assistance in building a railway line through Swazi territory linking it with the eastern Transvaal and the port of Richards Bay. It was reported that the project would make Swazi Railways profitable for the first time. In 1982, South Africa was purported to have paid a premium of R50 million (about $7 million) to Swaziland through the revenue sharing agreement under SACU (Davies and O'Meara 1985, 74). These incentives have been interpreted as overtures by South Africa to Swaziland in return for Swazi cooperation in matters of security. Thus in 1982 a secret non-aggression pact was signed between the two countries, which *inter alia*, stipulated that both states should commit themselves to combat terrorist insurgency and subversion individually and collectively and to call upon each other whenever possible for such assistance and steps as might be deemed necessary (Davies and O'Meara, 74). Subsequently, the Swazi government clamped down on the activities of ANC members within the kingdom by deporting or imprisoning them.

Swaziland's collaboration with South Africa was vindicated by the signing of the Nkomati Accord. By 1984, the two nations had exchanged trade missions which were viewed as leading to the establishment of diplomatic relations (Daniel and Vilane 1986, 64).

From the above it can be seen that Swaziland's foreign policy was motivated by rationalism and *realpolitik* perspectives from the period of independence well into the 1980s. The country's policy-makers made their policy choices with a view to safeguarding their economic, geographical, political and cultural identities. According to Morgenthau, "All nations are compelled to protect their physical political and cultural identity . . . " (Dougherty and Pfaltzgraf 1971, 76). Some of Swaziland's policies, detached from the level of political expediency, may seem to lack moral justification; but the acts of statesmen or political acts must be judged by rational criteria. In essence, the morality of the decisions of statesmen is determined by the national interest which they represent.

The Changing Context of Swaziland's External Relations: The 1990s Scenario

The end of apartheid and the establishment of a non-racial society in South Africa, the demise of communism and of the Soviet Union as a world power, the modern trend of economic globalization, trade liberalization and regionalism have all impinged on the formulation of Swaziland's foreign policy. Those who formulate Swaziland's external policies stress the importance of her economic relations with the outside world and aim for sustainable economic growth through trade and investment, cultural promotion (tourism), international cooperation and adherence to international law. In his New Year speech for 1999, the King stressed the need for foreign travel which should primarily be for the purpose of promoting trade and investment. He himself had embarked on a number of trips to countries such as Taiwan and Egypt for purposes of trade and investment. Re-echoing the central foreign policy objectives of Swaziland, in an interview with the *Times of Swaziland*, the Prime Minister, Sibusiso Dlamini, asserted that he had an "overall responsibility to ensure that the new policy [i.e. that envoys should only embark on foreign travel when on trade and investment missions] is being followed by the Ministry of Foreign Affairs and Trade." He would, he said, continue to monitor their travel until he was assured "that a satisfactory orientation towards trade and investment promotion has been achieved".[4]

The Domestic Context

The demise of apartheid and the establishment of a non-racial government has meant that South Africa's pariah status has come to an end. Furthermore, South Africa's rehabilitation means that investments and capital which were once diverted from the country to relatively stable countries like Swaziland have returned to South Africa and other more competitive countries within the region. As a result, there has been a decline in direct foreign investment in Swaziland with an attendant loss of revenue and jobs. The Prime Minister puts the predicament of the nation in perspective:

> Our economy grew at a reasonable pace in the 1980s mainly because of our proximity to South Africa at a time when many investors were avoiding that country. We were able to attract investment and our employment rates were reasonable. Following the lifting of sanctions against South Africa there was a decline in direct foreign investment in Swaziland. Now with the competition in the region we find that we can't keep pace and growth has slowed to around 3 per cent (*The Courier* 1999, 41).

A 1997 United Nations Development Programme (UNDP) report indicates that 66% of Swazis live below the poverty line, and that the rate of population growth is higher than the rate of economic growth.[5] Again, the Aids pandemic is not only increasingly removing the economically active segment of society, but it is also a huge drain on the nation's social services. It is against this background that the government launched its National Development Strategy in 1997, which has among its core aims the following: the acceleration of economic growth, poverty alleviation, the improvement of social services and the development and resettlement of rural communities. The overall objective of the programme is that by the year 2022 the country should be in the top 10 per cent of the medium developing economies founded on the principles of self-sustainable economic growth, social justice and political stability. It is in this context that a vigorous drive for trade and investment as the cornerstone of the kingdom's external relations becomes under- standable. External capital is sorely needed.

Again the emphasis on trade and investment is underscored by the fact that the economy is export-based. The main economic sectors are agriculture, industry based on sugar, citrus, wood-pulp, maize, cotton and mining (asbestos, coal, diamonds) (UNDP *Human Development Report* 1998). Sugar accounts for 20 per cent of Swaziland's exports. As part of the government's poverty alleviation strategy, many smallholders have been incorporated into the sugar and citrus industry. Such expansion entails the search for more or expanded markets. Also, the emphasis on trade and investment is necessitated by the Kingdom's preferential trade status with the European Union and the United States. Investments are being sought to take advantage of these external markets.

The Regional Environment

The Southern African regional environment has altered considerably since the demise of the apartheid regime in South Africa. The division and conflict that characterised that era has given place to a spirit of regional cooperation as embodied in the Southern African Development Community (SADC), which has as its core objective, a "cooperative philosophy" based on a desire to become part of a movement to create a new form of economic interaction in the region based on principles of mutual benefit and inter-dependence (ANC 1993). There has been cooperation in the fields of environment, security, infrastructure, trade and especially in transport. For example, the SADC Trade Protocol which was promulgated in January 2000 seeks to establish a Free Trade Area within 8 years.[6]

The content of Swaziland's external relationship with South Africa indicates a policy template for the sub-region. In a joint communiqué issued by the Foreign Ministers of the two countries, (Arthur Khoza of Swaziland and Alfred Nzo of South Africa) and signed in Mbabane on Friday 22 August 1997, the two countries *inter alia* expressed their desire to:

- develop equal relations between the two countries in accordance with the principle of sovereignty and non-interference in their internal affairs;
- reaffirm their bilateral relations, and cooperate in regional and international fora;
- consult, exchange opinion and information at the level of Foreign Affairs, Deputy Ministers of Foreign Affairs and other levels;
- extend and broaden bilateral cooperation in political, economic, scientific, technological, cultural, humanitarian and other spheres;
- cooperate within the framework of international and regional agencies and fora;
- promote relations and cooperation between their missions to third countries.

Undoubtedly, the key emphasis of the communiqué is cooperation and dialogue in diverse fields between the two countries whilst at the same time espousing the principle of 'sovereignty' and non-interference. The emphasis on cooperation is in response to Swaziland's social and developmental needs. An intra-regional investment is therefore a much needed imperative. South Africa's observance of this principle remains suspect, however, especially in light of a recent development: the South Africa Communist Party (SACP), (a coalition partner of the ANC), hosts the Swaziland Solidarity Network (SSN), which is the external arm of the opposition formation in Swaziland. In response to human rights violations in the kingdom, the ANC, through its representative, Terrence Goniwe, tabled a motion in parliament which, *inter alia,* condemned the gross violation of human rights in Swaziland and urged the South African president to bring pressure to bear to remedy the situation.

There have been a number of bilateral and multilateral ventures, involving South Africa, Mozambique and Swaziland. Examples are the Maguga Dam Project between South Africa and Swaziland, the Lubombo Spatial Development Initiative, a trilateral project involving Swaziland, Mozambique and South Africa, which was launched by the three heads of state in May 1998. It is a joint E600m project (about $85.7m) which aims to attract investments to eastern Swaziland, Southern Mozambique and parts of the South African province of Mpumalanga and KwaZulu-Natal. Among the projects envisaged are tourism and agricultural development since the area is reputed to have a unique ecosystem and a number of game parks.[7]

Swaziland's system of government is unique within the sub-region. It contains a distinctive blend of traditional and western political systems. This uniqueness is enshrined in the kingdom's political philosophy, which is radically different from that of the rest of the sub-region's. It is a policy which lays emphasis on political leadership systems and institutions based on the African traditional past. Swaziland's unique political system is due to the fact that the kingdom was not colonised in the same way that most colonised entities were. Rather, the indigenous political leadership extended an invitation to the British to protect them against the expansionist propensity of the Boers. When the country assumed protectorate status, the traditional leadership, institutions, systems and structures of the kingdom were left intact. The Minister for Foreign Affairs and Trade was reported in the *Swazi News* (Dec. 2, 2000) as saying: "When the British left in 1968 they handed over the political authority to the same authority which had invited them." As a result of this, it is the Swazi government's position that: "The development of political life and the evolution of political systems in Swaziland will inevitably be different from some other African countries including her neighbours".

The King (*Ngwenyama*) is the head of state. Party politics remains prohibited since the ban imposed by a royal decree of 1973. As would be expected there are pressures from regional neighbours for reforms, a fact acknowledged by Albert Shabangu, the Minister for Foreign Affairs and Trade.[8] By elevating the principle of sovereignty and non-interference in internal affairs of states as a policy concern, the Swazi government seeks to serve notice to regional neighbours, especially South Africa, to stay out of her internal political affairs. The country has initiated its own process of political reforms embodied in the establishment of a Constitutional Review Commission. There is no doubt that policy-makers are faced with the huge task of ensuring that whatever document is adopted is based on compromise — a document that would satisfy both internal and external stakeholders.

The International Environment

The changing context of the international environment undoubtedly impinges on the formulation and implementation of governmental policies. Economic globalization is more and more putting governments under pressure to bring their macro-economic policies in line with international economic institutions such as the World Trade Organization (WTO), the International Monetary Fund (IMF) and the World Bank. The Swazi government is no exception. It has had to establish global credentials to attract investments, to conform to the trade rules of the WTO and to embark on fiscal and structural reforms as recommended by the world economic organisations such as the IMF and World Bank.

Swaziland, along with her partners in the South African Customs Union (SACU), agreed in principle to bring the country's trade policies in line with the trade liberalization policies of the World Trade Organization as embodied in the General Agreement on Trade and Tariffs (GATT), in December 1993. This has enormous economic implications for Swaziland. Among other things SACU ensures the free passage of a number of goods and services within the customs area, whereas goods coming from non-member countries attract the imposition of tariffs. The revenue so derived is pooled and shared. Out of this arrangement comes about 50 per cent of Swaziland's revenue. However this is set to dwindle as a result of principles enshrined in GATT. For example, in line with GATT principles, SACU members are expected to drop their tariff on trade with other SADC countries from September 1, 2000. Goods with tariffs of between 0 per cent–17 per cent will be dropped to zero, whilst other tariffs are expected to be phased out in five years. In this scenario, only 2.4 per cent of the SACU market will remain protected by 2008 (*Business Times* August 6, 2000). The South Africa–European Union Cooperation on Trade, Development and Cooperation Agreement signed in October 1999, and the trade regime which it puts in place, is set to entail revenue loss to Swaziland as a SACU member. The Minister of Finance ominously pointed out in his budget speech: "It is expected to impact on Swaziland's trade pattern, the general price levels and revenue from trade taxes."[9]

The WTO also questions the Lomé Conventions, which allow free access to products such as beef, sugar, rum and bananas from Afro-Caribbean and Pacific countries to the European Union. Undoubtedly that may mean a huge revenue loss to Swaziland; under the special preferential sugar agreement between the European Union and the ACP countries, the kingdom sells 50,000 tonnes of sugar annually to the European Union. Should this special status be lost, she may have to sell on the open market where she may not be able to withstand the competition.

Thus Swaziland has had to embark on fiscal and structural policies in line with the principles of the world economic organization. The government's Economic and Social Reform Agenda (ESRA) first launched in 1997, was prepared in consultation with the IMF and World Bank (Matthews 1999, 1074). This is a 3-year economic development programme. The current programme, ESRA2, covers the period between 1999–2001. ESRA is undoubtedly a vehicle for the realisation of the country's overall objectives as spelt out in the National Development Strategy. It stresses efficiency and timely implementation of governmental programmes. It sets targets and time frames within which governmental goals are to be achieved. Undoubtedly ESRA bears the imprint of World Bank and IMF prescriptions seen through structural reforms of public enterprises, the emphasis on privatisation, retrenchment, nurturing of the private sector, governmental fiscal discipline and tight supervision of the banking system among other measures.

Obviously the growing influence of globalization presents policy-makers with a number of challenges. What measures, therefore, should policy-makers put in place, both in the short and long term, to counteract the effects of loss of revenue and markets, as the country, along with its regional partners, brings its trade policies in line with GATT? What effective policies are needed to mitigate the social cost of structural adjustment policies?

Foreign Policy Actors

In the light of the changing scenario as already described, the scope of foreign policy has indeed broadened in the kingdom. The broadening of international issues has also seen an increase in the number of actors in the field of foreign affairs. Thus both governmental and non-governmental organisations have become players in the formulation of foreign policy.

In the past in Swaziland, foreign affairs was the monopoly or the preserve of the head of state (the King) who delegated such responsibilities to the Prime Minister's office and other individuals whenever he found it expedient. The foreign affairs department within the Prime Minister's Office was elevated to a full Ministry in 1980 to cater for the broadening scope of external affairs. There are presently a host of actors whose activities impinge on the formulation and implementation of foreign policy.

The Monarch

The King, Mswati III, as an executive monarch is the head of state. He owes this position to a royal decree of 1973 known as The King's Proclamation. He was installed as King in 1986. As head of state therefore, he is officially in charge of foreign affairs along with the Minister of Foreign Affairs. It is therefore expected that he will play an active role in policy-formulation and the implementation process. There have been occasions when he has made statements on foreign policy and other international issues, and has represented

Swaziland in his official capacity as head of state in many international fora such as the Commonwealth, the United Nations (UN) and the Southern African Development Community (SADC). The King has made a number of statements on international issues and is noted for his support for Taiwan. He is sympathetic towards Taiwan's desire to be recognised by the UN and to be represented in the UN. Speaking on behalf of the King at the 54th session of the United Nations General Assembly, the then Foreign Minister Mr Arthur Khoza stated, "His Majesty King Mswati III has urged the United Nations to apply the principle of universality to all countries wishing to join the world body . . . I refer to the twenty million people of the Republic of China on Taiwan who believe that they are denied their right to representation in the United Nations" (*Swaziland Today* 1999). The exceptional trade ties that exist between Swaziland and Taiwan must have motivated the Kingdom's position on Taiwan. Taiwan has a number of investments in the country, and Swaziland recently established an embassy in Taipei.[10]

On donor attitude with regard to the release of funds to the developing world, King Mswati stated during the SADC Consultative Conference 2000 in Swaziland that donor funding should be released on time for developmental programmes without "unnecessary restrictive conditions." On security in the southern Africa region and the rest of the world he laid emphasis on preventive diplomacy, which entails peaceful co-existence with neighbours and peaceful negotiations to resolve conflict.[11]

Given the status of the King as an executive monarch with the royal prerogative of appointing the Prime Minister and other public servants, and the fact that the Swazi constitution places the King (*Ingwenyama*) and the Queen mother (*Indlovukati*) 'above the law' (The King's Proclamation, 1973), this could lead to a misperception that he is the sole determiner of the direction of policy decisions. However, the kingdom's decision-making process has an element of consultation embedded in it. The Prime Minister, Sibusiso Dlamini, in an interview with *The Courier* affirmed that:

> There has been criticism, which we are trying to address, that His Majesty is an absolute Monarch. That is not the case. Somebody who does not know the system might think that this is the situation, but the king does not take unilateral decisions. He consults the cabinet and other statutory and informal advisors. So whenever he makes a decision, he takes account of what his advisors are saying (*The Courier* 1999, 43).

The Swazi National Council Standing Committee (SNCSC)

This is a royal advisory body established in November 17, 1998. It is a 21-member body with membership drawn from all sectors of Swazi society. The members, known as royal councillors, include royalists, economists, lawyers, policy analysts and farmers, among others. The chairman of this body is Prince Tfohlongwane and its task is to advise the King on traditional, political, economic and social aspects of the country. In fact it has the prerogative to comment on parliamentary bills before they receive royal assent. It is therefore reputed to be the symbolic "eyes, the think-tank, feet, hands and mouthpiece of the King and the entire society." The King is reported to have stated that, as the body responsible for advising him, any fiasco in policy formulation and implementation should be traceable to the SNCSC. Its tasks include periodic consultative meetings with the King and members of cabinet and other bodies involved in the day-to-day running of the country in which policy issues are discussed. It offers advice on the formulation and implementation of national policies ranging from macro-economic management to the creation of a conducive environment for social and economic development. It is a body which is only answerable to the King and membership is by royal appointment. The constitutive document of the SNCSC indicates that as one of its central duties it has to ensure that any policies adopted contain a blend of traditional and modern elements. In fact it has been identified as the traditional watch dog of traditional institutions, customs and heritage. It could be spoken of as the traditional arm of government. It has its office at the royal headquarters at Lozitha.

The Prime Minister

The Prime Minister retains a powerful influence on foreign policy undertakings. As head of a government which has identified trade and investment as the centrepiece of its foreign policy, he has the task of ensuring, among other things, that the travels of foreign envoys between their duty stations are motivated by trade and investment. He retains the right to approve the postings and travels of foreign envoys. There have been jurisdictional conflicts between the Prime Minister and the Minister of Foreign Affairs and Trade. The Foreign Minister rejects what he sees as undue interference of the Prime Minister in the affairs of his ministry (especially with regards to trips by foreign envoys). In spite of this, the Prime minister insists: "I have an overall responsibility to ensure that the new policies are being followed by the Ministry of Foreign Affairs and Trade and will therefore continue to monitor their travel until I am assured that a satisfactory orientation towards trade and investment promotion has been achieved" (*Swazi News,* January 2000, p.8). He is responsible for the approval of foreign trade arrangements. He also embarks on foreign trips for the purpose of investment and trade. In 1997 the premier visited Taiwan to discuss new investment projects which resulted in the establishment of a Taiwanese Textile company, Tuntex. ESRA is the collaborative effort of the Prime Minister, the World Bank and the IMF. It has been reported that the idea of investors going to the particular state agency for all the information and assistance they need in the investment process was his brainchild.

The Ministry of Foreign Affairs and Trade

This ministry, by virtue of its expertise, is supposed to be the focal point of foreign policy formulation and implementation. However it has, on occasion, come under criticism from the press and other political commentators for its dearth of professionals with the necessary expertise in international relations. The attachment of the trade portfolio to the functions of the ministry reflects the extreme importance of trade and investment in the kingdom's foreign policy. It is therefore expected to give direction to the country's trade policies. The ministry, *inter alia* is charged with the responsibility of identifying new export market opportunities in order to facilitate the expansion and diversification of the export sector; to assist in the development of appropriate policies and measures to overcome problems encountered in the export markets; to arrange and co-ordinate participation in regional and international trade fairs, exhibitions and world expositions and to encourage local companies to produce commodities that are competitive and also conform to international standards. With investment as the other essential component of foreign policy, the ministry, through its foreign offices, is expected to play an active role in disseminating information on investment.

Swaziland Investment Promotion Authority

SIPA was established following the passing of the Swaziland Investment Promotion Act by parliament in 1998. It became imperative, especially with the identification of promotion of investments and trade as the cornerstone of the country's foreign policy, for a unit to be set up to give direction to the country's investment drive. Its constitutive document reveals wide-ranging powers, which *inter alia*, include initiating, coordinating and facilitating the implementation of government policies on investment.[12]

The Ministries of Economic Planning and Finance

The advent of economic globalisation has meant that these ministries have become important players in the foreign policy formulation and implementation process. They help to formulate economic and fiscal policies in line with global economic and monetary requirements. The Minister of Finance, John Carmichael, has said: "Developing countries have to formulate their economic policies in such a way that they take into consideration the implications of these economic policies that are implemented by the industrialised countries. Swaziland is no exception." Officials in these ministries therefore represent the country in world economic and monetary forums.

The Cabinet and Parliament

The relevance of cabinet in all matters of policy (including foreign policy) can be seen in the fact that the Prime Minister is obliged to discuss policy issues with his cabinet and meet the King and his advisory council every week — a forum which provides them with the opportunity to discuss policy issues. The body comprises the House of Assembly and the Senate. The king appoints 10 of the 65 members who constitute the House of Assembly. The remaining 55 members are elected to parliament from the various centres around the country, *Tinkundla*. (These are traditional rural administrative areas). In the absence of any political party framework candidates contest for the *Tinkundla* seat in their individual capacity. The Senate is composed of thirty members. Ten of the members are appointed by the House of Assembly whilst the remainder are appointed by the King. The royal appointees include chiefs and princes. In fact the members are reputed to be chosen to reflect the cultural, economic and social interests of the country. The Establishment of Parliament Order of 1992, Section 14 (5) instructs that "The King shall appoint the Senators after consultation with such bodies as the king may consider appropriate in an endeavour to appoint such persons who are able to contribute substantially to the good government of Swaziland." To some degree, therefore, the parliament can be seen as the representational vehicle through which the people express their opinions and are able to make inputs on all types of policy issues. Even though it has been criticised as a rubber stamp institution on some occasions, its relevance in the policy formulation and implementation process is demonstrated by the fact that it scrutinizes and oversees executive actions and evaluates all draft policy documents before they receive royal assent. It also ratifies treaties, appropriates funds and approves departmental budgets. The unit of parliament which has the expertise and formally deals with foreign affairs is the parliamentary sub-committee on foreign affairs. An official who wishes to remain anonymous lamented, "The only sub-committee which seems to be active is the Appropriation of Funds Committee; all the others are not functioning."

Defence

Defence has little role in foreign policy formulation and implementation. This is to be expected since, unlike countries plagued with both internal and external threat, where the defence force plays a crucial role, Swaziland is relatively peaceful. Again the unimportant role defence plays is explainable by the demise of apartheid and the ideological conflict that characterised the politics of the southern Africa region. As previously mentioned, during the apartheid era, Swaziland, on occasions, entered into security pacts with South Africa. Her military apparatus played an active role in the implementation of the pact, characterised by collaboration with the South African police against the ANC exile community in Swaziland.

Cross-border crime is very rife in southern Africa; Swaziland has an agreement with countries like South Africa and Mozambique which involves cooperation between security personnel across national borders to combat this type of crime. In June 1990, the governments of Mozambique and Swaziland signed an extradition agreement which provides for the repatriation of alleged criminals (Levin 1999, 1069).

Regional security is a *sine qua non* for regional economic development. As a result, economic blocs such as the Economic Community of West African States (ECOWAS) and the Southern African Development Community (SADC) have all adopted security protocols to deal with regional insecurities. The SADC, for example, subscribes to peace-keeping principles and the *Umbutfo* (Swaziland Defence Force) is set to play an active role in regional peace-keeping exercises and the formulation and implementation of security policies.

The Opposition

Political parties remain banned since the royal decree of 1973 which abolished the constitution adopted at independence. Among other reasons given for their abolition was that multi-partyism had polarised Swazi society and threatened its unity. However, the opposition had a new lease of political life after the death of Sobhuza II in August 1982, following acrimonious power struggles within the royal family. In some sense, the in-fighting within the royal family undermined the unquestioned loyalty that royalty and its institutions had hitherto enjoyed and paved the way for the re-emergence of opposition forces. The 1989 collapse of the Soviet Union gave added impetus to the activities of the opposition. Between 1989 and 1995 there was a series of acts of civil disobedience which sometimes degenerated into political violence. Demands included electoral reforms, abolition of the *Tinkundla* system of government, a constitutional monarchy and the establishment of a Constituent Assembly to draw up a new Constitution. It must be asserted that these activities — which received both regional and international support — contributed to the establishment by the government of a Constitutional Review Commission (CRC) in 1996.

There is a new development in the operation of the opposition. There is now a move towards internationalising the political situation in the country. The Swazi Solidarity Network (SSN) — the external arm of internal opposition — has been formed in South Africa. It is forging alliances with other political forces outside Swaziland and has its office next to the South African Communist Party (SACP). The aim of this organization seems to be to create international awareness and to whip up the community's support for its quest for meaningful political reforms. For example, it picketed the Swazi delegation during the Commonwealth Heads of State Conference in Durban.[13] However, it could be asserted that the influence of the opposition on foreign policy formulation remains insignificant by virtue of its illegitimacy. Other actors may include the business community, the press, the informed public, and home affairs.

The Labour Union

Though the government remains the predominant player in the field of external relations, there is a rising trend for non-governmental organizations to forge external links, alliances and coalitions to exert pressure on the national government to adopt policies favourable to them. The Swaziland

Federation of Trade Unions (SFTU) — which is an umbrella body for a host of labour unions – achieved notoriety in the 1990s for the series of industrial actions it embarked on to back its demands for both labour and political reforms. Over the years it has not only forged alliances with other regional labour organisations such as the Congress of South African Trade Unions (COSATU), but has also sought redress for labour grievances through the international forum that the International Labour Organization (ILO) provides. COSATU, on some occasions fraternized with SFTU and threatened to stop the flow of goods and services through Swazi-South Africa borders. In fact in March 1996, COSATU imposed a blockade on goods and services coming to and from the border with Swaziland. Though it lasted for only a day, the government was compelled to resume negotiations with the unions (Levin 1999, 1072). On November 6, 2000, COSATU facilitated a meeting of Swaziland's Trade Unions and other political formations in Nelspruit, South Africa, after the Swazi government placed a ban on such meetings in the country. The meeting ended in the adoption of a resolution, which has become known as the "Nelspruit Declaration." Among other things it called for the review of the amended Industrial Relations Act and appealed to bodies such as the OAU, the SADC and the Commonwealth to support the resolutions.[14]

The Internationalization of Swaziland's Industrial Relations

The Swaziland Federation of Trade Unions (SFTU) sought redress concerning its misgivings about a 1996 Industrial Relations Act, which it regarded as not containing adequate provisions for labour rights and to be in contravention of the Conventions of the International Labour Organisation (ILO). Swaziland is a signatory to the Conventions. In general terms, the Act was seen as very draconian as it made it impossible for any industrial disruption in the country. SFTU urged economic sanctions against Swaziland and at ILO fora it found a convenient and powerful ally — the American Federation of Labor and Congress of Industrial Organizations (AFL-CIO). Earlier on, AFL-CIO had succeeded in securing legislation through congress, which *inter alia* stipulated that developing countries whose laws contravene ILO rules and principles should not benefit from the Generalised System of Trade Preferences (GSTP) — a trade concession which the USA grants to developing countries. Such a concession grants unrestricted access for the American market of some products such as sugar and textiles. These products, which attract little or no tariffs, fetch more in terms of export revenue than they can fetch on the open market where there is great competition. In fact, one of the reasons Swaziland has attracted a number of investments is because it is a beneficiary of the GSTP.

The AFL-CIO presented SFTU's case before Congress which in turn threatened to revoke Swaziland's GSTP status unless the country brought its labour laws into conformity with the ILO standards. This development effectively ensures that the matter of industrial relations becomes as much an international affair as it is a domestic one, and therefore, whatever decisions are made become, in reality, a response to the demands of the external stakeholders. This is born out by the fact that the government of Swaziland promised to review the law as a result of international inducement.

The stakeholders — namely workers' organizations like SFTU, the Swaziland Federation of Labour (SFL), Swaziland Federation of Employers (SFE), government representatives, economists and observers from international labour organizations — sat down together to amend the law. The USA played a behind-the-scenes role through its ambassador in the country, Gregory Lee Johnson, who was reported as saying:

> Over the course of the four plus years this issue has been before the people of Swaziland, we have consistently and persistently advised the country's leadership that enacting a bill similar to the one now waiting approval is the best course to take (*The Sunday Times*, May 28, 2000, p. 11).

The draft document crafted by the review committee was hailed as a compromise bill. The decision-makers made the necessary compromises and the trade union federation struck a compromise with the employers' association. The 1996 law had denied SFTU the mandate to call for strike action, restricting this freedom only to the affiliated trade unions. For employers, the law imposed stringent penalties on employers who wrongfully dismissed workers. The employers' federation softened its stance on the restrictive conditions placed on SFTU's right to instigate strike action. In return, SFTU helped the employers' federation to relax the clauses which laid down stiff penalties to employers for unlawful dismissals. The document was duly passed by parliament.

The amended bill was then passed on to the Swazi National Council Standing Committee (SNCSC) which has the prerogative to examine bills before they receive royal assent. The SNCSC amended the bill after it had been in their possession for about a year. It has been noted that the advisory council was divided over the bill. The deliberation was characterised by intense lobbying for support of preferences. The 'hawks' within the council advocated a complete ban on trade unionism, whereas the 'doves,' sensitive to the reaction of the international community and the harm it might do to workers' bargaining position in the workplace, opposed it. After extensive royal consultations, a compromise emerged (*The Nation*, July 2000, p. 25). The labour federation's right to organise strikes was acknowledged; however, conditions were placed on this right. The amendment stipulated that workers should be liable for any losses in terms of profit incurred during strike action, whether such action is legal or not. It further stipulated that a decision to strike or take protest action should be preceded by a secret ballot or vote, in which all workers must participate; it wanted each enterprise to employ a royal representative (*Liso le-Nkhosi*) to an executive position, who would also chair workers' committees and disciplinary meetings (*Sunday Times May* 28, 2000: 30). A joint parliamentary session passed the amended bill which subsequently received royal assent. Prior to this decision, other stakeholders sought to influence the decision one way or the other. The press and the informed public urged for the adoption of the reviewed bill for the sake of the country's GSP status and were later incensed over the insertion of those clauses by the Swaziland National Council Standing Committee. They criticised the members for putting their personal interest before the national interest, referring especially to the clause which makes it mandatory for any enterprise to appoint a royal representative to an executive position (*Sunday Times of Swaziland*, May 28, 2000: 13). A joint delegation of the Federation of Employers and the Chamber of Commerce met the King in a two-hour session and advocated the signing of the bill.

The American ambassador to Swaziland argued for the adoption of the revised bill, because, in his estimation, it met ILO standards and qualified the country to continue benefiting from the GSTP. He reiterated the economic benefits that would accrue to the state: the continuity of business operations in the country and maintenance of the level of employment. The new legislation will also send a positive signal to investors who may see the country as offering the right investment climate; Swaziland would also qualify for the Africa Growth and Opportunity Act, signed by President Bill Clinton on May 17, 2000. This Act will ensure that textiles from developing nations enter the USA market free of quotas and at significantly reduced tariffs for a period of 8 years. On the other hand, Clinton ominously hinted that "if the Bill is not reviewed and ILO Conference legislates that the legal regime does not comply with international labour standards, a report will go to the US government which will then be obliged to undertake a review of

Swaziland's GSTP status. It is my positive view that we will not get to that point."[15] However, he acknowledged the King's prerogative to consult before signing the bill.

The business community, especially the sugar and textile industries, was in favour of the reviewed bill. These particular industries confirmed that they stood to lose the USA market and the revenue which accrued from it. If the trade concession was withdrawn, the sugar industry could lose as much as $40 million in annual revenue. Mike Matsebula, the chief executive officer of the Swaziland Sugar Association, indicated that the sugar industry could not afford a loss like that and pleaded:

> Each day passing by without this Bill promulgated into law has been agonising. Our plea is that the country must take a strategic decision, and that is get the Bill into the statue books and it can put in whatever amendments later on. There may be few necessary amendments, but they are nothing compared to the long term effects of having to be cut out (*Sunday Times of Swaziland*, May 21, 2000,: 2).

The sugar industry remains the largest employer in the country. In a similar case, the textile industry may lose about $1.2 million in revenue per month.

There seemed to be cabinet complicity in the insertion of the new clause into the Industrial Relations Bill. Earlier on, in what appears to be an effort to rally support from external stakeholders for decisional preferences of policy-makers, the Prime Minister, Sibusiso Dlamini, made a trip to the United States. Upon his return he held a press conference in which he asserted that he met with US government representatives and received assurances that there would be no sanctions against the state.[16] Much later, in an interview with the *Times of Swaziland* on August 14, 2000, he confidently affirmed that, "What should be made clear is that decisions on the GSTP are made by the US government — a government with which we have extremely warm relations." The Minister of Enterprise and Employment, Lutfo Dlamini, under whose jurisdiction the bill falls, supported the notion that the bill was amended to bring it into conformity with Swazi culture and expressed the view that his ministry was happy with the objectives of the law, meant to promote industrial harmony in the country.[17] Some political analysts argued that if the cabinet was not in favour of the amendment it could have influenced the decision during weekly cabinet meetings with the SNCSC and the Swazi monarch.

The amended labour bill will make it difficult for SFTU to call for successful strike action, since a call for protest action should be preceded by a mandate through the voting procedures in which all workers are obliged to participate. The difficulty arises when it is taken into account that there are two major labour federations in the kingdom — SFTU and the Swaziland Federation of Labour (SFL). There is a divergence of interest and perceived conflict between these two Federations. SFTU has been criticised for politicising labour issues, whereas the SFL, according to its Secretary-General, Ncongwane, wants labour to restrict itself to 'bread and butter' issues.[18] Therefore, seeking a mandate from the majority of workers may prove to be an uphill task for SFTU, which has always shown an unflagging propensity for protest action and has always been a political thorn in the flesh of government. It is therefore prudent for the government to be in favour of the amended bill.

The proponents and supporters of the amendments have argued that they were meant to ensure that Swazi custom and culture permeates the work place. A legislator, Mgabhi Dlamini, who has spoken in the House of Assembly in favour of the amendments, expressed the view that they represented the contributions from other stakeholders (i.e. traditionalists) who were not consulted when the bill was drafted.[19]

A consensus atmosphere pervaded the deliberation of the amended bill by a joint parliamentary session. It was an atmosphere, which, to a large extent, shut out any dissenting view. This assertion is substantiated by events which both preceded and followed the passage of the amended bill by the joint chamber by an overwhelming vote in favour. A Senator, Majahenkaba Dlamini, suggested that the amended bill should be altered, but this was rejected by the House. The Senate President, Muntu Mswane indicated that the House could only discuss or focus on SNCSC amendments, but doubted if parliament could introduce amendments. Stifled by the consensual atmosphere of the Chamber, he opted to walk out, rather than participate in the debate, which he saw as unnecessary. He was heard exclaiming '*Pho-ke*' a Swazi phrase which could be translated as 'why then?'[20] It was reported that most of the parliamentarians had reservations about the clauses which made it mandatory for royal appointees to be employed in the workplace; however, none voted against the amended bill with all its controversial clauses.

The amended Industrial Relations Act presented by the government delegation at the ILO conference was reviewed by ILO legal experts. Their brief was to ascertain whether it contained violations or not. After the review exercise, the team notified the government that the Amended Industrial Relations Act did not comply with ILO conventions, especially sections 40 and 52. Section 52 prescribes the setting up of a work council in the work place which could negotiate on behalf of any worker not affiliated to a union, on such matters as salary increments. This could have the effect of making the labour federation insignificant. Subsequently, the United States government advised that if the amended act was made operational without the Swazi government taking steps to remove the elements which contravened ILO conventions, the nation could lose its GSTP Status. Notwithstanding this, the amended act came into effect on 25 August 2000.

The government of the USA then warned that it was initiating a process to withdraw duty-free treatment accorded to imports from Swaziland under the USA GSTP. The kingdom was given a month to react to this warning. After consultation with technical experts from the USA and representatives from the ILO, the government modified the disputed clauses to bring them in line with ILO conventions and the labour laws of the USA. In the end, Swaziland retained its GSTP status. In fact the modified clauses partially addressed the labour unions' concerns. These were the clauses relating to a ballot before strike action and the work councils' and labour liability for losses incurred during strike action. For example, whereas the amended bill made it an obligation for all workers to vote before industrial action could take place, the modified clause instructs that there should be a quorum at both the level of the labour federation and at the affiliate level. Also, whereas the amended bill had made it obligatory for a work council to be established in the work place, the modified clauses, concede that a work council could only be established in a work place where no labour union existed. In fact the labour unions had rejected these modifications as inadequate.

What observations can be made about decision-makers in Swaziland from the Industrial Relations saga as discussed above? To begin with, their decisional behaviour has some affinity with Allison's bureaucratic model of decision-making (1969, 1971). This focuses on the following: divergence of preferences of policy-makers, their arguments and counter arguments, the multiplicity of decision-makers, the coalitions they build in their attempt to secure policy-preferences, the varied power, skills and knowledge they bring into policy-deliberations, and the compromises they strike. Arguably, most of these elements are present in the decisions which underpinned the passage of the Industrial Relations Bill. For example, the SNCSC and the cabinet — representing much power and possessing considerable decisional skills — managed to outmanoeuvre others in the decisional game. The amendments to the bill were made a year after it had been handed over to the SNCSC and tabled in Parliament only a day before the expiry date set by the ILO for the review of the bill, and a day before the government delegation was to leave for Geneva, in time for the ILO Convention. The timing, arguably, could not have been more propitious. Undoubtedly it may have created a panic situation within parliament. To delay the passage of the bill by arguing about the merits and demerits of the amended clauses and altering it would have had the potential danger of missing the deadline and inviting sanctions. This, in some sense, also explains the consensual temper of the chamber, that it was indeed pointless, at that late stage, to argue over the amended bill.

Upon close scrutiny, the amended clauses represent a half-way house between considerations of the government's interest and the demands of the external stakeholders. The clause for the labour federation to seek a worker's mandate through the vote is undoubtedly calculated to make it difficult for the SFTU to embark on industrial action loaded with political motives. For such action may not only threaten the survival of the government but will also have the effect of making the country less attractive to investors. On the other hand, the right to protest action (with those restrictions accorded SFTU by the policy-makers) represents a desire to appease international stake**holders.**

The government of Swaziland, as in other states, no longer has exclusive access to international fora. This means that decisional motives or motive statements of governments can be challenged by other actors. SFTU had to be represented at the ILO Convention. Its representative used the opportunity to draw delegates' attention to violations of ILO Conventions concealed in the amended version of the Industrial Relations Act. The Minister of Enterprise and Employment, who led the government delegation to the Geneva Conference, lamented upon his return from the conference:

> The only way these people [ILO members] could have known about the content was through a person who left this country and arrived there to report that the law that is on its way has serious violations of ILO Conventions. Nothing was raised by ILO on the SNC except by Jan [the Secretary General of SFTU] and his cohorts who even failed to explain the work of the SNC because his main aim was to discredit the way this country is governed (*Sunday Times* July 9, 2000 p.13).

The government of Swaziland's final agreement to modify those offensive clauses, indicates the power of the coalition of the trade unions and external actors to influence policy decisions.

Conclusion

As discussed above, the industrial relations saga has highlighted flaws in the policy formulation and implementation process of Swaziland. The weakness of the Kingdom's policy-formulation and implementation process is due, in part, to the traditional/modern nexus of Swaziland's policy decisions which can become problematic in the international sphere. Policies which have international ramifications, but contain the imprint of Swazi customs, practices and heritage, are bound to be rejected with dire economic consequences if they are found to be in breach of international conventions, and to be contrary to the interest of external stakeholders. The external milieu has uniformity of standards which leaves little or no room for the kingdom not to conform. This predicament is compounded by the fact that the kingdom has a dependence status in the global economic hierarchy. The interests of external actors, therefore, becomes indispensable in the formulation and implementation of policies, especially those with international ramifications. One of the obvious drawbacks of this position is that it limits the power of statesmen to negotiate and bargain successfully for their national interest.

The core objective of Swaziland's foreign policy is to promote trade and investment. To a very great extent, the means to achieve this lie in the external environment. Arguably, one of the attractions of Swaziland to investors is the trade concessions she enjoys in the European and North American markets. Policy-makers are, therefore, not only tasked with the responsibility to craft policies that will expand trade-cooperation, but must also act to consolidate existing ones. A case in point is the Industrial Relations drama. There seems to be a dangerous parochialism of decision preferences. It has now become imperative for decision-makers to eschew policy-preferences that are parochial in outlook and marshal political goodwill to harmonize their preferences in line with the objective national interest.

Swaziland's distinctiveness as a political entity marked by its blend of traditional and modern institutions remained largely unchallenged in a bipolarised world; however, with the end of the Cold War and the emergence of the democratisation of political systems, it is losing its *raison d'étre*. The kingdom's foreign policy objective of adhering to international laws and conventions has received a major setback as a result of the revelations of its human rights violations and lack of democratic credentials. It does still enjoy some measure of goodwill from the governments of the sub-region and the rest of the world, but this may not be guaranteed for long, given the zeal with which the political formations are lobbying national governments, states, human rights organizations and labour unions to pressurise the government to carry out meaningful reforms. Furthermore, the resolve of non-governmental forces to continue with protests demanding reforms may jeopardise the kingdom's image as a safe haven for investment. To forestall this scenario, it is suggested that Swaziland's policy-makers should emulate South Africa's formula of constructive engagement with dissenting groups which successfully brought an end to apartheid and led to the establishment of a genuinely democratic government. By so doing the kingdom is likely to continue to enjoy the goodwill of the international community whilst at the same time safeguarding the centrepiece of its foreign policy objectives.

Notes

1 *The Courier* (1999) Country Report — Swaziland March/April No. 174.
2 *Times of Swaziland* (1976) 8 October.
3 Dlamini cited in Daniel and Vilane 1986: 185.
4 *Times of Swaziland* (1999) May 17.
5 *Times of Swaziland* (2000) August 8.
6 *Times of Swaziland* (2000) February 29: 23.
7 *Sunday Times of Swaziland* (2000) November 12: 2.
8 *The Courier* (1999) No. 38.
9 *Times of Swaziland* (2000) February 29.
10 *Times of Swaziland* (2000) February 13.
11 *Times of Swaziland* (2000) April 19. *The King's Birthday Supplement*.
12 The Swaziland Investment Promotion Act (1997) S5.
13 *Times of Swaziland* (2000) July 18: 16-17.
14 *Times of Swaziland* (2000) November 6: 1.
15 *The Sunday Times* (2000) May 28: 11.
16 *Times of Swaziland* (2000) June 5: 2.
17 *Times of Swaziland* (2000) June 7: 36.
18 *The Nation* (2000) July. p. 25.
19 *Times of Swaziland* (2000) June 7: 36.
20 *Times of Swaziland* (2000) June 7: 1.

References

African National Congress. (1993) *Foreign Policy in New Democratic South Africa*. Johannesburg: African National Congress.
Allison, G.T. (1969) "Conceptual Models and the Cuban Missile Crisis." *American Political Science Review* 63: 689-718.

Allison, G.T. (1971) *Essence of Decision: Explaining the Cuban Missile Crisis.* Boston: Little Brown.
Bischoff, P.H. (1990) *Swaziland's International Relations and Foreign Policy: A Study of a Small African State in International Relations.* Bern: Peter Lang.
Daniel, J. and J. Vilane. (1986) "Swaziland's Political Crisis, Regional Dilemma." *Review of African Political Economy* 35: 54-66.
Davies, R. and D. O'Meara. (1985) "The Total Strategy — an Analysis of South African Regional Policy Since 1978." *Journal of Southern African Studies* 11.2: 57-471.
Dougerty, J.E. and R.L. Pfaltzgraf. (1971) *Contending Theories of International Relations.* Philadelphia: Lippincott.
Levin, R. (1999) "Swaziland, Recent History."*Africa South of the Sahara, 'Swaziland'.* 28th ed. London: Europa. 1069-1074.
Matsebula, J.S.M. (1980) *A History of Swaziland.* Cape Town: Longman.
Matthews, G. (1999) "Swaziland, Recent History, Economy." *Africa South of the Sahara, 'Swaziland.'* 28th ed. London: Europa. 1074-1085.
United Nation Development Programme. Development Report (1998). 29.

12 Zambian Foreign Policy-Making Process in the Post-1991 Multi-Party Dispensation: The Chiluba Presidency

KORWA G. ADAR

The defeat of the United National Independence Party (UNIP) of President Kaunda by the Movement for the Multiparty Democracy (MMD) in the 1991 multiparty elections ushered in a new epoch in Zambian political history. For nearly three decades the Zambian domestic political milieu, but particularly her foreign policy-making process, was dominated by the Kaunda presidency (Chan 1992; Burnell 1994; Herman 1987; Anglin and Shaw 1979). As Chan (1992, 147) argues, Kaunda hardly accommodated advice from his ministers, particularly on issues he considered to be of paramount importance to him and to Zambian national interest in general. It is this leadership style which, on a number of occasions, led to conflict between Zambia and other Front Line States (FLS), an informal organisation comprising Angola, Botswana, Lesotho, Malawi, Mozambique, Swaziland, Tanzania, Zambia and Zimbabwe. The FLS was established to promote the liberation and independence of countries in southern Africa and to coordinate efforts against the destabilisation of the region by the South African apartheid regime. President Kaunda made some overtures to South Africa, establishing mutual rapprochement with F. de Klerk's presidency without the acquiescence of the FLS (Chan 1992, 151-172).

However, the leadership style in which presidential dominance becomes the determinant key to the foreign policy-making process is not unique to the Kaunda presidency — it is a common phenomenon, not only in Africa, but also in other parts of the world. In the African context, studies have tended to focus our attention on the president as the key decision-maker (Jackson and Rosberg 1982; Korany 1986; Clapham 1977). According to this approach, an authoritarian and centralised foreign policy-making process constitutes one of the likely elements. The central concern of this chapter, however, is not the Kaunda presidency, but rather the extent to which the foreign policy-making process has been decentralised and democratised in Zambia in the post-1991 democratic multiparty dispensation under the Chiluba presidency.

The introduction of multipartyism in Zambia in 1991 provided an environment conducive to the restructuring of the Zambian foreign policy-making process by the Chiluba presidency. Indeed, the emerging paradigm shift away from the ideological confrontation in global relations reminiscent of the Cold War era, as well as the 1994 democratic dispensation in South Africa, have provided additional incentives for a more participatory, decentralised and democratic foreign policy-making process in Zambia. Military threats from the south faded with the collapse of the apartheid regime. However, this is not to argue that the civil wars which continue to rage in Angola and the Democratic Republic of Congo (DRC) pose no threats to Zambian stability and her socio-economic and politico-military *raison d'être*. President Chiluba's direct involvement in the peace initiatives in the DRC is indicative of his concern for the security of Zambia and the region as a whole (Liogno 1999). By 1999, there were over 27,000 and 15,000 refugees from Angola and the DRC respectively, residing in Zambia.

Taking cognizance of the Zambian multiparty dispensation, the Ministry of Foreign Affairs (MFA) published a document in 1996 which provides for, *inter alia*, a representative and non-partisan foreign policy-making process (Zambia 1996, 22). Reiterating its commitment to depart from the practice of the derogation of the principle of the separation of powers common during the UNIP era, the MMD has stressed that:

> . . . checks and balances have been strengthened by observing separation of powers. The Executive has become more accountable to Parliament. Presidential appointments to certain constitutional Offices are now subject to ratification by Parliament. The concept of party supremacy no longer exists (MMD Manifesto 1996: at 6.2).

The two documents put forward by the MMD and the Ministry of Foreign Affairs are clear testimonies to the concern of the Chiluba administration with the necessity of embracing an inclusive foreign policy-making process. Indeed, the establishment of the Mwanakatwe Commission in 1993 to collate the views of Zambians on questions pertaining to, among other things, good governance, was indicative of the desire by the Chiluba administration to achieve these objectives (Mphaisha 1996, 68). It needs to be stated that a decentralised foreign policy-making process is not of itself democratic.

This chapter examines Zambian foreign policy and the foreign policy-making process after the 1991 multiparty elections and is divided into two broad parts. The first part explores the domestic and international contexts of Zambian foreign policy. This is not to argue that there is a clear-cut dichotomy between the domestic and international contexts of Zambian foreign policy. Some of the issues associated with foreign policy are interrelated. The second part focuses on foreign policy-making actors, for example, the Presidency, the Cabinet, Ministry of Foreign Affairs, Parliament, and Ministry of Defence and their individual, collective and complementary impact on the Zambian foreign policy-making process. Specifically, this section examines the extent to which the actors are involved in the foreign policy-making process.

The Domestic Context of Zambian Foreign Policy

Whereas there are many factors that explain the domestic context of Zambian foreign policy, certain key attributes are of paramount importance. Zambia is not only a multi-ethnic and landlocked country, but one that like most other African countries, is both heavily indebted and maintains a colonial inherited mono-economy state system (DeLancey 1996). Being a landlocked country, Zambia regards the principle of good neighbourliness as one of its foreign policy priorities. The 1994 democratic dispensation in South Africa has altered the long-standing geopolitical and national security problems Zambia faced along its borders during the apartheid era. This is not to argue, however, that Zambia's national security is not threatened by the continued instability in the region. The National Union for the Total Independence of Angola (UNITA) led by Jonas Savimbi, continues to pose security threats to Zambia's western borders. Indeed, the construction of the Tanzania-Zambia Railway Authority (TAZARA) by the Chinese in 1976, was a clear testimony to Zambia's vulnerability as a landlocked country *vis-à-vis* its neighbours. The need for the establishment of a stable and viable transport system for the steady flow of its export-oriented economy was, and continues to be, a *sine qua non* for its national survival.

Between 1991-1997, Zambia's total external debt averaged more than seven billion dollars. Whereas in 1991, the total external debt reached $7,336m, in 1995, 1996 and 1997 it stood at $6,859m, $7,182m and $6,758m respectively (World Bank 2000, 176). By 1996 Zambia's debt-service payments accounted for 24.6 per cent of the value of exports of goods and services. This placed Zambia among eleven other sub-Saharan African countries with 'unsustainable' debt burdens (Van Buren 2000, 1171). Copper continues to be the mainstay of Zambia's source of foreign exchange income. For example, the total foreign exchange income from copper in 1991, 1994, 1995 and 1996 reached 93 per cent, 68 per cent, 69 per cent and 52 per cent respectively (Van Buren 2000, 1157). This level of dependence on copper continues to impose structural constraints on Zambian foreign policy, where dependence in this case refers to Zambia's continued reliance on external actors.

Zambia is not only vulnerable to the consumer economies of, especially the More Developed Countries (MDCs), but Zambian leaders are also wary of fluctuations in the price of copper on the international market. The annual copper earnings dropped from $851m to $568m and $430m in 1995, 1996 and 1998 respectively. Indeed, Kaunda's overtures to the apartheid regime in South Africa in the 1980s were partly influenced by Zambian economic vulnerability. Japan, the European Union (EU), the United States, South Africa, Saudi Arabia, Thailand and Malaysia are some of the principle importers of Zambian copper, with South Africa's Anglo-American company being one of the dominant players in Zambia's copper industry.

It was as a result of Zambia's indebtedness that the transition to pluralism was carried out under the shadow of the International Monetary Fund (IMF) restructuring package which required Zambia to institute deregulation, privatisation, and liberalisation (Szeftel 2000, 216). The IMF package directly challenged the neopatrimonial *ancien régime* of the Kaunda presidency, which had not only laid the foundation for personal rule and power, but also encouraged political patronage. The IMF and the World Bank had frozen $78 million in 1991 to force the Kaunda administration to institute reforms, which culminated in the deterioration of the economy and widespread protests (Ham 1992, 61). With the introduction of reforms under the Chiluba administration, the donors began to release funds to the new regime in Zambia. The World Bank alone increased its allocation to Zambia by more than $240 million (Ham 1992, 62). What needs to be stressed is that Zambia's internal situation — that is, its dependence on external financial sources — also explains her foreign policy *vis-à-vis* the donors, particularly with respect to the implementation of reforms. Increased donor involvement in democracy-governance issues in the post-1991 multiparty dispensation in Zambia has led to disagreements between the Chiluba administration and the donors over the years (Baylies and Szeftel 1997, 114). However, as we have explained above, Zambia's dependence on external financial resources makes it vulnerable to the donors (Van Donge 1995).

Apart from its landlocked position and dependence, Zambia, like most of the African states, is a multi-ethnic country. Even though the situation in Zambia with its over 70 ethnic groups has not reached a critical stage as in, among others, Kenya, Nigeria, the DRC, Sudan, Rwanda and Liberia — Zambians are becoming disillusioned with Chiluba's leadership. However, what is more worrying for the Chiluba leadership is the existence of secessionist movements. The Lozoi ethnic group in the Western Province of Zambia is demanding autonomy and land rights. The dominant secessionist movements are the Liseli Conservative Party (LCP), the Agenda for Zambia (AZ), and the Barotse Patriotic Front (BPF), which advocate change in Zambia (Chiluba 1995, 108).[1] Stable as Zambia may seem to be to observers, these internal fissures will continue to threaten the country's ethnic cohesion and stability. In 1992, for example, a splinter group from the ranks of the MMD known as the Caucus for National Unity (CNU), challenged Chiluba's appointment of cabinet ministers because of what the group perceived to be his administration's insensitivity towards ethnic considerations (Mthembu-Salter 2000, 1162). In the 1996 general elections, only the AZ of the pro-secessionist groups managed to secure two parliamentary seats, a clear indication of the unpopularity of the secessionists.

The military coup attempt of October 28, 1997 by army officers calling themselves the National Redemption Council (NRC) dubbed their action Operation Born Again (OBA). Once the coup was successfully quelled by soldiers loyal to the regime, President Chiluba, with the consultation of the Cabinet, invoked the State of Emergency as provided for in Section 30 of the Zambian Constitution. The declaration of the state of emergency gave him the right, under Section 31 of the Emergency Powers Act (Cap. 108) to institute emergency regulations as provided for in the colonial inherited Preservation of Public Security Act (Cap. 112). The coup leader, Captain Steven Lungu, alias "Captain Solo," and fifteen other soldiers were arrested. A broad spectrum of Zambians, including UNIP, the Zambia Democracy Congress (ZADECO), religious groups, the Law Association of Zambia (LAZ), and other civil society groups, condemned the coup attempt. Many people were, however, arrested. More than thirty-three people, including prominent opposition leaders such as K. Kaunda, Dean Mungomba, leader of ZADECO, and Princess Nakatindi Wina, a former minister and the MMD's chairperson for women, were detained. In direct violation of Article 15 of the Zambian Constitution, a number of detainees were tortured and subjected to degrading punishment.

It is important to note that these interlocking domestic issues have impacted on Zambia's foreign policy. In an attempt to ease tension between his administration and the internal pro-democracy and human rights movements, churches, opposition parties, as well as the donor community, Chiluba appointed the High Court Judge, Japhet Banda, to head the Zambian Human Rights Commission (ZHRC) established to investigate human rights violations. A number of detainees were gradually released and by early 1998 the figure had reached 104 (*Human Rights Watch* 1999). The state of emergency was lifted in March 1998, following protests from within Zambia as well as from the United States, the European Union (EU), the United Kingdom, Norway, Iceland, the Central and Eastern European countries connected with the EU and other countries. Denmark suspended a $43m aid project to Zambia. The World Bank informed the Chiluba administration that the donor Consultative Group (CG) meeting could only be held once the state of emergency was lifted (*Human Rights Watch* 1999). As we have indicated, the Chiluba administration lifted the state of emergency in March, 1998. Chiluba's conformity to the demands of donors is not unique to Zambia. As we have explained elsewhere, African states' foreign policy behaviour is increasingly being influenced by donor political conditionalities in the New World Order (Adar and Vivekananda 2000).

The reluctance of the Chiluba administration to institute tangible democratic changes, coupled with the reintroduction of the State of Emergency in 1993 and 1997, eroded the donors' confidence in Zambia as a "model for Africa". Of central concern to the donors' CG as well as to civil society in Zambia have been the following issues: democratic and accountable governance; the rule of law; constitutional review; and corruption (Baylies and Szeftel 1997, 124-125). Apart from the decision by the USA to cut aid amounting to $2.5 million prior to the 1996 general elections in Zambia, the other donors who suspended aid included, among others, Norway, the Netherlands, the United Kingdom and Germany. The failure of the Mwanakatwe Commission to incorporate the Bill of Rights into its report on the review of the Zambian Constitution and good governance were some of the contributory factors to the donors' ambivalence (Mphaisha 1996 and Zambia 1995). It is important to stress that Zambia has failed to bring its Constitution into harmony with the International Covenant on Civil and Political Rights (ICCPR), particularly with respect to its frequent states of emergencies. The states of emergencies are not invoked in conformity with

Article 4 of the Covenant (Beyani 1998, 106). Zambia, as a signatory to the ICCPR, recognises the competence of the Covenant as well as the 1966 Optional Protocol to the ICCPR.

The International Dimensions of Zambian Foreign Policy

In an attempt to depart from ideological considerations reminiscent of the Kaunda presidency, the Chiluba administration conceptualises the fundamental principles of Zambia's foreign policy within the contexts of self-determination, equality of races, human rights and fundamental freedoms, and good neighbourliness. These principles are articulated with a view to promoting Zambian national interests based on, among other things, sovereignty, national security, democracy and economic development (Zambia 1996a, 3-6). As a sovereign state, Zambia's survival is contingent upon, *inter alia*, the stability and security of countries in the region. Zambia has, therefore, played a prominent role in conflict resolution initiatives in Africa particularly in Angola and the DRC.

Intra-Continental Dimensions of Zambian Foreign Policy

The 1993 peace talks in Lusaka, Zambia, between Jose Eduardo dos Santos's Popular Movement for the Liberation of Angola (MPLA) and Jonas Savimbi's UNITA marked the beginning of the involvement of the Chiluba administration in conflict resolution initiatives in Angola. These initiatives finally culminated in the Lusaka Protocol signed on 20th November 1994 by Venancio da Silva Moura, the Angolan Minister of Foreign Affairs, Eugenio Ngolo Manuvalola, UNITA's Secretary-General and the Special Representative of the Secretary-General of the UN, Alioune Blondin Beye. The Lusaka Protocol contained a number of Annexes which provided for, *inter alia*, the integration of UNITA's 60,000 troops into the Angolan Armed Forces (FAA) and the creation of a Government of National Unity and Reconstruction (GNUR) in early 1997 (Zambia 1997, 39; Mills and Smith 1999, 338). The steps which provide for the reconciliation of the belligerents — that is, the MPLA–led government and UNITA — are inscribed in Annex 6 of the Lusaka Protocol. However, UNITA failed to honour its obligations and instead resorted to armed conflict, burying hope for the success of the Chiluba administration's regional diplomacy. The volatility of Angola's Moxico Province, which borders on Zambia, forced the Chiluba administration to dispatch troops to the area in 1993 to prevent frequent UNITA incursions into Zambia. As one high-ranking Zambian official admitted, the Zambian-Angolan border remains hostile and a 'no man's land' to civilians because of the presence of heavily-armed UNITA rebels.[2] Zambia's other concerns are centred on its border with Namibia around the Caprivi Strip. Armed clashes between the Namibian Armed Forces (NAF) and the separatist Caprivi Liberation Army (CLA) frequently spill over into Zambia.

Zambia's participation in some of the United Nations (UN) peacekeeping missions in Africa since 1993 is an attempt by the Chiluba administration to fulfil Zambian foreign policy objectives in international relations. For example, in 1993, 1994 and 1995 Zambia contributed 1,000, 852 and 520 troops to the UN peacekeeping operations in Mozambique, Rwanda and Angola respectively (Zambia 1997, 26-27). Apart from concern for its national security, it would be fair to argue that Zambian involvement in the UN peacekeeping missions in Mozambique, Rwanda and Angola was in conformity with its foreign policy objectives (Kapoma 1995). Zambia's foreign policy objectives in Africa are broadly conceptualised within the contexts of self-determination, democracy, human rights and fundamental freedom and the basic human liberties under siege in the civil war-torn countries. However, this does not mean that these fundamental freedoms are observed *in toto* by the Chiluba administration. The mandate for the UN peacekeeping missions in Mozambique (United Nations Operations in Mozambique-ONUMOZ), Rwanda (United Nations Assistance Mission for Rwanda-UNAMIR) and Angola (United Nations Angola Verification Mission-UNAVEM III) was to protect human rights and to maintain peace and stability. Yet, as in the case of other African countries, Zambia's concern for human rights abroad does not necessarily conform to its practice at home (Adar 2000).

Apart from national security, the principles of sovereignty and territorial integrity of Zambia and its neighbours also underpin the Chiluba administration's foreign policy priorities. When the civil war broke out in the DRC, Zambia was appointed by the Southern African Development Community (SADC) and the Organisation of African Unity (OAU) to co-ordinate conflict resolution initiatives in the crisis plagued countries. The Chiluba administration's peace initiatives in the DRC received an endorsement from the United States, the UN and the European Union (EU). The DRC ranks second as one of the major importers of Zambian goods in Africa. In 1995, for example, Zambia exported goods to Zimbabwe, the DRC, South Africa, Tanzania and Malawi which amounted to $32m, $27m and $24m, $22m and

$9 million respectively (World Bank 2000, 143-145). Regional stability is, therefore, of paramount importance to Zambia for econo-political and security reasons.

Zambia's conflict resolution efforts in the DRC culminated in the Lusaka Accord of 10 July 1999, which brought together most of the parties to the conflict. The Lusaka Cease-Fire Agreement was signed by the Presidents of Angola, the DRC, Namibia, Rwanda, Uganda and Zimbabwe and witnessed by the SADC, the OAU, and the UN representatives as well as some rebel factions. The Lusaka Accord was a diplomatic bonus for the Chiluba administration, particularly *vis-à-vis* the regional leaders and the donors. The European Union, in its recognition of the Chiluba administration's mediation efforts in the DRC, resolved to reimburse Zambia for all the costs associated with the civil war (Zambia 1999, 34). One of the major worries for Zambia was the question of refugees, who by 1999 reached nearly 200,000 in number (Zambia 1999, 9). Within the intra-African context of Zambia's foreign policy, the issues of econo-political and security considerations, it can be argued, are of paramount importance to the Chiluba administration.

Zambia's contribution to conflict resolution in the region notwithstanding, the Chiluba administration has been accused of pursuing a policy of alienation (Taylor 1997). During the 1997 SADC meeting in Blantyre, Malawi, President Mandela remarked that under his chairmanship the regional organisation would no longer condone member states whose domestic policies undermined democratic principles. President Mandela was tacitly making reference to the SADC member states such as Zambia which had resisted tangible democratic change. Chiluba's dismissal of the well-intentioned concerns of Mandela was not only ill-informed but also reflected his administration's incoherent foreign policy behaviour. In other words, the Chiluba administration has been more concerned with the issues of humanitarian and human rights situations abroad than with adherence to the same principles at home. Chiluba seemed to be more concerned with Mandela's perceived interference into Zambia's internal affairs than with the Zambia-South African long-term econo-political and security interests.

Extra-African Contexts of Zambian Foreign Policy

A careful perusal of public documents pertaining to Zambian foreign policy indicates that global peace and security, sovereign equality, non-alignment and economic interests take centre stage in her foreign policy priorities and pronouncements (Zambia 1996, 1-6). Pursuit of these foreign policy priorities in International Relations promotes Zambia's econo-political and security interests. Zambia's severance of diplomatic relations with Iran and Iraq in March 1993 demonstrated the Chiluba administration's uncompromising stance and sensitivity over issues associated with national security. Zambia accused Iran and Iraq of contravening the 1961 Vienna Convention on Diplomatic Relations because of what the Chiluba administration considered to be direct interference in the country's internal affairs (Zambia 1998, 19).

At the core of the diplomatic dispute between Zambia and Iran and Iraq was the 1993 military coup attempt. The Chiluba administration accused UNIP and other forces of plotting to overthrow the government with the financial help of Iran and Iraq. The military coup plan dubbed 'Zero Option' culminated in the declaration of the state of emergency and the arrest of leading UNIP officials, including three of Kaunda's sons. Other observers have, however, argued that the military coup was orchestrated by the fundamental Christian and anti-Muslim ranks within the MMD and the Chiluba administration.[3] These internal concerns for its national security are also in conformity with Zambia's global economic, political and security considerations. The Chiluba administration declared Zambia a Christian nation. The 1996 Constitutional Amendment declares Zambia a "Christian nation while upholding the right of every person to enjoy . . . freedom of conscience or religion" (Zambia 1996, preamble).

In a global environment still dominated by the major powers' econo-political and military interests in the post Cold War era, Zambia's foreign policy is articulated mainly within the frameworks of international forums such as the UN, OAU, the Non-Aligned Movement (NAM), the Group of 77 (G-77), the Africa, the Caribbean and the Pacific (ACP) and the Commonwealth. As he acknowledged in his 1999 report to the Zambian National Assembly, the Chairman of the Committee on National Security and Foreign Affairs (CNSFA), S. Mukupa, stated that in the New World Order, issues pertaining to the economic foundations of national interests will increasingly determine Zambia's foreign policy. According to Mukupa, Zambia's economic foreign policy priorities are centred on the promotion of exports; encouragement of foreign direct investment; membership of regional and international organisations and associations; and the role of economic diplomacy in the promotion of Zambia's image abroad (Zambia 1999, 3-4). Zambia has, therefore, expressed its unreserved views on salient issues affecting its interests abroad.

On the question of the restructuring of the UN, for example, Zambia supports the NAM and G-77 position, which call for, *inter alia*, transparency, accountability and democratisation of the Security Council (Zambia 1999: 24-25). This maximalist perspective is based on the proposal which calls for, *inter alia*, the expansion of membership of the UN Security Council (UNSC) from the current 15 to 26, with two permanent members from Africa. The supporters of this proposal, particularly the OAU, G-77 and NAM, are of the view that the monopoly of the UNSC by the permanent members (US, UK, France, Italy and China) is inconsistent with the post-Cold War New World Order. Apart from the question of the democratization of the UN decision-making hierarchy, foreign policy-makers in Zambia have also incorporated the issues pertaining to the volatile and conflict-prone regions of the world into Zambia's foreign policy agenda. For example, the Arab-Israeli conflict; the Korean problem; the collapsed state of Somalia; the civil wars in Angola, the DRC, Sierra Leone and Sudan; the situation in the former Yugoslavia; and the Eritrean-Ethiopian conflict, have remained priorities for the Zambian foreign policy-making establishment since the late 1990s.[4] Some of these issues, particularly the Palestinian question, conflicts in Angola, Somalia and the Ethio-Eritrean war took centre stage at the 1998 NAM Summit in Durban, South Africa.

Zambia's Foreign Policy-Making Process: The Role of Actors

Even though the Presidency is the dominant actor, there are other state actors, for example, Parliament, the Ministry of Foreign Affairs (MFA), the Ministry of Defence (MoD), the Ministry of Home Affairs (MHA) and the Intelligence Community (IC), as well as non-state actors or non-governmental organizations (NGOs), such as the media and political parties which play important roles at different levels in the Zambian foreign policy-making process. However, given their limitations, not all the actors are examined in this study. The foreign policy-making of any country is so replete with interlocking patterns that to assume a persistent and centralised presidential dominance is to underestimate and misperceive the complexities involved. In this section, an attempt is made to delineate, from analytical and conceptual perspectives, the input of actors involved in the Zambian foreign policy-making process. Taking a more Afro-pessimist perspective, Van Donge argues that the presidency in Zambia is still the central player in the domain of foreign policy-making, a situation which imposes limitations on the role of other actors in the post-1991 multiparty dispensation (Van Donge 1995, 193;

Szeftel 2000: 221-222). For example, Von Donge argues that the main stumbling block for the tangible institutionalization of a democratised foreign policy-making in Zambia is that the Chiluba administration has maintained a presidential as opposed to a parliamentary system of governance (Van Donge 1995, 208-210).

These observations do not provide adequate analyses of Zambian foreign policy-making structures. In any country, well established liberal democracies included, heads of state and government (presidents and prime ministers) take leading roles, particularly with respect to salient issues affecting national interest. For example, in the Zambian case, President Chiluba was directly involved when decisions were made to sever diplomatic relations with Iran and Iraq, with parliament merely sanctioning the decision. The Office of the President plays an important role in crisis situations, with parliament and the Ministry of Foreign Affairs taking proactive roles in other routine situations. Indeed, the formulation and implementation of Zambian foreign policy is the prerogative of the Ministry of Foreign Affairs. The fact that presidential dominance becomes apparent in crisis situations affecting Zambian national interest does not necessarily mean that other foreign policy-making institutions are not directly involved in the decisions at all levels. It is also important to stress that President Chiluba, like any other sovereign head of state, may still be involved in any foreign policy issue. This may take the form of an offer of advice after being briefed by officials within foreign policy-making structures. Even though Figure 12.1 (page 252) is not exhaustive, it provides a representative picture of Zambian foreign policy-making by different actors. It is drawn from my field research in Lusaka, Zambia, in March to April 2000. We do recognise that Zambian foreign policy-making is more complex than Figure 12.1 depicts, however, the figure approximates what takes place in crisis and routine situations. It is important to note that the levels of involvement by actors in the issue areas need not be interpreted to be sacrosanct. They may vary from time to time and with specific issue areas.

The Presidency

The presidency is the institution or simply the office of the presidency comprising the president, the vice-president, cabinet ministers, presidential advisers, the intelligence, and other personal staff. In the case of Zambia, the executive power of the president is provided for in Part IV, Article 33 (2) of the Constitution (Zambia 1996c, at 33 (2)). The president relies on these key

252 *Globalization and Emerging Trends*

individuals for the proper management and governance of the country. Apart from the president who normally chairs its proceedings, the other members of the Cabinet are the Vice President and Ministers (Zambia 1996c, at 49 (1)).

The Zambian Security Intelligence Act of 1998, Article 15(b) confers on the President, as the Chairman of the National Intelligence Council (NIC), the power to appoint the Director-General and three members of the

Figure 12.1 A Schematic Model of Zambian Foreign Policy-making

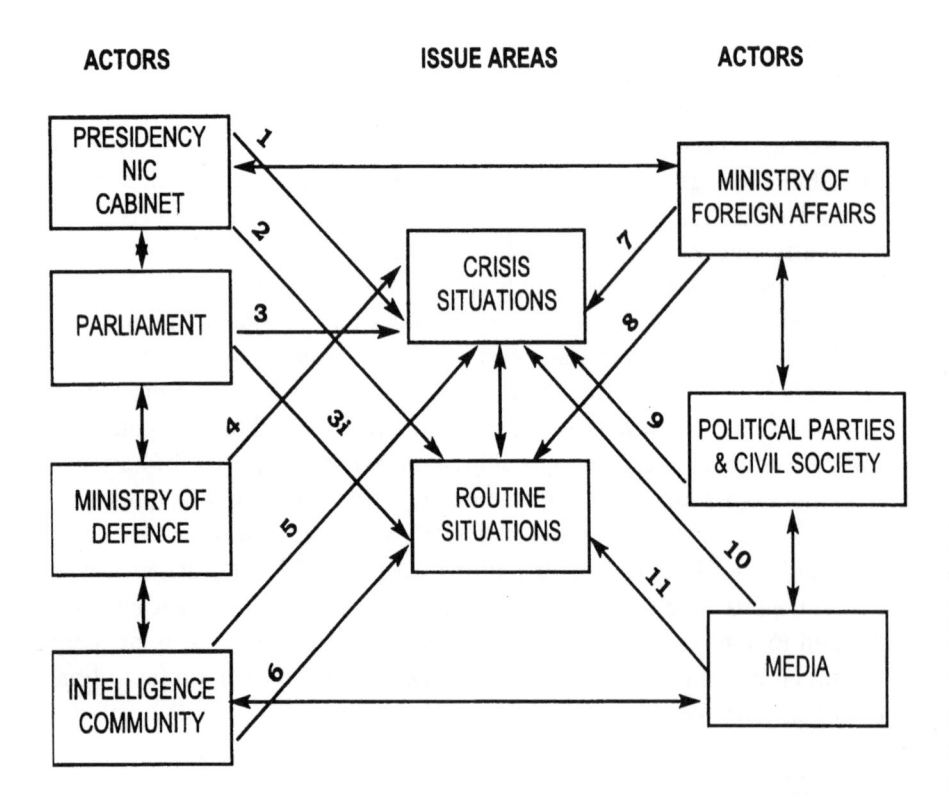

Levels of Decision-making: 1 Decision; 2 Support; 3 Investigative; 3i Investigative; 4 Implementation; 5 Investigative; 6 Investigative; 7 Implementation; 8 Formulation / Implementation; 9 Investigative; 10 Investigative; 11 Investigative.

Council. The three appointees serve at the pleasure of the President. The responsibilities of the NIC are provided for in Article 16 of the Act and include, *inter alia*, the formulation and review of intelligence as well as the coordination of activities relating to security intelligence of ministries or departments, the armed forces and the police force. The decision to sever diplomatic relations with Iran and Iraq, for example, was probably taken by the NIC in consultation with key members of the Cabinet. This suggests a State House-centred foreign policy-making process as opposed to what is reflected in Figure 12.1. Specifically, we are suggesting that it is likely that the NIC, chaired by Chiluba, made the initial decision before the Cabinet was involved. In crisis situations, presidents tend to institute *ad hoc* groups to deal with national security related issues before making them public. This is what is generally referred to as 'groupthink' (Janis and Mann 1977; Janis 1977 and Roberts 1988). Janis describes groupthink as "a mode of thinking that people engage in when they are deeply involved in a cohesive in-group, when the members striving for unanimity override their motivation to realistically appraise alternative courses of action" (Janis 1977, 8). The actual composition of those initially involved in decision-making during the Zambian–Iranian–Iraqi crisis may never be known. The other possible explanation is that all the members of the Cabinet, the NIC, and the president were present in the initial stages as depicted in Figure 12.1 above.

The discussions by the NIC and the Cabinet on the necessity to impose the State of Emergency led to divisions within the ranks of the Cabinet ministers. For example, the Minister for Legal Affairs, Roger Chongwe, the Minister Without Portfolio, Godfrey Miyanda, and the Minister for Labour, Ludwig Sandashi, among others, were opposed to the declaration of the State of Emergency (Ham 1993, 14). Two points need to be re-emphasised. Firstly, in crisis situations, decisions take place at the level of the presidency — in other words, presidential decision-making takes a centre stage. This is a president-centred or State House-centred foreign policy-making process. In this particular case, Chiluba, with the help of his key advisers, set the direction of the decision output. It is likely that Chiluba called the Cabinet crisis meeting with a pre-determined policy position. Secondly, the disagreements which emerged at the March 3, 1993 crisis meeting among members of the cabinet following Chiluba's request to impose a State of Emergency under Article 31 of the 1991 Zambian Constitution, can also be interpreted to mean that there was some degree of openness during the deliberations. In other words, Chiluba adhered to the constitutional provisions before he imposed the State of Emergency.

However, the disagreements among the members of the Cabinet may have occurred as a result of resentment over Chiluba's decision to pressure members into accepting his decision. President Chiluba not only proclaimed the State of Emergency under Article 31 on March 4, 1993, but on March 9, 1993 he also invoked the State of Public Emergency powers as provided for under Article 30 of the Zambian Constitution. He argued that the powers stipulated under Article 31 were not adequate (Chibangula 1998, 49). For most of its independent history, particularly under the Kaunda presidency, Zambia was governed under a State of Emergency, with far-reaching human rights violations (Chibangula 1998; Chanda 1998).

Parliament

Apart from the general deliberations on policy during parliamentary debates, the Committee on Foreign Affairs (CFA), renamed in 1999 the Committee on National Security and Foreign Affairs (CNSFA), is responsible for scrutinizing Zambian foreign relations. The power of the CFA is provided for in the National Assembly Standing Order No. 147(2) which stipulates that:

> . . . it shall be the duty of the Committee of Foreign Affairs to scrutinize Zambia's foreign policy. While the Government may make and ratify treaties or agreements without the authority or approval of the national Assembly, such treaties or agreements must be formally laid before the House, and the Government shall not proceed with the ratification until twenty-one days have elapsed after the treaties or agreements have been laid before the House (Zambia 1993(a), 1).

Standing Order No. 147(2) gives the government — specifically the presidency — more powers *vis-à-vis* parliament. However, in 1995, Standing Order No. 147(2) was amended to provide parliament with more powers in relation to the government. Specifically it provides that:

> . . . it shall be the duty of the Committee on Foreign Affairs to scrutinize Zambia's foreign policy and all treaties and agreements entered into by the Government. Except for treaties of a security nature, all other treaties entered into by the Government must be laid before the House within a reasonable period after ratification of such treaties and agreements by the Government (Zambia 1995, 1).

The revised Standing Order No. 147(2) is more specific with respect to the role of parliament on matters regarding treaties and agreements. Treaty ratification rests with parliament. As we have indicated, CFA was renamed CNSFA with responsibility for overseeing the activities of the Ministries of Defence, Home Affairs and Foreign Affairs (Zambia 1999, 1). Parliament is, therefore, empowered to scrutinize issues that deal with national security. The inclusion of the Ministries of Defence and Home Affairs whose responsibilities include, among other things, national security, gives Parliament additional influence *vis-à-vis* the Government.

The Committee of Foreign Affairs has the power to summon the Foreign Affairs Office or any other experts within the government to answer questions relating to Zambian foreign policy.[5] In this instance, as Figure 12.1 indicates, Parliament acts as an investigative institution. The Office of the President also has a mandate to initiate policy on important matters affecting the country. It was this prerogative that Chiluba invoked when he summoned the NIC and the Cabinet for a crisis meeting during the 1993 and 1997 military coup attempts. It is important to point out that one of the responsibilities of the Cabinet is to ratify policies before they are implemented by the Ministry of Foreign Affairs.

As shown in Figure 12.1, Parliament plays an investigative role, particularly if the foreign policy issues at stake do not border on national security questions. When Zambia severed diplomatic relations with Iran and Iraq in 1993, the then Minister of Foreign Affairs, V. J. Mwanga, informed the House that Zambia had made the decision because of the two countries' intention to "undermine the authority and legitimacy of our democratically elected Government" (Zambia 1993b, 1712). In this particular case, realists would argue that the Chiluba administration made a rational decision. The president, as the sovereign head of state, is endowed with the responsibility of making decisions on behalf of the state. Thus, the Zambian National Assembly merely sanctioned the Cabinet's decision.

It is important to reiterate that these interlocking foreign policy-making stages are not necessarily clear-cut. They may vary with issue areas. One should note that where national security is perceived to be at stake, in most cases policy-makers overlook fundamental principles of democracy. Specifically, even if such decisions contravene constitutionally established principles of democracy and human rights, national security issues generally take precedence. Zambia is, demonstrably, not alone in this practice. As a matter of fact, policy-makers usually find ways and means to justify their decisions. For his part, Chiluba has argued that his administration's decision to reintroduce the State of Emergency in 1993 was done with the approval of the constitutionally established institutional structures of Zambia. He has also pointed out that his administration's decision to institute the State of Emergency and to sever diplomatic relations with Iran and Iraq had a bipartisan endorsement from the political parties, the MMD included (Chiluba 1995, 107). It is important to note that the MMD had won 125 of the 150 parliamentary seats in the 1991 general elections which gave the party an overwhelming numerical strength in the Zambian National Assembly. Furthermore, Article 51 of the Constitution of Zambia requires "the Cabinet and Deputy Ministers to be accountable collectively to the National Assembly" (Zambia 1996, Article 51). It can be argued that the decision by the Chiluba presidency to table in the National Assembly, the 1993 and 1997 decisions pertaining to the State of Emergency and the other related policy decisions conformed to the spirit of the Constitution of Zambia.

Other Foreign Policy-making Actors

As we have indicated, the Chiluba administration has been involved in a number of conflict resolution initiatives, particularly in Angola and the DRC. Apart from the Office of the President, the other Zambian foreign policy actors involved in mediation efforts as well as other Zambian foreign policy interests include, *inter alia*, the Ministries of Foreign Affairs, Defence, Home Affairs and Finance. Indeed, the input of the Intelligence Community cannot be ignored. The Ministry of Foreign Affairs constitutes the central locus in as far as the formulation and implementation of Zambian foreign policy is concerned. Even in crisis situations, as was the case in the 1993 severance of diplomatic relations with Iran and Iraq, it was the prerogative of the ministry to implement the government's decision. Indeed, the Ministry of Foreign Affairs in conjunction with the Ministries of Home Affairs and Defence, the Office of the President and the Intelligence Community, was instrumental in setting in motion the 'proximity talks' between the MPLA-led government and UNITA.[6]

Proximity talks refer to a situation in which negotiations involving belligerent parties are held separately before the parties are brought together face-to-face at the same table. In the case of the October 1993 to 1994 negotiations in Zambia involving the MPLA and UNITA, proximity talks took more than three months before the belligerent parties agreed to sit down together.[7] Kapoma was directly involved in the intensive negotiations. Zambia had been requested by the UN to offer its good offices to resolve the civil war. The participants in the peace negotiations included not only the belligerent parties but also observers from the USA, Russia and Portugal, as well as from the UN, the OAU and the SADC. The DRC ceasefire negotiations in Zambia paved the way for the adoption of UN Security Council

Resolution 1291 of 24th February 2000 in which 5,537 peacekeeping troops were to be deployed in the civil war-torn country (Zambia 2000).

Instability in the region has made it imperative for the Office of the President, the Intelligence Community, Home Affairs and Defence to be more active participants in Zambian foreign policy-making process. Table 12.2 below, indicates the gradual decrease in military spending by the Chiluba presidency in comparison to that of Kaunda. Except for the civil war-torn countries, military spending by most countries in Africa has generally declined in the post Cold War era. Whereas the numbers of the Zambian armed forces have remained at an average of 17,000 between 1992 and 1999, Zambia's military spending has dropped markedly from $104 million in 1992 to $41 million in 1997. Between 1997 and 1999, the Independence armed forces increased to over 20,000.

Zambia is not only worried about instability, but the military strength of both the civil war-torn neighbours and the insurgent movements as well. For example, between 1987 and 1997, Angola maintained an army of an average of over 118,000 and spent an average of more that $1.46 million annually in the same period. UNITA, with an estimated 60,000 militia, controlled 70% of Angola's $1.2 billion diamond production in 1996. What is important to note is the frequent Zambian-Angolan border incursions by the FAA in pursuit of UNITA. Angola also claims that Independence armed forces frequently cross into Angolan territory. The two countries established the Angola-Zambia Joint Permanent Defence and Security Commission in 1998 to deal with the volatile border issue. The Zambian Defence Minister is responsible for Zambian national security interests in the Commission. The Zambian Ministry of Home Affairs and the Zambian Chief of Staff, as well as the Zambian Security Intelligence Service (ZSIS) are also involved in the Commission's security deliberations. The Zambian Ministry of Home Affairs is involved in Commission deliberations primarily because of the influx of Angolan refugees into Zambia.

Apart from contributing troops to the UN peacekeeping operations in Angola, Mozambique and Rwanda, Zambia also dispatched observers and military contingents to the United Nations Observer Mission in Sierra Leone (UNOMSIL) in 1998. Zambian participation in UN peacekeeping missions is perceived by the Ministry of Defence and other Zambian foreign policy-making actors in a number of ways. The benefits — especially to the Zambian Armed Forces — include "professional, corporate, and image-building" benefits (Zambia 1999, 19). In the areas where they operate, the UN peacekeeping troops are involved in various activities which expose the

Table 12.1 Zambian Military Expenditure and Armed Forces

YEAR	MILITARY EXPENDITURE (Million Dollars)	ARMED FORCES	ME %GNP	ME %CGE
1987	96*	17	3.5	9.2
1988	101	17	3.3	9.8
1989	149	17	4.7	14.6
1990	131	16	4.1	12.6
1991	90	16	2.9	3.9
1992	104	16	3.3	9.3
1993	58	16	1.7	5.5
1994	68	16	2.0	7.2
1995	56	16	1.7	5.9
1996	43	16	1.2	4.7
1997	41	21	1.1	3.9
1998	58**	21		
1999	25	21		

Sources: *U.S. Bureau of Arms Control, *World Military Expenditures and Arms Transfers 1998* (Washington DC: Bureau of Arms Control, 1998);
**SIPRI Yearbook 2000, *Armaments, Disarmaments and International Security* (London: Oxford University Press, 2000).

Zambians to civilian and humanitarian concepts of conflict resolution. Within southern Africa, the Inter-State Defence and Security Committee (ISDSC) of the SADC provides an important forum for Zambia's Ministry of Defence and other foreign policy-making actors to participate in fostering peace, stability and harmony in the region (Chiluba 1998, 12).

The influence of the NGOs, particularly political parties, the church, trade unions, and the media on Zambian foreign policy cannot be underestimated. After all Chiluba, as Chairman of the powerful Zambia Congress of Trade Unions (ZCTU), ascended to the presidency with the support of the trade union movement. Apart from the ZCTU, the other active trade unions that have influenced Zambian post–1991 politics include the Zambia Industrial and Commercial Association (ZINCOM) and the Mineworkers Union of Zambia (MUZ). It was because of the pressure of trade unions, religious groups such as the Christian Council of Zambia (CCZ), the Evangelical Fellowship of Zambia (EFZ), the Zambia Episcopal Conference (ZEC) and the Roman Catholic Church, that Kaunda agreed to institute multiparty democracy. In conjunction with other NGOs and the donor community, these actors continue to play important roles in the Zambian foreign policy-making process. The decision by some of the donors to withhold funds after the 1996 Zambian general elections was influenced by the NGOs (Kabwe 1997). The elections were considered not to be free and fair by a number of local and international observers. However, the multiplicity of political parties (which have reached twenty in 2000) and laws restricting freedom of the media, continue to undermine the impact of these NGOs on Zambian foreign policy. Even the ZCTU, (an ally of the ruling party, the MMD), has observed that "you cannot talk about accountability and transparency in the absence of a free press . . . Control measures introduced against journalists is not a healthy development at all" (Chirwa 1997, 14). The Constitution of Zambia, Amendment Act, 17 and 18 of 1996 did not incorporate the recommendations of the Mwanakatwe Commission which dealt extensively with the freedom of the press. These limitations notwithstanding, the press and the media remain important watchdogs of the government.

Conclusion

In this chapter we have examined Zambian foreign policy and foreign policy-making process during the Chiluba presidency. We have dealt with Zambia's intra- and extra- African states foreign policy interests. In as much as these foreign policy interests are distinct, we have also explained that they are interrelated. For example, Zambia's econo-political and security interests have an impact on its foreign policy behaviour. Zambia's direct involvement in conflict resolution initiatives in the region is determined by its internal and external needs. The international borders are increasingly becoming permeable in this era of globalization. One of the consequences of this is that conflicts in Angola and the DRC become Zambia's problems, particularly because of the security implications.

Whereas it would be incorrect to underestimate the influence of the President in Zambia's foreign policy-making process, we have demonstrated that other actors, namely the Ministries of Foreign Affairs, Defence, Home Affairs, the Cabinet, Parliament, and the Intelligence Community are also important players. These actors are involved in Zambian foreign policy-making at different levels, with the Presidency and the Cabinet constituting the central loci for decision-making in crisis situations. We have examined Zambian foreign policy-making actors in relation to the responsibilities conferred on them by the Constitution. The 1993 military coup attempt which culminated in Zambia's severance of diplomatic relations with Iran and Iraq and the imposition of the State of Emergency, provided a good example of situations in which these actors were involved. Indeed, the impact of non-state actors in Zambian foreign policy-making cannot be ignored. In many ways, the non-state actors in Zambia, as in other parts of Africa, have mainly advocated the institutionalization of democracy and human rights.

Notes

1 See *Jane's Sentinel Security Assessments* (http://www.newsite.jane...sentinel/southern-africa/zambia.shtml, 8/19/00).
2 Interview with T. C. Kapoma, Deputy Permanent Secretary, Ministry of Foreign Affairs, Lusaka, Zambia in April 2000.
3 *Africa Confidential* 14 May 1993: 1; also see *Echo of Islam*, March 1993: 11-12.
4 Zambia 1996, 1997, 1998 and 1999.
5 Interview with Joe Muntanga, Deputy Principal Clerk, National Assembly of Zambia, Lusaka, Zambia in April 2000.
6 Interview with T. C. Kapoma, Deputy Permanent Secretary, Ministry of Foreign Affairs, Lusaka, Zambia in April 2000.
7 Interview with T. C. Kapoma, April 2000.

References

Adar, Korwa G. (2000) "The Internal and External Contexts of Human Rights Practice in Kenya: Daniel arap Moi's Operational Code." *African Sociological Review* 4.1: 74-96.
Adar, Korwa G. and Vivekananda, Franklin. (2000) "The Interface between Political Conditionality and Democratization: The Case of Kenya." *Scandinavian Journal of Development Alternatives and Area Studies* 19.2/3: 71-104.
Anglin, Douglas G. and Timothy M. Shaw. (1979) *Zambia's Foreign Policy: Studies in Diplomacy and Dependence*. Boulder: Westview Press.
Baylies, Carolyn and Morris Szeftel. (1997) "The 1996 Zambia Elections: Still Awaiting Democratic Consolidation." *Review of African Political Economy* 24.71 (March): 113-128.

Beyani, Chalok. (1998) "International Law and the Lawfulness of Derogations from Human Rights during States of Emergency in Zambia." *Zambia Law Journal*, Special Edition: 103-119.
Burnell, Peter. (1994) "Zambia at the Crossroads." *World Affairs* 157: 19-28.
Chan, Stephen. (1992) *Kaunda and Southern Africa: Image and Reality in Foreign Policy.* London: British Academic Press.
Chanda, Alfred W. (1998) "Human Rights in Zambia in Third Republic: An Overview. *Legality Journal* 1998: 59-77.
Chibangula, Gary D. (1998) "The Protection of Freedom from Torture under a Declared State of Emergency." *Legality Journal* 1998: 49-58.
Chiluba, Frederick J.T. (1998) Speech of the Official Opening of the Second Session of the Eighth National Assembly. 6th January 1998. Lusaka: Government Printers.
———. (1995) *Democracy: The Challenge of Change.* Lusaka: Multimedia Publications.
Chirwa, Chris H. (1997) *Press Freedom in Zambia: A Brief Overview of the State of the Press During the MMD's First Five Years in Office.* Lusaka: Zambia Independent Media Association.
Clapham, Christopher, ed. (1977) *Foreign Policy Making in Developing States.* Farnborough: Saxon House.
DeLancey, Virginia. (1996) "The Economies of Africa." *Understanding Contemporary Africa*. Ed. April A. Gordon and Donald L. Gordon. Boulder: Lynne Rienner. 91-127.
Echo of Islam. "A Second Look at Iran—Zambia Relationship." No. 129 (March 1995): 11-12.
Gertzel, Cherry, Carolyn Baylies and Morris Szeftel. (1984) *The Dynamics of the One-Party State in Zambia*. Manchester: Manchester University Press.
Ham, Melinda. (1992) "End of the Honeymoon." *Africa Report* 37: 61-63.
———. (1993) "History Repeats Itself." *Africa Report* 38: 13-16.
Hawkins, Margaret G. (1987) "Assessing the Foreign Policy Role Orientations of Sub-Saharan African Leaders." *Role Theory and Foreign Policy Analysis.* Ed. Stephen G. Walker. Durham: Duke University Press. 161-198.
Human Rights Watch, World Report (1999) Zambia: Human Rights Developments (http://www.hrw.org/hrw/worldreport99/africa/zambia.html).
Jackson, Robert and Carl G. Rosberg. (1982) *Personal Rule in Africa: Prince, Autocrat, Prophet, Tyrant.* Berkeley: University of California Press.
Janis, I.L. (1997) *Victims of Groupthink.* Boston: Houghton Mifflin.
Janis, I.L. and L. Mann. (1977) *Decision Making: A Psychological Analysis of Conflict, Choice and Commitment.* New York: Free Press.
Kabwe, Tiyaonse Chisanga. (1997) *Kenneth David Kaunda: Founder President of the Republic of Zambia. Perspectives of his Exit from Office.* Harare: SAPES Books.
Kapoma, T.C. "Zambia's Foreign Policy." A paper presented by Mr T. C. Kapoma, Deputy Permanent Secretary (Political) at the Zambia Institute of Diplomacy and International Studies (ZIDIS), Lusaka, Zambia, 17 December 1995.
Koraney, Bahgat ed. (1986) *How Foreign Policy Decisions Are Made In The Third World: A Comparative Analysis.* Boulder: Westview Press.
Liongo, André A.A. (1999) *The Lusaka Cease-Fire Agreement and Perspectives for Peace in the DRC.* Johannesburg: Institute for Global Dialogue.
Mills, Greg and Johann Smith. (1999) "Angola: the Resurrection of UNITA?" *South African Yearbook of International Affairs 1999/2000.* Johannesburg: South African Institute of International Affairs. 337-343.
Movement for the Multiparty Democracy (MMD). (1966) *Movement for the Multiparty Democracy Manifesto 1996; Movement for Multiparty Democracy: The Better Way.* Lusaka: W.L. and Co.

Mphaisha, Chesepo J.J. (1996) "Retreat from Democracy in post One-Party State Zambia." *Journal of Commonwealth and Comparative Politics* 24.2: 65-84.

Mthembu-Salter, Gregory. (2000) "Zambia: Recent History." *Africa, South of the Sahara 2000*. 29th ed. London: Europa Publlications. 1160-1166.

Non-Aligned Movement. Final Document XII, NAM Summit. Durban, 29 August-3 September, 1998.

Roberts, Jonathan M. (1988) *Decision-Making During International Crises*. London: Macmillan.

Shaw, Timothy M. (1976) "The Foreign Policy System of Zambia." *The African Studies Review* 19.1: 31-66.

Szeftel, Morris (2000) "'Eat With Us': Managing Corruption and Patronage under Zambia's Three Republics, 1964-1999." *Journal of Contemporary African Studies* 18.2: 207-224.

Taylor, Ian (1997) "Zambia and the Foreign Policy of Alienation." *Contemporary Review* 271 (1582): 238-242.

Van Buren, Linda. (2000) "Zambia: Economy." *Africa South of the Sahara 2000*. 29th Ed. London: Europa Publications. 1166-1182.

Van Donge, Jan Kees. (1995) "Zambia: Kaunda and Chiluba: Enduring Patterns of Political Culture." *Democracy and Political Change in Sub-Saharan Africa*. Ed. John A. Wiseman. London: Routledge. 193-219.

World Bank. (2000) *African Development Indicators 2000. World Bank Africa Database*. Washington, DC: World Bank.

———. (1993) National Assembly of Zambia. *Parliamentary Debates of the 22nd Session of the 7th National Assembly, 15th January-18th March 1993*. Lusaka: Government Printer. 1712-1713.

Zambia. (1993) National Assembly of Zambia. *Parliamentary Debates of the 22nd Session of the 7th National Assembly, 15th January-18th March 1993*. Lusaka: Government Printer. 1712-1713.

———. (1993a) National Assembly of Zambia. *Report of the Committee on Foreign Affairs for the Second Session of the Seventh National Assembly Appointed on the 20th January 1993*. Lusaka: National Assembly of Zambia.

———. (1995) *Summary of the Recommendations of the Mwanakatwe Constitution Review Commission and Government Reaction to the Report*. Government Paper No. 1 of 1995. Lusaka: Government Printer.

———. (1996) The Constitution of Zambia, Amendment No. 18 of 1996. Lusaka: Government Printer.

———. (1996a) Ministry of Foreign Affairs. *Zambia's Foreign Policy*. Lusaka: Government Printer. 31 January.

———. (1997) National Assembly of Zambia. *Report of the Committee on Foreign Affairs for the First Session of the Eighth National Assembly Appointed on 23rd January, 1997*. Lusaka: National Assembly of Zambia.

———. (1998) National Assembly of Zambia. *Report of the Committee on Foreign Affairs for the Second Session of the Eighth National Assembly Appointed on 22nd January 1998*. Lusaka: National Assembly of Zambia.

———. (1999) National Assembly of Zambia. *Report of the Committee on National Security and Foreign Affairs for the Third Session of the Eighth National Assembly Appointed on 3rd February 1999*. Lusaka: National Assembly of Zambia.

———. (2000) Speech delivered by the Zambian Minister for Foreign Affairs, Mr. S.K. Walubita, at the 71st OAU Council of Ministers Meeting in Addis Ababa, Ethiopia, 8-10 March 2000.

"Zambia: The Model Democracy Loses Its Shine." *Africa Confidential* 34.10 (14 May 1993): 1-3.

13 Post-Cold War Zimbabwe's Foreign Policy and Foreign Policy-Making Process

KORWA G. ADAR, ROK AJULU AND MOSES O. ONYANGO

The collapse of the Soviet Union and the end of the Cold War in the 1980s ushered in shifts in the global balance of forces, changes which have had tremendous effects on regional as well international interactions. In southern Africa, the Southern African Development Community (SADC) countries witnessed similar shifts in the balance of power: not only did these shifts engender the transition from the old Southern African Development and Coordinating Committee (SADCC) to the more developmentally-orientated SADC, but more critically, thoroughgoing changes at the political level were equally discernible. Namibia, Lesotho and South Africa all went through successful transitions, culminating in the historic South African democratic elections of 1994. In Mozambique, Frente de Libertacao de Mozambique (FRELIMO) and Resistancia National Mocambicana (RENAMO) ceased hostilities, leading to the first multi-party elections in 1994. These shifts in the balance of forces, particularly the end of apartheid, and the advent of democratization in the region have had tremendous influence on foreign policies and policy-making processes in the countries of the southern Africa region. Against this background, Zimbabwe, a former leader of the region, has had to adjust its policies to meet the changed circumstances.

This chapter attempts to trace changes in Zimbabwean foreign policy and policy-making processes since the advent of democratization and globalization in the region. It is argued that policy shifts away from support for liberation in the sub-continent to an emphasis on protection of its economic interests together with the predatory activities of the small kleptocratic class that has ruled the country since independence in 1980, has been the most distinctive feature of the last decade. It is further argued that in charting a new role for itself, the Zimbabwean regime has pursued an aggressive economic and military policy in the region which has led it into engagement in Angola, and more recently, in the Democratic Republic of Congo (DRC), with possible consequences of friction with other regional players, as well as western-led global institutions of governance. At the multi-lateral level, these policy changes have led to direct confrontation between the regime and the two Bretton Woods institutions, the World Bank and the International Monetary Fund (IMF), and uneasy relations with most of the western donor nations.

Zimbabwe's foreign policy behaviour is thus quite expansive. In this chapter however, we propose to limit our analysis to the issues mentioned above in an to attempt to explain aspects of current Zimbabwean foreign policy.

The Regional Context of Zimbabwe's Foreign Policy

At independence in 1980, Zimbabwe emerged as the most important player in the region. It will be recalled that the role of independent Zimbabwe was critical in the disbandment of Pretoria's idea of a Constellation of Southern African States (CONSAS). As the largest economy in the region after South Africa, Zimbabwe was largely perceived as the leader of both the SADCC and the then Front Line States (FLS). Both the FLS and SADCC had two principal econo-political foreign policy goals: first, to reduce the dependence of member states on South Africa, and second, to isolate the apartheid regime from the international community, so that South Africa would either unconditionally abandon its apartheid policy or see its whole political system crumble and give way to a new political dispensation. Zimbabwe thus made it clear that political and diplomatic support would be given to the opposition movements in neighbouring South Africa. It was thus an important player in the struggle against colonialism and racism in Southern Africa. One of the reasons advanced for this has been that since most African countries had rallied behind Zimbabwe's nationalists in the struggle for liberation, independent Zimbabwe was conscious of its indebtedness for that support (Nkiwane 1999, 207-208). As a landlocked state, Zimbabwe also understood only too well that as long as the racist regime was in power in Pretoria, it would remain forever a hostage state.

It is against this background that Zimbabwe's involvement in the region can best be appreciated. Even before the merger of the Zimbabwe African

National Union (ZANU) and the Zimbabwe African People's Union (ZAPU) in 1988, relations with the African National Congress (ANC) had already thawed to the extent that despite years of suspicion between the two liberation movements, *Realpolitik* necessitated that the ANC should be granted a presence in the country and accorded diplomatic support. Zimbabwe was partisanly involved on the side of Mozambique in South Africa's proxy war. However, by the 1990s, Zimbabwe had lost some of the regional pre-eminence it had enjoyed since its independence in 1980. This loss of clout was due to the political transformations in South Africa that ushered in a democratic government. In 1992, President Robert Mugabe maintained a hardline stand on South Africa after he was elected as a leader of the Front Line States (FLS) all of which were members of the SADCC. President Mugabe's tough policies *vis-à-vis* South Africa continued in spite of the political transformation of that country. Nelson Mandela had been released and there were expectations of successful constitutional talks (Weiss 2000, B 725). However, Mugabe's uncompromising stance rested on his mistrust of the sincerity of the apartheid regime and, even more, on his determination to ensure that South Africa did not reverse its decision on transformation. Zimbabwe-South Africa relations remained shaky during the Mandela Presidency because of South Africa's concern over the issues of democracy and human rights in Zimbabwe. President Mbeki has, however, taken a conciliatory approach to Zimbabwe.

Irrespective of the internal pressure by some interest groups within South Africa for that country to take a more proactive role on the land crisis in Zimbabwe, President Mbeki has adopted an approach of quiet diplomacy towards Mugabe as the central premise of his foreign policy (Sadie and Schoeman 2000, 266). It is imperative to note that South Africa is Zimbabwe's major trading partner (Chapter 14) and controls the main routes for fuel and other supplies to the landlocked country (Sadie and Schoeman, 2000). During a SADC summit which was held in Windhoek, President Mugabe mobilised SADC member states to call for international assistance to finance his land reform plan. In a show of solidarity with Zimbabwe, the SADC acquiesced to Mugabe's proposals. It is worth noting that Mbeki had earlier embarked on an international diplomatic mission to win funding for the land takeovers (*Southscan* August 2000). Mbeki and his counterpart, President Muluzi of Malawi, were asked by the SADC to help to secure support from the United Kingdom for Zimbabwe's land reform programme. Indeed, the accommodative approach emerging amongst the SADC *vis-à-vis*

Zimbabwe on the land question can be viewed as one of the major foreign policy successes of the Mugabe Presidency.

Charting a New Foreign Policy

As we have indicated above, Zimbabwe's involvement in international affairs began with a strong commitment to the total liberation of the African continent (Nkiwane 1999, 204). Working to liberate their countries, Zimbabwe joined forces with the Organization of African Unity (OAU) in support of the peoples of Namibia and South Africa. Zimbabwe's liberation policy can best be explained within the context of the country's past experience of getting tremendous support from the FLS in its fight for independence (Thompson 1985).

Mozambique

Following changes which began in the sub-continent in the 1990s, Zimbabwe would appear to have shifted its foreign policy to focus on the areas closely tied to its immediate national interests. Mugabe played a crucial role in the peace process between FRELIMO and RENAMO. RENAMO's leader, Alfonso Dhlakama, met Mugabe in Malawi for the first time in January 1992. The two had further contacts, as Mugabe assisted in the ongoing talks in Rome for a resolution of the Mozambican problem. The Mozambican conflict affected Zimbabwe due to the influx of refugees into Zimbabwe, and the threat posed to transport routes. The cost of maintaining Zimbabwean troops in Mozambique was also a problem, hence Mugabe declared that Zimbabwean troops would not be left in Mozambique once the peace process had been completed. He successfully persuaded Dhlakama to call off his boycott of the general election in 1994 (Weiss, 2000 B725).

Under the terms of a ceasefire, Zimbabwean troops who had been stationed in Mozambique since 1982 were to be withdrawn between 1992 and early 1997. It was estimated that 250,000 Mozambican refugees were sheltering in Zimbabwe by 1992. In March 1993, plans for the repatriation of some 145,000 Mozambican refugees were announced. The United Nations High Commissioner for Refugees (UNHCR) played a big role in this exercise and the repatriation was completed during the mid-1990s. Zimbabwe's refugee population had been reduced to an estimated 1,400 by January 1997. This outcome was of great importance to the Zimbabwean economy. To this end the SADC has engaged the support of private business interests, including Zimbabwean companies, for the Beira corridor rehabilitation project in Mozambique (Weiss, 2000 B725).

When it was confirmed in April 1995 that a group of armed Zimbabwean dissidents (known as *Chimwenjes*) had occupied abandoned RENAMO bases in Mozambique, and that in July 1995 hundreds of former RENAMO rebels had joined them, the Zimbabwean government in collaboration with the Mozambican government confronted the *Chimwenjes* who were mounting attacks on both countries (Weiss 2000, B725). This demonstrates further the extent to which the Beira corridor is of national interest to Zimbabwe.

Angola

Zimbabwean forces have also been engaged in Angola. Zimbabwean troops participated alongside *Forcas Armadas Angolanas* (FAA) troops in the battle of Bailundo and Andulo on the central plateau of Angola on November 5 1999. Zimbabwe has more than 2000 combat troops, including 20 military intelligence officers, deployed in Angola. These forces were initially based in the DRC. The troops were battle-hardened in the DRC and sought to capture UNITA leader Jonas Savimbi personally in an attack on his highlands bases. Zimbabwe utilised the heavy weaponry it has acquired from North Korea and China in engagements in Angola (*Southscan* July 1999).

Democratic Republic of Congo

The Zimbabwean government dispatched troops and arms to the DRC to support the regime of the late Laurent Kabila against advancing rebels. This action followed the SADC summit in Harare in mid-August 1998. As Chairman of the SADC Organ on Politics, Defence and Security, Mugabe insisted that Zimbabwean troops were in the DRC as part of a SADC mission. This claim was later denied by other SADC states who claimed that Zimbabwe's action was unilateral. It is estimated that from July 1999 about 10,000–11,000 Zimbabwean troops were deployed in the DRC. This estimated figure is inclusive of 3,000 troops which were added in May 1999 to counter a rebel offensive against the diamond-rich town of Mbuyi-Mayi (*Southscan* July 1999). The total army available for deployment at any time is around 35,000. Each soldier gets an allowance of US$12 for each day spent in the Congo. The soldiers are also awarded a month's home leave for every three days spent at the front. Helicopters deliver special shipments of cigarettes, soap and other items, to the soldiers. The allowance for being at the front alone costs US$132,000. Because of a lack of infrastructure in the DRC, the entire force has to be supplied by air. This in turn inflates the price. The daily living allowance for the soldiers is in the region of US$ 250,000–300,000. This estimate excludes the contract costs. The cost of ammunition, weapons, replacing lost equipment etc. could trebble the living costs for the soldiers (*Southscan* July 1999).

In the deal that led to the deployment of Zimbabwean troops in the DRC, the late President Kabila had agreed to contribute to the living costs of the Zimbabwean forces and had also agreed to pay the entirety of the daily allowance for the troops engaged at the front. In this deal, Kabila agreed to share the revenue of the diamond mines around Mbuyi-Mayi with each of his allies, including Angola and Namibia. Mugabe believed that he will receive the biggest share of the proceeds since he is contributing most of the forces defending the diamond fields from the rebels (*Southscan* July 1999). However, Kabila did not honour the deal: he did not contribute as much as was promised towards the daily allowance for the troops at the front.

Meanwhile, Zimbabwe had spent at least US$13 million on its military intervention. The action has placed Zimbabwe's military resources under considerable strain and it is domestically unpopular, given Zimbabwe's internal economic realities. Troop withdrawals were to follow after a ceasefire was signed in Lusaka, Zambia on July 1999. This did not happen, and both the rebels and allies in the DRC were accused of violating the accord. Even though, a SADC commission was formed later to monitor the ceasefire, the economic interests of Zimbabwe in the DRC *vis-à-vis* the demobilisation of the immense number of troops at home determines the timetable of troop withdrawal from the DRC (Weiss 2000, 1189).

Zimbabwe faces problems in cutting down its immense military force which had been reduced to 51, 000 from 130,000 at independence. The IMF-World Bank conditions require Zimbabwe to further reduce this force to 20,000. Nevertheless, Zimbabwe's involvement in the DRC delivers some benefits for the Zimbabwe economy, hence Mugabe maybe unwilling to pull the Zimbabwean troops out soon. The military companies involved in the freighting and supply of goods to the DRC are reaping economic benefits. Zimbabwean defence force generals are involved in big business although there was a setback in the control of Gecamines[1] (the state mining corporation) by Zimbabweans (*Southscan* November 1999). Elsewhere, the Zimbabwean government has encouraged other prominent businesses, for example the Congo-Dukwa to trade in the DRC (*Southscan* October 1999). The Zimbabwe army-owned firm, Osleg Ltd, entered into a joint mining venture with the Kabila army's Comiex Ltd in the diamond rich area of Senga-Senga in the DRC (*Southscan* July 1999).

Others who have benefitted from this adventure are the soldiers at the front. The senior officers and some of the soldiers have become rich from diamonds. Some of these soldiers smuggle minerals back home. Young men are known, in some cases after serving in the DRC, to have improved their lifestyles in comparison to those left at home, where unemployment and poverty is a big problem. Other kinds of trade are known to be developing too. It has been established that a group of Zimbabwean businessmen were taken to the DRC diamond centre of Mbuyi-Mayi in 1999. This group was led by the the Zimbabwean Justice Minister, Emmerson Mnangagwa, who urged them to begin establishing commercial links with local businessmen in the DRC. Mnangagwa is known to be the power behind the intervention and the business deals in the DRC (*Southscan* July 1999). Even though the issues of regional stability and the preservation of sovereignty constituted some of the main foreign policy priorities for Zimbabwean involvement in the DRC, President Mugabe had his own personal economic interests. However, the Zimbabwe–DRC quagmire need not overshadow Zimbabwe's long-standing national interests and foreign policy objectives, namely support for de-colonization and self-determination.

The Continental Environment

The manifestation of this commitment has been demonstrated in Zimbabwe's assistance elsewhere in Africa. Therefore, in its external relations and interactions, Zimbabwe has strongly promoted the non-negotiable principle of self-determination for all the peoples of Africa (Nkiwane 1999, 205). Zimbabwe has been a positive and uniting force in the OAU councils. Although, in some instances Zimbabwe has tried to avoid taking sides on African issues, it has given an unequivocal support to the principles enshrined in the OAU charter. This unequivocal support extends to adherence to the Non-Aligned Movement (NAM) (Gregory 1988 and Windrich 1987). In this regard, Zimbabwe strongly criticized the continued imperialism, superpower hegemony and meddling in African affairs among others. Over the years, Zimbabwe continued to uphold her commitment to African issues in dealing with the northern industrialised countries (socialist and non-socialist) as set out by the OAU and NAM (Nkiwane 1999, 206).

For example, in a conference on good governance at the historic European-African summit in Cairo, it was reported that tensions over conditions attached to aid by former colonizers was brought to the fore by a number of African leaders. At this conference the OAU Secretary-General, Salim Ahmed Salim, reminded participants that the last time Europeans got together to talk was at the 1884-85 Congress of Berlin where they carved the continent up among themselves. Salim reiterated that, "the destiny of Africa was determined without the participation of Africans" (*Southscan* April 2000). At this conference, Mugabe responded to British criticisms that his officials had not done enough to protect opposition-owned farms from unauthorised squatters. He expressed the view that Britain had no right to suggest to the world that Zimbabwe is a failure, and pointed out that Zimbabwe is not the only developing country with problems (*Southscan* April 2000).

The Extra-Continental Context of Zimbabwe's Foreign Policy

Zimbabwe has been less than willing to adopt market-oriented strategies, and only circumstances beyond its control have forced it to abide by the conditions imposed by the IMF and the World Bank. Foreign policy in Zimbabwe has continued to be dictated by the ideas that emerged from the liberation struggle and has proved resistant to pressure from other sectors of society (Nkiwane 1999, 206). This explains Mugabe's negative attitude to the market-oriented economic requirements of the IMF and the World Bank.

Land redistribution and rehabilation of the trust lands seemed likely to provide the greatest challenges to Zimbabwe's new government's aspirations and authority after Zimbabwe gained independence from Britain in 1980 (Brown 2000, 1184). The struggle for independence, for most Zimbabweans, had been about recovering the land. The later stages of the guerrilla war brought this land issue into clear perspective. The strategic power and importance of the established commercial farming sector made the problem of acquiring land for the masses impossible. Drought, manpower shortages and the restrictive provisions in the Lancaster House agreement also slowed the pace of resettling the masses. This land issue was to come up later.

Western aid donors and the powerful white dominated Commercial Farmers Union (CFU) were vehemently opposed to the Mugabe Administration's promulgation of the 1992 Land Acquisition Act which, *inter alia*, paved the way for the compulsory acquisition of land by the state (Brown 2000, 1186). The decision, in April 1993, to designate 70 commercially-owned farms under the 1992 Land Acquisition Act for purchase set the stage for tangible confrontation between the Mugabe Administration and the CFU and their western allies. Many of these farms were productive holdings which were understood by the farmers to be exempt from compulsory purchase. However, Mugabe continued with his land reforms in the following years regardless of criticism, challenging the United Kingdom in its role as a former colonial power to take responsibility for assisting those whose land had been appropriated. A list of 1,471 properties to be reallocated was published in November 1997. However, the IMF demanded an assurance from the Mugabe Administration that it would respect the constitution during the land resettlement as a condition for the release of financial assistance in January 1998 (Brown 2000, 1188). It is worth remembering that at the time of independence in 1980, the Compensation Clause attached to land reform was strongly opposed by the Patriotic Front (PF), and was accepted only after assurances had been given by the British about a future multinational fund to assist in the urgent problems of land redistribution (Brown 2000, 1184).

Zimbabwean Foreign Policy-Making Process: The Role of Actors

According to Nkiwane (1999, 212), Zimbabwe's foreign policy is a creature of the ruling party, the Zimbabwe African National Union-Patriotic Front (ZANU-PF). The Ministry of Foreign Affairs and the diplomatic missions execute the declarations and pronouncements of the party hierarchy.

The foreign policy-making process in Zimbabwe is basically a response or reaction to internal and external influences. Prior to the 2000 multiparty parliamentary electoral dispensation, Zimbabwe remained what would best be characterised as a *de facto* one-party state largely because the opposition parties in the country had disintegrated or were less influential, thus restricting foreign policy-making to the ruling party, and the presidency in particular. Because of the overwhelming dominance of ZANU-PF, the president has remained the dominant player in foreign policy-making. After the adventure in the DRC, where Zimbabwe was entangled in the Great Lakes War, it has become clear exactly what Mugabe's interests and principles in foreign policy are.

The Presidency

Mugabe adopted a conciliatory stance in the immediate period following his victory in 1980. To restore stability, he quickly stressed the need for reconciliation, disavowed rapid transformation to his socialist goals, emphasized non-alignment in foreign affairs, and included two whites in his Cabinet. Nevertheless, the new government was faced with formidable problems arising from the ravages of war and the expectations aroused in the struggle against colonial rule (Hull 1988, Nkiwane 1993 and 1997).

The 1988 merger of Nkomo's Zimbabwe African People's Union (ZAPU) and Mugabe's ZANU into ZANU-PF laid the foundation for the centralization of power within the Office of the President (OP). The ceremonial presidency was thereafter transformed through constitutional reforms into an executive presidency, with Mugabe at the helm (Sithole 1992). According to the agreement, the new party was to be committed to the establishment of a one-party state with Marxist-Leninist doctrine as the guiding econo-political doctrine (Willet 1997, Engel 1994). Even though the existing opposition parties and trade unions — the Conservertive Alliance of Zimbabwe (CAZ), the Zimbabwe Unity Movement (ZUM), the United Parties (UP), the Forum Party of Zimbabwe (FPZ), the Zimbabwe African National Union-Ndonga (ZANU-Ndonga) and the Zimbabwe Congress of Trade Unions (ZCTU) — persistently challenged the dictatorship of Mugabe's presidency, the country remained largely an authoritarian *de facto* one party state (Herbst 1990 and Sithole 1992). The introduction of the Land Acquisition Act (LAA) of 1999 has since pitted the presidency against the white dominated CFU and the United Kingdom as alluded to earlier in the chapter. The enactment of the LAA enhanced the president's power *vis-à-vis* other institutions for governance in Zimbabwe, with the presidency persistently ignoring court rulings made against the government.

According to Article 27 of the Zimbabwean Constitution (1996), the "President shall be Head of State and Head of Government and Commander-in-chief of the Defence Forces," and the "President shall take precedence over all other persons in Zimbabwe." One of the executive functions of the President as provided for in the 1996 Constitution is that, subject to the provisions of the Constitution of Zimbabwe, the President shall have power to "appoint, accredit, receive and recognize diplomatic agents and consular officers; and to enter into international conventions, treaties and agreements; and to declare war and to make peace" (Zimbabwe, 1996 Article 3 H at (4) a-d). "In the exercise of his functions, the President shall act on the advice of the Cabinet, except in cases where he is required by the Zimbabwean Constitution or any other law to act on the advice of any other person or authority" (Zimbabwe, 1996: Article 3 H (5)). Mugabe invoked these rights when he committed the Zimbabwean troops to the DRC.

Over the years, the presidency has over-shadowed parliament and the judiciary, particularly on matters considered salient by Mugabe, exhibiting what we call State House-centred foreign policy-making process, that is, foreign policy-making centred in the Office of the President. As we have explained, the Zimbabwean military involvement in Mozambique, Angola and the DRC was a decision taken mainly by the presidency. This State House-centred foreign policy-making style became the subject of debate in parliament at the end of the 2000 parliamentary elections. The issue was raised in parliament by Tendai Biti of the Movement for Democratic Change (MDC). Central to the disagreement between ZANU-PF and the MDC in parliament was what the MDC considered to be an unconstitutional decision by the presidency to commit the Zimbabwean troops abroad without the acquiescence of parliament. A member of the MDC stated in parliament *inter alia*, that, "We on this side of the house do not prescribe to devalue the values but we believe strongly that an adventure such as that of the DRC which has messed up our foreign policies is not worth it in terms of human lives".[2] Even though the Minister for Defence, Moven Mahachi, was responsible for the deployment of the Zimbabwean troops in the DRC, it was Mugabe himself whose decisions carried the day (Southscan April 1999:70).

However, this trend of Presidential dominance continues to face internal challenges, particularly during the 1990s. Indeed, it has been observed that "from 1990 onwards the public had began to criticize not only the party, ZANU-PF, but also Mugabe, dispelling the myth that Mugabe was omnipotent, omniscient and indispensable" (Weiss 2000, B725). The post-2000 multi-party electoral dispensation is witnessing the rapid transformation of Executive-Legislative relations. Even the civil society led by the religious organizations, particularly the Zimbabwe Council of Churches (ZCC) are advocating the democratization of the institutions for governance and respect for human rights. It was as a result of the internal pressure by, among others, the non-governmental organizations (NGOs) that Mugabe acquiesced to the 1998-1999 constitutional reform project (Mafundikwa 1998). The debate over the constitutional review continues to polarize Zimbabweans, with the government and NGOs supporting parliament-centred and people-centred constitution-making projects respectively. The draft constitution submitted by a team of 400 government-appointed commissioners, was rejected by over 53% of the vote by the supporters of the National Constitutional Assembly (NCA, a conglomeration of religious organizations, opposition parties and NGOs in general). The NCA advocates a people-centred constitution-making project. Coupled with the success of the MDC, led by Morgan Tsvangirai, in the 2000 parliamentary elections, the challenges facing Mugabe are admittedly real (Southscan, October 2000).

The Ministry of Defence: Consolidation of the Military and Zimbabwe's Foreign Policy

The consolidation of the military became important after Zimbabwe achieved independence. It was necessary to consolidate the peace by integrating the three large, hostile and undefeated armies of the Rhodesian Front (RF), ZAPU and ZANU-PF. Integration appeared to be successful after the initial problems and violent clashes resulting in several hundred deaths, by late 1981. The creation of a specialist army, the Fifth Brigade, led to a lot of criticism mounted against ZANU-PF by Zimbabweans, particularly by the pro-democracy and human rights movements. This specialist brigade was composed largely of Shona and they were trained by advisers from North Korea. However, Mugabe justified the action by citing the "internal and external threats posed by disaffected supporters of the former regime, by unresolved tensions within the governing coalition, and by South Africa" (Brown 2000, 1184; Weiss 2000; De Waal 1990). For example, the ZANU-PF headquarters had been destroyed in a bomb attack in December 1981. Subsequently, important transport routes and petroleum facilities in Mozambique were sabotaged, the homes of government ministers were also attacked, and a substantial part of the air force was destroyed. These events seemed to justify even more, the creation of the specialist army brigade.

Dissidents from ZAPU's former guerrilla army, who had deserted from the new national army, perpetrated numerous indiscriminate acts of violence in 1982. It was alleged that members of the former regime's forces who had moved to South Africa were providing a ready supply of personnel for covert operations, which the South African government was also suspected of supporting (Brown 2000; Weiss 2000). Early in 1983, and again in 1984, serious allegations of indiscipline and atrocities against civilians were made against the Fifth Brigade as it sought to suppress the dissidents and to protect the mainly white, commercial farming sector on which so much of the government's overall economic strategy rested (Weiss 1994 and Moyo 1994). Controversy over human rights issues continued when adverse reports — from Amnesty International in 1985, and from the USA-based Lawyers' Committee for Human Rights — were rejected by Mugabe.

In addition to the desire to dislodge ZAPU from its regional stronghold, the fear that a South African-backed dissident movement might reach the same devastating proportions as those already operating in Angola and Mozambique, probably lay behind the government's decision to mount a forceful military campaign in Matabeleland in spite of the risk of alienating the province's mainly Ndebele-speaking population. The Ndebele constitute Zimbabwe's principal minority language group (Brown 2000, 1185; Moyo 1992).

Under considerable international and domestic pressure, the government officially began to reduce the numbers of the armed forces from 51,000 to 40,000 by the end of 2000. The demobilisation of the troops was phased in over a period of time to prevent problems from arising. At the end of the liberation war there were roughly 130,000 combatants: 97,000 in the Rhodesian Security Forces, 20,000 in the ZANU-PF military wing and 10-12,000 in the ZAPU military wing (Willet 1997, 25). Following the election in 1980, elements of the three factions were merged to form a new national army, the Zimbabwean Defence Force (ZDF) some 51,000 strong. However, demobilising large numbers too quickly was perceived to be unwise, as few ex-combatants would be likely to find jobs (Willet 1997, 25).

Zimbabwe's military involvement in Mozambique, Angola and the DRC are clear testimonies to the importance the Mugabe Administration attaches to the military as an instrument of the country's foreign policy and foreign policy-making. For example, during the 1992–1995 United Nations Operation in Somalia (UNOSOM I and UNOSOM II), established under Resolution 751 of 24 April 1992 (and other subsequent resolutions), Zimbabwe dispatched over 85% or 5939 troops of the 7000 strong African contingent (Adar 1998, 42-43). The Zimbabwean contribution of troops to the UN Angola Verification Mission (UNIVEM I) and the UN Observer Mission in Angola (MONUA) peacekeeping missions was based not only on her econo-political and military interests in the region, but also as a vehicle to promote her regional and global status. Zimbabwe's 1993 joint military training maneuvers with 26 US Fort Bragg commandos can be understood in this broad context. Since the 1990s, the Ministry of Defence, in conjunction with the Office of the President, is increasingly emerging as an important actor in the Zimbabwean foreign policy-making process. In April 1997, the Alliance des Forces Democratiques Pour la Liberation du Congo (AFDL), led by Laurent Kabila, received between $30 million to $200 million from

Zimbabwe.[3] Zimbabwe also provided the AFDL with food, uniforms and boots. Most of the ammunition and land mines supplied to the AFDL were provided by the state-owned Zimbabwe Defence Industries (ZDI). President Mugabe insisted that deployment in the DRC in early 1999 was a result of Rwanda's escalation of the war, particularly around the diamond-rich area of Mbuyi-Mayi.[4]

The Zimbabwe Defence Industries (ZDI) produces small arms, ammunition and explosives. In 1993 it was privatised in line with the State's privatisation programme, and in 1994 ZDI was reported to have exported ammunition and explosives to at least six African countries (*Herald* 1995). Since then, ZDI has been trying to commercialise its operations in response to the downturn in military expenditure. France and China are reported to have helped ZDI with the production of high explosives and small arms (*Economist Intelligence Unit* 1995).

As part of wider reform plans, overall defence expenditure was targeted for a 40 per cent reduction, reportedly encouraged both by the World Bank and IMF. As Table 13.1 (opposite) indicates, national military expenditure declined from about 4.6 per cent of GNP in 1990 to about 3.4 per cent in 1994, largely due to the greater stability in the region, not least because of the diminished threat from its post-apartheid neighbour, South Africa, and the fact that Zimbabwean troops had been withdrawn from Mozambique as a result of the onset of peace and political transition in that country (Willet 1997, 22).

Table 13.1 shows that military expenditure in Zimbabwe was high between 1987 and 1991, but this is the period during which Zimbabwe deployed between 6,000 to 12,000 troops in Mozambique to guard the main trade routes against RENAMO attacks, particularly the Beira Corridor and the port of Beira, a lifeline for Zimbabwe's exports.

Zimbabwe's military operations in Mozambique absorbed an estimated 70 per cent of the defence budget during the period of 1987 to 1991 (Willet 1997). (South Africa's regional destabilisation programme was the main preoccupation of Zimbabwe's security until the early 1990s. In this regard, Zimbabwean troops often fought side by side with FRELIMO forces against the South African-backed RENAMO (Willet 1997, 26).)

The table also shows that military expenditure declined from 1992 to 1996. This could be attributed to peace in the region following the political transformation in South Africa. The increase in expenditure in 1997 could be attributed to the disbursement of US$210 million to War Veterans.[5]

Table 13.1 Zimbabwe: Military Expenditure and Armed Forces

Year	Military Expenditure (ME) Constant 1997 ($ millions)	Armed Forces (Thousands)	ME GNP %	ME Central Government Expenditure %	ME Per Capita $ 1997 Constant
*1987	367	45	6.0	16.1	40
1988	337	45	5.1	15.0	35
1989	335	51	4.8	15.0	34
1990	340	45	4.6	14.8	34
1991	303	45	3.9	12.6	30
1992	269	48	3.8	10.1	26
1993	251	48	3.5	9.9	24
1994	257	43	3.4	11.5	24
1995	283	40	3.8	10.4	27
1996	232	40	2.8	8.9	22
1997	320	40	3.8	11.9	29
**1998	173	–	2.7	–	–
1999	213	–	3.4	–	–
2000	401	–	–	–	–

Source: *United States, Bureau of Arms Control, *World Military Expenditures and Arms Transfers, 1998* (Washington, DC: Bureau of Arms Control, 1998). The data covers 1987-1997.
** SIPRI Yearbook 2000: Armaments, Disarmament and International Security (Oxford: Oxford University Press, 2000). The data covers 1998-2000.

ZANU-PF

Zimbawean foreign policy initially revolved around the ruling party, ZANU-PF. This is in conformity with the historical background of the party. In 1962, whites in Southern Rhodesia (now Zimbabwe) voted into office the newly-formed Rhodesian Front (RF), dedicated to upholding white supremacy and demanding full independence from the United Kingdom and the retention of the existing minority-rule constitution. When the United Kingdom refused independence on this basis, the RF appointed Ian Smith as Prime Minister. Smith carried out the long-threatened Unilateral Declaration of Independence (UDI) in November 1965, renaming the territory 'Rhodesia' (Whyte 1990 and Morris-Jones 1980). Repressive measures preceding this had seriously weakened the African nationalist opposition, which in 1963 had split into the ZANU, led by Rev N Sithole (and subsequently, Robert Mugabe), and the original ZAPU led by Joshua Nkomo.

These nationalists embarked upon a 'people's war' to overthrow the Smith regime. ZAPU, based mainly in Zambia, received training and armaments from the USSR, although its operations within Zimbabwe were confined mainly to majority Ndebele areas. ZANU developed strong links with the FRELIMO movement fighting the Portuguese in Mozambique, and with the People's Republic of China. It concentrated on infiltration and rural mobilization in the Shona-speaking areas in the north-east, and later in the eastern and central areas of the country. From 1976, a combined struggle was waged in the name of the Patriotic Front, an alliance formed by ZAPU and ZANU and backed by the FLS. Within the country, mounting economic difficulties, resulting in large part from the imposition of economic sanctions by the international community (with the exception of South Africa), together with declining white morale and guerrilla inroads in the rural areas, led the Smith regime in 1979 to fashion what was termed an 'Internal Settlement' (Brown 2000, 1184; Weiss 2000). Within less than a year all the parties to the conflict agreed to participate in the Lancaster House Constitutional Conference under the chairmanship of the British Secretary of State for Foreign and Commonwealth Affairs. An agreement which was to lead to the emergence of the independent state of Zimbabwe was reached.

The control of ZANU-PF over the years by Mugabe, imposed limitations on the party's ability to exert its influence over Zimbabwe's foreign policy. Mugabe's unwillingness to allow opposition within ranks of the party hierarchy was manifested during the 1992 meeting of the Central Committee of ZANU-PF. Some members of the Central Committee opposed the five-year Economic Structural Adjustment Programme (ESAP) launched in 1991 and backed by a total of $700 million donor funds (*Bulawayo Chronicle,* 28 March 1992). It was because of the influence of the Presidency vis-à-vis ZANU-PF that the ESAP programmes were sanctioned from 1992. In the Zimbabwean case, it is fair to observe that on matters pertaining to foreign policy-making the functions of the Presidency and ZANU-PF are intertwined.

Summary and Conclusion

This chapter has demonstrated certain central underpinnings of Zimbabwe's post-Cold War foreign policy-making process. First, Zimbabwe's foreign policy emanates from its experience during the liberation struggle. The country's military involvement in Angola and Mozambique clearly indicates the Mugabe Administration's unreserved commitment to support their former allies during the liberation struggle. Zimbabwe is the only country in Africa that frequently deploys troops in war-torn areas within the region irrespective of the casualties the country's military personnel may incur. Second, Zimbabwe's involvement in Angola, the DRC and Mozambique was influenced not only by the country's econo-political interests, but also because of concerns for stability in the region. Third, ever since he took over the presidency, but more so after the 1988 merger between ZANU-PF and ZAPU, President Mugabe has remained the key figure in matters pertaining to Zimbabwe's foreign policy and foreign policy-making process. The control of the other institutions for governance namely, the Legislature and the Judiciary by the Executive Branch, has been made possible by constitutional amendments over the years. However, with the unexpected overwhelming success of the opposition parties, particularly the MDC, in the 2000 Parliamentary elections, the Mugabe Administration is increasingly being challenged to democratize the institutions for governance.

Notes

1   Gecamines is a Congolese parastatal running most of the mines held by the pro-Kabila forces. Chaired by Billy Rautenbach a Zimbabwean tycoon, Gecamines got into deep trouble and was thought to be sinking under debts of up to US$ 1 billion. Rautenbach was appointed to head Gecamines immediately after Mugabe began his adventure in the DRC in August 1998 (*Southscan* July 1999. 14/02).
2   See http://www.afrol.com/news/zim041-drc-parliament:htm,02/25/2001.
3   See Public Education Centre, "Central Africa: The Influence of Arms and the Continuation of Crisis, A Background Report for Journalists." May 1998. http://www. publicedcentre.org/nsns/afrca/index.html, 51.
4   International Crisis Group, "Africa's Seven Nation War." 21 May 1999. http://www.crisisweb.org.
5   See "The Arms trade, debt and development." www.than.onthepc.co.uk/whatshappening/research/development-Body.html#6

References

Adar, K.G. (1998) "From Nations to Nation-State to Nations: The Withering Away of Somalia." *Politics Administration and Change* 30 (July-December 1998): 30-47.
Brown, Richard. (1999) "Zimbabwe: Recent History." *Africa South of Sahara 2000*. Ed. R. Brown. London: Europa Publications.
De Waal, V. (1992) *The Politics of Reconciliation: Zimbabwe's First Decade*. London: Hurst, 1990; Harare: Longman Zimbabwe, 1992.

Engel, U. (1994) *Foreign Policy of Zimbabwe*. Hamburg: Institute of African Affairs.
Gregory, C.L. (1988) *The Impact of ideology on Zimbabwe's Foreign Relations (1980-1987)*. Johannesburg: University of Witwatersrand, unpublished MA Dissertation.
Herald. "Mugabe commissions ammunition factories." 17 February 1985.
Herbst, J. (1990) *State Politics in Zimbabwe*. Harare: University of Zimbabwe Publications.
Hull, R.W.(1988) "Overcoming Zimbabwe's Vulnerabilities." *Current History* 87(529): 197-239.
Mafundikwa, E. (1998) "Church Leaders Forcing Zimbabwe to Reform Constitution." *Ecumenical News International*, 2 November (http://www.umr.org/Htzimcon. Htm).
Morris-Johns, E.H. ed. (1980) *From Rhodesia to Zimbabwe*. London: Cass.
Moyo, J.N. (1992) *Voting for Democracy: A Study of Electoral Politics in Zimbabwe*. Harare: University of Zimbabwe Publications.
Moyo, S. (1994) *Economic Nationalism and Land Reform in Zimbabwe*. Harare: Southern African Printing and Publishing House.
Nkiwane, S.M. (1993) "Development of Zimbabwe's Foreign Relations, 1980-90." *The Round Table* (326): 199-216.
——. (1997) *Zimbabwe's International Borders: A Study in National and Regional Development*. Harare: University of Zimbabwe Publications.
——. (1999) "Zimbabwe's Foreign Policy." *African Foreign Policies*. Ed. Stephen Wright. Colorado: Westview Press.
Sadie, Y. and M. Schoeman. (2000) "Zimbabwe: Lessons for and Responses from South Africa and the Region." *South African Yearbook of International Affairs 2000/01*. Johannesburg: South African Institute of International Affairs: 261-267.
Sithole, M. (1992) *Democracy and the One-Party State in Africa: The Case of Zimbabwe*. Harare: SAPES books.
Southscan: "Talk inside the military is of Mugabe's private war again." 14. 30 April 1999.
"Violent military reaction appears to confirm story of coup plot." 14.2. 22 July 1999.
"Mugabe counts mounting costs of his Congo intervention." 14.15. 23 July 1999.
"Military companies reveal aim of profiting from Congo link." 14.20. 1 October 1999.
"Zimbabwean troops involved in central highlands fighting." 14.23. 12 November 1999.
"Good governance Zimbabwe-style to the fore at Cairo summit." 15.7. 7 April 2000.
"Election results appears best for stability and transition." 15.13. 30 June 2000.
"SA tied in closer to Mugabe's game plan." 15.16. 11 August 2000.
"Showdown looms as opposition hands Mugabe a hostage to fortune." 15.20. 6 Oct. 2000.
The Economist Intelligence Unit. (1995) *Zimbabwe 2nd Quarter*. Economist Intelligence Unit.
Thompson B. Carol. (1985) *Challenge to Imperialism: The Frontline States in the Liberation of Zimbabwe*. Harare: Zimbabwe Publishing House.
Weiss, R. (1994) *Zimbabwe and the New Elite*. London: British Academic Press.
Weiss, R. (2000) "Zimbabwe: Turning of the Tide for President Mugabe." *Africa Contemporary Record* 24 *(1992-94)*. New York: Africana Publishing Company.
Whyte, B. (1990) *Yesterday, Today and Tomorrow: A 100 Years History of Zimbabwe, 1890-1990*. Harare: David Burke.
Willet, Susan. (1997) "Military Spending Trends and Developments in Southern Africa: Angola, Zimbabwe, Mozambique and South Africa." Revised ed. Ottawa Symposium on Military Expenditures in Developing Countries, July 1997.
Windrich, E. (1987) "Zimbabwe: Towards Socialism and Non-Alignment." *Africa in World Politics: Changing Perspectives*. Ed. S. Wright and J. Brownfoot. London: Macmillan.
Zimbabwe. *The Constitution*, revised ed. (1996) Harare: Government Printer.

PART II
REGIONAL AND GLOBAL CASE STUDIES

14 How Far, Where To? Regionalism, the Southern African Development Community and Decision-Making into the Millennium

PAUL-HENRI BISCHOFF

Regionalism embraces two movements: transnational relations across a region; and cooperative forms of policy-coordination and integration by nation-states. In southern Africa, regionalism exists in both these forms. This suggests that foreign policy decision-making here includes non-state actors and happens along a continuum of non-state-non-state-state-state relations. From amongst a typology of trans-governmental coalitions, individuals, the epistemic community and non-governmental organisations (NGOs), the latter would seem to be most prominent as a 'linkage actor' in region-building (Mingst 1995, 234–6). But southern African states which are at various stages of democratization largely remain outside the grasp of organised civil society. The state as such predominates in foreign policy-making and retains the ability to either promote or impede the regional project in a situation where — paradox as it may seem — states themselves rather than the people can often be the source of the region's problems (Van Nieuwkerk 1999, 2). Under the aegis of the Southern African Development Community (SADC), the most formal and inclusive expression of Southern African regionalism, the disposition of member states remains crucial in determining and enforcing common policy parameters to make regional cooperation and the further growth of transnational relations possible (Makoni 1994, 17; Soederbaum 1998, 83).

The way in which states respond to the SADC forms part of their foreign policy response. The need to respond to a region-in-the-making is greater than ever since devoting foreign policy resources to the region is part of a wider response to global change (Shaw and Nyang'oro 1999, 242). It is a measure of governments making fewer decisions on their own. Vital decisions surrounding economics or security need increasingly to be made in consultation with others in the world at large, including international and regional institutions or, for that matter, transnational actors rather than domestic constituencies.[1] Here functionalist convention around regional decision-making has it that states in piecemeal fashion surrender some of their decision-making powers to a higher regional body (Nye 1971).

However, in the case of the SADC and foreign policy-making, this would not as yet, seem to be the case. SADC's region–region relations with the European Union (EU), USA, North American Free Trade Agreement (NAFTA), Association of South East Asian Nations (ASEAN), Economic Community of West African States (ECOWAS), Common Market for Eastern and Southern Africa (COMESA) and Nordic countries do exist or are being explored,[2] as does its security mechanism, the Organ for Politics, Defence and Security (OPDS). In the context of the functions and the general power its institutions are allowed to possess, the SADC's foreign policy is a nascent one however,[3] but trade matters in particular do provide the fuel for a future foreign policy role.[4] As a foreign policy actor, the SADC is only likely to come to the fore when it is called upon to defend the emergent SADC Free Trade Area, and when institutions at the centre of the organisation (such as the OPDS) are broadened and strengthened.

This chapter addresses the varied forms and changing nature of decision-making within the SADC. It does so by looking at the environmental context of inter-state foreign policy decision-making, its structure and political culture. Comment is then made about the quantity and quality of decisions informing a greater regionalism in Southern Africa at the beginning of the millennium.

Inter-Governmental Decision-making: SADC's Aims and Objectives

The SADC as a regional organisation evolved out of the Southern African Development Coordination Conference (SADCC). The SADCC in turn was created by a political grouping, the Front Line States (FLS). The *raison d'être* for both was strategic. Whereas the SADCC sought regional autonomy outside a South African sphere, the SADC seeks to consolidate Southern Africa's position in a changing world economic environment.

The SADCC was meant to create for itself its own economic space to free the region from its dependence on the apartheid economy. In doing so, the SADCC opted for functional cooperation and attracted overseas economic aid, whilst on the political side, the Front Line States articulated the notion of greater security for southern Africa from apartheid, as well as of fundamental change aimed at the liberation of both Namibia and South Africa.

The SADC in turn marked a wider response to the emergence of regional economic blocs and the perception of Africa's overall marginalization in world affairs during the first half of the 1990s (Olufemi 1994, 186). It also intended to address new security issues in a post-apartheid region. The political and economic liberalization taking place in the region (with a number of new governments elected in parliamentary elections, including those of Namibia, Zambia, Angola, South Africa, Malawi and Mozambique), and a situation where virtually all member states are subject to Structural Adjustment Programmes (SAPs), would seem to lay the basis for regional cooperation at a higher level of integration.

Starting with the end of the Cold War and the unbanning of all political opposition in South Africa in 1990, regional hostilities were replaced by a growing anticipation about promoting the common interests of the region. The major threat to stability could now be perceived to come from common issues: human displacement, poverty, economic migration, environmental degradation, HIV-AIDS, drug running and organised crime, the proliferation of small arms and abandoned personnel mines left in the aftermath of war and conflict.[5]

The Community was now to concentrate on expanding the process of cooperation and development started by its predecessor. In this it was to build on the convergence of interests and values achieved by all the national liberation movements and their successor states. Integration centred on trade was made urgent by economic openings for government donors and foreign investors elsewhere in the world (such as in the Community of Independent States (CIS) and Eastern Europe). A number of areas in which cooperation towards integration was to take place were therefore spelt out. These included:

- human resources development, science and technology;
- agriculture, food security, natural resources and environment;
- infrastructure and services;
- industry, finance, investment and trade;

- social welfare, information and culture;
- popular participation in region-building;
- solidarity, peace and security;
- national and regional institution-building;
- **international cooperation with Northern partners.**[6]

Importantly too, Article 5/1a of its Declaration and Protocol signed at Windhoek in 1992 points out how the SADC is meant to serve as a vehicle of support for the socially disadvantaged in the region and, as such, accommodate civil society in putting on the regional agenda issues such as respect for human rights, the redress of gender inequality, the promotion of people-centred development and the fight against poverty and inequality in the region.[7]

All this presupposed ways and means of coordinating the broad, macro-policies in the member states of the area. It was to be done by counting on a spirit of solidarity and common purpose which characterised the politics of liberation in the region, as well as on the modest successes of regional sector cooperation under the SADCC, particularly in the areas of energy, food and agriculture, transport and communications.

Moreover, the SADC's ultimate challenge is to be able to fully mobilise the region's human, material and organizational resources in order to make the region a serious player in the world economy. In order to achieve this, it is necessary to create a framework amongst state and non-state actors which encourages a regional market for trade and investment, but also the holding of free and fair elections, the adherence to constitutionality and the rule of law the outcome of which is a shared commitment to democracy and democratic governance. Given the disparities in the region, the active promotion of human and social rights anticipates an outcome where the alleviation of poverty, and a much broader participation in national and regional affairs becomes possible for the majority (including women). As such, inter-state and transnational cooperation and growing forms of solidarity can be seen to be elements necessary to bring about a sense of 'regionness' to produce a regional identity.

Whilst the SADC had, in its first eight years of existence, formulated eleven regional policy frameworks (covering areas such as mining, education, energy, transport and communication, trade, the combat of drug trafficking, immunities and privileges, shared watercourse systems, the SADC Tribunal and its rules of procedures and legal affairs), and had responded to issues revolving around gender and HIV/AIDS, this amounted to policy cooperation (much of it still to be credibly implemented,) rather than actual, deep-seated integration. If at all, integration continued to develop in its own, mostly spontaneous way, but — as shown by the increase in South African business activities in the region — this simply intensified the economic imbalances which characterise the region because of country trade imbalances with South Africa. In the opinion of some, therefore, the institutional framework inherited from the SADCC has so far not been sufficiently changed to match ambitions of state-driven integration. Expanding the organisation from 12 to 14 members in 1997 only stretched the instrumental limits further. As such, the SADC is generally seen as inadequate to the tasks of further integration (Georgala and Tostensen 1996, 10), something which repeatedly prompted the Summit into wishing to tackle institutional reform. Clearly, the SADC is at the point where political and economic integration has reached a delicate phase. National sensitivities continue to characterise negotiations in the attempts made to reform or strengthen the organisation at its centre (Seymour 1997).[8]

SADC: The Nature of Decision-Making

The SADC is a traditional inter-governmental organisation. Its character is defined by the nature of its membership and reasons for existence. States are prime actors in it and membership is expanding. From the original nine members, its membership now stands at fourteen and includes Anglophone, Francophone and Lusophone states, island states such as the Seychelles and Mauritius and states such as the Democratic Republic of Congo (DRC) and Tanzania, traditionally seen as Central and East African states respectively.[9]

The preponderance of the state clearly shapes the SADC: the body is largely treated as an extension of the individual needs of member states. Those needs primarily revolve around achieving economic security by way of obtaining multilateral or bilateral aid through the regional body. The SADC, which has little autonomy as a policy body, remains a multilateral diplomatic forum and instrument of the often rather limited national interests of its members. Those interests relate to the business of safeguarding strategic interests, obtaining aid or deriving economic gain.

The importance given to the state as the driver of the regional body is accompanied by the insistence that each member state's view is of equal and absolute importance. The SADC, like its predecessor the SADCC, therefore continues to follow a consensus model of deliberation where consensus is "a general convergence or harmonisation of views reflecting the broadest concerns of a ... meeting ... it is both a process and a final compromise formula and is shaped by prior consultations, discussions and negotiations into a generally agreed position" (cited in Rajan 1990, 42). Whilst this was seen to work at the time of a smaller SADCC engaged in more modest forms of cooperation, this can now sometimes be viewed as an obstacle to full-blown integration. However, the parameters of decision-making are not only constrained by a consensus model of deliberation — something only potentially undercut by the existence of the Tribunal in the SADC Treaty to be constituted for dealing with the adjudication of conflict — but also by a continued dependence on the 'external factor' made up of foreign donors.

When it comes to policy and structure, the SADC like many regional organisations situated in the South, is in part a creation of its Northern donors on which it has relied heavily for up to 90% of its funding[10] whilst the member states mobilise few resources for the organisation. In this context, it is the outside world which broadly determines the direct benefits of membership and the relevance of the SADC decision-making to the welfare of states and their citizens. Donors have a say on what is given where and who gets what.[11] At the same time, the Northern discourse on the strategic policy framework regional organisations adopt in a globalizing world has a profound impact on regionalization (Soederbaum 1998, 78) and plays a part in undermining the cohesion of African regional groups (Babarinde 1999, 220). The SADC Declaration stated that the SADC would need to continue to rely on foreign assistance and, unlike the SADCC at its founding in 1980, no longer found it useful to make greater financial self-sufficiency and independence from donors an organisational objective (Georgala and Tostensen, 1996, 7). Thus, the larger international policy context in which decisions affecting SADC are made would seem to consist of a number of ostensibly Northern actors with their own demands and expectations.

The troika of world financial institutions — the International Monetary Fund (IMF), World Bank and World Trade Organisation (WTO) — led by the IMF against the backdrop of a massive debt and mostly through the imposition of, and adherence to, the Structural Adjustment Programmes (SAPS), has, since the 1980s, set down the parameters for what constitutes "good governance" in fiscal, development and trade policy in the region. Accompanying this are the donor expectations and policies set out by the EU states, the USA and Japan at fora such as the SADC-EU ministerial donor conferences, the SADC-USA donor forum or bilateral talks on assistance held with Japan.[12]

In addition, there are the periodic interventions of conferences and reports. The calling of SADC fora to attract foreign private investment — such as the Southern African Forum hosting 700 participants held in Berlin in April 2000 — has SADC governments respond to foreign investor needs and perceptions. Similarly, world think tanks of the North such as the World Economic Forum set terms and conditions by which to measure SADC performance.[13] This predisposes the SADC states to take decisions which are likely to anticipate or respond to Northern concerns and policy postures. The 1998 SADC summit, for instance, encouraged member states to establish autonomous and accountable anti-corruption regimes[14] in order to counteract falling levels of aid and the falling off of Foreign Direct Investment (FDI) from ostensibly Northern states.[15] Similarly, the 2000 Summit noted its satisfaction with the observation that investment in the SADC had improved in the 1990s as governments actively sought to bring about a "more attractive policy environment for investors."[16] However, the whole region's reputation in a world of would-be-investors can be affected detrimentally by instances where, as in Zimbabwe in the lead-up to the elections of June 2000, property rights were under challenge; or, as in the Democratic Republic of Congo (DRC) where effective customs systems are not in place (Wackernagel, "SADC must get to basics." *Mail and Guardian*, 12-18-9.97).

Clearly, at a time of globalization, the region is being reincorporated into the world economy. The SADC and its member states are meant to pursue policies within an increasingly transnational environment encroaching on social and political relations across the region. The issue here is a long-standing one, whether the SADC like the SADCC at the end of this process will be able to shape their relations with the outside world, or whether the outside world will continue to mould these relations (Stadler 1987, 10). It is argued that economic policies and political systems have converged mainly as a consequence of the adoption of economic reform programmes in line with Structural Adjustment Programmes and changes in global development ideology. This convergence is seen to favour the coming together of similarly run states (Soederbaum 1998, 79). Whilst this similarity may have its uses in joint calls for debt relief by multilateral institutions (such as the one made at the Windhoek Summit of 2000), the *raison d'être* for regional organisation, here as elsewhere in Africa, often lies outside the region. In the context of an African renewal, the challenge is how to promote the greater effective African ownership of regional organisations such as the SADC which, ultimately, can work against the marginalization of Africa and contribute towards a pan-African Economic Community modelled on the

European Community as envisaged under the Abuja Treaty of 1991 (Babarinde 1999, 221).

The Structure of Decision-Making

The mechanisms or structure on which the SADC is based include the Summit, the Council of Ministers, the Sectoral Ministerial Committees, the Organ on Politics, Defence and Security, as well as multilateral instruments such as the Trade and other protocols.[17]

Annual Summit of Heads of Government The Summit meets once a year and is the supreme policy-making body. Decisions are arrived at by consensus. On occasion, extraordinary summits have been called to deal with issues of crisis management.[18]

Periodic Meetings of the Council of Ministers supported by a Standing Committee of Officials on Regional Economic Development Matters. Before the Summit, the Council of Ministers, mostly composed of Foreign Ministers, meets in order to finalise the agenda of the Summit.

Sectoral Committees of Ministers chaired by a sector coordinating country. Each sector coordinating country will call meetings on the design and implementation of projects falling under one or the other sector. For every sector there is a Sector Coordinating Unit (SCU).[19] In order to minimise the size of the SADC secretariat, each country makes use of its own administration to identify, implement or monitor regional projects. As such, technically speaking, Sector Coordinating Units run within national administrations of member states are not formally regional institutions, but national entities engaged in regional work. As such, even though they form the backbone of the work that SADC does, they are not mentioned in the founding treaty of the SADC (Georgala and Tostensen 1996, v).

Organ for Political Cooperation, Defence and Security. This constitutes meetings of what are usually Ministers of Foreign Affairs chaired by one Head of State (not the Chair of the SADC Summit), supported by a Rotating Secretariat (see Figure 14.1). The Organ has met only irregularly since its inception in 1996, in part because of differing interpretations on whether or not it enjoyed any autonomy *vis à vis* the Summit. Falling under the Organ are meetings of the Inter-state Defence and Security Committee (ISDSC, a hangover of the Front Line period and still to be integrated into the Organ proper).

Figure 14.1 Proposed SADC Organ Structure (1999)

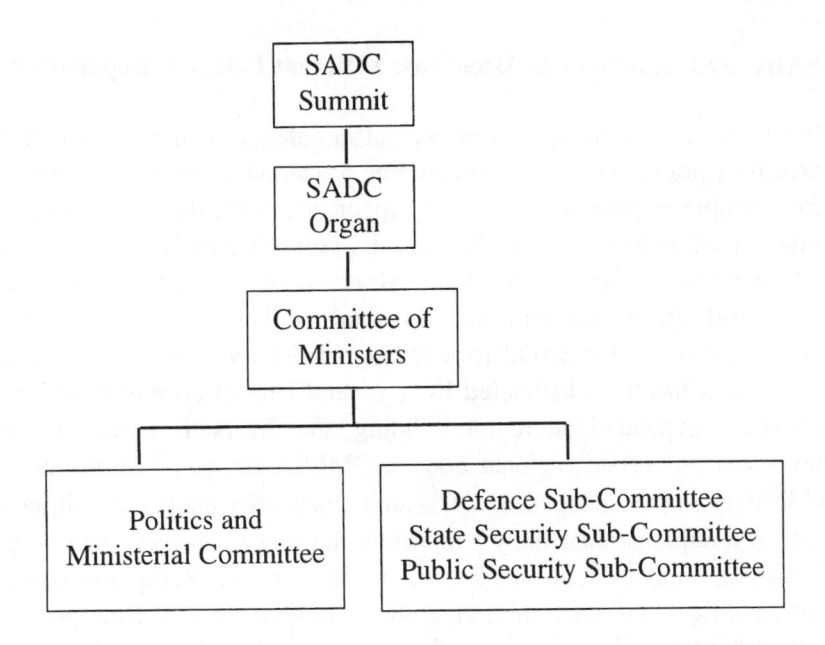

```
          ┌─────────────┐
          │    SADC     │
          │   Summit    │
          └──────┬──────┘
                 │
          ┌──────┴──────┐
          │    SADC     │
          │    Organ    │
          └──────┬──────┘
                 │
          ┌──────┴──────┐
          │ Committee of│
          │  Ministers  │
          └──────┬──────┘
        ┌────────┴────────┐
┌───────┴────────┐ ┌──────┴──────────────────┐
│  Politics and  │ │  Defence Sub-Committee  │
│   Ministerial  │ │ State Security Sub-Committee │
│   Committee    │ │ Public Security Sub-Committee │
└────────────────┘ └─────────────────────────┘
```

Regional treaty instruments There are a number of protocols which, when ratified, compel members states to adhere to their prescriptions. By 2000, eight out of eleven SADC projects had been ratified e.g. the all important Trade Protocol which came into force in September 2000. This is meant to lead to the constitution of a Free Trade Area which envisages that all tariffs be abolished by 2012.[20] The SADC has a small secretariat financed by subscriptions from member states. The secretariat has little more than a coordinating role since —in the interests of reducing the SADC bureaucracy — various member countries are responsible for the coordination of sectoral functions within their own line function departments. Additionally, financed by national budgets, Sector Coordinating Units (SCU's) in each country are responsible for arranging meetings, distributing information and performing other sector-coordinating functions.[21] Moreover, since the state-centred system of control has favoured the national control of foreign aid projects, member states have generally resisted devolving powers to the Secretariat.[22] Thus the Secretariat is not the administrative centre of the SADC in all its parts. This puts the organisation at some disadvantage as a decision-making /

policy-making unit, and lowers its capacity to retain an institutional memory important for the purposes of strategic planning.

SADC and Development Decisions: Different Points of Departure?

It is to be remembered that from the outset, integration in the SADC(C) was driven by political rather than economic or market-driven factors. This may, for example, explain why political expedience rather than the SADC's own rules of admission allowed for the admission of Kabila's Congo in 1997 (*Business Day* 4 September, 1997). Moreover, cooperation is cast in a predominantly functional, inter-governmental mould which pervades the logic of cooperation in the SADC (Soederbaum 1998, 89). Yet cooperation along these lines has been hampered by a general lack of economic and human resources expended on region-building, the diversion of already scarce resources on a rival regional body, COMESA (some of whose aims and objectives mirror those of SADC)[23] and a hesitancy about committing oneself to a supranational body[24] in which the bigger players, such as South Africa or Zimbabwe, are likely to have the most say. Because of these factors, political and economic integration has reached a delicate phase, and national interests have increasingly come to clash with the regional agenda (Seymour 1997, 2). This situation is compounded by tenuous political or military situations in Lesotho, the DRC, Swaziland, Zimbabwe and Angola where democracy and stability are challenged. Here, first attempts by President Mandela, as chair of the SADC, to impose sanctions on members such as Zambia or Swaziland for obstructing democratic practices were singularly unsuccessful. Military spending by individual member countries of the SADC varies enormously as Tables 14.1 and 14.2 below clearly illustrate.

All the same, mobilising domestic support for regional integration is increasingly necessary as foreign willingness to contribute to donor aid programmes diminishes and the need to promote a regional environment conducive to attracting regional and foreign direct investment increases. The restructuring of the ACP-EU relationship with its emphasis on trade rather than aid is one such indicator in the early part of the new century. South Africa has encouraged regionalism by diverting a major project away from South Africa to Mozambique,[25] whilst others, such as Tanzania, are making their own decisions about region-building (the latter has expressed a preference for entering into free trade agreements with its neighbours Kenya and Uganda (who are not members of the SADC) in its more immediate region.

Table 14.1 Military Expenditure by the Members of the Southern African Development Commuity (US$ millions)

COUNTRY	1987	1988	1989	1990	1991	1992	1993	1994	1995	1996	1997
ANGOLA	1310	1580	1790	1470	1100	1570	734	1200	1150	1370	1550
BOTSWANA	118	130	121	168	182	183	235	231	215	239	241
LESOTHO	NA	NA	35	51	NA	34	27	23	24	28	32
MALAWI	32	28	29	24	23	21	21	29	17	23	26
MAURITIUS	5	6	8	10	11	12	12	13	14	13	12
MOZAMBIQUE	126	118	141	140	125	126	134	154	69	66	73
NAMIBIA	NA	NA	NA	48	70	65	57	55	60	69	90
SOUTH AFRICA*	4630	4870	4870	4770	3970	3570	3210	3560	2990	3010	2320
SWAZILAND	11	12	12	19	19	24	28	26	27	30	32
TANZANIA	133	105	105	97	102	117	101	NA	87	103	87
ZAMBIA	96	149	149	131	90	104	58	68	56	43	41
ZIMBABWE	367	337	335	340	303	269	251	257	283	231	320

Source: United States, Department of State, Bureau of Arms Control, *World Military Expenditures and Arms Transfers 1998* (Washington, DC: Bureau of Arms Control, 1998).
*Note: Figures for South Africa prior to the 1994 democratic dispensation are included.

At the core of economic cooperation, sectoral cooperation based on inter-governmental cooperation continues. In 1997, 425 projects were being implemented in the region.[26] Many of these are small, or amount to national rather than regional projects. Since many projects have only national connotations, they do not directly contribute to a broader regionalism. As such, the SADC simply remains one other avenue through which individual members can obtain donor funding for individual projects.

All this suggests that not only does the scale and content of these projects need to be discussed, but it also raises the issue of whether the organisation and management systems inherited from the SADCC are suited to meeting the goals towards integration the SADC has set itself (Davies 1994, 11). Officially this issue was recognised by the Summit in 1996 and brought about a Presidential Review Commission (consisting of Mozambique, Namibia and Tanzania) resulting in a report in 1997. This report contained proposals for a renewed secretariat and a move away from project and sectoral

Table 14.2 Armed Forces of the Members of the Southern African Development Community (millions)

COUNTRY	1987	1988	1989	1990	1991	1992	1993	1994	1995	1996	1997
ANGOLA	74	107	107	115	150	128	128	120	100	95	95
BOTSWANA	4	4	6	6	7	7	7	7	7	7	8
LESOTHO	2	2	2	2	2	2	2	2	2	2	2
MALAWI	7	7	7	7	8	10	10	10	10	8	8
MAURITIUS	1	1	1	1	1	1	1	1	1	1	1
MOZAMBIQUE	65	65	65	65	65	50	50	11	12	11	14
NAMIBIA	NA	NA	NA	NA	8	8	8	8	8	8	8
SOUTH AFRICA*	102	100	100	85	80	75	75	75	75	75	75
SWAZILAND	3	3	4	3	3	3	3	3	3	3	3
TANZANIA	40	40	40	40	40	46	46	50	50	50	35
ZAMBIA	17	17	17	16	16	16	16	16	16	16	21
ZIMBABWE	45	45	51	45	45	48	48	43	40	40	40

Source: United States, Department of State, Bureau of Arms Control, *World Military Expenditures and Arms Transfers 1998* (Washington, DC: Bureau of Arms Control, 1998).
*Note: Figures for South Africa prior to the 1994 democratic dispensation are included.

co-operation to involve private market forces and aim at greater financial self-sufficiency (Breytenbach 2000, 88). However, it raised fears that this would endanger the notion of economic development integration and mean greater political weight for the most developed member states.[27] As such, the SADC's final report on restructuring has to date led to little movement on institutional reform.[28]

Given the modest coordinating functions the Secretariat possesses, innovative practices at the the centre of the organisation to establish the SADC's credentials as a body promoting pluralism have been incremental. The establishment of a gender unit at the Secretariat in 1997 works towards implementing the Summit's declaration on gender and development with its commitment to ensure that by 2005 at least 30% of MPs and ministers will be women (the current respective figures are 15% and 12%).[29] Local Government Ministers in 2000 proposed to form a SADC Forum on Local Government, whilst the 2000 Summit saw an interactive session between Heads of State and SADC business leaders.[30] The SADC Parliamentary

Forum in existence since 1996, recently put itself on a firm footing by establishing a Secretariat based in Windhoek. Working on the premise that informed people are more likely to participate and contribute to regional integration, it aims to popularise the work of the SADC amongst a wider public, dispatch electoral observers to help sustain fair electoral processes and embark on a first five year programme on how to promote integration around the management of natural resources in the region.[31] Importantly, a draft human rights charter is to accompany the eventual setting up of a proposed SADC Human Rights Court which is meant to entrench and enforce a regional code on rights provided there is the political will among members to subordinate their constitutions to the final charter.[32]

SADC Security Decisions: A Lack of Common Objectives?

The origin of a regional definition of security lies in the constitution of the Front Line grouping of states to coordinate a policy response to an apartheid South Africa between 1979–1992. The expansionism of apartheid South Africa in its pursuit of a Constellation of Southern African States (CONSAS) had made this a necessary response. With the end of apartheid, and following SA's accession to the SADC, it was decided at the SADC summit in August 1994 to disband the Front Line States as the entente which had served as the effective political arm of the SADCC in the struggle against apartheid, and replace it with a new framework for political and security cooperation. What remained of the Front Line grouping — the Inter-State Defence and Security Committee (ISDSC) — was meant to be part of any new regional security architecture.

With the removal of the apartheid security threat, and having reached the threshold of a security community (Soederbaum 1998, 89), the issue of what body could take care of both old and new security issues was addressed. In the knowledge of the structural weaknesses of the Organisation of African Unity (OAU) which "plainly lacked the capability of handling conflicts . . . and sometimes even the political interest to do so . . . ." (Henrikson 1995, 147-8) there was a need for a sub-regional approach on security even though some have argued that such initiatives undermine overall African solidarity (Grauman 1998, 6).

The meeting of SADC Foreign Ministers which was convened in Harare in March 1995 proposed the establishment of an Association of Southern African States (ASAS) which would become the primary mechanism for dealing with conflict prevention, management and resolution in Southern Africa. ASAS was meant to complement, not replace, OAU mechanisms. It was to operate independently of the SADC Secretariat, but report directly to the SADC (Heads of Government) Summit. Its Chair rotated amongst member states every two years; heads of government constituted its decision-making authority, and all its decisions were implemented by two Committees (serviced by the Foreign Ministry of the Chairing state) — one for political and one for defence and security matters.

The latter was intended to focus upon training and cooperation — conflict management — rather than on the creation of either a regional peacekeeping force or any form of regional command. Nonetheless, it was to be a multilateral organisation able to provide the intelligence support for preventive diplomacy initiatives in the case of pending or actual conflicts. It was also able to plan combined operations and work towards security arrangements on specific issues such as countering weapons smuggling.

However, South Africa came to play an increasingly significant role in the re-orientation of the region towards "peace-making." This built on a commitment made by the SADC at its founding to establish a framework and mechanisms aimed at strengthening regional solidarity and provide for mutual peace and security. In line with this concern, ASAS was changed to the Organ on Politics, Defence and Security (OPDS) at Gaberone and constituted in June 1996. Its brief was to complement, not replace, OAU mechanisms for resolving security issues. It operated independently from the SADC secretariat (Bischoff and Southall 1999, 174).

The OPDS, which operates at both a ministerial and technical level, briefs SADC Heads of Government Summits on matters affecting regional security. The question of whether it is subordinate to the Summit or enjoys its own policy-making autonomy remains open to contending interpretations. The Blantyre Summit had President Mandela as Chair hold that the Summit could never have intended to enable such a "Frankenstein monster" not to be under its control (*Sunday Independent* 14 September, 1997). By March 1998, the Summit had set up a working group to discuss the entire security concept and create consensus on the basic principles, political values and objectives underlying its establishment. It was only in late 1999 at the ISDSC meeting in Mbabane that the matter was, in principle at least, resolved in favour of the Organ's subordination to the General Summit (although the Windhoek Summit of August 2000 chose not as yet, to finalise the matter).

The Chair constitutes its decision-making authority — the first and so far only Chairperson is Zimbabwe's President Robert Mugabe — and is intended to rotate amongst heads of government on an annual troika basis. At the same time, the Inter-State Defence and Security Committee (ISDSC), a body held over from the disbanded Front Line states, is meant to form part of the OPDS, though here actual integration has still to be achieved.

The OPDS is to safeguard the region from instability, both internal as well as external, but has yet to begin to operate effectively and proactively in either instance.[33] Its history indicates competition and conflict for leadership on security matters contrary to the principle of consensus underlying the SADC wider economic integration efforts. On the one hand, it is a contest for national leadership between the former and present leading power in the SADC(C), and on the other, it is about differences on definitions of security and how inclusive the discussions on security should be.[34] However, there are concerns that what amounts to a preoccupation with rather narrowly conceived state-centric security concerns deflects from one of the provisions of the terms of reference set up for the Organ: "the observance of human rights, democracy and the rule of law" and the "peaceful settlement of disputes by negotiation, mediation"[35] both of which provide avenues for the participation of non-state actors.

At a practical level, the OPDS through the ISDSC, promotes police, security and defence cooperation around inter-border crime and specific issues such as weapons smuggling, drug trafficking or stock theft. Recognising that preventive diplomacy, mediation, arms control and peace-keeping activities also form part of its brief, it is recognised that this multilateral organisation ought to work towards providing the intelligence support needed for initiatives aimed at preventive diplomacy. In addition, in a somewhat ambitious move, the OPDS eventually wants to bring about a defence pact and thereby create a collective security capacity for itself comparable to that of the North Atlantic Treaty Organization (NATO) (*Daily Despatch*, 11 September 1997). All these elements are present in recent SADC activities and have been the source of differences on what emphasis to attach to either peace-making or peace enforcement. In a first step towards creating a multinational peacekeeping capability and, with British technical support, regional peacekeeping manoeuvres — dubbed Blue Hwange — were held amongst seven SADC states in eastern Zimbabwe during April 1997. Repeated with logistical European, American, and Indian support in Operation Blue Crane two years later in South Africa, ten SADC countries actively took part in the exercises (*Business Day*, 11 February 1999).

In keeping with a more statist driven approach in defining regional security interests, a troika of members within the OPDS, Zimbabwe, Angola and Namibia, launched a military intervention in defence of embattled President Kabila and his forces in the Congo during the second half of 1998. The military intervention was dubbed a SADC initiative by its proponents on the strength of a meeting by the OPDS alone but, controversially for some, without reference to the SADC Chair.[36]

Even though the Organ does, as yet, not have the competence to take concrete action against countries which fall foul of the principles enshrined in the SADC Treaty (Graumans 1998, 6), Mugabe saw the Organ as having "sweeping powers to intervene in domestic disputes," whilst Mandela (with the support of Botswana) insisted the Organ "remain a consultative body assisting member states in dealing with their internal disputes through political means" (Goncalves 1997, 10).[37]

Following some deft regional diplomacy from South African Defence Minister Lekota, a special ministerial meeting of the Inter-State Defence and Security Committee (ISDSC) and SADC Ministers of Foreign Affairs in Mbabane in late 1999 agreed that the disputed organ was part of the SADC and should report to the SADC Summit meeting. The final shape of the Organ was to be worked out on the basis of the Draft Protocol on Politics, Defence and Security of 1996. Further deliberations were to look at the composition, structure and principles by which the organ should operate.[38] The Windhoek Summit of August 2000 postponed the matter for further consideration. However, the trend would seem to be towards a pluralist as opposed to a more realist mindset in SADC thinking regarding regional security.

What remains unresolved at the level of OPDS is the status for the SADC of the Zimbabwean–Congolese–Namibian defence pact and, in more general terms, the terms under which intervention by SADC members takes place. The absence of clear procedures means there need be no consensus or unanimity for defence ministers to agree on intervention in a member state. Zimbabwe's, Angola's and Namibia's intervention in the DRC in 1998 was to support Kabila's government in Kinshasa, whilst South Africa's sudden military intervention (aided by Botswana) in Lesotho in 1998 was to save an embattled but ostensibly democratically elected government. In both instances, these acts were legitimised as SADC interventions. Whilst the intervention in the DRC was (regardless of the political complexion of the DRC government) justified in terms of defending the sovereignty of a member state, the one in Lesotho was ostensibly a response to a call from an elected government struggling to maintain law and order. Both the similarities and differences in the two acts of intervention testified to the absence of any standard operating procedure on decision-making regarding intervention and the dysfunctional nature of the OPDS. Above all, in this foreign policy vacuum, it signified the underlying ideological mix between a realist impulse to defend any member state, regardless of its democratic credentials, suitable to one's own national interests, and a pluralist desire to uphold democratic norms and elected government in the region.

The absence of a functioning Organ has had its political costs in resisting the implementation the 1999 Lusaka ceasefire agreement. Even though the SADC Summit did play a part in putting pressure on President Kabila to implement the agreement during 2000, all attempts at bringing peace to the Congo and the Great Lakes region — Africa's greatest internal conflict since independence — did not originate from the SADC (Breytenbach 2000, 90), and COMESA in a rival bid to address issues of ongoing instability in the region also covered by the SADC, announced plans of establishing its own security mechanism.[39]

Conclusion

At the beginning of the 1990s, the SADC was a potential model for a new form of South-South cooperation based on the solidarity that was the experience of the state-non-state-non-state alliances formed during the struggles for liberation. Regional organisation had exemplary potential at the close of the apartheid era and at the dawning of a liberated sub-continent (Saul 1990, 163). However, the durability of national interests and intensification of transnational influences have not helped the SADC as a model of regional organisation. The durability of the national interest is in part explained by the diversity of states in the region and their common vulnerability: "No African state is sheltered from centrifugal explosions and internal implosions today" (Ki-Zerbo 2000, 5). The intensification of transnational influences in turn is due to the acceleration of the forces of globalization.

There are two political poles in the sub-region. At one end there are states such as Angola or the DRC who exercise little real control over their territory or over the movement of people and goods across their borders. Indeed, their preoccupation is with political survival which, in turn, depends on the state's ability to fend off military threats. This "paradox of the state" (Jackson 1990, 117) where governments cannot provide security, but insist on the national interest as paramount, means they have, in effect, little to add to the give-and-take of regional decisions and the transformation of regional relations. Counterposing this are states such as South Africa and Zimbabwe who economically are the most important states, able in concert with others, to do much towards transforming the region. Yet, by the same token, South Africa's sheer economic and military size and potential capacity to reinforce vertical relations in the world economy is a source of insecurity for all other member states (Weisfelder 1989, 159). This diversity in the region affects the nature and content of regional deliberation.

As such, two tendencies dominate regional deliberation, that of state-centred realism and that of a nascent pluralism. The realist position wants regionalism to add political and economic value to the resources available to each state. Decision-making is first and foremost about defining and projecting the national interest. Similarly, African unity is conceived of as the unity of Africa's states and its governments.

The other, institutionalist position is one where decision-making is part of an ongoing process of policy consultation and policy integration between state and non-state actors at a sub-national and regional level. It is based on an evolving understanding of what an all-encompassing regional commonwealth entails, the re-emergence of an Africa in charge of its own development at different political and social levels of governance.

Such differences in approach are driven by disparities in the region and differences of opinion about how best to resolve them; only South Africa and Zimbabwe have appreciable industrial sectors and even here South Africa's manufacturing sector is fifteen times bigger than that of its neighbour. Issues of transformation are issues about who stands to benefit in a situation of relative scarcity. As a result, regional organisation remains highly politicised. This influences the level of integration and encourages extensive rather than intensive forms of cooperation.

These differences have been taken into the security sphere by the somewhat hasty inclusion of a newly formed and politically weak Democratic Republic of Congo (DRC) in 1997. Not only did the SADC become directly embroiled in the Central African crisis — an event which directly drew other SADC states including Angola, Zimbabwe, Zambia and Namibia into the physical contestations of the DRC — but interpretations on how to resolve the issue initially revolved around whether states took a realist or pluralist approach.[40]

In the absence of an optimal decision-making environment in which all participants feel secure, much that passes as regional deliberation is actually about the politics of mutual affirmation. States which are self-conscious about their weakness and vulnerability as nation-states are often very concerned about the recognition of their sovereignty and the status accorded to their leaders. The preoccupation is with confirmation. Here the summit which lends itself to the politics of affirmation serves as a useful tool. Accompanied by a decision-making culture based on consensus, tough decisions are likely to be played down and rules sidestepped.[41] The result is often extensive rather than intensive forms of regional cooperation, since the latter may mean taking painful decisions. The SADC, needing to develop a regional decision-making environment which promotes intensive forms of integration, should have the wherewithal to transcend this scenario.

The structure of regional cooperation in the SADC and its predecessor, the Southern African Development Coordination Conference (SADCC), is based on functional forms of cooperation. Individual projects often favour individual donor-recipient relations instead of the region. The SADC's structure favours a nation-based and realist view of SADC decision-making.

There is resistance to having regional cooperation with its connotations of equality — embodied by the functional-sectoral model of cooperation carried over into the SADC — superseded by integration and supranationality. Leadership is by rotation; decisions in the SADC are reached by consensus and all, regardless of capacity, contribute equally small membership dues. Given the general lack of economic capacity to contribute to regional economic development, members can contribute little to region-building. Since its bigger members have no special role and South Africa is the only possible motor for integration (Vale 1989, 4), the SADC lacks a strong centre (Oden 1997, 27-48).

If the SADC is to grow, a deep-felt consensus on vital issues regarding peace, security and development is necessary. Only this will allow for the depoliticization of issues, greater functionalism, participation by civil society and deeper forms of integration. In the wake of regionalism elsewhere, the challenge is how to transform the decision-making environment in a way which builds confidence and trust, goes beyond summitry and presidential diplomacy, and institutionalises broader forms of participation lower down to strengthen regional loyalties. Whether this can happen organically in the context of a dynamic relationship between the SADC and regional civil society, or whether it will come through demands within a transnationalised political setting which wants to coopt regional élites, remains to be seen (Cox and Sinclair 1996, 139).

The challenge for the SADC, therefore, is to make use of a growing democratic space in the region in order to promote, not just regional inter-governmental cooperation, but also regional networks of solidarity supported by relevant policies and protocols at the regional level. As such, the SADC can, and should, become an organisation that demands greater contributions and becomes more participatory, that builds up institutions such as its inter-parliamentary forum and a proposed SADC Human Rights Court based on a human rights charter, and which makes greater institutional space for regional, nonprofit NGOs. The SADC should encourage its epistemic community or network of professionals and individuals to have an input in the deliberations and diplomacy surrounding human and state security, conflict prevention and conflict resolution; further, it should encourage development aimed at integration in the endeavour to build a regional community capable of being its own respondent in world affairs.

Notes

1   Domestically, after thirty years of independence, nation-building has achieved much that it set out to do. In an ideological, economic and social climate where the state has submitted itself to the regime of structural adjustment, adapts itself to a situation where it is no longer a major participant in the economy nor administers amounts of aid as in the past, it is forced to look outwards. In doing so, a major concern is setting up policy parameters which promote and regulate market activity across national borders. Doing this in tandem with neighbours, makes the region an important setting for addressing the issue of how to respond to the world market and how the latter is set to regard and use the region.

2   The Berlin Initiative launched in September 1994 identified areas of cooperation relating to investment, trade and economic development. The EU organised regional seminars and workshops on regional integration to facilitate a dialogue between itself and the SADC. There have been three SADC-EU ministerial conferences held in Berlin (1994), Windhoek (1996) and Vienna (1998). There are also provisions for a regular political dialogue on general matters of foreign policy with a view to promoting peace and long term stability in the region. A framework of cooperation exists with Nordic countries including matters relating to development assistance policy, business, trade and investment. Two cooperation agreements were signed between the USA and the SADC in December 1995 and February 1996. The US-SADC Forum intends to be an annual event to discuss issues around law enforcement, the environment and health (SADC, *Industry and Trade Report*, Windhoek 9–10.2.1997; A. Graumanns 1998; *The Citizen*, 15 April 1999). Relations with Mercosur are still exploratory (S.Chetty, "Southern links probed," *The Sowetan*, 29 June 1998). The SADC has signed protocols with African regional organisations including ECOWAS, IGAD and COMESA in the context of the development of an African Economic Community (AEC). This implies the exchange of information and intra-bloc cooperation (*Daily News*, 3 March 1998). On COMESA, the SADC, after the initial recommendation to its members in 1994 to withdraw from the organisation, was only partially successful (only Lesotho and Mozambique followed the recommendation),

subsequently advocating the continued existence of the two bodies although efforts to come to an agreement on the aims, objectives and functions of the two organisations after that remain inconclusive (Sidaway and Gibb 1998).

3 In the case of relations with the EU for instance, a Joint Council of Senior Officials has three SADC states and the SADC Secretariat meet a troika of EU states and the EU Commission in-between ministerial meetings, but this is an arrangement only meant for the EU.

4 As shown by the SADC's Secretary-General's rare type of response in regard to the negative effects a EU-SA trade deal for instance (*Business Day*, 16 April 1999).

5 By the 1990s, the recognition that these are shared difficulties has provided some substantial basis for regional cooperation. For instance, the increasing awareness of the need for a counter-offensive against the growing influence of international crime cartels which, riding upon the massive inter-state movement of people triggered by the end to apartheid, and by the rapid expansion of SA's air and trade links, led to regional measures to jointly combat the use of the region as a major trans-shipment centre for a wide variety of narcotics. Similarly, whilst a decision by the new Mandela government was to allow migrant workers from the SADC who had worked in SA continuously for five years to claim permanent residence disturbed the government of Lesotho (which depends heavily upon migrants' remittances), it was indicative of a wider realisation that the movement of migrants needs to be regulated by way of regional measures.

6 Declaration by the Heads of State of Government of Southern African States, *Towards the Southern African Development Community* (Windhoek, 17 August 1992: 7–9; Chapter 7, Article 21/3 *Treaty of the Southern African Development Community* Windhoek, 19 August 1992).

7 See Articles 6 Clause 2, Article 5 Clause 1a, *Treaty of the Southern African Development Community*, Windhoek, 19 August 1992.

8 The Windhoek Summit of August 2000, which received a report on institutional change, thought the matter needed further consultation.

9 SADC members after 1998 include Angola, Botswana, Democratic Republic of Congo, Lesotho, Malawi, Mauritius, Mozambique, Namibia, Seychelles, South Africa, Swaziland, Tanzania, Zambia and Zimbabwe.

10 *Southern African Economist*, February 1998:6.

11 *Business Day* 20.5.1998, 3.7.1998.

12 See 2 above. Japan has extended assistance amounting to $1.95 billion from 1991–1996 (*Daily News*, 18 March 1998).

13 *Business Report*, 18.11.1998.

14 *SADC Today* 2/4 (November 1998 : 9).

15 *SADC Today* 2/4 (November 1998: 1).

16 2000 SADC Summit, *Final Communique*, 7 August 2000, Point 19.

17 To date, protocols have been signed and ratified. The trade protocol was ratified in September 2000.

18 An example would be the 'mini-summits' convened on the DRC in Maputo on 16 January 2000 or 21 April 2000 to discuss the implementation of the Lusaka Peace Accord of 1999.

19 Each sector can have a number of sub-sectors. Thus, under the sector of Food, Agriculture and Natural Resources there are sub-sectors such as Wildlife (coordinated by Malawi) or Marine Fisheries (coordinated by Namibia).

20 See SADC. "Free Trade Area on Track." *Panafrican News Agency*, 11 May 2000.

304   *Globalization and Emerging Trends*

21   UNISA, Bureau Market Research. *The SADC Research Report*, 244/1997.
22   *South African Economist*, February 1998: 6.
23   Angola, Botswana, Lesotho, Malawi, Namibia, Swaziland, Zambia and Zimbabwe are SADC members who belong to COMESA.
24   *South African Economist*, February 1998: 6.
25   *Business Africa*, 1-31.12.1998.
26   Foreign Service Institute, SADC Workshop, 20-21 January 1997.
27   J. Dludlu, "Mixed feelings over Paper on SADC's Restructuring." *Business Day*, 5.8.1997.
28   Personal communication, 20 January 2000.
29   Athalie Molokomme, "Women on the Rise in SADC's Political Life." *The Sunday Independent* 16 April 2000: 15.
30   This lead to the signing of a memorandum of understanding between the SADC and the Association of SADC Chambers of Commerce and Industry.
31   SARDC, D. Marunduze, *The SADC Parliamentary Forum*, 3 April 2000.
32   The draft human rights charter provides for the extension of rights to individuals to safeguard their liberty, their freedom to engage in political activity, enjoy freedom of speech and conscience, protect them from all forms of discrimination, safeguard their privacy, allow them access to information, education and provide access to and protection from the law (T. Nyaki, "A Blow for Human Rights." *West Africa* 13–19 May 1996: 743).
33   Whilst in the wake of civil war or political instability, Mozambique, with the help of SADC leaders, was able to bring its principal opponent into the political process and conduct multi-party elections (Bischoff and Southall 1999, 175), similar efforts by individual SADC leaders in Angola and Swaziland were unsuccessful. South Africa and Botswana's military intervention during Lesotho's military and political crisis in 1998 was undertaken in the name of the SADC, but the decision to intervene was not taken as result of either a crisis summit or a meeting of the OPDS. The political crisis promoted around the post-colonial ownership of land in Zimbabwe following the ruling ZANU-PF party's defeat in a referendum over a new constitution in April 2000, had a reverberating effect on the region. However, the SADC's behind-the-scenes diplomacy in and around a SADC summit on the DRC held at Victoria Falls seems to have achieved little in controlling subsequent events.
34   Zimbabwe, for instance, feels the OPDS should be separated from the rest of the SADC since this helps to exclude SADC donors from the discussions on security.
35   Quoted from the *Financial Gazette* 25.9.1997: 3.
36   Complicated by a mutual defence pact involving Zimbabwe, the DRC and Namibia, this led to disagreement — ostensibly involving Zimbabwe and South Africa — about whether or not the OPDS should indeed fall under the SADC Summit. For a year the side which saw the OPDS as its own decision-maker on regional security affairs persisted.
37   F. Goncalves, "Deadlock in Blantyre." *SAPEM*, 15 October 1997. Only once Mozambique assumed the chair of the SADC in 1999 could what was ultimately seen as a personal rift between the chair of SADC — Mandela of South Africa — and the chair of the OPDS — Mugabe of Zimbabwe be resolved.
38   *Business Day*, 29 October 1999.
39   COMESA works on security mechanism (*Panafrican News Agency*, 25 April 2000).
40   Zimbabwe, Angola and Namibia together with Kabila's DRC followed a realist line and saw that resolution lay in a military solution intended to defend the state in the DRC. Countries like South Africa opted for a pluralist approach which sought to initiate an all

inclusive political process which would bring about an all inclusive political dispensation in the DRC.
41 The SADC has a set of rules stipulating the conditions which states applying for membership need to fulfil. Yet in 1997, at a meeting of foreign ministers, the pressure to reach a consensus — new members are admitted only unanimously — allowed members to forego those rules regarding the admission of the DRC. The decision ultimately weakened the SADC's integration efforts since the DRC was, amongst other things, unable to participate as a fully fledged SADC member in the years after its admission.

References

Barbarinde, O. (1999) "Regionalism and African Foreign Policies." *African Foreign Policies.* Ed. S. Wright. Boulder: Westview.
Bischoff, P. and R. Southall. (1999) "The Early Foreign Policy of the Democratic South Africa." *African Foreign Policies*. Ed. S. Wright. Boulder: Westview.
Breytenbach, W. (2000) "Failure of Security Cooperation in SADC: the Suspension of the Organ for Politics, Defence and Security." *South African Journal of International Affairs* 7.1.
Cox, R.W. and T.J. Sinclair. (1996) *Approaches to World Order.* Cambridge: Cambridge University Press.
Davies, R. (1994) "Creating an Appropriate Institutional Framework." *Prospects for Progress.* Ed. M. Venter. Cape Town: Longman.
Georgala S. and A. Tostensen. (1996) *Mobilising Resources for Regional Integration in Southern Africa: Towards a SADC Capacity-Building Fund.* Fantoff-Bergen, Norway: Michelsen Institute.
Goncalves, F. (1997) "Deadlock in Blantyre." *Southern African Political and Economic Monthly*, 15 October 1997.
Graumans, A. (1998) *Political Dialogue between the EU and SADC.* ECDPM Working Paper No 61. Lisbon: ICP, September 1998.
Henrikson, A.K. (1995) "The Growth of Regional Organizations and the Role of the UN." *Regionalism in World Politics.* Ed. L. Fawcett and A. Hurrell. Oxford: Oxford University Press.
Hodges, M. (1978) "Integration Theory." *Approaches and Theory in International Relations* Ed. T. Taylor. London: Macmillan.
Jackson, R.H. (1990) *Quasi States.* Cambridge: Cambridge University Press.
Ki Zerbo, J. (2000) "The Historic Framework of Governance in Africa." *AAPS Newsletter,* January–February 2000: 2–6.
Mingst, K. (1995) "Uncovering the Missing Links: Linkage Actors and their Strategies in Foreign Policy Analysis." *Foreign Policy Analysis.* Ed. L. Neack, J. Hey and P. Haney. Englewood-Cliffs: Prentice-Hall.
Nkiwane, T. (1999) "Contested Regionalism: Southern and Central Africa in the Post-Apartheid Era." *African Journal of Political Science* 4.2: 126-142.
Nye, J. (1971) *Peace in Parts.* Boston: Little.
Oden, B. (1997) "Is South African Hegemony a Condition for Regionalisation?" *African Journal of International Affairs and Development* 2.7: 27–48.

Ollapally, P. (1995) "Third World Nations and the US after the Cold War." *Political Science Quarterly* 110.
Olufemi, V. (1994) "The Politics of Global Marginalisation." *Journal of Asian and African Studies* 29: 186–204.
Rajan, M.S. (1990) *Non Alignment and Non Aligned Movement.* New Delhi: Vikas.
Saul, J.S. (1990) *Socialist Ideology and the Struggle for Southern Africa.* New York: Africa World Press.
Shaw, T. and J. Nyang'oro (1999) "African Foreign Policies and the Next Millennium." *African Foreign Policies.* Ed. S. Wright. Boulder: Westview.
Sidaway, J. and R. Gibb (1998) "SADC, COMESA and SACU." *South Africa in Southern Africa.* Ed. D. Simon. London: Curry.
Stadler, A. (1987) *The Political Economy of Modern South Africa.* Beckenham: Croom Helm.
Vale, P. (1989) *Integration and Disintegration in Southern Africa.* IDASA Occasional Paper.
Van Nieuwkerk, A. (1999) "Promoting Peace and Security in Southern Africa: is SADC the Appropriate Vehicle?" *Global Dialogue* 4.3:1–2.
Weisfelder, R.E. (1989) "SADCC as a Counter-dependency Strategy." *South Africa in Southern Africa.* Ed. E.J. Keller. London: Boulder.

15 Britain and Southern Africa: A 'Third Way' or Business as Usual?

RITA ABRAHAMSEN AND PAUL WILLIAMS

During the summer of 1999, as financial speculators in New York were celebrating their profits after the Bank of England's latest gold bullion sales, thousands of miners in Pretoria took to the streets in protest against the gold sales. By triggering a sharp drop in gold prices as part of the process of Third World debt relief, business as usual at the Bank of England had forced thousands of South African miners to join the ranks of the unemployed (Beresford 1999).

The fate of the South African miners is a good illustration of the difficulties involved in New Labour's desire to add an 'ethical dimension' to British foreign policy. After their election victory in May 1997, the Labour Party promised not only a radical change on the domestic arena, but also an innovative approach to foreign policy. The party had been elected on a renewed commitment to the principles of social justice — to security, health, education and equality, and these principles were also to form the basis of New Labour's international relations. In a world characterised by accelerating globalization and interdependence, the government announced that foreign policy could no longer be based on a narrow conception of 'the national interest,' but had to pay serious attention to the ethical implications of Britain's actions abroad. Henceforth, New Labour argued, foreign policy was to be understood as inextricably linked to the government's programme of domestic renewal. Since 1998 this project has coalesced around the idea of a 'third way.'

This chapter focuses on New Labour's attempts to implement the idea of a 'third way' in relation to southern Africa. Rather than address the foreign policy-making process in any great detail, the chapter examines the way in which British foreign policy under New Labour's stewardship has affected the southern African region.[1] It does so in two stages. The first section explores the concept of the 'third way' and how such ideas have been translated into the debate about British foreign policy. The second section discusses how such general pronouncements relate to Africa, and we identify and elaborate on three core themes of New Labour's 'third way' in southern Africa, namely peace, prosperity and democracy. We conclude that although New Labour's claims about a 'third way' foreign policy have succeeded in giving Britain a higher profile in the international arena, the implementation of such a policy is intrinsically difficult.

The 'Third Way' in British Foreign Policy

The debate about how Britain should seek to balance the traditional goals of foreign policy (national security and commercial prosperity) with an 'ethical dimension' was initiated by the Foreign Secretary, Robin Cook, only ten days into New Labour's term in office (1997a). Similar concerns about ethics were also discernible within the Ministry of Defence (MoD) (Robertson 1997, 40). One year later, in a speech to mark New Labour's first year in government, Cook unequivocally attached himself to the "Blairite credo" of the "third way" (Richards 1998, 22).

Talk of a so-called 'third way' is not new (it dates back to the end of the 19th century), nor has it been confined to Britain. However, along with Bill Clinton, Tony Blair has been one of the concept's most vocal advocates, and the 'third way' has become the central axis of New Labour's policies. The recent debate about the 'third way' in Britain emerged from a number of sources, most notably in the writings of several left-wing thinkers (Hutton 1996; Giddens 1998; Hargreaves and Christie 1998; Finlayson 1999). These writers sought to move political debate beyond the sterile disputes between 'old left' socialists and 'new right' Thatcherites which were increasingly indicative of high levels of political apathy and alienation. For Anthony Giddens, one of the concept's main proponents, the 'third way':

> . . . refers to a framework of thinking and policy-making that seeks to adapt social democracy to a world which has changed fundamentally over the past two or three decades. It is a 'third way' in the sense that it is an attempt to transcend both the old-style social democracy and neo-liberalism (1998, 26).

The 'third way' is designed to help citizens and their representatives steer a path through the major revolutions of our time, which, according to

Giddens, revolve around globalization, transformations in personal life, and our collective relationship to nature. In short, the 'third way' prescribes a set of flexible, but identifiable values designed to guide action while preserving "a core concern with social justice" in a fluid political sphere (Giddens 1998, 65).

But as Giddens acknowledges, thinking alone cannot produce the desired social, economic and political outcomes, and under Tony Blair's leadership, the Labour government has sought to operationalise the 'third way' through concrete political strategies. For Blair, increased globalization gives rise to the need for a 'third way', which he regards as "an attempt to make realistic sense of the modern world." It seeks to "equip people for change, to shape its impact, . . . [and] embrace it in order that we can make it work for us" (1998b). In his opinion, the 'third way' is the best label for "a new politics arising from the ashes of the struggles of the 20th century between traditional views of capitalism and of socialism," a politics that "seeks to combine economic dynamism with social justice" (1999a). Blair further contends that the 'third way' "is founded on the values which have guided progressive politics for more than a century – democracy, liberty, justice, mutual obligation and internationalism" (1998a, 1). In particular, it is designed to meet four broad objectives: a dynamic knowledge-based economy which harnesses the market to serve the public interest; a strong civil society; a modern government of partnership and decentralisation; and a foreign policy based on international co-operation (Blair 1998a, 7–18).

Crucially then, the 'third way' is not just about what happens in Britain, but has a strong international dimension. Global interdependence is a recurring theme in New Labour's policy discourse and it is frequently argued that in an increasingly globalized world, Britain's ethical and practical commitments can no longer stop at the water's edge. In the same way that distant events can have a direct and immediate impact on the daily lives of Britons, the decisions and actions taken by the people and government of Britain are likely to affect the choices and possibilities of other states and societies. Global warming, deforestation, polluted and over-fished oceans, and the spread of AIDS are only some examples of challenges that show no respect for national frontiers. As the boundary between the national and the international is becoming increasingly blurred, so the traditional distinction between domestic and foreign policy is also eroding. It is this recognition that has led New Labour to rethink Britain's international relations, and to argue that foreign policy "should not be seen as some self-contained part of government in a box marked 'abroad' or 'foreigners.' It should complement and reflect our domestic goals. It should be part of our mission of domestic renewal" (Blair 1997). For the Foreign Secretary, this means that the "Labour Government does not accept that political values can be left behind when we check in our passports to travel on diplomatic business" (Cook 1997a).

Despite these pronouncements, relatively little attention has been devoted to addressing the implications of the 'third way' in foreign policy. This is partly because of a deep-seated scepticism about the possibilities for a significant shift in British foreign policy (Martin and Garnett 1997). The former Foreign Secretary, Douglas Hurd gave voice to this scepticism when arguing that, despite all the rhetoric, New Labour had merely adjusted the foreign policy compass by "two or three points." What Hurd found most annoying was the pretence "that a shift of two or three degrees is a shift of 180 degrees and that all [New Labour's] predecessors were immoral rogues" (Hurd 1997, 25). Recently, however, the links between the 'third way' and foreign policy have generated more interest. For instance, a number of publications have appeared, some critical (Curtis 1998; Herring 1999; Pilger 1998; Vickers 1999; Whittingham 1998), others more sympathetic (Frost 1999; Wheeler and Dunne 1998, 1999). The emerging debate about the 'third way' in foreign policy is also evident in other ways. In 1999 the British International Studies Association convened a workshop on the issue, while a selection of academics and policy makers were invited to a conference at Wilton Park in 1999 to discuss the issue of governance in Africa. In addition, a new Foreign Policy Centre (FPC) has been established and the Foreign Affairs Select Committee (FASC) has issued several substantial reports on the conduct of foreign policy under New Labour. As part of this debate, it has been suggested that a number of ideas and values can be identified as key characteristics of New Labour's 'third way' in foreign policy. These include (i) internationalism, (ii) accountability, and (iii) the priority of human rights (Wheeler and Dunne 1999). Each of these themes merits a brief discussion, before we turn our attention to how the 'third way' relates to southern Africa.

(i) Internationalism

The Labour Party has a long history of pursuing an internationalist stance (Vickers 1999), and following its election in 1997 the new government was keen to end the isolationist policies of the last twenty years. At the launch of the Foreign and Commonwealth Office (FCO) Mission Statement, Cook declared that in an age of internationalism Britain needed a foreign strategy to support its domestic goals and that New Labour wanted to project a forward-looking, progressive identity for Britain on the international stage. Accordingly, Britain should become a key player in transnational issues such as the environment, drugs, terrorism, crime, human rights and development, and work to solve global problems by working with, rather than against other countries. As Cook put it, "I want our people to be proud of our country. Not proud because other countries are afraid of our might" (1997b).

(ii) Accountability

Under New Labour, the foreign policy process has been characterised by an unusual degree of openness. There has been nothing short of a multimedia bombardment informing the public about the ends and means of foreign policy, as well as unprecedented access to official speeches through the web sites of various government departments. The Government has also deepened the FCO's commitment to a process of dialogue with several human rights NGOs such as Amnesty International and Save the Children, and through the MoD, it has attempted to develop "a wide consensus on defence policy" through the Strategic Defence Review (SDR) (McInnes 1998; Robertson 1997). Another sign of this greater accountability is the publication of an annual report on human rights via the FCO. While the first report[2] represented a rather superficial triumph of style over substance, the 1999 report shows definite signs of improvement in terms of its structure and scope. However, it remains somewhat short on substance, preferring brief thematic discussions to more systematic and detailed reports on British activities in specific countries.

Future policy commitments also remain rather vague. Nevertheless, one of the effects of this new openness has been a higher profile for foreign policy issues, as by setting out its aims and objectives the government has provided the media and interested observers with a yardstick against which to measure its performance.

(iii) The Priority of Human Rights

One of the most noticeable elements in Labour's international relations is the promise "to put human rights at the heart of . . . foreign policy" (Cook 1997a). The government has stressed that sovereignty should no longer provide gangster states with the ability to erect what R. J. Vincent (1986) called "no trespassing" signs to conceal their abuse of human rights from international scrutiny (Blair 1999b). Instead, Britain has vowed to act as "a champion of the oppressed" (Cook 1997b) and to "support the demands of other peoples for the democratic rights on which we insist for ourselves" (Cook 1997a). The Government has taken the view that human rights standards, as enshrined in the Universal Declaration of Human Rights (UDHR 1948) are universal. For Cook, the UDHR should therefore provide the benchmark against which states are judged within international society.

Labour's commitment to human rights has found expression in several initiatives, including the establishment of a Human Rights Project Fund, supporting the use of sanctions (and sometimes force) applied by the international community, providing resources for the International Criminal Court, supporting media under threat from authoritarian regimes, and (at least a rhetorical) refusal to supply arms to regimes which deny the human rights of their peoples (Cook 1997a, 1998). It should be noted, however, that this is not the first British government to make the promotion of human rights a key element of their foreign policy. For example, the Callaghan government (1976-79) was keen to place human rights higher up the diplomatic agenda, and Douglas Hurd was responsible for establishing the first free-standing human rights policy department at the FCO.[3]

The 'Third Way' in Africa

A commitment to an ethical foreign policy is by implication a commitment to the poorer countries of the world. The extent to which the 'third way' has occasioned a substantial change in Britain's relationship with Africa thus becomes an important question. Britain has of course long been an important bilateral actor in Africa. As the dominant colonial power in southern Africa, Britain has maintained close links with the region and these have been reinforced through the Commonwealth. Britain also remains a major trading partner with South Africa, and consequently a significant source of internal investment in the southern African region. For example, according to a recent survey, British companies employ some 128,000 South Africans (or 42 per cent of all South Africans working for foreign companies) and have investments in South Africa totalling some $20 billion (R120 billion). In the post-Cold War era, however, the African continent has become increasingly marginalised as both its economic and strategic importance has declined, and the Labour government has stated its intention to give the continent "a new priority on the international agenda" (Lloyd 1999).

In its most general pronouncements, the 'third way' in Africa is about promoting and supporting positive change through equitable relationships based on mutual respect. Positive change is here defined with reference to the accepted tenets of contemporary development discourse, namely "good governance, human rights and sound economic policies" (Lloyd 1999). In more concrete terms, the 'third way' in Africa is designed to build lasting peace, prosperity and democracy. According to New Labour, these are the three key challenges facing Africa at the dawn of the 21st century, and consequently they form the core of British policy towards the continent (Cook 1998b; Hain 1999; Lloyd 1999). The rest of this chapter is devoted to a more detailed discussion of these policies as they relate to southern Africa.

Building Peace – The 'Third Way'

According to the FCO, peace is the first precondition of a successful future for the continent. Yet as a UN Secretary General's report highlighted, in one single year, one in four African countries experienced conflict and half of the worldwide deaths from conflict were in Africa (Cook 1998b). In Lloyd's opinion, present African wars are not about liberation, nor do they contribute to lasting security. Instead, they tend to fuel instability and feed off the resources of already devastated countries. It is clear, therefore, that building peace requires not only the resolution and management of existing conflicts, but also a long-term commitment to their prevention and to post-conflict reconstruction. Consequently, New Labour has recognised that "the most effective way to end human rights violations in conflict is by preventing conflict in the first place" (FCO 1998a, 19).

Britain has committed itself to help build peace by providing political support for conflict resolution, giving practical help to consolidate peace through demobilisation, disarmament and rehabilitation, by pursuing responsible arms export policies, and by boosting Africa's own long-term peacekeeping ability. A number of ministries are involved in these projects including the FCO, the Department for International Development (DFID) and the MoD, and as the FCO has highlighted, Britain contributed over 6.5 per cent of the cost of UN Peacekeeping Operations in 1997 (FCO 1998, 19).[4] However, it is significant that despite being plagued by several major conflicts, southern Africa has received relatively little of the UN's peacekeeping budget in comparison with other areas of the globe. In addition, the commitment of just six British personnel to the UN mission to the

Democratic Republic of Congo (DRC) similarly indicates that Africa remains at best of secondary interest to Britain.

On a more positive note, an Action Programme for southernAfrica has been launched following a May 1998 workshop on the subject of light weapons. The workshop was sponsored by DFID and organised by two NGOs, Saferworld and the South African Institute for Security Studies, and the Action Programme includes a commitment to "reverse the culture of violence" in southern African states (Cooper 1999, 14). British ministers have also recently endorsed the European Union's (EU) programme on Illicit Trafficking in Conventional Arms at the EU/Southern African Development Community (SADC) Summit (November 1998).

However, there remain important obstacles to tackling the issue of light weapons in the region. First, without significant change in the attitudes and policies of some African states, these initiatives will have relatively little impact on a continent where in 1997, only 8 countries submitted an entry to the UN register of conventional arms. Secondly, if it is to take the ethical dimension to foreign policy seriously, Britain should work to reduce its own arms sales to Africa. Although the government has declared that it will not give any more licences for arms exports that might be used for internal repression or torture, in the long-term, peace and security requires demilitarisation. As one South African analyst recently argued, "arms sales simply perpetuate the Cold War mentality of international military competition and wasteful expenditure on weapons systems that cannot guarantee security" (Shelton 1998, 36). Yet, at the same time as the DFID conference, the British government was engaged in an aggressive and successful campaign to persuade the South African government to purchase UK arms as part of a larger package amounting to some US$4.8 billion (Cooper 1999, 14). As this chapter is being written, the British defence industry is hosting the *Defence Systems and Equipment International '99*, one of the biggest arms fairs in the world (Sellars 1999).

Britain's stance on the arms industry illustrates the difficulties involved in trying to implement an ethical foreign policy. Britain has one of the largest arms industries in the world, employing some four hundred thousand people across the country. The government's responsibility towards the job security of these people stands in an uneasy relationship with the commitment to protect the human rights of foreigners. As long as Britain maintains an export oriented defence industry a fundamental tension will be contained within New Labour's desire to promote peace and human rights abroad.

In practice, Britain has been most active in southern Africa through DFID and its development activities, which are discussed in more detail below. Nevertheless, there has also been some activity in relation to peace building in southern Africa. For one, the FCO and DFID have begun to undertake "conflict appraisals" when preparing country development assistance programmes. Such initiatives are linked to a broader continent-wide strategy where Britain has been assisting the OAU in drawing up a capacity building programme for its Conflict Management Centre.

Other projects established to contribute to peace building include initiatives in South Africa, Zimbabwe and Lesotho. For instance, part of British aid is directed to reorganising South Africa's armed forces, including a British Military Advisory and Training Team (Barber 1998, 69). In Zimbabwe, Britain has helped establish a military training centre to support the OAU in its peacekeeping initiative in southern Africa, while in Lesotho, Britain is supporting security sector reform through efforts to deliver an effective and accountable community-based police service. Britain has also publicly discouraged the use of mercenaries on the continent. However, in 1997 the 'Arms to Africa' scandal concerning FCO activities in relation to Sierra Leone has done much to discredit New Labour's stance on this issue.

Support for such peace building projects is by no means exclusive to the present government. In 1994, for example, the Conservative Prime Minister, John Major, supported the establishment of a peace-keeping force of between 1,000-1,500 African troops, trained, equipped and financed by France and other European powers, and eventually the EU (Rye Olsen 1997, 314). Similarly, the "good government" strategy of the previous administration also included support for police training and so on in southern Africa.

Viewed in a wider regional context, New Labour's positive contributions such as military training and security sector reform are of relatively minor significance. Examples of southern African conflicts (such as Angola) are frequently used to demonstrate the difficulties involved in building peace and the intractability of intra-state conflict. New Labour, and international society in general, may therefore be relieved that such conflicts are occurring at a time when proponents of an African Renaissance are calling for "African solutions to African problems." While enhancing Africa's limited peace-keeping and peace-enforcement capacity would undoubtedly be a useful starting point, one needs to be aware that calls for 'African solutions' might also serve as an excuse for disconnecting from Africa at a time when the continent is becoming increasingly marginalised in the global economy.

The 'third way' also entails a recognition that economic deprivation is a cause of violent conflict, and that peace therefore requires economic improvements (FCO, 199a, 34). In the words of Cook, "If we want armed parties to a conflict to lay down their arms, then realistically we must demonstrate to them that they also have a better economic future in peace" (1998b). Processes aimed at post-conflict reconstruction are thus an integral part of building stable, long-term peace. New Labour's approach, however, like that of its predecessors, continues to revolve around persuading the International Monetary Fund (IMF) and the World Bank to strengthen their assistance to countries shattered by violent conflict. As we will see below, this approach is not without its problems.

Building Prosperity – The 'Third Way'

According to the Foreign Secretary, the government's commitment to reduce poverty at home "confers on us a moral obligation to fight poverty abroad" (Cook 1998b). In line with New Labour's recognition of increasing global interdependence, moral duty abroad is easily reconciled with 'hard-nosed' national self-interest, as a wealthy and prosperous Africa is seen to benefit not only Africans, but also Britons and the world in general. The global economy, according to Cook, is not a zero sum game — "If we are all prosperous, we all win. If there is widespread poverty, we all lose" (1998b). This, then, is the rationale behind the second aim of British policy in Africa, namely to build prosperity on the continent.

Britain's strategy for encouraging economic growth includes three main elements: the promotion of free and fair trade; the reduction of debt; and the enlargement and refocusing of the development aid programme. Among these goals, it is perhaps Britain's leading role in the initiative to reduce the debt burden of the world's poorest and most indebted countries that has attracted most attention. The Chancellor, Gordon Brown, was instrumental in securing agreement for a new debt relief package at the G8 Summit in Cologne in June 1999. The proposals will increase the number of countries eligible for debt write-offs, and will also speed up the implementation of relief so that three-quarters of the eligible countries will be able to reap the benefits by the end of 2000. While falling short of the demands put forward by debt campaigners, the Cologne initiative represents a small step in the right direction.

In terms of development, Labour has established a separate Department for International Development (DFID) and the Minister for Development, Clare Short, has helped make development a more prominent issue in British politics. The Labour government has also published the first White Paper on development for over 20 years, which described the overall aim of DFID as "the elimination of poverty in poorer countries" (DFID 1997). While the publication of the White Paper was a significant indication of New Labour's commitment to development, there is little new in the Paper itself. Its policy proposals and prescriptions are rather general, emphasising traditional areas such as primary education and health, whereas the key target to halve the proportion of the world's people living in extreme poverty by 2015 signals at best good intentions, at worst an empty promise given the current structural imbalances in the global economy.

As part of its commitment to the prosperity of other peoples, the Labour government has pledged to increase its aid budget by 28 per cent in real terms by 2001, bringing the total to more than £3,000 million a year. In the longer term, Britain is also committed to reaching international targets for aid spending, set by the UN at 0.7 per cent of GNP, but has given no date as to when this aim will be achieved (FCO 1999b). Britain's aid fell to 0.26 percent of GNP under the Tories, but is set to rise to only 0.3 per of GNP in the year 2000 (Elliott & Denny 1999).

Not only are such promises rather limited and disappointing, New Labour's policy proposals for stimulating economic growth in Africa also contain little that is new and remain steeped in economic liberalism. Like most western donor countries, the government follows the World Bank's lead when it comes to development policy. Since the late 1980s, the World Bank has established itself as the intellectual leader of the donor community (see Gibbon 1993), and the Bank has been the driving-force behind the formulation and refinement of contemporary development orthodoxy, the so-called "good governance" agenda. Although this agenda represents a move away from the crude economic liberalism of the 1980s, in that it pays more attention to the state and its relationship to society, current development policy retains a strong commitment to economic liberalisation (World Bank 1989, 1992). The central tenet of the good governance agenda is that democracy is not only a human right, but a necessary precondition for economic growth and prosperity. Political and economic liberalisation are regarded as two sides of the same coin, and a reformed and democratised state is expected to be more successful at implementing economic adjustment measures. Current World Bank recommendations are thus for a more efficient and democratic state, as well as continued structural adjustment. This was clearly stated in the Bank's 1994 report *Adjustment in Africa: Reforms, Results and the Road Ahead*, which argued that "adjustment is the necessary first step on the road to sustainable, poverty-reducing growth" (1994, 15).

This view also informs New Labour's development policy. The White Paper speaks of a "virtuous state" and "pro-poor" growth, and thus seeks to bridge the gap between the old ideological divides of capitalism versus socialism. At the same time, the government recognises that the IMF and the World Bank will be at the centre of future development efforts and endorses the IMF's contributions to the establishment of "sound macro-economic and financial policies" in developing countries (DFID 1997, 1.16; 2.10).

The corollary of this view is that there is no contradiction or conflict between economic liberalism and social justice. Indeed, this represents a central feature of the 'third way' and its effort to bridge the gap between traditional notions of capitalism and socialism. During his visit to South Africa in 1999, Tony Blair stated that the 'third way' not only combines economic dynamism and social justice, but that each depends on the other. In short, "If a country generates no wealth, it cannot afford social justice" (Blair 1999a). Such views have led New Labour to endorse not only the structural adjustment measures advocated by the World Bank and the IMF, but also to praise the African National Congress' shift away from the socialist principles that guided its thinking during the liberation struggle towards the neo-liberal economic policies it pursues today. According to Blair, South Africa's "Growth, Employment and Redistribution" (GEAR) strategy has set the country "on a course to tackle the needs of the disadvantaged, while retaining the confidence of the market." Indeed, Blair was so enamoured of GEAR that he dubbed it the 'third way', South Africa style" (Blair 1999a).

Measured against New Labour's declared commitment to reducing poverty and protecting the disadvantaged, however, such statements are problematic. The negative social consequences of structural adjustment programmes are by now well documented. While the fiercest critics condemn such programmes as a form of "economic genocide,"[5] it is widely reported that such policies tend to worsen the living standards of the already poor by depressing employment and real incomes. At the same time, the introduction of user fees in order to cut the cost of public services reduces poor people's access to health and education (Cornia, Jolly and Stuart 1987; Caufield 1997; Chossudovsky 1997 and Hoogvelt 1997). Although safety nets for the poor and vulnerable have now been incorporated into the structural adjustment package, the overall design of the programmes remains largely unaltered, and in many countries in southern Africa strict adherence to the policy prescriptions of the Bretton Woods institutions has significantly increased the suffering of the majority of the population.

In Zambia, for example, the economic policies of President Chiluba's government have led to a dramatic increase in unemployment and poverty. Through one of Africa's most ambitious privatisation programmes, designed with substantial assistance from western donors, the government has succeeded in privatising about 90 per cent of state-owned companies and public utilities. The result has been widespread retrenchment, increased poverty and inequality. De-industrialisation has also emerged as a trend, as trade liberalisation has caused small-scale businesses to collapse in the face of foreign competition. Various welfare and religious organisations in Zambia have criticised the government's economic policies as irresponsible and as leading to "economic apartheid" (Burnell 1994, 1995; *The Economist* 1993).

In relation to GEAR in South Africa, the criticisms of its negative social and political consequences have been equally damning (Marais 1998). Not only has GEAR failed to meet its specified targets, it has also brought rising inequality, increased unemployment and job insecurity, and has privileged the demands of internationally mobile capital over the interests of South Africa's poor. Given their position on the relationship between economic dynamism and social justice, New Labour is left with virtually no room to criticise the negative social consequences of economic liberalism in southern Africa. In this way, the poorer sections of society appear to lose out from a policy that claims to bridge the left/right divide and to be based on cosmopolitan ethics and a moral obligation to alleviate poverty.

The same tension between New Labour's commitment to social justice and economic liberalism resurfaces again over the issue of free trade. As part of its pledge to promote prosperity in Africa, Britain has promised to demand that African countries get a fair deal in international trade negotiations. In the words of Cook, "free trade must also be fair trade" (1998b). More often than not, however, rhetorical appeals to 'free trade' mask the highly legalistic and protectionist policies of the richer countries to secure their vital interests (as witnessed in the recent US-EU trade dispute), and the dismantling of trade barriers and import controls frequently benefits the economically stronger countries rather than the weaker. This issue became a source of conflict at the Commonwealth Summit in Edinburgh in October 1997, when a call by the richer member states for a new round of world trade negotiations was thwarted by the poorer members, including South Africa. Although the Summit eventually agreed on its first economic charter committing the Commonwealth to free market principles, the document entitled *Promoting Shared Prosperity* revealed a clear division between the poorer countries and the more wealthy members. While Blair described the charter as "an important and exciting" opportunity for the Commonwealth to play a dynamic part in global trade and investment, Nelson Mandela cautioned that the declaration was not binding and that many delegates had reservations about or were opposed to free market principles. Chief Emeka Anyaoku, the Secretary General, also warned that the benefits of globalization had been unequally distributed and that for many developing countries, globalization meant further marginalization (Johnson 1997). This conflict is telling, in that it illustrates the difficulties of combining a commitment to poverty reduction with the traditional liberal values of free trade. Although New Labour portrays itself as the champion of the rights of the underprivileged, poor countries themselves frequently perceive proposals for free trade as a threat to their interests.

In some respects, the same reservations apply to New Labour's call for debt reduction for the most heavily indebted countries. According to the proposals, debt reduction only comes into play once a country has followed the economic policies stipulated by the World Bank and IMF. Currently, a country must have a record of six years of satisfactory economic adjustment before qualifying for debt relief, but this period is set to be reduced to three years according to the Cologne initiative. In any event, neo-liberal economics remains a condition for debt relief, and as discussed above, years of structural adjustment measures can significantly reduce the welfare of the poorer sections of the population. The benefits of debt relief for the poor should not therefore be exaggerated, as the economic conditions set by the Bretton Woods institutions might prove to be counter-productive.

Building Democracy – The 'Third Way'

The promotion of democracy is another key aim of New Labour's policy in Africa. The Government has promised to be a "friend of democracy" on the continent and to "work for the observance of the Harare principles of human rights and democratic government" (Cook 1998b). In this respect, however, there is nothing particularly new or innovative about New Labour's policies. Following the publication of the World Bank's 1989 report *Sub-Saharan Africa: From Crisis to Sustainable Growth*, democracy or "good governance" has become the buzzword of development discourse. While paying relatively little attention to the structural imbalances present in the global economy and the negative effects this has had on Africa, the World Bank report identified "bad governance" as the root cause of Africa's development predicament, and argued that democracy was a precondition for prosperity and sustainable development on the continent. Accordingly, the Bank urged bilateral donors to direct their aid only to countries pursuing sound and sustained reform programmes, and within a year of the report's publication most major donor countries and multilateral institutions had made development assistance conditional on reforms towards good governance and liberal democracy. In the post-Cold War era then, the promotion of democracy has become an integral part of development policy, with the previous Conservative government in Britain being one of the first to endorse this new agenda. Already in June 1990, former Foreign Secretary Douglas Hurd announced that "Countries which tend towards pluralism, public accountability, respect for the rule of law, human rights, [and] market principles should be encouraged," and that governments that persist with repressive policies "should not expect us to support them in their folly with scarce aid resources" (in ODI 1992, 1).

On the issue of democracy New Labour can thus be seen to follow in the footsteps of the previous administration, and also to correspond to the accepted tenets of contemporary development discourse. A slight change in terminology can nevertheless be detected between the two British administrations; where New Labour speaks of democracy, their predecessors frequently preferred the more vague term "good government".[6] This change of terminology does not, however, indicate a significant shift in policy, but rather reflects the greater acceptance of democracy as a foreign policy goal in the late 1990s, when the initial criticisms of political aid conditionality as an infringement of national sovereignty have largely abated.

For New Labour, the promotion of democracy in Africa is largely unproblematic. While recognising that Africa is a diverse continent, and claiming respect for that diversity, New Labour regards certain principles and values as universal. Referring to the UDHR, these rights include people's ability to choose their leaders, their human rights, their basic freedoms and the rule of law. Again the notion of global interdependence informs the government's position; these are "rights that we claim for ourselves and which we therefore have a duty to demand for those who do not yet enjoy them" (Cook 1997c). Accordingly, Britain has directed its development assistance towards areas that can help build and sustain an open and free society. In southern Africa, this has involved the provision of electoral monitors, media training, funding for civil society groups, support for an independent judiciary and help in tackling corruption.

In contemporary development discourse, democracy appears as an unproblematic concept, an unquestionable good about which there is little or no difference of opinion. This is also the case in New Labour's policy pronouncements, where democracy is presented as a universal human right. While not wishing to address the issues of cultural imperialism or the cultural particularity of liberal democracy, we want here to draw attention to the contested nature of the concept of democracy. Contrary to the representations in New Labour speeches and in current development discourse, democracy is one of the most contested and controversial concepts in political theory. Put simply, there is not one, but many, frequently conflicting, democratic discourses and democracy can mean different things to different people (Abrahamsen 1997; Gallie 1995-6; Held 1987). In line with current development orthodoxy New Labour promotes and advocates a particular form of democracy. More specifically, they promote a form of liberal democracy that is compatible with continued economic liberalisation. This vision of democracy, which may well be endorsed by domestic élites in many countries in southern Africa, is not necessarily the form of democracy sought by the majority of poor people in the region.

It has been widely reported that popular movements for political change in southern Africa frequently originated from a deep dissatisfaction with deteriorating standards of living, and that 'bread and butter' issues dominated many campaigns for political reform (Bratton and Van de Walle 1992). Popular protests were thus not only directed against African incumbents, but were simultaneously revolts against structural adjustment programmes as a main contributor to the escalation of poverty and suffering. This was clearly the case in Zambia, where mass riots against President Kenneth Kaunda's one-party state were first triggered by the decision in June 1990 to remove food subsidies in accordance with demands from the Bretton Woods institutions. As a result, the price of maize meal more than doubled, and mass civil unrest, in which at least thirty people died, broke out in Lusaka and in other, regional towns on the Copperbelt (Ihonvbere 1996; Baylies and Szeftel 1992).

Popular demands for democracy in Zambia, as well as in many other countries in southern Africa, were not only demands for political rights, but also for concrete social and economic rights. For the thousands of people who took to the streets in Lusaka and other towns and cities, democracy was not only about the right to vote, but also about the right to a decent way of life for themselves and their families. Lest we should be misunderstood, this is not to dismiss electoral democracy as unimportant, nor to say that poor people do not care about how they are governed. Democracy may offer protection against oppression by a tyrannical state and this is of course of immeasurable importance, but so is freedom from hunger, ignorance and ill-health. The majority of impoverished people value political and civil rights not only because they offer protection from oppression, but also because they open up political space for demanding social and economic rights. Seen in this light, political rights are a means to the end of a decent way of life.

The contested nature of democracy thus becomes apparent. Whereas popular demands for democracy in many southern African states embodied clear social-democratic, welfarist aspirations, the Bretton Woods institutions and the Labour government regard democracy as intrinsically linked to economic liberalism. By locking democracy to continued economic adjustment in this manner, New Labour and the international donor community in general may rule out reforms towards a more just and equitable social order (Robinson 1996). In this way, the democracy advocated by New Labour may not only be at variance with the vision of democracy held by the majority of people, but it may also increase the suffering of vast sections of the population, at least in the short term.

Conclusion

When New Labour took office in May 1997, the Foreign Secretary Robin Cook vowed to make Britain "a force for good in the world" (1997a). Britain was to become "a champion of the oppressed," a defender of peace and democracy (Cook 1997b). After nearly three years in office, how are we to assess New Labour's foreign policy in relation to southern Africa?

It is clear from the above discussion that the Labour government has attempted to define a 'third way' in foreign policy and to combine national interest with a concern for the welfare of other countries and their peoples. The 'third way' has not only led to more openness about foreign policy, but it has also given Britain a higher profile internationally and stimulated a debate about the ethical dimensions of foreign policy. While this debate is to be welcomed, the achievements of New Labour's 'third way' should not be exaggerated. In the post-Cold War era, most western countries have become more concerned with democracy and human rights, or what can be referred to as the "ethical dimensions" of foreign policy. After having fought the

Cold War in the name of democracy and freedom, these goals could not easily be abandoned at the time of capitalism's historic victory over communism. The promotion of democracy thus became an intrinsic part of the liberal triumphalism that permeated the western world at the beginning of the decade, as witnessed for example in the writings of Fukuyama (1989, 1992). As we have seen, this goal was also endorsed by the previous Conservative administration, and in this respect New Labour merely follows in the footsteps of their predecessors.

While the Labour government appears committed to giving the "ethical dimension" a higher priority in foreign policy and has made some genuine attempts to implement their policies, it should also be recognised that the image of New Labour as the "ethical party" has been assisted by the employment of efficient 'spin-doctors' and marketing consultants. The Labour government has been very successful in 'branding' itself, and as this chapter has argued, many of its promises of a 'third way' in southern Africa have yet to translate into concrete action and financial commitments. Where such action has occurred it continues to share much in common with the approach of the Bretton Woods institutions.

Apart from such concerns, an ethical foreign policy is also intrinsically difficult to implement for at least two reasons. First, domestic responsibilities frequently clash with commitments to promote human rights abroad. The need to protect jobs in Britain's large defence industry versus the desire to support peace is only one example of such a conflict, and illustrates how adherence to an ethical foreign policy could necessitate political choices that might jeopardise Labour's prospects for re-election. Second, to live up to their stated moral commitment to be a "champion of the oppressed," New Labour must ultimately do more than provide Africa with increased levels of aid. In the longer-term, it is necessary to give Africans themselves a genuine voice in the major institutions of global governance such as the UN, the IMF, the World Bank and the World Trade Organisation (WTO). However, such a process of democratization would not only require the support of other countries (most notably the United States), but would also entail diminishing Britain's currently powerful status within these institutions.

A final obstacle to implementing a 'third way' foreign policy arises from a longstanding, unresolved issue within liberal philosophy, namely how to balance a commitment to liberal political and social values with the commitment to economic liberalism and market freedom. As this chapter has shown, the 'third way' constitutes an attempt to transcend the binary opposition of capitalism versus socialism. But while efforts to move political debate forward and to stimulate new thinking in a rapidly changing world should be welcomed, New Labour has failed to appreciate the way in which economic liberalism frequently exacerbates poverty and inequalities. Beyond the rather simplistic and formulaic statements that economic dynamism and social justice are mutually reinforcing, New Labour has neglected or glossed over the deeper tensions contained within their liberal internationalism. The ethical content of their foreign policy is frequently undermined by the commitment to economic liberalism and further economic globalization, and in relation to southern Africa at least, the 'third way' represents little new. Perhaps then, 'business as usual' is a more apt description of New Labour's southern Africa policy.

Notes

1. For discussions on the history of the British foreign policy-making process see Jenkins, S. and A. Sloman, *With Respect, Ambassador: An Inquiry into the Foreign Office* (London: BBC, 1985); Cromwell, V. "The Foreign and Commonwealth Office," in Z. Steiner Ed. *The Times Survey of Foreign Ministries of the World* (London: Times Books, 1982), 541-573; and Allen, D. "United Kingdom — The Foreign and Commonwealth Office: Flexible, Responsive and Proactive?" in B. Hocking Ed. *Foreign Ministries: Change and Adaption* (London: Macmillan, 1999), 207-225.
2. FCO, *Annual Report on Human Rights* (FCO and DFID, 1998).
3. Thanks to Nick Wheeler and Tim Dunne for drawing our attention to this point.
4. FCO, *Annual Report on Human Rights*, p. 19. The total UN Peacekeeping budget peaked at $4 billion in 1993 and has steadily declined from $1.4 billion in 1996 to $1.3 billion in 1997, and is expected to decline further to $900 million in 1998. Figures obtained at www.un.org/Depts/dpko/.
5. Michael Chossudovsky, cited in Thomas C. "International Financial Institutions and Social and Economic Human Rights: an Exploration," in Tony Evans Ed. *Human Rights Fifty Years On: A Reappraisal* (Manchester: Manchester University Press, 1998), p. 171.
6. See Chalker, L. "Good Government and the Aid Programme." Speech by the Minister of Overseas Development at the RIIA, 25 June 1991; Hard, D. "Promoting Good Government," *Crossbow* (Autumn 1990), pp. 4-5; and ODA, "Taking Account of Good Government," Overseas Development Agency Technical Note No. 10 (London: ODA, 1993).

References

Unless otherwise stated, all speeches and other FCO material have been obtained from the FCO's website at http://www.fco.gov.uk/

Abrahamsen, R. (1997) "The Victory of Popular Forces or Passive Revolution? A Neo-Gramscian Perspective on Democratisation." *Journal of Modern African Studies* 35.1: 129-152.
Barber, J. (1998) "Britain and South Africa: A Comfortable Relationship." *South African Yearbook of International Affairs, 1998/9*. Braamfontein: South African Institute for International Affairs [SAIIA]). 65-71.
Baylies, C. and M. Szeftel. (1992) "The Fall and Rise of Multi-Party Politics in Zambia." *Review of African Political Economy* 54: 75–91.
Beresford, B. (1999) "Speculation Fuels Gold Slump." *The Mail and Guardian*, Johannesburg, 9 July.
Blair, A. (1997) "The Principles of a Modern British Foreign Policy." Speech at the Lord Mayor's Banquet, London, 10 November.
———. (1998a) "The 'Third Way': New Politics for a New Century." London: Fabian Society Pamphlet 588.
———. (1998b) "The 'Third Way'." Speech to the French National Assembly, Paris, 24 March.
———. (1999a) "Facing the Modern Challenge: The 'Third Way' in Britain and South Africa." Speech, Parliament Building, Cape Town, South Africa, 8 January.
———. (1999b) "The Doctrine of International Community." Speech to the Economic Club of Chicago, 22 April.
Blumenfeld, J. (1999) "The Post-Apartheid Economy: Achievements, Problems and Prospects." *After Mandela: The 1999 South African Elections*. Ed. J. E. Spence. London: Royal Institute of International Affairs [RIIA]). 33–48.
Bratton, M. and N. van de Walle. (1992) "Popular Protests and Political Reform in Africa." *Comparative Politics* 24: 419–442.
Burnell, P. (1994) "Zambia at the Crossroads." *World Affairs* 157.1: 19-28.
———. (1995) "The Politics of Poverty and the Poverty of Politics in Zambia's Third Republic." *Third World Quarterly* 16.4: 675–690.
Caufield, C. (1997) *Masters of Illusion: The World Bank and the Poverty of Nations*. London: Macmillan.
Chalker, L. (1991) "Good Government and the Aid Programme." Speech by the Minister for Overseas Development at the RIIA, 25 June.
Chossudovsky, M. 1997. *The Globalization of Poverty: Impacts of IMF and World Bank Reforms*. London: Zed Books.
Cook, R. (1997a) "British Foreign Policy." Speech at the launch of the Foreign Office (FCO) Mission Statement, Locarno Suite, FCO, London, 12 May.
———. (1997b) "Britain's New Approach to the World." Speech to the Labour Party Conference, Brighton, 2 October.
———. (1997c) "Human Rights into a New Century." Speech at the Locarno Suite, FCO, London, 17 July.
———. (1998a) "Human Rights: Making the Difference." Speech to Amnesty International Human Rights Festival, London, 16 October.
———. (1998b) "Promoting Peace and Prosperity in Africa." Speech to the UN Security Council, 24 September.
Cooper, N. (1999) "New Labour and the Arms Trade." Paper presented to the British International Studies Association [BISA] 'Ethics and Foreign Policy' workshop, Bristol, 8-9 June.

Cornia, G.A., R. Jolly and F. Stewart, eds. (1987) *Adjustment with a Human Face. Protecting the Vulnerable and Promoting Growth.* Oxford: Oxford University Press.
Curtis, M. (1998) *The Great Deception: Anglo-American Power and World Order.* London: Pluto Press.
DFID. (1997) *Eliminating World Poverty: A Challenge for the 21st Century.* DFID, White Paper on International Development.
Economist, The (1993) "Zambia: The Miseries of Modeldom." 20 February.
Elliott, L. and C. Denny. (1999) "No Longer Far Away or Little Known." *The Guardian* London, 18 June.
FCO (1998a) *Annual Report on Human Rights* (FCO and DFID).
FCO (1998b) *Tackling Poverty in the 21st Century: Britain's Role.* Background Brief, January.
FCO (1999a) *Human Rights: Annual Report 1999* (Cm 4404 with DFID).
FCO (1999b) *The Cologne Debt Initiative.* (*Focus International*, August).
Finlayson, A. (1999) "'Third Way' Theory." *The Political Quarterly* 70.3: 271–279.
Frost, M. (1999) "Putting the World to Rights: Britain's Ethical Foreign Policy." *Cambridge Review of International Affairs* XII(2): 80-89.
Fukuyama, F. (1989) "The End of History?" *The National Interest* 16.3: 15.
———. (1992) *The End of History and the Last Man.* London: Hamish Hamilton.
Gallie, W.B. (1955/6) "Essentially Contested Concepts." *Proceedings of the Aristotelian Society* 56: 167–198.
Gibbon, P. (1993) "The World Bank and the New Politics of Aid." *European Journal of Development Research* 5.1: 35-62.
Giddens, A. (1998) *The 'Third Way': The Renewal of Social Democracy.* Cambridge: Polity Press.
Hain, P. (1999) "Africa: Backing Success." Speech at the Challenges for Governance in Africa Conference, Wilton Park, 13 September.
Hargreaves, I. and I. Christie, eds. (1998) *Tomorrow's Politics.* London: Demos.
Held, D. (1987) *Models of Democracy.* Cambridge: Polity.
Herring, E. (1999) "Response to Mervyn Frost: The Systematic Violation of Ethical Norms in British Foreign Policy." *Cambridge Review of International Affairs* XII(2): 90-92.
Hoogvelt, A. (1997) *Globalization and the Postcolonial World: The New Political Economy of Development.* London: Macmillan.
Hurd, D. (1990) "Promoting Good Government." *Crossbow*, Autum, 4–5.
———. (1997) "Foreign Policy and Human Rights." *Foreign Affairs Committee.* 16 December.
Hutton, W. (1996) *The State We're In.* London: Vintage.
Ihonvbere, J.O. (1996) *Economic Crisis, Civil Society and Democratisation: the case of Zambia.* Trenton: Africa World Press.
Johnson, A. (1997) "Promoting Shared Prosperity." *The Mail & Guardian.* Johannesburg, 31 October.
Lloyd, A. (1999) Speech to the Africa Day Conference, Lancaster House, London, 26 May.
Marais, H. (1998) *South Africa – Limits to Change: The Political Economy of Transformation.* London: Zed Books.
Martin, L. and J.C. Garnett. (1997) *British Foreign Policy: Challenges and Choices for the 21st Century.* London: Pinter/RIIA. 82-85.
McInnes, C. (1998) "Labour's Strategic Defence Review." *International Affairs* 74.4: 823–845.

ODA. (1993) "Taking Account of Good Government." Overseas Development Agency Technical Note No. 10. London: ODA.

ODI. (1992) *Aid and Political Reform.* London: Briefing Paper, Overseas Development Institute, January.

Pilger, J. (1998) *Hidden Agendas.* London: Vintage. 115–152.

Richards, S. (1998) "Interview: Robin Cook." *New Statesman and Society* 1 May: 22–23.

Robertson, G. (1997) "The Strategic Defence Review." *Journal of the Royal United Services Institute for Defence Studies* 142.5.

Robinson, W.I. (1996) *Promoting Polyarchy: Globalization, US Intervention and Hegemony.* Cambridge: Cambridge University Press.

Rye Olsen, G. (1997) "Western Europe's Relations with Africa Since the End of the Cold War." *Journal of Modern African Studies* 35.2: 299–319.

Sellars, K. (1999) "Lethal Weapons." *The Guardian*, London, 16 September.

Shelton, G. (1998) *South African Arms Sales to North Africa and the Middle East – Promoting Peace or Fuelling the Arms Race?* Braamfontein, SA: Foundation for Global Dialogue Occasional Paper No. 16.

Thomas, C. (1998) "International Financial Institutions and Social and Economic Human Rights: an Exploration." *Human Rights Fifty Years On: A Reappraisal.* Ed. Tony Evans. Manchester: Manchester University Press. 161–185.

Vickers, R. (1999) "Labour's Search for a 'Third Way' in Foreign Policy." Workshop, Bristol, 8–9 June.

Vincent, R.J. (1986) *Human Rights and International Relations.* Cambridge: Cambridge University Press.

Wheeler, N.J. and T. Dunne. (1998) "Good International Citizenship: A 'Third Way' for British Foreign Policy." *International Affairs* 74.4: 847–870.

———. (1999) "The Blair Doctrine: Advancing the 'Third Way' in the World." Paper presented to the "Ethics and Foreign Policy" Workshop, Bristol, 8–9 June.

Whittingham, P. (1998) *New Labour, New Hope?: The Development Policy of the New British Government.* Braamfontein, SA: FGD Occasional Paper No. 12.

World Bank. (1989) *Sub-Saharan Africa: From Crisis to Sustainable Growth.* Washington DC: World Bank.

World Bank. (1992) *Governance and Development.* Washington DC: World Bank.

World Bank. (1994) *Adjustment in Africa: Reforms, Results and the Road Ahead.* Washington, DC: World Bank Policy Research Unit. 15.

16 Continuity and Change in the United States' Foreign Policy Towards Southern Africa

PETER J. SCHRAEDER

Nelson Mandela's inauguration as President of South Africa on May 10, 1994 served as a crucial turning point in African history with important implications for the future of United States (USA) foreign policy toward southern Africa. For decades American policy-makers and their critics had viewed USA policy in southern Africa through the prism of South Africa's inherently unjust apartheid system. Whereas members of the executive branch had a tendency to view South Africa's apartheid system as a necessary evil in America's global confrontation with the Soviet Union and its allies during the Cold War era, the USA Congress became the focal point of an anti-apartheid movement that demanded the imposition of comprehensive economic sanctions against the Afrikaner regime, a policy ultimately enacted into law in 1986 over the strenuous objections (and veto) of the Reagan administration. Mandela's election in 1994 — five years after the fall of the Berlin Wall and the effective end of Cold War conflict in Africa — signalled a sea-change in southern African politics and international relations, and raised expectations among Africanists, both within the USA government and the wider African affairs community, that Washington would pursue a more balanced, proactive set of policies no longer constrained by the racial and ideological blinders of anti-apartheid and anti-communism.[1]

The changes in policy expected by Africanists were seemingly captured in a speech that President William Jefferson Clinton gave in Gaborone, Botswana, on March 29, 1998, as part of his historic eleven-day presidential visit to the African continent that also included stops in Ghana, Rwanda, Senegal, South Africa, and Uganda. Clinton's speech described Botswana as an exemplary model of democracy and economic development led by a far-sighted and dynamic leadership, and suggested that democracy was making gains throughout the subregion, most notably in Namibia and South Africa.

"We have seen the promise of a new Africa whose roots are deep here in your soil, for you have been an inspiration to all who cherish freedom," proclaimed Clinton before more than 5,000 people at the Botswana State House in remarks designed to highlight Botswana's special role as Africa's oldest democracy. "Africa needs more Botswanas, and America is determined to support all those who would follow your lead."[2]

An important paradox embodied in Clinton's speech is that rhetoric praising Botswana's special role as a democratic model historically has led Botswanan policy-makers to expect the further strengthening of USA–Botswanan bilateral relations, expectations which were further enhanced by the end of the Cold War and the decline of apartheid in South Africa. The Cold War's end particularly raised local expectations that the Clinton administration would make the promotion of democracy and human rights the cornerstones of a reinvigorated USA foreign policy toward the African continent, and in so doing recognize, build upon, and reward Botswana's special efforts in this realm, not to mention those of Namibia and South Africa, two other leading democracies within the southern African region. To the chagrin of numerous Botswanan policy-makers, however, a significant gap has existed between the rhetoric and the reality of the USA commitment to strong bilateral relations with Botswana. "We realize, of course, that Botswana is not the country of greatest importance to America, and that during the Cold War Americans were preoccupied with communism," explained one member of the Ministry of Foreign Affairs.[3] "But the Cold War is now over, and democracy is supposedly one of your chief foreign policy goals, yet we are still not seeing the level of commitment to Botswana that would suggest that words are finally being matched by deeds."[4] Another Botswanan diplomat was much more blunt: "We are always the model, but we are always neglected".[5]

The critiques of USA foreign policy offered by Botswanan policy-makers are echoed in varying degrees by their counterparts throughout southern Africa, not to mention Africanists in the USA and the other Northern industrialized democracies (Schraeder 1998; Minter 2000, 200-210). Part of the reason for these criticisms is that the Clinton administration, like its Democratic Party predecessors (the Kennedy and Carter administrations) and liberal counterparts in other Northern industrialized democracies, was extremely critical of the Africa policies of its Republican predecessors and extremely vocal about the need for more enlightened USA relations with the African continent. Such foreign policy pronouncements, regardless of whether made by Democrats in the USA, Socialists in France, or Labour Party members in Great Britain, not surprisingly lead to raised foreign policy expectations among Africanists that, more often than not, remain unfulfilled (at least to the degree desired by proponents of change), ultimately fostering rising criticisms among groups previously presumed to be each administration's closest domestic allies (Schraeder 1998, 1-7).

An equally (if not more) important reason for criticism has been the Clinton administration's failure to craft a proactive set of policies that are both coherent and consistently applied — a foreign policy failing typical of USA Africa policies regardless of whether one focuses on Democratic or Republican administrations. "Policies instead remain highly reactive, particularly with respect to crises requiring humanitarian assistance," explains Korwa Gombe Adar, a Kenyan specialist of USA foreign policy. In the case of Nigeria, for example, Adar argues that the Clinton administration missed an important opportunity when it failed to impose comprehensive economic sanctions against the authoritarian regime of Sani Abacha, despite the fact that such sanctions were imposed against other countries in Africa. Indeed, Adar rightfully concludes that "perhaps the lives of [Ken] Saro-Wiwa and other democracy and human rights activists would have been spared if the [Clinton] administration had sent the right signal when the 1993 elections were annulled in Nigeria" (Adar 1998, 73).

The primary purpose of this chapter is to offer some initial thoughts on changes in USA foreign policy toward southern Africa during the evolving post-Cold War/post-apartheid era to complement the case studies on African foreign policy. The analysis builds upon a series of field interviews that were conducted during July 1996 with USA diplomats in Botswana, South Africa, and Zimbabwe. The first two portions of the chapter establish the evolving regional context of USA foreign policy toward southern Africa. Trends are highlighted by focusing on the region's portrayal in the USA media and the evolution of foreign aid ties. The remaining sections of the chapter highlight five specific trends in USA foreign policy toward southern Africa: the centrality of trade, the 'regionalization' of foreign policy initiatives, bureaucratic dominance of the USA policy-making process, reassessments of direct USA involvement in African conflicts, and an uneven approach to democracy promotion. These trends are principally highlighted by drawing on the case studies of Botswana, South Africa, and Zimbabwe, although reference is also made to Angola, Lesotho, Malawi, Mozambique, Namibia, and Zambia. A final section offers general conclusions.

Evolving American Perceptions of Africa

Despite the rising numbers of USA citizens who have lived and worked on the African continent during the post-World War II era, there still exists a gap of knowledge concerning Africa among the majority of elected officials charged with the task of overseeing USA foreign policy throughout the world. This lack of knowledge is especially acute at the level of the mass public, which maintains what can be called a *National Geographic* image of the continent (Lutz and Collins 1993). Although some topics, such as racial politics in southern Africa, receive regular press coverage and have somewhat improved the public's awareness of African political and economic issues, the mention of Africa typically conjures up stereotypical images of lush jungles and wild animals, poverty and famine, corruption and 'tribal' warfare, and rampant sexuality leading to the explosion of AIDS. These stereotypical images are further reinforced by the nature of USA media programming which, when it does focus on Africa, usually concentrates on the sensationalist and often negative aspects of the continent.[6]

An Evolving Foreign Aid Regime

An analysis of USA foreign assistance trends portrays evolving 'official' (i.e., governmental) interests in southern Africa. These trends can be divided into four historical periods: Cold War I (pre–1947); Cold War II (1974–1989); post-Cold War era (1989–1994); and post-apartheid era (1994–present). During the first period — Cold War I (pre–1947) — the relatively weak intrusion of great power competition into southern Africa ensured that only modest amounts of foreign aid were provided to independent countries within the region. Whereas the USA provided a yearly average of $9.1 million in aid from 1965 to 1969, this amount had roughly doubled to $18.8 million by the 1970-74 period. This aid was distributed among five countries within the region (Botswana, Lesotho, Malawi, Swaziland and Zambia), with Botswana emerging as the largest aid recipient during the 1970–74 period ($7.1 million a year or 38 percent of the total). These figures must be kept in perspective, however, in that aid to southern Africa only constituted 5.8 percent of all USA aid to Africa during this period, which in turn constituted a very small portion of a global foreign aid budget.

The 1974 coup d'état in Lisbon ushered in a new era — Cold War II (1974–1989) — in southern African international relations that witnessed the massive intrusion of great power competition and the dramatic expansion of USA foreign aid activities. After the military victory of a self-proclaimed Marxist regime in Angola was followed by the emergence of ideologically similar regimes in Mozambique and Zimbabwe, a succession of USA administrations worried that ideologically and racially inspired guerrilla movements would lead to communist victories in Namibia and South Africa. As a result, the yearly averages of USA aid towards southern Africa increased to $53.7 million in 1975–79, $154.4 million in 1980–84, and $209 million in 1985-89. One analyst aptly captured the influence that the perceived threat of communist victories in southern Africa exerted upon senior USA policy-makers: "It was as if a map of that part of the world had come alive".[7]

The irony of rising USA attention to southern Africa in the post-1974 era was that formerly Marxist Mozambique eventually emerged as the largest recipient of USA foreign aid by the end of the 1980s (receiving 21 percent of regional aid or a yearly average of $44.6 million), followed by Malawi (16 per cent; $33.1 million) and Zambia (14 per cent; $29.1 million). In each of these cases, single-party regimes were on average receiving more aid than historically democratic Botswana, which was almost tied with single-party Zimbabwe for fourth place in the regional pecking order of USA aid.

The fall of the Berlin Wall in 1989 and the effective end of USA–Soviet competition in southern Africa signaled the emergence of the post-Cold War era (1989–1994) and prompted another dramatic increase in USA foreign aid to a yearly average of $413.9 million during 1990–94 (more than double the amount disbursed during the previous five-year period). Ironically, political and economic stability in Botswana prompted a decline in USA foreign aid to that country ($15.2 million or 4 per cent of the regional total). USA policy-makers were instead more concerned with promoting transitions to democracy in Malawi ($58.4 million; 14 per cent) and Zambia ($41.7 million; 10 per cent), aiding in the resolution of civil wars in Mozambique ($102 million; 25 per cent) and Angola ($29.4 million; 7 per cent), or promoting the liberalization of Zimbabwe's heavily statist economy ($54.8 million; 13 per cent).

The most significant change in USA regional priorities during the 1989–94 period revolved around South Africa's emergence as the second largest recipient of USA foreign aid. The willingness of the apartheid regime to work with the African National Congress (ANC) to ensure the peaceful transition to a multiracial democratic regime was rewarded by the provision of a yearly average of $75.3 million or 18 percent of the regional total. "The irony of the USA attention lavished on South Africa during this period," explained one member of the Botswanan Ministry of Foreign Affairs, "is that they [the South Africans] in reality were being rewarded for having stopped their wars of aggression against neighbouring states, including Botswana, whereas we, the victims, were being ignored".[8] This diplomat's statement was only partially true in that the most notable victims of South Africa's policies of destabilization during the 1980s — Angola, Mozambique, and Zimbabwe — actually witnessed increases in both the actual amounts and percentages of foreign aid along with South Africa, and only historically democratic Botswana along with the micro-states of Lesotho and Swaziland witnessed a decline in both the actual amounts and percentages.

The formal end of apartheid and its replacement with a multiracial democratic regime under the leadership of President Nelson Mandela in 1994 reinforced changes that had already begun to emerge with the end of the Cold War. The most notable development associated with the emergence of the post-apartheid era (1994–present) was the dramatic increase in South Africa's yearly aid average to $112 million (32 per cent) in 1995–96, making it the largest recipient of USA aid in southern Africa. In sharp contrast, every other southern African country except Angola, experienced a decline in aid programs that, in any case, were indicative of a declining foreign aid budget for southern Africa as a whole (receiving a yearly average of $348 million for 1995–96). The primary reason for Angola's exceptional doubling of aid levels from its 7 per cent share in 1990–94 to a 14 per cent share in 1995-96 (a yearly average of $50 million) was the ongoing pressure of conservative members of Congress to maintain support for Jonas Savimbi and his UNITA forces (Union for the Total Independence of Angola) in their power-sharing bid with the formerly Marxist government of Angola.

The continued downward trend in southern Africa's place within the USA foreign aid hierarchy is clearly demonstrated by the Clinton administration's foreign aid request for the Fiscal Year (FY) 2000. The overall budget request (which inevitably will be pared down by the USA Congress) envisions a total of $290 million for the southern African region, a nearly 17 per cent decline from the average for 1995-96 ($348 million). The majority of the region's decline in aid was the direct result of a much smaller aid request for South Africa — $68.9 million in 2000 as opposed to $112 million for 1995–96 — suggesting a more normalized foreign aid relationship after the initial euphoria surrounding South Africa's transition to a multi-party, multiracial democracy in 1994.

Centrality of Trade

An important factor in declining USA foreign aid toward Africa has been the emergence and strengthening of trade and investment as the preferred tools of USA foreign economic policy. To its credit, the Clinton administration in 1996 unveiled the first formal, comprehensive trade policy for aggressively pursuing new markets throughout Africa.[9] This report included the formal launching of an interagency Africa Trade and Development Coordinating Group, which is jointly chaired by the National Economic Council (NEC) and the National Security Council (NSC). The centerpiece of this economic strategy is congressional legislation — the Africa Growth and Opportunity Act — designed to enhance USA–African trade. Although sharply criticized by African leaders, such as South African President Nelson Mandela, as well as influential members of the USA African affairs constituency, most notably the Congressional Black Caucus (CBC), a compromise bill was passed by the both the USA House of Representatives and the Senate in 2000.

The formal announcement of the Clinton administration's trade policy was preceded by a series of highly publicized speeches rejecting Washington's past support for Europe's privileged economic role in its former colonies in favor of a more aggressive approach to promoting USA trade and investment. "The African market is open to everyone," explained former Assistant Secretary of State for African Affairs, Herman Cohen, in a 1995 speech in Libreville, Gabon. "We must accept free and fair competition, equality between all actors." Towards this end, senior administration officials increasingly agree that foreign policy should serve as the facilitator of USA private enterprise throughout the African continent. According to what is often referred to as the "big emerging markets" strategy, regional economic leaders — most notably South Africa in southern Africa — particularly should be courted by USA policy-makers and private business.

An important outgrowth of the Clinton administration's aggressive trade policy is the intensification of economic competition between the USA and the other northern industrialized democracies in their search for economic influence and markets throughout Africa. This economic competition has become especially pronounced in terms of USA–French relations, most notably in the highly lucrative petroleum, telecommunications, and transport industries in Francophone Africa. In the eyes of French policy-makers, the penetration of American and other western companies constitutes "at best an intrusion" and "at worst an aggression" into France's perceived *domaine réservé* (privileged realm) throughout Francophone Africa (Glaser and Smith 1994). All foreign observers agree, however, that southern Africa constitutes the richest future African market. It is precisely for this reason that France, the USA and the other great powers increasingly focused their economic sights on southern Africa beginning in the 1990s.

An important aspect of the burgeoning USA trade policy in southern Africa is the willingness of the USA ambassador to serve as an advocate for USA business. In the case of Botswana, former USA Ambassador Howard F. Jeter was recognized as a very effective advocate of the Clinton administration's trade priorities throughout the subregion. According to Michael A. Weaver, Manager of Plant Operations for a pipe-making subsidiary of Owens-Corning that opened in Gaborone in 1994, Ambassador Jeter and the more aggressive policy of the Department of Commerce contributed in no small part to his company's decision to locate in Gaborone. "In the past the USA government was not as willing to serve as an advocate for business, and as a result Americans were here [Botswana] in name only, at least as concerns trade and investment," explained Weaver. "This definitely has changed under the Clinton administration — they most notably aided us by helping to keep the local playing field level against the often unfair economic practices of our competitors, and working with and facilitating our access to key government officials interested in what we could bring to Botswana."[10]

For its part, the Clinton administration is equally effusive concerning the Owens-Corning decision to locate their pipe subsidiary in Botswana. As underscored by Secretary of Commerce, Ron Brown, when he visited Botswana in early 1996 as part of a five-country tour of Africa designed to promote USA trade and investment, the creation of the Owens-Corning plant in Gaborone constituted an example of 'true partnership' between an American company and the Botswana Development Corporation that would be financially lucrative for both countries — most notably due to the fact that Owens-Corning received a Botswanan government contract worth approximately $75 million to fabricate all the pipes necessary for the completion of the North-South Carrier Project. In addition to the obvious job creation for Botswana and the financial benefits that will accrue to a USA company, Brown was especially pleased to note the collateral impact on job creation in the USA. "I understand that the resin and the glass [for fabricating the pipes] come principally from the USA," explained Brown. "So here we have a situation where there has been investment in Botswana, creating jobs in Botswana, and raw materials coming from the United States creating jobs for Americans."[11] Other examples of high-profile deals brokered by the Clinton administration include the decision of Barden International (a USA firm headquartered in Detroit, Michigan) to open in March 1998 a multi-million dollar, righthand drive GM vehicle conversion plant in Windhoek, Namibia (the largest USA investment in Namibia during the decade of the 1990s); the expansion of an existing, USA-firm operated oil field (Block Zero) in the Cabinda province of Angola (expected to yield billions in revenue); and the signing of a wide array of bilateral investment treaties, such as the December 1998 treaty signed with Mozambique.[12]

A more aggressive business policy is especially highlighted by the Clinton administration's willingness to participate in a variety of high-profile regional events, such as the African/African-American Summit. Originally conceived by the Reverend Leon Sullivan as a vehicle for strengthening cultural ties between African-Americans and their African counterparts, the African/African-American gathering has evolved into a burgeoning forum for encouraging trade and investment between the USA and Africa. The inaugural summit was held in Abidjan, Coté d'Ivoire, in 1991, followed by summits in Libreville, Gabon (1993), Dakar, Senegal (1995), Harare, Zimbabwe (1997), and Accra, Ghana (1999). The Harare meeting (which also included several coordinated events in Johannesburg, South Africa) was attended by more than 3,000 participants, including African heads of state from Botswana, Ethiopia, Senegal, Swaziland and Uganda, as well as notable African-American politicians, such as two-time presidential candidate Reverend Jesse Jackson, David Dinkins, Marion Barry and Coretta Scott King. The official USA government delegation was led by Secretary of Transportation, Rodney Slater, and was joined by Jack Kemp. The trade and investment exhibition of the summit was dedicated to the memory of Secretary of Commerce, Ron Brown, who took the initiative in building USA-African relations before he died in a plane crash in Bosnia in 1995.

The renewal of USA trade ties with South Africa — perceived in Washington as the most advanced and the most lucrative economy on the African continent — serves as the focal point of the Clinton administration's business initiatives in the southern African region. As discussed below, an important regional dimension of USA foreign policy is to ensure that South Africa's economy is closely "knitted" to those of the other southern African Development Community (SADC) countries, thereby enhancing the rise of a regional market that would be more attractive to USA investors and capable of absorbing greater levels of USA exports.[13] "The economic logic behind such an approach, especially if we focus on the case of Botswana, is obvious," explained Steven M Lauterbach, Public Affairs Officer (PAO) at the USA Embassy in Gaborone. "A market of only 1.4 million people cannot expect by itself to be a target of USA trade and investment — the Botswanans and other members of the SADC must realize that their economic futures are tied to that of South Africa, and that USA businesses will be more likely to invest in a regional market offering more lucrative profits for USA businesses."[14] The Owens-Corning project is a perfect case in point. Although based in Gaborone, this subsidiary is taking advantage of economies of scale throughout the SADC region. As a result, contracts were signed to provide pipeline to the Hartley Platinum Mine and the Pungwe Water Scheme in Zimbabwe, and to the Namibian Department of Water Affairs for a variety of national projects.

An analysis of trade statistics clearly demonstrates why South Africa plays such an important role in USA economic calculations concerning southern Africa. Since the easing in 1991 of economic sanctions associated with the 1986 Comprehensive Anti-Apartheid Act, USA exports to South Africa have increased dramatically, including a 25 percent increase in 1995, and are expected to continue at such a pace throughout the first decade of the new millennium.[15] Indeed, the 1995 figure for USA exports to South Africa — $2.75 billion — represented 51 percent of all USA exports ($5.4 billion) to the African continent. The only other countries in southern Africa to even approach such trade levels were Angola and Zimbabwe, which absorbed $159 million (2.9 percent) and $122 million (2.3 percent), respectively, of USA exports during the same period. In sharp contrast, Botswana absorbed approximately one-half of 1 percent ($29.5 million) of USA exports to the region, with only Lesotho, Swaziland and Malawi maintaining smaller bilateral trade relationships with the USA.[16]

Regionalization of Foreign Policy Initiatives

The 'regionalization' of foreign policy initiatives serves as an important component of USA foreign policy towards southern Africa. In an attempt to do 'more with less,' the USA moved the now defunct southern Africa Regional Program (SAREP) from its original headquarters in Harare, Zimbabwe, to Gaborone, Botswana, and renamed it the Initiative for southern Africa (ISA). SAREP was originally conceived as a vehicle for supporting cross-national development projects of the southern African Development Coordination Conference (SADCC), a regional organization designed to enhance cooperation among the Front Line States (FLS) and reduce their economic dependence on the apartheid regime of South Africa. With the end of apartheid, the ISA was presented as the cornerstone of USA support for the SADC, the regional successor to the SADCC which includes South Africa in its membership and is headquartered in Gaborone. According to Brian Atwood, former Director of USAID, the ISA reflects the USA vision of "the promise and potential of the southern Africa region upon the transition to democracy in South Africa, the end of the conflicts in Mozambique and Angola, and the movement toward more open economies and political systems throughout the region".[17]

The primary logic behind the creation of the ISA as the coordinator of USA activities in the SADC region is to avoid the obvious duplication of activities (and costs) that would accompany the funding of major USA initiatives in each of these countries, a factor which is especially relevant now that the USA has terminated bilateral development aid programs in Botswana, Lesotho, and Swaziland. The ISA's specific connection to the SADC is also consistent with an emerging USA tendency to rely upon regional African organizations to take the lead in a variety of economic, political, and even military sectors, as witnessed by the Cinton administration's support for the SADC to take the lead in military intervention in Lesotho following the breakdown of civil order after the elections of 1998. Unfortunately, the ISA and its predecessor, SAREP, remain confronted by the same budgetary logic leading to decreased levels of USA bilateral aid to individual southern African countries. Whereas funding for what in essence constitutes one ongoing organization increased from roughly $50 million in 1994 to a peak of $85.3 million in 1995, funding had declined to $32.4 million in 1996 with a request for only $24.8 million in 2000.[18]

A noteworthy aspect of the ISA's short history to date was the decision to move the headquarters of what was originally known as SAREP from Harare to Gaborone. Members of the Zimbabwean Ministry of Foreign Affairs were predictably unhappy with this decision, and their Botswanan counterparts not surprisingly expressed praise.[19] The official reason for ISA's relocation is that Gaborone is the headquarters for the SADC, and therefore should be the site of the principal USA liaison office for regional cooperation. A more important, unspoken reason for the shift, however, was the desire to counter the perception by the Botswanan policy-making élite of declining USA interest relative to other countries within the region, especially in the light of declining aid levels, the closure of the bilateral USA Agency for International Development (USAID) office, and the recent termination of all bilateral development aid to Botswana. Although no USA official admitted the need to 'compensate' Botswana for past 'losses,' Wendy A. Stickel, Deputy Director of USAID's Regional Center for southern Africa which administers the ISA, nonetheless explained the decision to locate the ISA in Gaborone as part of a desire to "send a strong signal" to the Botswanan policy-making establishment that they have played an "exemplary role" within the region.[20]

It is interesting to note that the decision to move the ISA — which had significant implications for USA relations with Botswana and Zimbabwe — not surprisingly was made by USAID Director Atwood after a period of internal bureaucratic debate. Whereas proponents of maintaining the center in Harare underscored the need to reward Zimbabwe's historic contribution to the anti-apartheid struggle, they simply did not carry the same bureaucratic clout as proponents of Botswana who could point to that country's historic commitment to multiparty democracy and free-market enterprise — especially in the emerging post-Cold War/post-apartheid environment. As aptly explained by Peter Benedict, Director of USAID in Harare, the transition to democracy in South Africa in 1994 meant that Zimbabwe's perceived shortcomings, most notably the maintenance of an increasingly corrupt and authoritarian single-party regime, could no longer be downplayed in bureaucratic debates over allocating scarce resources.[21] This perception was strengthened throughout the State Department and the other bureaucracies of the executive branch at the beginning of 2000 as a result of the Mugabe regime's manipulation of racial (white-black) tensions to deflect rising internal dissension with an increasingly authoritarian and economically bankrupt regime.

Bureaucratic Dominance of the Policy-making Process

A further trend of the post–Cold War era is the rising importance of USA bureaucracies in the formulation and implementation of policy. The White House and Congress historically have been uninterested in the day-to-day management of USA foreign policy toward Africa relative to other regions of perceived greater concern, most notably Europe, the former Soviet Union and its successor states, and the Middle East. As a result, their involvement in policy-making related to Africa has been sporadic, most notably during times of crisis and extended humanitarian crisis.[22] In order to best understand continuity and change in USA foreign policy toward southern Africa, one must therefore focus on the policies and interactions of the African affairs bureaus of the traditional national security-oriented bureaucracies, such as the State Department, the Defense Department, and the Central Intelligence Agency (CIA), as well as of their counterparts within the economic and cultural realms, most notably the Department of Commerce.

One important result of what can be referred to as bureaucratic dominance of the policy-making process is the tendency towards the promotion of the status quo in favor of existing policies, even after a new administration takes office. The impact of this bureaucratic reality was clearly demonstrated by the Clinton administration's early policy toward Angola. During the presidential campaign of 1992, candidate Clinton called for 'strong' USA support for whoever emerged victorious in the Angolan presidential elections to be held in September 1992. Yet when Savimbi rejected his initial defeat in these elections (which international observers regarded as "generally free and fair") and returned the country to civil war, the newly elected Clinton administration delayed recognizing the Popular Movement for the Liberation of Angola (MPLA) government until May 19, 1994. The primary reason for the delay was the continuation of a failed pro-Savimbi policy advanced by one portion of the State Department that stood in sharp contrast to a growing recognition in other quarters of Savimbi's unwillingness to accept anything short of total victory — if not in the electoral arena, then on the military battle-field. According to the latter interpretation, the proper policy response, which would have been warmly accepted by the Africanist community in both the USA and abroad, should have been "prompt recognition" of the Angolan government immediately following the elections to leave no doubt in Savimbi's mind that the USA "fully supported the democratic process".[23]

During the Clinton administration's second term in office, however, the constellation of bureaucratic forces gradually evolved in favor of more forcefully supporting the MPLA regime and decreasing historically close ties with Savimbi's guerrilla movement — most notably after the breakdown of the Lusaka Protocol peace agreement and the re-emergence of full-scale warfare between Savimbi's guerrilla forces and the MPLA regime. The cornerstones of this new bureaucratic constellation of forces were twofold (Prendergast 1999). First, the State Department's Bureau of African Affairs under the leadership of Susan Rice captured the sentiment of the national security bureaucracies when it proclaimed profound American disbelief at Savimbi's refusal to abide by the painstakingly negotiated Lusaka Protocol peace agreement. Any remaining bureaucratic clout that Savimbi enjoyed with his traditional bureaucratic patrons — the Pentagon and especially the CIA — was effectively terminated. Second, and perhaps of even greater importance, the Commerce Department has served as the focal point of an increasingly trade/investment oriented strategy which recognizes the importance of the Angolan oil industry to USA national security interests. New oil discoveries in Angola have ensured a dramatic increase in oil production to nearly 2.5 million barrels of oil per day by 2015 (more than Kuwait's current production). It is estimated that this expansion will require between $40–60 billion in private investments, and that the companies getting in on the ground floor will realize outstanding profit margins. Most important, the USA currently imports nearly 7 per cent of its daily oil needs from Angola — a figure that is expected to double by 2004 (Prendergast 1999, 3). In short, a bureaucratically inspired consensus around Angola's economic importance has ensured the emergence of a new policy that was embraced by the Clinton White House.

The Defense Department's approach to security in southern Africa further highlights the importance of bureaucracies in the day-to-day fashioning of policy. From the Joint Chiefs of Staff (JCS) to the Office of International Security Affairs (the de facto State Department of the Pentagon), the military establishment agrees that southern Africa is marginal at best to USA security concerns in the post-Cold War era, and therefore military commitments should be minimal at best in an era of declining military resources. As a result, USA bilateral military aid to the southern African region represented a paultry 1 per cent of all USA bilateral aid provided to the region from 1965 to 1996, which reached its peak during the 1985-89 period when the combined yearly average for all countries was $4.6 million. Although a focus on bilateral (i.e., government-to-government) military aid obviously masks significant Defense Department involvement in the USA–funded paramilitary war in Angola during the 1970s and the 1980s, as well as earlier support for Portuguese counter-insurgency campaigns in their colonies prior to 1974, it nonetheless captures the bureaucratic mindset of Defense Department officials that extensive, long-term USA military commitments in southern Africa should be avoided.[24]

However, one area of military cooperation consistently supported by the Defense Department in southern Africa and all other regions of the African continent is the training of local military officers in the USA under the auspices of the International Military Education and Training (IMET) program.[25] The following amounts were budgeted in 2000 for the southern African region: Angola ($100,000); Botswana ($450,000); Lesotho

($75,000); Malawi ($335,000); Mozambique ($180,000); Namibia ($175,000); South Africa ($800,000); Swaziland ($75,000); Zambia ($150,000) and Zimbabwe ($300,000). Whereas at first glance these amounts appear to be relatively insignificant, the cumulative impact of this program over time in some cases has been nothing less than extraordinary. In the case of Botswana, for example, USA Embassy personnel are extremely proud of the fact that 85 percent of the Botswanan officer corps has received military training in the USA, and has returned to Botswana presumably more inclined to be sympathetic to USA interests within the southern African region.[26]

The IMET program, which constituted the centerpiece of extremely small USA military aid programs throughout southern Africa during the 1980s and the 1990s, is indicative of an approach that emphasizes the cultivation of personal ties between the officers of the host country and their American counterparts. "In a continent that for three decades was plagued by military coups d'état and the establishment of military based regimes, as well as the ongoing influential role of militaries in transitions to democracy in the post-Cold War era," explained Lieutenant Colonel James Oliver Smaugh, Chief of the Office of Defense Cooperation at the USA Embassy in Gaborone, "it seems only logical that we seek to ensure close ties with the **military leaders of tomorrow".[27] Although Smaugh emphasizes that the most** important goal of the IMET program is to create an officer corps respectful of civilian control over the military, and therefore capable of strengthening the democratization process in southern Africa, it is clear that the promotion of a cohort of pro-USA military officers presumably sensitive to USA foreign policy interests constitutes the true essence of USA military activities within the region. Apart from the IMET program, the Defense Department has adopted a relatively low-key approach to military involvement in southern Africa that nonetheless includes a wide array of other activities, including the transfer of excess military stocks and weapons programs to select southern African countries, and the funding of Joint Combined Training Exercises (JCTE), such as the biannual Blue Crane military exercises carried out in conjunction with SADC members.

Uneven Approach to Democracy Promotion

Entering office at a period in which democratization movements were multiplying throughout the African continent, the Clinton administration also was expected by Africanists to make democratization one of the critical elements of its Africa policies. A variety of observers warmly noted that "democracy" was one of the "common threads" linking Clinton's campaign speeches during the presidential elections, and strongly greeted his statement in a Milwaukee, Wisconsin campaign stop that "we should encourage and nurture the stirring for democratic reform that is surfacing all across Africa from the birth of an independent Namibia to the pressure for democratic reforms in Kenya".[28] The Clinton administration even went so far as to codify USA support for the democratization process into an official doctrine — the "policy of enlargement" — intended to replace the outmoded strategy of containment (Lake 1993). Toward this end, the Clinton administration clearly has made democratization an important aspect of policy pronouncements concerning Africa, and several cases, such as USA support for South Africa's transition to a post-apartheid democratic system, indicate that this rhetoric is being transformed into viable policies.

As demonstrated by current Clinton administration policy toward Congo-Kinshasa, however, democratization rhetoric does not always conform with actual policies. The cornerstone of administration policy is a permutation of the 'Mobutu or chaos' thesis that dominated State Department, Pentagon, and CIA thinking from the 1960s through the 1980s (Schatzberg 1991). This bureaucratically inspired consensus embodied the firm belief that 'chaos' — meaning territorial disintegration, regional instability, and ultimately, communist expansion into the heart of Africa — was the only alternative to Mobutu's continued hold over power. The 'Mobutu or chaos' thesis suggests the necessity for a strong (but not necessarily democratic) leader if the region is to avoid socio-economic and political-military chaos. "Regardless of the fact that we are no longer faced with a communist threat," explained a member of the State Department's Africa Bureau, "the destabilization of Zaire [Congo-Kinshasa] — which borders nine other African countries — could have a tremendously negative impact on regional stability" (Schraeder 1994). With the experiences of Somalia and Rwanda still etched in their minds, the Africa specialists of the national security bureaucracies have successfully argued the need to tread softly as, according to another member of the State Department's Africa Bureau, the situation in Congo-Kinshasa "could easily turn into a Somalia and a Rwanda rolled into one, although this time in one of Africa's largest and most populous nations".[29]

It is particularly striking to hear members of the State Department's Africa Bureau argue that, like his predecessor at the beginning of the 1990s, Kabila is both "part of the problem and part of the solution" to resolving the crisis in the Great Lakes region. Once again returning to current manifestations of the 'Mobutu or chaos' thesis, there is a tendency for USA diplomatic personnel to argue against pushing Kabila too hard or too fast for fear that USA efforts will intensify an already chaotic political-military situation. Indeed, as is the case with USA support for other members of the 'new bloc' of African leaders, initial USA support for the Kabila regime placed a heavy premium on his promise to create a "responsive and accountable" (but not necessarily democratic) government capable of restoring order and ensuring the territorial integrity of the nation. In this regard, USA policy toward Congo-Kinshasa continues to emphasize (in the following order): stability, territorial integrity, and the cessation of transborder threats, even if the successful achievement of all three comes at the short-term expense of democracy.

The potential contradictions in the Clinton administration's support for democratization are nicely demonstrated by a comparison of Clinton's presidential trip to Africa with that of an earlier trip by Secretary of State Albright in December 1997. Clinton's itinerary was purposely whittled down to emphasize his administration's commitment to democratization throughout the African continent. Indeed, four of the six countries visited — Botswana, Ghana, Senegal, and South Africa — are among the leading democracies on the African continent. If one focuses on the countries visited by Albright, however, a very different and undemocratic picture emerges of USA priorities in Africa. Six of the seven countries — Ethiopia, Uganda, Rwanda, Congo-Kinshasa, Angola, and Zimbabwe — are ruled by leaders who seized power by the barrel of the gun rather than by democratic elections. According to critics, the message sent by the Albright visit was that the Clinton administration's true priority is the cultivation of strategically located, pro–USA regimes capable of maintaining stability where civil wars and ethnic conflicts once raged.

The often contradictory nature of the Clinton administration's support for democratization in Africa is clearly demonstrated by the State Department's budget request to the USA Congress for the funding of all USA foreign operations (i.e., diplomacy) in 2000. At the beginning of each budget request for individual countries, a priority is typically placed on one of three major sets of objectives: promotion and strengthening of democracy; promotion of USA trade and investment; and humanitarian concerns. In the case of Mozambique, the budget request underscores the overriding importance of humanitarian concerns over democracy promotion, emphasizing the necessity first and foremost of responding to natural disasters —

an acceptable priority for most Africanists. In the case of Botswana, the emphasis is placed on strengthening democratic practices in that historically democratic country. However, in the case of Angola, a country still beset by internal civil war, an emphasis is placed first and foremost on promoting USA trade and investment, followed by the strengthening of democracy. The inherent potential problem with this latter case, similar to the nature of USA policy during the Cold War era, is that when the strategic objective of maintaining access to Angolan oil clashes with the normative goal of democracy promotion, oil access will presumably win out over democracy. In short, proponents of a clear-cut policy in favor of democracy promotion have decried the Clinton administration's selective application of this standard, especially in countries deemed to be of overriding economic importance to the United States.

Towards the Future

Three concluding remarks capture the essence of evolving USA foreign policy toward southern Africa. First, the Clinton administration's presidential visit to the African continent in 1998 clearly heralded rising USA interests in Africa, as well as setting a standard by which all future administrations will be judged. These interests, however, are principally economic in nature, leading to our second theme and perhaps the greatest change in USA foreign policy toward Africa during the second half of the twentieth century: the growing centrality of USA trade and investment in shaping the contours of USA/Africa policies. Although USA policy toward some countries (e.g., the Sudan) continues to exhibit a Cold War mindset (i.e., containment of the perceived threat of Islamic fundamentalism), economics increasingly are at the forefront of the USA diplomatic agenda in all regions of the world, including southern Africa. It is precisely for this reason that USA political-military strategic thinking increasingly has emphasized the necessity of African countries to take the lead in resolving conflict on the African continent. The USA will be willing to assist in such endeavours (witness support for ACRI), but typically will look to either regional organizations (e.g., the SADC in southern Africa) or regional hegemons (e.g., South Africa) to take the lead in their respective regions.

Principal Interviews

Benedict, Peter. Director, USAID, USA Embassy, Harare, Zimbabwe. July 9, 1996.
Carragher, James J. Deputy Chief of Mission, USA Embassy, Harare, Zimbabwe. July 10, 1996.
Craig, Theodore J. Vice Consul and Second Secretary, USA Embassy, Gaborone, Botswana. July 17, 1996.
Doggett, Jr., Clinton L. Program Officer, USAID, USA Embassy, Harare, Zimbabwe. July 9, 1996.
Garwe, Edmund Richard Mashoko. Minister of Education, Harare, Zimbabwe. July 11, 1996.
Gochani, Victoria. Cultural Affairs Specialist (CAS), USA Embassy, Gaborone, Botswana. July 18, 1996.
Goche, Nicholas T. Deputy Minister of Foreign Affairs, Harare, Zimbabwe. July 12, 1996.
Hayes, Grant C. Lieutenant Colonel, USA Army, and Defense Attaché and Army Attaché, USA Embassy, Harare, Zimbabwe. July 11, 1996.
Lauterbach, Steven M. Public Affairs Officer (PAO), USA Embassy, Gaborone, Botswana. July 18, 1996.
Lemar, Bryan G. General Manager, Owens-Corning Pipe Botswana (Proprietary) Limited, Gaborone, Botswana. July 19, 1996.
Olson, Peter M. Democracy Officer, Regional Center for Southern Africa, USAID, USA Embassy, Gaborone, Botswana. July 19, 1996.
Palmer, Virginia E. Political Section Chief, USA Embassy, Harare, Zimbabwe. July 10, 1996.
Smaugh, Jr., James Oliver. Lieutenant Colonel, USA Army, and Chief, Office of Defense Cooperation, USA Embassy, Gaborone, Botswana. July 17, 1996.
Stickel, Wendy A. Deputy Director, Regional Center for Southern Africa, USAID, USA Embassy, Gaborone, Botswana. July 19, 1996.
Weaver, A. Michael. Manager, Plant/Operations, Owens-Corning Pipe Botswana (Proprietary) Limited, Gaborone, Botswana. July 19, 1996.

Notes

Acknowledgements. The analysis builds upon field interviews that were conducted in July 1996 in Botswana, Zimbabwe and South Africa, thanks to generous funding from the Institut Francais de Recherche en Afrique/Harare (IFRA/Harare) and the Fulbright Foundation, Washington, DC.

1   For an introduction to the general literature on USA foreign policy towards southern Africa, see Schraeder (1994); for an analysis treating the initial impact of the end of the Cold War, see Hull (1990).
2   "Remarks by the President at Reception in His Honor, Lawn of the State House, Gaborone, Botswana," March 29, 1998. Text obtained from[http://www.whitehouse.gov/Africa/ 19980330-1654.html].
3   Confidential interview, Gaborone, Botswana, 1996.
4   *Ibid.*
5   Confidential interview, Gaborone, Botswana, 1996.
6   For an overview, see Hawk, 1992 and 1994.

7   Quoted in Elise Forbes Pachter, "Our Man in Kinshasa: US Relations with Mobutu, 1970-1983; Patron-Client Relations in the International Sphere." PhD dissertation, Baltimore, Md, the Johns Hopkins University, 1987: 239.
8   Confidential interview, Gaborone, Botswana, 1996.
9   Department of Commerce, "A Comprehensive Trade and Development Policy for the Countries of Africa. A Report Submitted by the President of the United States to the Congress," February 1996.
10 Interview, July 19, 1996, Gaborone, Botswana.
11 Quoted in "Secretary Brown's Visit to Owens Corning — Botswana, Saturday 24/02/96 -08H00 AM." Document provided by the USA Embassy, Gaborone, Botswana.
12 See USA State Department, "Congressional Presentation for Foreign Operations Fiscal Year 2000," 1999.
13 Interview with Peter M. Olson. Democracy Officer, Regional Center for Southern Africa, USAID, USA Embassy, Gaborone, Botswana, July 19, 1996. See also Tilton (1996).
14 Interview, July 18, 1996, Gaborone, Botswana. For a discussion of opportunities and constraints in the post-apartheid era, see Chipasula and Chilivumbo (1993).
15 See Department of Commerce, "A Comprehensive Trade and Development Policy for the Countries of Africa," 1996.
16 Figures provided by the USA Department of Commerce.
17 Statement provided by the USA Embassy, Gaborone, Botswana.
18 Statistics provided by USAID, Washington, DC.
19 Confidential interviews, Gaborone, Botswana; and Harare, Zimbabwe, 1996.
20 Interview, July 17, 1996, Gaborone, Botswana.
21 Interview, July 9, 1996, Harare, Zimbabwe.
22 See Schraeder, United States Foreign Policy Toward Africa (1994). For a recent analysis of this trend as applied to USA foreign policy toward Somalia, see also Schraeder (1998).
23 Human Rights Watch/Africa, "Human Rights in Africa and US Policy," 1994, 4.
24 See, for example, Scott (1996).
25 Ibid.
26 Interviews, July 17, 1996, Gaborone, Botswana; and July 11, 1996, Harare, Zimbabwe.
27 Interview with Smaugh, July 17, 1996, Gaborone, Botswana.
28 Ibid.
29 See M.G. Schatzberg, *Mobutu or Chaos? The United States and Zaire, 1960-1990* (Lanham, MD: University Press of America, 1991).

References

Adar, K.G. (1998) "The Clinton Administration and Africa: A View from Nairobi, Kenya." *Issue: A Journal of Opinion* 26.2.
Chipasula, J. and A. Chilivumbo, eds. (1993) *South Africa's Dilemmas in the Post-Apartheid Era*. Lanham, MD: University Press of America.
Glaser, A. and S. Smith. (1994) *L'Afrique sans Africains: Le rêve blanc du Continent Noir*. Paris: Editions Stock.
Hawk, B.G., ed. (1992) Africa's Media Image. New York: Praeger.
———, ed. "The News Media and Africa." Special Issue. *Issue: A Journal of Opinion* 22.1.

Hull, R.W. (1990) "United States Policy in Southern Africa." *Current History* 89.547: 193-96, 228-231.
Lutz, C.A. and J.L. Collins. (1993) *Reading National Geographic*. Chicago: University of Chicago Press.
Minter, W. (2000) "America and Africa: Beyond the Double Standard." *Current History* 99.637: 200-210.
Prendergast, J. (1999) "Angola's Deadly War: Dealing with Savimbi's Hell on Earth." *United States Institute of Peace Special Report*, October 12. (www.usip.org).
Schatzberg, M.G. (1991) *Mobutu or Chaos? The United States and Zaire, 1960-1990*. Lanham, MD: University Press of America.
Schraeder, P.J. (1994) *United States Foreign Policy Toward Africa: Incrementalism, Crisis and Change*. Cambridge: Cambridge University Press
————, ed. (1998) "Trends and Transformations in the Clinton Administration's Foreign Policy Toward Africa (1993-1999)"; "The Clinton Administration and Africa (1993-1999)." Special Issue. *Issue: A Journal of Opinion* 26.2.
————. "Ally to Orphan: US Intervention in Somalia under the Bush and Clinton Administrations." *After the End*. Ed. J.M. Scott. Durham, NC: Duke University Press (forthcoming).
Scott, J.M. (1996) *Deciding to Intervene: The Reagan Doctrine and American Foreign Policy*. Durham: Duke University Press.
Tilton, D.J. (1996) *USAID in South Africa: Learning Lessons, Continuing Debates*. Ed. J. Carson. Washington, DC: Africa Policy Information Centre.

Index

Action Programme for southern Africa 314
African/African-American Summit 337
Africa Crisis Response Initiative (ACRI) 86
Africa Growth and Opportunity Act 232, 335
Africa Trade and Development Coordinating Group (ATDCG), 335
African Development Bank (ADB) 79
African National Congress (ANC) 8, 25, 38, 60, 120, 138, 156, 174-180
  globalization, attitudes to 157-158
  neoliberalism 179
  and Swaziland 215
  and USA, 333
African Renaissance
  and Britain, 315
  Mbeki, Thabo 190
Agenda for Zambia (AZ) 244
Alliance des Forces Democratiques pour la Liberation du Congo (AFDL) 276
Alliance for Democracy (Malawi) 81-82
American Federation of Labour and Congress of Industrial Organizations (AFL-CIO) 230
Amnesty International 275, 311
Anglo-Mauritian Agreement 94
Angola 13—33
  Armed Forces 19
  Central Committee 14
  civil war 13, 20
  diamond smuggling 23
  foreign policy 16
  Futongo de Belas 16
  Moxico Province 246
  multi-party politics 16
  Parliament, Party Congress 14
  Political Bureau 15
  Presidency 15
  single party era 14
  Namibia, relations with 25, 142-143
  South Africa, relations with 26
  USA, relations with 28-31, 332-334, 337, 341-343

Angola-Zambia Joint Permanent Defence and Security Commission 257
Apartheid 24, 63, 103, 122, 126, 137, 173, 181, 295, 329, 338
Association of Southern African States (ASAS) 293

Banda, Hastings Kamuzu 72, 76-79, 80
Bank of Botswana (BoB) 47
Barden International 335
Barotse Patriotic Front (BPF) 244
Basutoland African Congress 55
Basutoland Congress Party 55, 65
Basutoland National Party (BNP) 51, 54, 59, 65-67
Basutoland Progressive Association (BPA) 55
Berlin Initiative 300n
Best-Loser System, and Mauritius 97, 99
Beye, Alioune Blondin 246
Bicesse Peace Accord 16
Bi-national Commission 153, 190
Blair, Tony 318, 320
Botswana 34—50
  bilateral economic relations 38, 330
  Bureau of Standards 43
  capacity-building 36
  Financial Assistance Policy (FAP) 41
  foreign policy-making 36
  globalization, effects of 36-37
  Industrial Development Policy 35
  information technology 36
  Ministry of Commerce and Industry (MCI) 40
  Ministry of Finance and Development Planning (MFDP) 46
  Ministry of Foreign Affairs 43
  Office of the President 45
  National Development Plan 8, 35
  Trade and Investment Promotion Agency (TIPA) 41
  and USA, relations with 333-334, 338-340, 343, 346

Botswana Confederation of Commerce and Industry (BOCCIM) 42
Botswana Development Corporation (BOC) 41, 336
Botswana Export Development and Investment Authority (BEDIA) 41
Bretton Woods 5, 35, 264, 319, 322
Britain 78, 91, 271, 277-278
  'Third Way', in Africa 307–328
  accountability 311
  building democracy 320-323
  building peace 313-316
  building prosperity 316-320
  economic deprivation 316, 319
  ethics of 307, 312, 314
  Foreign Policy Centre (FPC) 310
  foreign policy 307-310, 325n
  and globalization 309
  and human rights 311-312
  internationalism 310
  New Labour 307-311, 313-323
British Military Advisory and Training Team (BMATT) 315
British Overseas Development Administration (ODA) 79
Brown, Ron 336-337

Caprivi Liberation Army (CLA) 149
Caprivi Liberation Movement (CLM) 247
Caucus for National Unity (CNU) 244
Central Intelligence Agency (CIA) 341-342, 344
Chiluba, F.J.T.
  Presidency 240-242, 250-254
China (*see* People's Republic of China)
Chipeta, Mapopa 82
Chissano, Joaquim 120, 127-129, 133
Clinton Administration (*see* United States of America)
Cold War 1, 6, 77, 91, 135, 214, 241, 263, 324, 329
Comite Militar de Resistencia de Angola (COMIRA) 23
Common Market for Eastern and Southern Africa (COMESA) 284, 292, 299, 302n, 304n
Commonwealth Summit 1997, 319

Community of Independent States (CIS) 285
Congress of South African Trade Unions (COSATU) 157-158, 161
Congressional Black Caucus (CBC) 335
Constellation of Southern African States (CONSAS) 264, 295
Cook, Robin 308, 312, 316, 319, 320, 323
Creoles (Mauritian) 92, 95-100, 105, 108-109, 112, 115n
Cuba, and Angola 18, 27, 30

Democratic Republic of Congo (DRC) 200, 241, 314
  Namibia, relations with 143-145
  and SADC 288, 292, 298, 300, 304n
  and Zimbabwe, 264, 268-269, 273
Democratic Turnhalle Alliance (DTA) 147
Department for International Development UK (DFID) 313-315, 317
Destabilisation 60, 334
Dlakama, Alfonso (RENAMO) 267
Dlamini, Makhosini Prince 215
Dos Santos, Jose Eduardo 28, 30
Duval, Gaetan 94, 102, 114n

Economic Community of West African States (ECOWAS) 228, 284, 302n
East Asia, and Botswana 39
European Development Fund (EDF) 79
European Union (EU) 84, 284, 314, 319
  Berlin Initiative (SADC) 302n, 303n
  and South Africa 182, 198-199
Export Processing Zones (EPZ) 101,111

Federation of Rhodesia & Nyasaland 72
Forcas Armadas Angolanas (FAA) 267
Foreign Direct Investment (FDI) 111, 162, 289
Forum of Development in Africa 160
Fowler Report 22
France 104, 111, 114n
Frente de Libertacao de Mocambique / Front for the Liberation of Mozambique (FRELIMO) 20, 118-122, 124, 215, 266, 278

Frente Nacional de Libertacao de Angola /
National Front for the Liberation of
Angola (FNLA) 20-23, 142
Front Line States (FLS) 119, 126, 240, 264, 278, 284-285, 295, 339G8 Summit 314

General Agreement on Trade and Tariffs (GATT) 38, 222
General Peace Accord 120
Generalised System of Trade Preferences (GSTP) 230
Germany, and Namibia 136-137
Globalization 3-6, 34, 52, 289, 320
   defined 154-155
   élite perceptions of 155-158
   and GNU 154
   and Lesotho 63-69
   middle-powermanship 167-170
   and New Labour 305-318
   public response (SA) 158-167
   sovereignty, loss of 158-161
Government of National Unity (GNU) 162-163, 171n
Government of National Unity and Reconstruction (GNUR) 153-156, 174, 246
Group of 22, 202
Group of 77 (G-77) 249
Growth, Employment and Redistribution Programme (GEAR) 205, 318-319

Highly Indebted Poor Countries (HIPC) 71
HIV/AIDS 200, 285-286, 309, 332
Holden, Roberto (FNLA) 23, 142
Human Rights Commission (Malawi) 80
Hurd, Douglas 321

India 105, 115n
Indian Ocean Commission (IOC) 107
Indian Ocean Rim Association for Regional Cooperation 107
Initiative for Southern Africa (ISA) 338
International Court of Justice 142
International Covenant on Civil and Political Rights (ICCPR) 245
International Financial Institutions (IFIs) 5, 159

International Labour Organization (ILO) 230, 236
International Military Education and Training (IMET) 86, 342
International Monetary Fund (IMF) 5, 95, 126, 159, 202, 221, 243, 264, 268, 270, 274, 288, 316, 318, 320
Inter-state Defence and Security Committee (ISDSC) 295-297

Jack Report 78
Joint Combined Exchange Training (JCET) 86, 343

Kabila, Laurent 24, 143, 268-269, 276, 304n, 344
Kaunda, Kenneth 240, 322

Lancaster House Agreement 119, 269, 276
Lara, Lucio 15
Law Association of Zambia (LAZ) 244
Lawyers' Committee for Human Rights 275
Leabua, Jonathan Chief 51, 55-56, 60
League of Nations 136
Lekhanya, General 51, 61, 67
Lesotho 51–70, 315
   collaborationist policies 56-58
   economic decline 65
   election (1993) 65; (1998) 66-67
   foreign policy 56-63, 66
   globalization, effects of 63-69
   Operation Boleas 201
   and South Africa 51-54, 56-63, 201
   sovereignty, loss of 63, 68
Lesotho Congress for Democracy (LCD) 66-68
Lesotho Council of NGOs 67
Lesotho Highland Water Project 52
Lesotho Liberation Army (LLA) 60
Lesotho National Development Corp. 57
Letsie III, King 65-67
Liseli Conservative Party (LCP) 244
Lomé Agreement 183, 222
Lusaka Agreement (1974) 119
Lusaka Manifesto (1969) 212
Lusaka Peace Accord (1999) 17, 248, 299
Lusaka Protocol 246, 341

Machel, Samora 120, 124-125, 215
Major, John 315
Malawi 71-90
  aid donors 78-79, 85
  Alliance for Democracy (AFORD) 81-82
  election (1961) 74
  foreign policy-making 76, 80, 83
  globalization, effects of 72, 88
  National Rural Development Programme 79
  single party state 74
  Republic of Malawi Constitution 75, 80
  United Democratic Front (UDF) 81
Malawi Congress Party (MCP) 72, 74
Mandela, Nelson 107, 131, 248, 320, 335
  foreign policy principles 175, 202
  globalization, attitude to 156-160, 170
  inauguration 329
  and SADC 292, 296, 304n
  stature 189-190, 204
  Two-China policy 177
Marema-Tlou Freedom Party (MFP) 59, 66-67
Mauritian Labour Party (MLP) 94, 96, 100
Mauritian Militant Movement (MMM) 96, 111
Mauritian Social Democratic Party (PMSD) 96
Mauritius 91–116
  'Communalism' 115n
  Constitution (1968) 96
  democracy 97
  foreign policy-making 105-110
  historical overview 94
  human rights 110-111
  independence 91, 102
  lobby politics 112
  military, the 98
  parliament 99
  and South Africa 108
  Supreme Court 97
  structure of government 96
Mbeki, Thabo 8, 132, 177, 190, 204
  foreign policy (G-7) 183, 195-200, 265
  globalization, attitude to 157, 170, 170n
Mboweni, Tito 157
Militant Socialist Movement (MSM) 96
Military Intelligence Agency SA 192
Mobutu Sese Seko 22-23, 344

Mocambique African National Union (MANU) 118
Mogae, Festus 34, 45, 150
Mokhehle, Ntsu 66-67
Mondlane, Eduardo 118
More Developed Countries (MDCs) 243
Movement for Democratic Change (MDC) 272
Movement for Democratic Change (MDC) (Zimbabwe) 273-274
Movement for the Multi-Party Democracy (MMD) 240, 256
Movimento Popular de Libertacao de Angola / Popular Movement for the Liberation of Angola (MPLA) 14, 17, 30, 142, 246, 341
Mozambique 117–134, 332, 337
  civil society 130
  civil war 129
  destabilization 119
  elections, multiparty 129
  external actors 131
  foreign policy 121-122, 126-132
  independence 119
  Presidency 124, 127-128
  political parties 128
  refugees 130
  and South Arica 119-120, 123, 131
  and USA 331, 335, 343
Mpinganjira, Brown 83
Mswati III, King 223-224
Mugabe, Robert 8, 123, 125, 132, 264-278 297-298
Multilateral Agreement on Investments (MAI) 5, 85
Multilateral Investment Guarantee Agency (MIGA) 5
Muluzi, Bakili 81-84, 88, 265

Namibia 135–152
  and Angola (civil war) 142-143
  boundary disputes 140-142
  civil society 149
  DRC, involvement in 145
  economy 137-140, 335
  election (1999) 148
  independence 135-137, 147

foreign policy 137
ministries 146
political parties 147-149
presidency 144-146
South Africa, relations with 136, 138, 146
SWAPO, role of 147-149
Namibian National Students' Organization (NANSO) 149
National Constitutional Assembly (NCA) 272
National Conventional Arms Control Committee (NCACC) 184
National Economic Council (NEC) 335
National Front for the Liberation of Angola (FNLA) *(see Frente Nacional de Libertacao de Angola)*
National Intelligence Agency (NIA) 192
National Intelligence Coordinating Committee (NICOC) 192
National Redemption Council (NRC) 244
National Security Council (NEC) 335
National Society for Human Rights (NSHR) 148
National Union for the Total Independence of Angola (UNITA) *(see Uniao Nacional Para Independencia Total de Angola)*
National Union of Namibian Workers (NUNW) 149
Neto, Agostinho 15, 20, 23, 28, 29
New Labour *(see* 'Third Way')
New World Order 249
Nkomati Accord 120, 124-125, 216
Nkomo, Joshua 271, 276
Non-Aligned Movement (NAM)
 and South Africa 153, 169, 179, 202-203
 and Zambia 249-250
 and Zimbabwe 269
Non-Governmental Organisations (NGOs) 193-194, 203, 205, 250, 259, 273, 283, 302, 311, 314
North American Free Trade Agreement (NAFTA) 284
North Atlantic Treaty Organisation (NATO) 297
Nuclear Non-Proliferation Treaty (NPT) 153
Nujoma, Sam President 142-145, 151

Nyerere, Julius 125, 202
Nzo, Alfred 177

Operation Blue Crane 297
Operation Born Again (OBA) 244
Organ for Politics, Defence and Security (OPDS) 192, 200, 205, 284, 296-299, 304n
Organization of African Unity (OAU) 143, 179, 201, 206, 213, 247, 266, 269, 295-299, 315
 13th Summit 103
 Lesotho, intervention in 66
Ottawa Treaty 153
Owens-Corning 336, 338
Ox-Bow Hydro Electric Scheme 57

Parti Mauricien Socialiste Democrate (PMSD) 94, 103
Patriotic Front (PF) 271
Peace Accord, Angola 30
People's Republic of China 39, 111, 118, 177, 207n, 278
Popular Movement for the Liberation of Angola (MPLA) *(see Movimento Popular de Libertacao de Angola)*
Portugal
 and Angola 13, 20
 and Mozambique 117-119
Presidential Review Commission 293

Ramgoolan, Seewoosagur 95, 100, 102, 108
Ramgoolan, Navin 100
Rand Monetary Area (RMA) 212
Reconstruction and Development Programme (RDP) 156, 162-166, 176, 182
 White Paper 1994, 185
Republic of Malawi Constitution Act 75, 80
Resistance Nationale de Mocambique
 National Resistance of Mozambique (RENAMO) 119-120, 123-130, 132, 266-267, 274
Rhodesian Front 274, 277-278
Roman Catholic Church 55, 129
Rome Statute 153
Rubadiri, David 83
Russia *(see* United Soviet Socialist Republic)

Savimbi, Jonas (UNITA) 17, 20-21, 30, 267, 336, 343
Sector Coordination Unit (SCU) SADC 291
Social Democratic Party of Mauritius 114n
Sotho State 52-53, 59, 65
South Africa 153–210
  and the Abacha regime 178
  arms sales in Africa 179, 192
  Bi-national Commission 153
  civil society 193-195
  Dept of Foreign Affairs (DFA) 181-185, 189
  Dept of Trade & Industry 184, 191
  Defence & Intelligence Community 191-192
  diplomatic missions 183
  elite, defined 155, role of 170n
  Foreign Direct Investment (FDI)
  foreign policy-making (1994-1999) 174-186; actors 187-193, 195-200
  free trade areas 198-199
  GEAR (see Growth, Employment and Redistribution Programme)
  and globalization 154, 155-159, 186
  international role 203
  middle-powermanship 167-170
  Parliament 190-191
  Reconstruction and Development Programme (RDP) 156, 162-166, 176, 182
  and USA, trade relations with 335-338
South African Communist Party (SACP) 220
  and Botswana 38
  and Swaziland 212, 222
South African National Defence Force (SANDF) 25, 192
South African Secret Service (SASS) 192
Southern Africa Regional Program (SAREP) 338
Southern African Customs Union (SACU) 53, 139, 183, 199, 207n
Southern African Development Community (SADC) 3, 6, 8, 139, 179, 219, 283, 337
  aims and objectives 284
  Association of Southern African States 295
  Blantyre Summit 296
  'Blue Hwange' 295
  Consultative Conference 2000, 224
  decision-making 287-292; structure of 290-291
  Declaration 288
  donor conferences 288
  DRC, admission of 292, 298, 300, 305n
  early warning and monitoring system 132
  free trade area/protocol 219, 284, 291, 303n
  Human Rights Court 295, 302, 304n
  Lesotho, intervention in 65, 66-68, 298, 304n, 339
  member countries 287, 303n
  and Mauritius 107, 113
  and Mozambique 131-132, 292, 304n
  Namibia, trade relations with 138-140
  OPDS (*see* Organ for Politics, Defence and Security)
  peace-keeping 201, 228, 296-298
  Presidential Review Commission 293
  regional policy frameworks 286
  security decisions and protocols 228
  and South Africa 153, 182, 185, 198, 202, 337
  Summits 293-299, 302n, 303n, 304n, 314
  Southern African Forum 289
  Trade Protocol 291, 303
  US-SADC Forum 302
  Windhoek Summit 286, 296, 298, 303n
  and Zambia, 247
  and Zimbabwe, 263-267, 294, 304n
Southern African Development Coordination Conference (SADCC) 119, 214-215, 264, 282-287, 299, 336
South West Africa National Union (SWANU) 137, 147
South West African People's Organisation (SWAPO) 25, 137, 142-147
Strategic Defence Review (SDR) 311
Structural Adjustment Programmes (SAPs) 285, 288-289, 318
Swazi National Council Standing Committee (SNCSC) 225-231
Swaziland 211–239
  Constitutional Review Commission 229
  defence 228
  economic policies 213-214, 218

Economic and Social Reforms Agenda 222
foreign policy 215-224
King's Proclamation 1973, 223-224
Industrial Relations 230-236
Labour Union 229-237
Lubombo Spatial Development Project Initiative 220
Maguga Dam Project 220
Ministry of Foreign Affairs 226
National Development Strategy 219-223
Nelspruit Declaration 230
Opposition parties 229
Parliament 227
South Africa, relations with 211-221
Taiwan, relations with 213, 224, 226
Swaziland Federation of Trade Unions (SFTU) 230-236
Swaziland Federation of Labour (SFL) 230-236
Swaziland Federation of Employers (SFE) 230-236
Swaziland Investment Promotion Authority (SIPA) 226-227
Swaziland Solidarity Network (SSN) 220

Tambo, Oliver 215
Tanzania African National Union (TANU) 242
'Third Way' (*see* Britain)
Trade and Development Cooperation Agreement (TDCA) 199
Trans-Caprivi Highway 140
Trans-Kalahari Highway 140
Travail pour Tous 101
Tripartite Task Force (TTF) 67
Tsvangirai, Morgan (MDC) 274
Uniao Democratic Nacional de Mocambique (UDENAMO) 118
Uniao Nacional Para Independencia Total de Angola (UNITA) 16, 20-21, 25, 29, 142, 149, 242, 245, 334
Uniao Nacional Africana de Mocambique Independente (UNAMI) 118
Unilateral Declaration of Independence (UDI) 277-278
UNITA-Renovada 17
United Kingdom (*see* Britain)

United National Independence Party (UNIP) Zambia 240
United Nations (UN) 21, 84, 136-137, 179, 320
  peace-keeping missions 247
  register of conventional arms 314
  South Africa, relations with 153, 206
United Nations Angola Verification Mission (UNAVEM) 247, 275
United Nations Assistance Mission for Rwanda (UNAMIR) 247
United Nations Conference on Trade and Development (UNCTAD) 153, 179, 202, 205
United Nations Development Programme (UNDP) 71, 218
United Nations High Commission for Refugees (UNHCR) 266
United Nations Observer Mission in Sierra Leone (UNOMSIL) 257
United Nations Operation in Mozambique (UNOMOZ) 120, 247
United Nations Security Council (UNSC) 203, 250
United Nations Transition Assistance Group (UNTAG) 26, 137
United Soviet Socialist Republic (USSR) 28, 102, 148, 276
United States Agency for International Development (USAID) 79, 339
United States of America (USA) 245, 329-349
  aid regime in Africa 332-335, 339
  and Angola 28-29, 332-334, 337, 341-342
  and Botswana 330, 332-334, 338-340, 343, 346
  bi-lateral relations 342
  bureaucracies, role of 340-343
  Clinton Administration 329-337, 341-346
  democracy, promotion of 343-346
  foreign policy 332, 338-340, 343, 345, 347n
  Mauritius, relations with 92, 96, 114n
  Malawi, relations with 87, 332-333
  military involvement 342-343
  'Mobutu or chaos' theory 344

Mozambique, relations with 333, 337, 345
'regionalization' 338-340
South Africa, relations with 329, 333-335, 337-338
Universal Declaration of Human Rights (UDHR) 312

Walvis Bay: Joint Administration Authority (JAA) 141, 146
World Bank 5, 84-85, 221, 243, 263, 270, 274, 288, 316, 317
  Consultative Group (CG) 245
  debt relief 322
  'good governance' 317, 320, 325n
World Development Report 1999-2000 (IBRD 1999) 71
World Economic Forum 157, 159, 289
World Health Organisation (WHO) 177, 221
World Trade Organisation (WTO) 5, 186, 202, 288, 324

Zaire, and Angola 22-23
Zambia 240–262, 317, 320, 331
  Angola, relations with 246-247, 256
  Committee of Foreign Affairs 254-255
  conflict resolution 256
  copper 243
  and Democratic Republic of Congo 247
  external debt 242
  foreign policy 246-254
  Iran and Iraq, relations with 249, 253, 255
  military spending 257-258
  Ministry of Foreign Affairs 241
  multipartyism 241, 259,
  Mwanakatwe Commission 241, 245
  Office of the President 251, 255
  Parliament 254
  seccessionist movements 244
  States of Emergency 244-245, 253
  trade unions 259
  Zambia Democracy Congress (ZADECD) 244
  Zambian Human Rights Commission (ZHRC) 245
  Zambian Security Intelligence Act 252
Zimbabwe 263-280, 289, 315, 333, 339-340
  Angola, relations with 267
  Chimwenjes 267
  DRC, involvement in 264, 267-269, 276
  Commercial Farmers Union (CFU) 270
  Economic Structural Adjustment Programme (ESAP) 278
  Fifth Brigade 274-276
  foreign policy 274-278
  Land Acquisition Act 1999 (LAA) 272
  land reform 264, 270-271
  military strength 266, 274-278
  Mozambique, involvement in 266-267
  opposition parties 272-274
  Presidency 272-274
  and SADC 263-268, 289
  and South Africa 265, 274
Zimbabwe African Nationalist Union (ZANU) 122, 265
Zimbabwe African National Union-Patriotic Front (ZANU-PF) 8, 265-274, 277-278, 304n
Zimbabwe African People's Union (ZAPU) 8, 272-274
Zimbabwe Congress of Trade Unions (ZCTU) 272
Zimbabwe Council of Churches (ZCC) 273
Zimbabwe Defence Industries (ZDI) 276
Zuma, Nkosazana 177, 195, 201